The Dorian Aegean

States and Cities
of Ancient Greece

Edited by

R. F. WILLETTS

Argos and the Argolid   R. A. Tomlinson
The Foundations of Palatial Crete   K. Branigan
Mycenean Greece   J. T. Hooker
Sparta and Lakonia   P. Cartledge

The Dorian Aegean

Elizabeth M. Craik

Department of Greek
University of St Andrews

Routledge & Kegan Paul
London, Boston and Henley

First published in 1980
by Routledge & Kegan Paul Ltd
39 Store Street,
London WC1E 7DD,
Broadway House,
Newtown Road,
Henley-on-Thames,
Oxon RG9 1EN and
9 Park Street,
Boston, Mass. 02108, USA
and Printed in Great Britain by
Redwood Burn Ltd
Trowbridge and Esher
© Elizabeth M. Craik 1980

British Library Cataloguing in Publication Data

Craik, Elizabeth M.

The Dorian Aegean. – (States and cities of
ancient Greece).
1. Dorians – Civilization
I. Title   II. Series
939. 1'01   DF136.D6   79–42836

ISBN 0 7100 0378 1

Contents

PREFACE   vii

            PART I INTRODUCTION   1

1 SETTING   3

2 RESOURCES   14

3 HISTORY   22

            PART II ACHIEVEMENTS   45

4 LANGUAGE AND SCRIPT   47

5 LITERATURE   63

6 MEDICINE AND SCIENCE   107

            PART III RELIGION   147

7 MYTHS   149

8 CULTS   168

9 ADMINISTRATION   193

APPENDIX: CULT TITLES   209

CONTENTS

ABBREVIATIONS   225

BIBLIOGRAPHY   230

NAMES INDEX   252

SUBJECT INDEX   261

Preface

There are now many students – and others – interested in
Greek civilization but not specializing in Classics. It
is hoped that they, as well as the conventional classicist,
will find this book helpful. It embraces all aspects of
the culture and traditions of an interesting and lively
outlying region of the Greek world: the Dorian islands of
the Aegean.

Chapters 1-3 are introductory, dealing with the geographical setting, natural resources and historical
development of the area. After a brief survey of
linguistic usage and local scripts (Chapter 4), the
regional contribution to Greek literature (Chapter 5)
and to medicine and science (Chapter 6) is examined and
assessed. Chapters 7-9 discuss the religious traditions
and practices of the islands, under the headings myths,
cults and administration.

Two interrelated aims have determined the format and
approach of the book: breadth and perspective. I have
long believed that too many books on classical subjects
are too narrow. However, it is difficult to attain
breadth without sacrificing depth, especially with the
degree of specialization normal in modern scholarship.
I have tried throughout the text and in the bibliography
to present the most important and up-to-date views (not
always coincident) on all topics treated; but the coverage
is inevitably uneven, and doubtless some will find the
emphasis misplaced. As to perspective, my aim has been
to present the regional contribution not only *per se*, but
within its wider cultural context, in relation to that of
other communities, both Dorian and non-Dorian.

Wide as the book is in scope, some may regret the
exclusion of the visual arts, in view of Rhodian
excellence in sculpture and pottery. I share this regret,
but plead considerations of space and an inclination to

vii

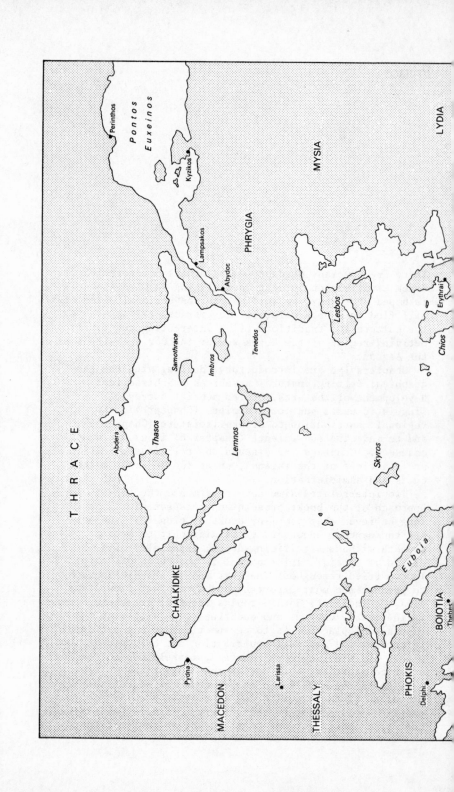

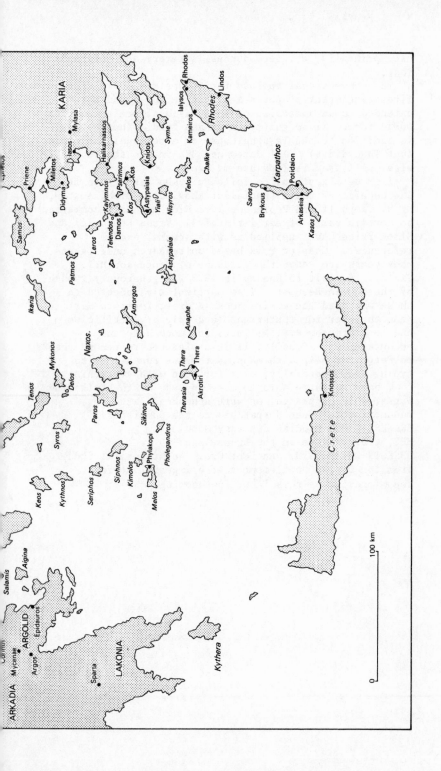

use, primarily, written sources, literary and epigraphical.

The conventional apology for inconsistency in trans-
literating Greek proper-names must be made, and here
extended to an admission of an occasional preference for
Doric forms. I am guilty of Athana Lindia (but Helios)
in addition to the less heinous, or more usual, Hekataios
(but Thucydides). All dates are BC, unless stated otherwise. All translations are my own.

I am very grateful to colleagues who have given me
the benefit of their specialist knowledge: Dr M. Austin,
Mr M. Campbell and Professor I.G. Kidd have all commented
on certain parts of earlier drafts. Vassa Kontorini and
Simon Price have supplied me with several useful
references. Chapter 9 is based on research undertaken
many years ago under the guidance of Professor M.I.
Finley. A visit to Rhodes in 1973 was generously funded
by the Duncan Bequest. I am particularly indebted to
those who read the entire book in draft form; to Sir
Kenneth Dover for forthright (and salutary) criticism
and to Professor R.F. Willetts for much help and
encouragement. Finally, it is a pleasure to record thanks
to Peter for help with maps, Katharine for help with
typing and, especially, Alex for help with everything.

I have not been able to make any use of the following
works, which appeared, or were announced, after my
manuscript had been despatched to the publishers:
FRASER, P.M., Rhodian Funerary Monuments
MEE, C.B., Rhodes in the Bronze Age
SHERWIN-WHITE, S.M., Ancient Cos. An Historical Study
from the Dorian Settlement to the Imperial Period. But
see my review of this last, forthcoming JHS.

The Dorian Aegean

Part I
Introduction

1 Setting

This book explores the culture of Rhodes, Kos and the
other Aegean islands which were Dorian in classical
times. It aims to describe and assess the collective
achievement of this area and to set it in the context of
Greek civilization as a whole; to isolate peculiar local
elements and to demonstrate affinities with Greek culture
as it developed elsewhere. Attention is paid both to the
distinctive characteristics of the islands' contribution
and to its place in Greek thought.

We see Greek civilization primarily through Attic
eyes. While the importance of fifth- and fourth-century
Athens in Greek cultural development is undeniably
immense, it is too often forgotten that Athens was only
one of the many small states which made up Greece; and
emphasis on the Athenian achievement tends to obscure
the contribution of other regions.

The contribution of the Dorian islands was different
at different times. In the archaic period, the islands
were important as stepping-stones: Near Eastern and
Levantine influences filtered through the Greek communities of the Asiatic seaboard and the islands to mainland
Greece. This influence is discernible in writing (the
adoption of the alphabet), in literature (especially
epic and philosophical thought), in religion (myth motifs
and cult titles), as well as in the artefacts of the
potter and metalworker. Later, contacts between the
islands and mainland Greece demonstrate the interaction
of Greek states, tangibly in trade (where the islands
had a monopoly of certain markets) and intangibly in
such areas as literature, medicine, technology and
religion. Similarities between the islands and mainland
Greece illumine the influence of mother city on colony
(this is particularly discernible in cult); differences
aid an understanding of Greek constitutional development.

3

In the Hellenistic period, the islands had a cultural
momentum of their own, associated with the activity in
Alexandria.

Other islands or groups of islands would repay similar
study. Larger islands, self-contained and independent,
often show a particularly interesting development in
terms of their own impetus and their interaction with
other communities. Samos might be singled out as one of
many which had a lively and varied intellectual, cultural
and artistic life.

The grouping of islands adopted here (on the basis of
Dorian origins) may seem novel, as such terms as Cyclades,
Sporades and Dodekanese offer more familiar lines of
demarcation in the Aegean. Grouping by these names was
initiated by the ancient geographers, but the terms were,
and still are, used without precision or consistency
(Str.10.5.14; Plin.'HN'4.12.65-71; cf.Ptol.'Geog.'5.2.8
and 19). The term Dodekanese (literally, 'twelve
islands') was coined to denote an administrative division
of the Byzantine Empire in the eighth century AD. It has
had some vogue in modern times, but again there is disagreement of reference among those who use it as to which
twelve islands it embraces, and indeed whether there are
only twelve in the group.

The Dorian islands were taken as the subject of this
book in the belief that criteria of origins and dialect
allow a more meaningful grouping than vague geographical
labels. Here, the Dorian islands are intended as those
which were settled in the eighth century BC by Dorian
immigration from the Peloponnese - from the states around
the Isthmos or from Sparta - and which then used the Doric
dialect. It will, however, be argued (Chapter 3) that
the settlements of the Mycenaean period were also Dorian.

The Dorians cannot be dismissed as the rude horde whose
emergence heralded the end of Mycenaean civilization, and
who subsequently lived, in the Peloponnese and elsewhere,
a life of different (and inferior) values from those of
other Greek ethnic groups. It is probable that the
conflicts of the Bronze Age left a residue of bitterness
which surfaced in the fifth century with the wars between
Athens and Sparta: at this time, the gulf between Ionian
and Dorian widened, and underlying tensions were exacerbated. The differences, then and later, were both
political and cultural.

In writing about the Dorians, one raises the spectre
of the Teutonic view of Spartan values and virtues (see
Will, 1956 and Rawson, 1969 for evaluations of Müller,
1824, tr.1930). However, there were more Dorians than
ever lived in Sparta. The complex process of interaction

with and reaction against other communities underlies
this book. It will be evident that the Dorian culture
of the Aegean islands evolved along different lines from
that of the Peloponnese, or that of Sicily, though certain
affinities persist.

While the Dorian islands are far from homogeneous, and
the islanders of antiquity were not a cohesive group,
there was undoubtedly some feeling of solidarity with an
ethnic basis. Otherwise, the 'Doric Hexapolis' (Lindos,
Ialysos, Kameiros, Kos, Knidos and Halikarnassos, a
federation with a shared cult of Apollo) could scarcely
have existed (Hdt.1.144.1; cf. 1.6.2, 7.93). The people
of Halikarnassos, who used the Ionic script and dialect
by the middle of the fifth century (SIG 45) still regarded
themselves, by virtue of their ancestry, as Dorian, even
if Halikarnassos' membership of the Hexapolis was shortlived. The Dorians of the west in Italy and Sicily were
chauvinistic about their origins - and they were of
Aegean, as well as mainland, antecedents (Th.6.77.1;
cf. Pi.'P'1.60-8; Theoc.15.91 and 28.17). As late as
the first century AD, the rhetorician Aristeides, in an
address to Rhodes, reminded the islanders of their Dorian
and specifically Argive ancestry (Aristid.24.23, 27, 45,
57; cf.[Aristid.] 25.42).

The Dorian islands lie in a band across the south of
the Aegean, from Melos in the west to Rhodes in the east,
with Kalymnos the furthest north of the group. Included
are - to proceed from the westernmost to the easternmost
members - Melos, Kimolos, Pholegandros, Sikinos, Thera
with Therasia, Anaphe, Astypalaia, Kalymnos, Kos, Pserimos,
Nisyros, Telos, Karpathos with Kasos and Saros, Chalke,
Syme, with Teutlunssa, and Rhodes. Crete too is Dorian;
its culture and institutions already extensively studied
(Willetts, 1955, 1962, 1974, 1977). Kythera is also Dorian,
but it is close to the shores of the Peloponnese (off
Cape Malea) and was under direct mainland domination,
first of Argos, then, from about the middle of the sixth
century, of Sparta. Dorian communities on the west coast
of Asia Minor - Halikarnassos, founded from Troizen, and
Knidos, from Sparta - which share many cultural and
constitutional features with the islands were reluctantly
excluded, as was the part of the mainland later subject
to Rhodes as the 'Peraia'. However, these regions are
mentioned where appropriate.

The Aegean islands have always been influenced by their
position, collectively in relation to the civilizations
to the east and west and individually in relation to one
another. Settled conditions have prevailed only when the
interests of east and west have been in harmony, and when

the influence of the larger islands has been benign.   The
heroic Trojan War; the wars of Greece against Persia;
fifth-century Athenian aggrandizement; the domination of
Alexander and rivalries among his successors; the Roman
conquests - all of these profoundly affected the Aegean.
   The distinctive culture of the individual islands was
shaped by their different geographical locations and
their varying physical features (Cary, 1949, pp.100-2;
Myres, 1953, pp.271-338). Rhodes' commercial prosperity,
the source of her cultural vitality, arose from her key
position as a port of call for ships plying between the
great landmasses to east, west and south. Thera, by
contrast, with the main town of the classical era built
on a ridge away from the sea, was bound to be a more
isolated inward-looking community. Karpathos, with its
sheer cliffs, lack of good natural harbours and stormy
straits never achieved an importance commensurate with
its size (second only to Rhodes in our group). Volcanic
Melos and Nisyros, mountainous Kalymnos and Astypalaia,
fertile Kos set different patterns of life for their
inhabitants. Rhodes and Kos are much affected by the
east; Thera and Anaphe show affinities with Crete.
Kalymnos has certain 'Ionian' features in her constitution - for instance, the presence of an official called
the 'stephanephoros', unique for a Dorian community.
(Leros to the north - and a mere two km. of sea separates
the islands - was Ionian and a deme of Miletos.) Some
of the islands were in the Rhodian orbit: Chalke,
Karpathos, Kasos, Nisyros, Syme and Telos were included
at various times as demes of Rhodes, though Rhodian
domination was sporadic (Fraser and Bean, 1954).
Similarly, Kalymnos certainly and Pserimos probably became
demes of Kos. Islands to the west preserved independence
from their neighbours (apart from Therasia, close to and
linked with Thera), but all were subject to the advances
of successive sea-powers from the Greek mainland and
beyond.
   The Greeks were always intrepid sailors. That the
earliest Aegean peoples were sophisticated in shipbuilding
and seafaring is demonstrated by the presence of obsidian
(a tough sharp volcanic glass superior to flint for weapon
manufacture and a prized raw material in Stone Age and
Early Bronze Age communities) in areas far from its source.
Even in the 'aceramic' phase - that is, before they could
make pottery - peoples acquired obsidian from a distance
rather than make do with poor quality local flint.
Obsidian from Melos - the main Aegean source of this
material - is found in strikingly early contexts on the
mainland (Peloponnese, Macedonia and Thessaly) as well as

at Knossos in Crete. Yiali, an islet between Kos and
Nisyros, is another source of obsidian, but was apparently
not known till much later; obsidian of this composition
type appears in Minoan Crete (Renfrew, Cann and Dixon,
1965; cf. Cann and Renfrew, 1964), where stone vases
inlaid with white shell were manufactured in imitation of
its curious pumice-flecked appearance.

    That an accurate knowledge of local conditions and
terrain prevailed in the late Bronze Age is demonstrated
by the Homeric Catalogue of Ships in 'Iliad' 2, a list of
Agamemnon's allies against Troy. The descriptive epithets
attached to the places named are brief but apt, giving a
maximum of information in a minimum of words (Page, 1959).
Kameiros is 'arginoeis', 'bright-shining', 'white' (or,
as some suggest, 'argiloeis' from 'argilos', 'white clay'),
with reference to the conspicuously white soil of the
region used in Rhodian pottery manufacture. In the fifth
century, the Athenians found it feasible to administer
and control a confederacy embracing many Aegean islands,
and to extract from its members annual revenues of cash
or contributions of ships. In the third and second
centuries, a benevolent Rhodian protectorate policed the
sea, assisting small states threatened by bigger powers,
curbing the illicit activities of powerful cities and
keeping the menace of piracy under control. Rhodes used
Tenos as a naval headquarters; the Ptolemaic fleet made
similar use of Thera, and the Romans of Astypalaia.

    However, communications in the Aegean were unpredictable
at best. Hesiod, giving advice on seafaring, reckoned it
was best avoided ('Op.' 646 sqq.), and long sea journeys
were not undertaken in the winter months. Many epitaphs
of travellers lost at sea testify to the hazards of
ancient navigation, as does the stock theme in 'propemticon'
('send-off') verse of the wish for a journey free from
storms. Traders involved in litigation at Athens tried
to win sympathy by emphasizing the dangers of their
occupation (D.33.4, 56.1; cf.34.31, 52.3). In the
Hellenistic period, bad weather or illness were acceptable
as excuses for actors' failure to turn up in accordance
with their contract (Pickard-Cambridge, rev. Gould and
Lewis, 1968, pp.316-17). The danger of piracy added to
natural hazards.

    In the fourth century, the voyage from Athens to Rhodes
might take three weeks, with long delays occasioned by
adverse winds and periods of sailing at random in the
direction dictated by successive squalls, according to
Aischines ('Ep.'1, a late forgery but undoubtedly a
description which would seem plausible, if not authentic):

We left Mounychia in the evening with a very fine west
wind and around midday reached Koresos in Keos. We
stayed there nine days, for the wind was unfavourable,
then having set sail again in the evening we reached
Delos at dawn.... While it was still night, we
left.... Storm and violent wind fell upon us and took
us off course to Crete, near Psamathos. However, when
we were already in sight of land, a wind from Libya
blew us away. Then, as the gale blew from the north
again, we were five days at sea before putting in at
Thera.... From there, in four days' time, we reached
a harbour on Rhodes.

(The text is uncertain at the point where I suggest 'Thera'
which lies due north of Crete: the mss readings Ἀερώνη H,
Ἀτόρων ἢ f, Τορώνη B may be corruptions of Θηραίων
νήσῳ).

Similarly, Cicero once took two weeks to reach the
Peiraieus from Ephesos ('Att.' 6.9.1). The voyage from
Rhodes to Athens demanded a first class vessel: the case
of the defendants in a Demosthenic speech apparently
rested on the contention that their ship, though seaworthy,
was not good enough to undertake the long haul across the
Aegean (D.56.21, 23).

Rhodian sea-captains travelled far with their warships;
the names of many are known from the historians who
recorded the rise of Rome and the part played in this –
often fighting on different sides – by men of Rhodes.
Many acted as escorts too – for instance Erastos,
commissioned by the emperor Hadrian for his voyages in
the Aegean (SIG 838).

The many travellers of the classical period to endure
the vicissitudes, dangers and discomforts of travel by
sea did not record their experiences. The merchants who
brought grain to the Greek mainland (exporting wine,
pottery, olives and honey) were probably not highly
literate. The Hippokratic writers were keen observers of
their surroundings, but give in the 'Epidemiai' descriptions of environmental conditions, not of regions as such.
Herodotos, who was interested in places as well as people,
goes into detail about Egypt, but has little of geographical interest to say about regions nearer home; born in
Halikarnassos, he had the Dorian islands on his doorstep.
The sophists who travelled widely did not record local
impressions either.

After the conquests of Alexander, the Greeks became
more aware both of the extent and character of the wider
world and of regional differences in Greek lands.
Descriptive and mathematical geography came into existence.
Travel literature was another product of improved communi-

cations, and from this time on some subjective impressions
were recorded. The Hellenistic poet Philitas, who lived
in Kos, may be drawing from personal experience in writing
(fr.13, Coll.Alex.p.93):
> The gods will reveal land once more, but at the moment
> there is to be seen only the domain of gale-force winds.

However, Horace 'Sat.' 5, an extended accound of a difficult journey, has no known Greek model.

Theokritos - equally at home in Sicily, Kos and
Alexandria - in Idyll 7 describes a visit to a farm in
Kos. The names of Haleis (a district) and Bourina (a
fountain, cf.Philitas fr.24, Coll.Alex. p.95) are
authentic topographical details, as is probably Pyxa also.
The region is indicated with enough precision to identify
the spot to anyone familiar with the island: a crossroads,
the farm of Phrasidamos, the cave of the Nymphs (130-46):
> He took the turning to the left and went along the
> road to Pyxa, while Eukritos, the handsome Amyntichos
> and I turned off for Phrasidamos' place. We reclined
> amid deep couches of fragrant reed, rejoicing in the
> new-cut vine leaves. Many poplars and elms swayed over
> our heads. Nearby, the sacred stream of the Nymphs,
> trickling down from a cavern, murmured. Amid the shady
> boughs the dark cicadas chattering went about their
> toil. The tree-frog far off croaked in the thick
> thorny growth of brambles. Larks and songbirds were
> singing, the dove was moaning, tuneful bees were
> flitting around the spring. Everything was redolent
> of summer with its riches, redolent of autumn. Pears
> at our feet, apples by our sides rolled in profusion;
> the branches laden with sloes hung down to the ground.

Diodoros, writing in the first century BC, described
Kos as a place of some account (D.S.15.76.2):
> The Koans moved to the place they now inhabit and made
> it remarkable; walls were built at great expense and
> a harbour of note. From this epoch it constantly went
> from strength to strength in public revenues and
> private fortunes; and, to sum up, it came to rival the
> foremost Greek cities.

Strabo, in his long treatise entitled 'Geography', writing
a few decades after Diodoros, also praises Kos singling
out the Asklepieion, with its art treasures, for special
mention (Str.14.2.19):
> The city is not large, but it is the most beautiful
> of all settlements, and presents a most pleasing
> appearance as one sails to land.

Rhodes is given even more fulsome treatment (Str.14.2.5):
> The city of the Rhodians lies on the eastern promontory
> and it is so far superior to others in harbours, roads,

walls and other amenities that we cannot describe any
other city as even nearly its equal, far less superior
to it.
Pliny too enthused about Rhodes ('HN' 5.132):

But Rhodes, which is free, is the most beautiful
place.

Rhodes must have made a peculiarly dramatic impact on
arriving travellers when the Kolossos, a statue of Helios
thirty-two metres high, stood at the harbour mouth
(Gabriel, 1932). Completed in 281, it was destroyed by
earthquake in around 227. Passages in Lucian demonstrate
that it was remembered for centuries after it fell. A
speaker in his satirical description of a flight to
heaven and the view of earth from above remarks ('Icar.'
12; cf. 'J.Tr.'11-13):

And if I had not seen the Kolossos of Rhodes and the
lighthouse of Pharos, be assured that I should not
have recognized the earth at all.

The temples of Rhodes, especially that of Dionysos, also
attracted the attention of visitors. A dialogue of Lucian
describes a 'sightseeing' trip, with chance encounters
with acquaintances from Corinth and Athens also holidaying
in Rhodes (Luc. 'Am.'7-8; cf.Str.14.2.5. X.'Eph.'5.12 and
Plin.'HN' 34.17.36, 18.41-2 for further comment on the
votive offerings and statues to be seen at Rhodes):

When we reached Rhodes, the island of the Sun-god, we
decided to rest for a little from our continuous
voyage. And so the oarsmen hauled the vessel to land
and pitched their camp nearby. With accommodation
secured opposite the temple of Dionysos, I strolled
at my ease, filled with tremendous enjoyment. For it
really is the city of Helios, with a beauty appropriate
to the god. As I did the rounds of the porticoes in
the temple of Dionysos, I gazed at each painting,
reminding myself of the tales of the heroes, while I
enjoyed their visual impact.

Other writers refer to the splendours of Rhodes. Dio
(D.Chr.31.146) alludes to the Rhodian civic pride, based
on:

first of all your laws and the stability of your
constitution; then, I suppose, on such things as
temples, theatres, dockyards, walls and harbours.

Aelius Aristeides (or, rather, the anonymous writer of
the treatise 'Rhodiakos' preserved in the corpus of
Aristeides' works, a lament for Rhodes' past glories,
generally regarded on stylistic grounds as spurious;
see Keil, ed., 1898; Boulanger, 1968) praises the precincts
of the gods, temples, offerings, statuary, paintings,
acropolis and broad streets of the town.

The different aspects of different islands from the
sea is striking - Melos, with its vast bay ringed with
mountains; Thera, which forms part of the rim of a huge
volcanic crater, with the rim partially continued in
Therasia across the bay and, in the bay itself, several
islets, uninhabited and uninhabitable, as tangible
reminders of the still active volcanic core; Astypalaia,
with its fine natural harbour, modern Maltezana, sheltered
by the landmass behind and by two islets out to sea in
front; Kos with its gentler aspect, the town by the sea
and hills rising behind. The seascapes have changed much
in the seismic and volcanic region of Thera, as was already
the case in antiquity and remarked by Pliny ('HN'.4.12.70;
cf.D.C.56.7):

When Thera first emerged, it was called Kalliste.
Later, Therasia was torn away from it, and soon Automate
came into existence between them, as did Hiera, and,
in our day, Thia came into being near them.

The landscapes have changed too, from antiquity to the
present day, with changing areas of settlement and levels
of cultivation. In many islands, the areas settled in
the Bronze Age - by Minoans from Crete and Mycenaeans from
the mainland - were not the sites chosen by later settlers
for their towns. In Thera, the Minoan town, destroyed in
the great eruption of c.1500 BC, was concealed under
tephra on the south-west tip of the island, while the
Peloponnesian settlers occupied a new site on a mountain
ridge facing south-east, away from the sheer cliffs
ringing the submerged crater of the volcano. Perhaps they
preferred not to be reminded of the ever-present menace in
the bay. In Melos, the prehistoric settlements were in
the west of the island, at Phylakopi, while the acropolis
of Dorian Melos was on the hill of Prophet Elias. In
Rhodes, the main areas of settlement remained the same
until the fifth century: Lindos in the east, Ialysos in
the north-west and Kameiros in the west. The city of
Rhodes, founded by synoecism in 408, quickly prospered,
with its coastal site well placed for overseas communications. On Karpathos, the Dorian towns were Karpathos
(not yet certainly located, but the port Potidaion was
probably at Pigadhia, on the south-east coast, a fine
harbour used also by the Bronze Age settlers; cf.Hope
Simpson and Lazenby, 1962), Brykous in the north-west and
Arkaseia in the south-west. The group Eteokarpathioi,
who occupied a locality of their own - probably in the
hilly interior - may represent an indigenous population
pushed out by the Dorians from the strategic coastal
regions. In Kos, the settlers who had used the (protogeometric) cemetery known as the Serraglio, in the eighth

century, situated above the Mycenaean settlement in the
east of the island, gave way before a new group, who
established themselves in the west. Despite being
unfavourably placed for commerce, this settlement
(Astypalaia) remained the main town until the synoecism
in the fourth century (Bean and Cook, 1957). The eastern
town was known as Kos Meropis, and the island continued
to have Meropis as an alternative name (D.S.13.42.3). In
Kalymnos, Damos, where Mycenaean tombs were found, is
distant from the area in the north which has yielded
classical remains.

Excavation in the islands, and publication of finds,
has proceeded at an uneven place. (For useful summaries
and brief bibliographies, see, on the individual islands,
'The Princeton Encyclopedia of Classical Sites', ed.
R. Stillwell, 1976.) In the nineteenth century, much lay
on the surface, as the German traveller Ross was among
the first to discover (Ross, 1840-5). The memoirs of
such travellers, with a more or less casual interest in
antiquity, often contain acute observations with reports
of sites explored, or copies of inscriptions discovered.
Some works of this kind are having a deserved reprinting
(Leake, 1824, repr.1976; Fellows, 1852, repr.1975;
Ramsay, 1895, repr.1975). In the years 1852-9, Sir Charles
Newton, a diplomat appointed to the vice-consulship of
Mitylene, and simultaneously commissioned by the British
Museum to acquire antiquities, explored Rhodes, Kos and
Kalymnos as well as the west coast of Asia Minor (Newton,
1862 and 1865). His finds of Mycenaean tombs and pottery
on Kalymnos deserve to be remembered: this was before
Schliemann excavated at Mycenae and Troy. Among the first
systematic explorations on the islands were those of a
British expedition at Phylakopi in Melos, 1896-9, briefly
renewed in 1910 (Atkinson et al., 1904; Dawkins and Droop,
1910-11; cf. Barber, 1974). Duncan Mackenzie, who soon
afterwards accompanied Arthur Evans on his more celebrated
excavations at Knossos, was a prominent member of this
team. Meantime, Hiller von Gaertringen explored Thera
(Hiller von Gaertringen, 1902a). On Kos, inscriptions
were copied and published by W.R. Paton (IC=Paton and
Hicks, 1891). Paton's collection was followed by the
discovery of the site of the Asklepieion - on the outskirts
of the town, just as Strabo had described it (Str.14.2.19) -
and of many inscriptions there by R. Herzog (Herzog, 1898,
etc.). On Rhodes, a Danish expedition led by C. Blinkenberg made a thorough exploration at Lindos. The most
significant find of this expedition was the long inscription which has come to be known as the 'Lindian Chronicle',
a record of donations made to Athena at Lindos, from pre-

historic times down to the third century, erected in
99 BC (Blinkenberg, 1941, II Inscriptions, 2, 'Chronique
du temple'; cf. Forsdyke, 1957, pp.44-6). Further excavations by Italian archaeologists during their country's
occupation of the Dodekanese yielded copious additional
material (see esp.ClRh passim; also the work of Maiuri,
Pugliese Carratelli, Segre = NS, NSER, SER, TC, TCam,
TCamS). Unfortunately, these finds have not yet been
fully published (cf. Craik, 1969, pp.323-4).

Inscriptions from the islands are published in various
collections and in many different periodicals. The great
compilation 'Inscriptiones Graecae', originally envisaged
as a collection to include all Greek inscriptions, embraces
Rhodes, Chalke and Karpathos, IG XII 1 (1895); also Syme,
Telos, Nisyros, Astypalaia, Anaphe, Thera, Pholegandros
and Melos, IG XII 3 (1898). Included in this volume are
the few inscriptions found as yet on Saros, Kasos (off
Karpathos), Seutloussa (off Syme), Therasia (off Thera)
and Kimolos. It was originally intended that the
inscriptions of Kos and Kalymnos would form Volume XII 2
of IG. For Kalymnos, an impeccable collection by Segre
(TC, 1944-5) fills the gap. For Kos, as has been seen,
the situation is very different.

The Greek Archaeological Service has forged ahead with
excavation in the islands, recording finds in the journals
EAE and PAAH. The discovery and exploration by S. Marinatos
of Minoan Akrotiri has engendered most interest in
scholarly circles and beyond. Since the untimely death
of Marinatos in 1974, his work has been ably continued by
C. Doumas. Also on Thera, N. Zapheiropoulos has uncovered
much new material at the site of the classical town. On
Rhodes, G. Konstaninopoulos and his assistants renewed
excavation in 1973, and every year adds to their discoveries.
While few new inscriptions have been discovered in recent
years, work continues on the edition, interpretation and
release of the epigraphical material in the museum at
Rhodes (Kontorini, 1975a and b, etc.; cf. Peek, 1969).

2 Resources

Information about the islands' natural resources comes
from inscriptions and, more directly, from late descriptive works. Strabo's 'Geography' and Pliny's 'Natural
History' are of this factually descriptive type.
Athenaios, writing about AD 200, is a mine of information
on food and drink of all kinds, as well as relaying,
through citations, the content of many earlier writers.
Some incidental information about the area is contained
in Ovid's poems. Ovid's style and subject matter are
heavily influenced by Hellenistic verse and his interest
in the region may be an indirect aspect of his imitation
of poets who lived there.

By ancient standards, the islanders ate well, with a
diet relatively rich in protein from fresh fish and dairy
products. By modern western standards, they ate little
meat. The diet of the island Greeks in antiquity
resembled that of rural Greeks today, with cheese and
eggs more common than meat, honey as a sweetener, olives
and olive oil, a high consumption of bread. Meat was not
cooked in the home, but, after a sacrifice to the gods,
the sacrificial beast was roasted and the people feasted.
As there were many gods, honoured assiduously by the
islanders with regular state festivals and more informal
private sacrifices, beef, lamb, pork and goat-meat were
frequently available. The temples were both abattoirs
and banqueting halls, with personnel who could act as
butchers and cooks. The grassy uplands of Kos and Rhodes
provided good pasture. At a sacrifice to Zeus in
Hellenistic Kos, the victim was chosen from herds of
eligible animals; there was clearly a plentiful supply of
good beef cattle (IC 37). The shepherds and goatherds who
figure in the contemporary poems of Theokritos would find
a ready market in town for their animals - not, however,
an aspect of rural life that a pastoral poet would care to

mention. A certain prodigality is apparent in some of
the detailed provisions for sacrifice: only a rich farming
community would sacrifice a ewe about to lamb, as in the
offering to Demeter and to Rhea at Kos (IC 37.60, 38.3).
The young goats of Melos were a prized delicacy in later
times (Ath. 1.4c; Poll.6.63). Anaphe and Astypalaia were
famous for their game, hares and partridges - excellent
for the pot, but a menace to crops. Athenaios records an
anecdote, quoted from Hegesander of Delphi (Ath.9.400d =
FGH IV.421):

> In the reign of Antigonos Gonatas there came to be so
> many hares in Astypalaia that the Astypalaians
> consulted the oracle about them. The Pythia told them
> to keep dogs and hunt; in a single year more than 6,000
> hares were caught. This multitude of hares was the
> result of the introduction of two hares into Asty-
> palaia by a man from Anaphe; he did this because earlier,
> after a man from Astypalaia had introduced two
> partridges into Anaphe, there came to be so many
> partridges on Anaphe that the inhabitants were in danger
> of being driven out.

A somewhat similar story was told of Karpathos, which also
suffered a plague of hares. Rhodes was 'good for fish',
with the small fish of the region particularly prized
(Lynkeus ap. Ath.8.360d, Ath.7.285c, e, 294e-295a).
Astypalaia too was 'surrounded by waters rich in fish'
(Ov. 'AA' 2.82): its mussels and snails were famous, as
was the 'skaros' fish of Karpathos.

Theokritos' eloquent description conjuring up the heady
autumnal fragrance of a Koan orchard confirms Strabo's
description of Kos as 'rich in fruit' (Theoc.7.144-6;
Str.14.2.19). In the fifth century, Athens imported
raisins and dried fruit from Rhodes; in the third century
Alexandria imported Rhodian dried figs (Athens: Hermippos
ap. Ath.1.27e; Alexandria: PCair.Zen.59.110.23, 24; cf.
Ath.3.75e, 80c, 14.652d). The cultivation of olives began
in prehistoric times. One of the earliest beam-presses
used for the extraction of olive oil yet discovered in
Greece was found in Therasia, dating to the late Helladic
period, c.1600-1100 BC (Forbes, 1965, III2 p.133). Nuts
(especially almonds) and vegetables (especially onions)
gave variety to the diet. Later, Rhodes gained a reputation for fine vegetables, with cabbage a particularly
successful crop (Ath.9.369f). The honey of the islands
was - as it still is - of excellent quality, especially
that of Kos and Kalymnos (Str.10.5.19; Ov.'AA' 8.222).
Spices and herbs were cultivated, some for export. The
herbal perfumes of Rhodes and Kos were famous: Rhodian
saffron, Koan essence of marjoram and quince (Ath.15.688e;

cf.NS 466). Telos produced celebrated unguents (Plin.
'HN' 4.12.69). A medicinal herb of the arbutus family
('erysiskeptron') was cultivated at Nisyros and Rhodes.

Regional variations in the names for foods and in the
preparation of them were widespread. Rhodian bread was
unusual, in particular a sort of hot toast with a savoury
spread; also so-called Atabyrian bread (named after the
mountain Atabyros) and '"echinos" cake' (cake in the shape
of a sea-urchin); Kos had its own name, 'paisa', for a
type of bun (Lynkeus of Samos ap. Ath.3.109d-e, id. ap.
Ath.14.647b, 646f; cf. Sopater of Paphos ap. Ath.4.158d
on the unavailability in Rhodes of lentil bread, common in
Alexandria). The people of Thera sprinkled pulse instead
of barley-meal on their wine, a peculiar regional additive
approved by ancient gourmets (Ath.10.432c-d).

The island wines were distinctive and those of Kos and
Rhodes especially famous. Vergil approved Rhodian wines
as fit for the feasts of the gods, while Strabo and Pliny
rated those of Kos second to none (Verg.'E' 2.102;
Str.14.2.19; Plin.'HN' 14.10.77). Athenaios was less
appreciative of the Koan and Rhodian wines because they
were treated with sea-water. This practice was intended
to counteract the acidity of the product (other additives
with the same effect being turpentine, chalk and resin).
Characteristically, Pliny alleges that sea-water was first
added by a bibulous slave trying to conceal the inroads
he had made on his master's casks. Athenaios allows Koan
wines faint praise for their digestive and laxative
qualities; Rhodian wine he regards as better, but still
'useless' (Ath.1.32e; Plin. 'HN' 14.10.78).

By the end of the fifth century, viticulture was
industrialized to the extent that professional wine-
merchants conducted the business and wine could be exported
only in sealed and stamped vessels (cf. Forbes, 1965, III2
p.112). Widespread finds of Rhodian amphora handles
suggest that Rhodes had an important part in this trade.
There is fourth-century literary evidence for a flourishing Koan wine-trade: ships from Athens collected wine from
Kos and traded this for corn in the Pontos region (D.35.31).
This procedure of direct exchange was common in the
classical period, there being no sophisticated balance of
imports and exports, no international credit system and
no universal standard coinage (cf. Finley, 1973, pp.132-9,
166-8). In the second century, the price of grain rose,
while that of oil and wine fell. This damaged the island
wine-merchants for a time, but they survived. Even under
the Romans - despite the attempt of the chauvinist Cato
to turn Italian wine into 'Koan' by processing (Plin.'HN'
14.10.79) - the islands continued to purvey quality wines

to the West, though their share in the mass vin ordinaire
market dwindled. Wine was for centuries the most significant island export. The export of dried fruit and honey
was probably only to wealthy urban areas (fifth-century
Athens, third-century Alexandria), making a small contribution to the economy. Most communities would consume the
poorer quality produce of their own area; just as today
they grow their own olives rather than purchase choice
supplies from Kalamata.

The islands were self-supporting for foodstuffs, with
one important exception - grain. In this, they reflect
the situation obtaining generally in the ancient world.
Grain was a significant component in the diet. There was
no awareness of the relative value of different types of
food, and protein foods went unrecognized. The treatises
on regimen in the Hippokratic Corpus recognize the
importance of the consumption of the 'right' foods for
the individual's condition, but this was a luxury for the
leisured and wealthy. For most people, bread - perhaps
accompanied by fish, cheese or eggs - and porridge were
the staple foods; filling broths were also made from beans
and pulses. Few ancient communities could grow enough
grain for their needs, and this was imported from Sicily,
Egypt and the Pontos region. All populous areas of Greece -
Athens, the Peloponnesian states, the towns on the coast
of Asia Minor - had to make arrangements for their supply.
In the speeches of Demosthenes (against Dionysodoros,
Lakritos, Phormio, Zenothemis), merchants and money
lenders, many of them foreigners, feature in the carrying
trade. Enterprising metics, debarred by law from holding
land in Attica, made money by turning to the shipping
trade, or to manufacturing, or to speculation in the local
silver mines. The speeches written for Demosthenes'
clients play on the popular fear of famine, if corn were
to become unobtainable or very expensive.

Kos, providing wine for the Athens-based grain-trade of
the fourth century, had some influence to exert over
securing her own corn supply at this time. There is third-
century epigraphical evidence for imports to Kos of grain
from Thessaly and Cyprus (NS 433; Segre, 1934b). Herodas'
second Mime, from around the same period, represents a
brothel-keeper, prosecuting the owner of a merchant ship
for assault. The plaintiff suggests his opponent may
urge in his defence (16-17):
    'I came from Ake (a port in Phoenicia) bringing wheat,
    and checked miserable famine.'
Throughout, there are elements of parody of the type of
arguments used in Attic forensic speeches, but the claim
clearly had verisimilitude for local conditions of the day.

The 'case' is between foreigners living in Kos, just as
known fourth-century cases are disputed between aliens
in Attica (where a law forbade residents to import corn
to any foreign port).

For several centuries - from the fourth to the middle
of the second - Rhodes played an important part in the
international grain-trade (Casson, 1954). The island was
accessible from Egypt and Cyprus when the open Aegean could
not be crossed by merchant ships. At times, unscrupulous
dealers used the island as a depot to stockpile supplies
of corn, creating a shortage and pushing up the price
(see D.56.7-10 and 16-17, on the racket of Kleomenes,
governor of Egypt). Rhodes received gifts of grain in
time of trouble - from Ptolemy Soter during the protracted
siege of the island at the end of the fourth century; and
from Ptolemy Euergetes, Hiero II, Seleukos II and
Antigonos Doson after the serious earthquake of the decade
230-220 (D.S.20.96.1-3; Plb.5.88-9). The supply at Rhodes
was assured by the state's commercial prosperity, and
safeguarded by the great powers' interest in preserving
the status quo: a prosperous Rhodes could afford to police
the seas. As at Athens, commerce attracted foreign
entrepreneurs. A speaker in an Attic court case of 330 BC
(Lycurg.15; cf.D.56.21) alludes to:
'the city of Rhodes and merchants residing there, who
sail round all the inhabited world on their business'.
A prominent banker, Apollodotos son of Herakleitos,
honoured at Rhodes around 200 BC, was from a family with
Samian connections, not a pure Rhodian. Also, as at
Athens, speculators and shipowners were linked; a Rhodian
who lent money free of interest for the transport of grain
from Rhodes to Delos was probably using his own ship and
waiving interest on his capital in return for profit on
the cargo (Casson, 1954; IG XI 4, 1055, c.225 BC).

The eastern islands had good natural resources of
timber for ship- and housebuilding. It was from the south
Aegean - Karpathos and Crete - that Athens imported cypress
wood, doubtless the finest available, to roof her temples
(IG XII 1, 977; Hermippos ap. Ath.1.27f). Kos too had
forests of cypress, coveted in 32 BC by a Roman admiral
seeking to rebuild his fleet (Val. Max.1.1.19; D.C.51.8.3).
The worship of Asklepios had original associations with
'Apollo of the Cypress' and the locality of the Asklepieion
long retained the name Kyparissos (IC 43; HG 11; cf.
Herzog, 1905 and Laumonier, 1958, pp.691-5). Plane-trees,
which give dense shade in the summer months, grew well in
Kos, and were favoured by writers as 'studies'.
Contemporary sources had it that Philitas wrote his verse
under a plane-tree, and that Hippokrates had his surgery

under one. Kalymnos too was well wooded in antiquity
(Ov. 'AA' 2.81).

Local marble was quarried for temples and for
inscriptional records. Much of that used in Rhodes came
from Lartos, near Lindos (IG XII 1, 677, etc.). Kos,
Kalymnos and Syme had plentiful limestone, and Nisyros
was famous as a source of millstones and pumice (Str.
10.5.16). There were rich mineral deposits in the
volcanic soil of Melos, Kimolos and Nisyros (Pettinger,
1977). The obsidian of Melos and Yiali, of great
functional importance in the Stone and Early Bronze Age,
was later prized for its decorative appeal. Small
deposits of gold have been found in Kimolos, Melos and
Thera, but these were probably unexploited in antiquity
(Forbes, 1964, VIII p.163). The iron ore now known to
exist on Melos, Rhodes and Kos may not have been worked
either (Forbes, 1964, IX p.182). Fine pottery clay was
plentiful and Rhodes had a flourishing industry in the
manufacture of amphoras and crocks for the export of wine
and other materials; or perhaps these were exported as
empty containers (Rostovtzeff, 1941, p.680 and n.97;
PA I p.166 and II p.281 n.262). A natural earth of the
china clay type, used by painters as a white pigment, was
widely exported from Melos; also from Melos came alum,
used for medicinal purposes (Plin. 'HN' 35.19.37,
52.188-90, etc.; cf. Forbes, 1965, III2 p.227). Kimolos,
with Crete, supplied the ancient world with fuller's
earth, 'a natural, finely divided, hydrated aluminium
silicate' (Forbes, 1964, IV2 p.85, Plin.'HN' 34.46.155,
35.57.196-8) used in ancient dry-cleaning and retexturing
establishments. It was also used by Roman matrons as a
cosmetic, a face-powder less lethal than the poisonous
white-lead affected in Athens (Plin. 'HN' 35.56.194;
Hor. 'Epod',12.10; Mart.6.93.9; 8.33.17; Lys.1.14).
Rhodes was a source of lead according to Pliny ('HN'
34.54.175-7; cf.Forbes, 1965, III2 p.235).

The prosperity of Kalymnos and Syme was based on the
export of sponges, these islands having a monopoly of the
'world' market. Sponges were known in the Bronze Age –
they are depicted in frescoes and mentioned by Homer –
and familiar throughout the classical period ('Od.'1.111;
'Il.'18.414; Ar.'V'600; 'Ach.'463 etc.; Arist.'HA' 487b9,
588b20; IG XI 2, 144A37 – Delos, fourth century BC).
A reference in Pliny to 'Rhodian' sponges suggests that
Rhodes exploited the resources of Syme, at this time a
dependency ('HN' 31.11.47). Asia Minor was the centre of
the textile industry: Milesian wools and Lydian
embroideries were sought after by wealthy Greek households
(Ar.'Lys.' 729). The mountainous interior was sheep

country and conditions in the coastal regions were
favourable for flax growing. Purple dye, extracted from
a small shellfish (as a colourless secretion from a vein,
darkening on exposure to the air) was processed in the
same area, with Tyre as the main source (cf. Forbes, 1964,
IV2 p.119). Materials were grown, spun, woven, dyed and
made up in the region. The offshore islands had a share
in the textile trade. Kos and Rhodes had purple-dyeing
establishments (cf.IC 309; NS 571), as did Chalke (an
island named after the dye-producing shellfish, Kalche
becoming Chalke by metathesis).

By the fourth century, Kos was producing silk.
Aristotle tells us ('HA' 551b):
    It is said that the first woman to weave silk was
    Pamphile, daughter of Plateus, in Kos,
and his words are paraphrased by Pliny ('HN' 11.76-7).
It has been argued that the silk of Kos came not from the
famous Chinese silkworm, but from either the 'saturnia
pyri' (which gave a strong silk, dark brown in colour)
or the 'pachypasa otus' (which gave a paler and finer
silk, more difficult to card), or from both of these:
Pliny's account lists with the mulberry (which still
grows in Kos) plants including the food of both species
(Forbes, 1930). But for the chance aside of Aristotle,
which suggests that in his time Kos had a long-established
silk industry, it might have been supposed that silk came
much later from the east to Greece in general and Kos in
particular. There are frequent allusions in the Augustan
poets of Rome and in prose moralists to the costliness
of Koan silk and the blatant sensuality of those who wore
garments in this almost transparent material (Ov.'AA'
2.298; Prop.1.2.2; Sen.'Ben.' 8.9.5, etc.). The silence
of the intervening centuries, and of writers before
Aristotle, seems total. Herodas' ladies might have been
expected to mention silks, but do not; orators who make
insinuations in the Attic lawcourts about their opponents'
sexual aberrations do not either. Yet it may be supposed
that silks were worn by sybarites and prostitutes, by the
discerning or decadent wealthy of Greece before they were
exported to Rome. A difficulty in the way of determining
whether silk was known in classical Greece is that Greek
had no word for 'silk' for a long time after it existed.
The Greeks typically identified fabrics by the name of
the locality where they were produced: a list in a
lexicographical compilation of the second century AD
(Poll.7.77) includes stuffs of Crete, Sicily, Phrygia and
other regions. It has been suggested that the 'garments
from Amorgos' worn by Aristophanes' characters in
'Lysistrata' are silk (Richter, 1929; others treat this as
a colour reference).

Thera too had a share in the textile trade. Pollux
and other late writers mention a variegated Theran tunic
('chiton'). According to Pollux, it was worn in the
satyric drama; according to Theophrastos, it was worn at
the Attic dancing festivals of Delian Apollo in whose
honour the Thargelia was celebrated (Poll.4.118, cf.7.48,
77; Theophrastos ap. Ath.10.424e = fr.119, Wimmer;
cf.Hsch., Phot.; Schol.Ar.'Lys.' 150). 'Variegated', the
adjective commonly applied to the Theran garment, might
refer to dyes (multi-coloured), weave (intricately woven),
or decoration (richly embroidered); it is applied also to
stuffs from Cyprus, Carthage and Sicily. (The word is
also commonly used of animal hides, 'dappled' and but for
the term 'tunic' following might have been taken to refer
to the fleece worn by Silenos in satyric drama. Some
suggest that Theraios or Theraikos is connected with
'ther', 'beast', not with the island Thera.)

The flourishing trade of the islands brought many
benefits. Both Kos and Rhodes were prestigious banking
centres. An epitaph from about 200 commemorates the
banker Apollodotos (NS 19, dated by the 'signature' of
the Cretan sculptor Timocharis):

Having scrutinized at close quarters this living
bronze, remember this man's sacred probity. For, for
thirteen years he kept safe the gold of foreigners
and citizens alike, with pure honesty....

In the Mithridatic Wars, the Jews of Asian Minor deposited
large sums of money on Kos for safe keeping (J.'AJ' 14.7.2).

The legal systems of Kos and, especially, Rhodes were
celebrated. These islands were in demand as arbitrators
in international disputes (cf. Laurenzi, 1941, pp.27-30,
no.1). Rhodian power at sea was reinforced by a code of
laws governing naval affairs. This code was influential
for centuries: the Byzantine text recording the 'Rhodian
Sea-Law', known in medieval Venice, incorporated fragments
of the Rhodian maritime code (Ashburner, 1909). The
Athenian legal system can be reconstructed from the
evidence of forensic oratory; for Rhodes and Kos (IC 26;
KF 190) there are references to trials, but no records of
speeches delivered or verdicts given (see, however, Fraser,
1972). For many centuries, Rhodes shared with Athens a
reputation for fair dealing in internal management and
foreign affairs (Arist. 'Pol'. 1304b; Str.14.2.5; cf.
Mahaffy, 1887, Chapter 15).

3 History

Excavations at the Franchthi cave in the Argolid have
revealed material covering some 15,000 radiocarbon years;
Palaeolithic, Mesolithic and Neolithic (Jacobsen, 1973).
Finds of Melian obsidian in Mesolithic levels show that
the Cyclades were visited from the mainland as early as
7000 BC. Similarly, obsidian from Melos is found in
neolithic strata in Crete (Doumas, 1976). Extensive
Neolithic settlements flourished in north Greece (notably
Thessaly) from the sixth millennium onwards and on Crete
(especially at the site later Knossos) from the fifth
(Weinberg, CAH I3 pp.557-618). While the mainland and
Cretan settlements are unrelated to each other, the affinity
of both with cultures of the Near East is recognized: it
seems that over a long period of time successive bands of
settlers arrived from the East, bringing at different
stages a knowledge of the practices of crop growing and
animal rearing, new pottery techniques and skills in
seafaring and shipbuilding. The orientation of the mainland settlements to the east and to the sea is shown by
the siting of villages on the east coast, or in places
readily accessible from the sea; and by evidence that
communications at sea were better than those inland. In
Crete too, settlement began in the east of the island and
spread westwards; in Evans' much-quoted words, the island
became 'an insular offshoot of an extensive Anatolian
province' (Evans, 1921, I p.14).
  As yet, evidence for prehistoric settlement of the
islands is scanty (cf. Honea, 1975, on an early site on
Kythnos, 7500-6500 BC; also Evans and Renfrew, 1968;
Caskey, 1962, etc.; Coldstream and Huxley, 1972; Isler,
1973 and especially Renfrew, 1972 for other island sites).
This is probably attributable to a low population density.
At all periods in their history, the smaller islands have
been more sparsely populated than Crete, Cyprus or the

adjacent landmasses: periods of complete depopulation are
known. Melos was evidently much visited by people in
search of obsidian, but there is no indication of a local
Melian exploitation of this material, or of settlement on
Melos before around 2000 BC. It may be conjectured that
Rhodes, Karpathos and Kasos, lying in the path of travellers
from the East to Crete, were familiar to seafaring bands
throughout the Neolithic period, but they have as yet
yielded no trace of settled habitation. The earliest known
settlements are cave dwellings in Kos and Kalymnos, dating
perhaps from 3000 BC. (This is not a radiocarbon date,
and there is some disagreement about its validity.)
Already the siting of these communities indicates a
certain command over the available resources: the settlement in Kalymnos lies beside the largest and most fertile
valley of the island (Jacopi, 1928). The pottery which
has survived is hand-made and decorated, some of it finely
incised: it is similar to that of Samos, Chios and Lesbos
at this period and has decided Anatolian affinities
(Burton Brown, 1947; Furness, 1956; cf. Hope Simpson and
Lazenby, 1973, p.170). Such affinities are apparent also
in the earliest buildings in Melos (Hoeckmann, 1975) and
in the wide distribution of Cycladic figurines (Branigan,
1971). In general, there is good archaeological evidence
for an Aegean cultural rapport in the Early Bronze Age
(Coleman, 1974).

Material remains from our area in the Bronze Age show
the fortunes of the islanders dependent, as so often in
their history, on those of the great sea-powers of the
time. Minoan cities have now been discovered outside
Crete - on Kythera (Kastri), Melos (Phylakopi), Rhodes
(Trianda) and Thera (Akrotiri). Minoan occupation
preceded Mycenaean settlement on Kos and Karpathos;
Kalymnos was occupied by Mycenaeans and it would be no
surprise if Minoan influence were to come to light there
too. (Trianda was excavated by Italian archaeologists -
see Monaco, 1941 - and the implications of the finds are
discussed by Furumark, 1950. There is a summary by
Marinatos of his finds at Akrotiri, 'Late Minoan Thera',
in Phylactopoulos, 1974, pp.220-8. On Phylakopi, see
Atkinson et al., 1904; Dawkins and Droop, 1910-11; Barber,
1974; on Minoan and Mycenaean finds in the other islands,
Hope Simpson 1965; Hope Simpson and Lazenby, 1962, 1973.)

Pottery finds provide the basis for the chronology of
this period. From the ceramic evidence, it may be
concluded that Knossos started colonizing activity in the
Aegean in the middle of the sixteenth century, and that
there was a gradual growth of Mycenaean settlements alongside Minoan ones. On Rhodes, relations between Trianda

and the neighbouring Mycenaeans were at first amicable,
as the presence of Minoan and Mycenaean pottery side by
side indicates. Then, at about the time of the fall of
Knossos, Trianda was deserted. After this time, there is
no further trace of Minoans on the island. A similar
pattern may be traced in the other islands: they passed
from the Minoan to the Mycenaean sphere in the fourteenth
century or somewhat earlier. It is not clear why, after
a time of apparently peaceful coexistence, the Minoan
sites were destroyed or abandoned, leaving the Mycenaeans
in possession, but there are sinister implications in the
archaeological record of the desertion of Trianda,
abandoned in a hurry.

The picture is complicated by natural as well as man-
made destruction. Cretan civilization was weakened - if
not completely demolished - by the effects of the
cataclysmic eruption of the Santorini volcano. Marinatos
was first to suggest - before he discovered the remains
at Akrotiri - that the eruption was the direct cause of
the fall of Knossos and the demise of Minoan power, and
many have found his thesis attractive (Marinatos, 1939).
However, there is a serious chronological problem: the
disaster which buried Minoan Thera under volcanic ash
seems to antedate the fall of Knossos by at least a
generation (cf. Page, 1970). In ceramic terms, the
latest pottery from Akrotiri is of the LMIA style
(c.1550-1500 on Evans' scale), whereas Crete has LMIB
(c.1500-1250) and Trianda has 'sub-Minoan IA'. To meet
this difficulty, it may be argued that there were several
phases in the eruption: earth tremors affecting the Theran
settlement (and there is evidence of the repair or
demolition of damaged buildings); followed by eruption,
burying the town under a massive layer of ash; followed
finally by the formation of the caldera, setting up shock-
waves which destroyed the towns in Crete (Doumas, 1974).
Alternatively, it may be argued that the chronological
gap is not serious: that the difference between LMIA and
LMIB pottery styles has been exaggerated; that some LMIB
has been found at Thera; that in the unsettled conditions
prevailing in Thera's last phase fine Cretan ware would
not have been imported (Luce, 1976, suggesting that the
eruption proceeded to its climax in months, rather than
years, destroying both Akrotiri and Knossos c.1470 BC).
A brave attempt by geologists to isolate and assign a date
to Theran tephra on Crete proved rather inconclusive
(Vitaliano and Vitaliano, 1974; Pomerance, 1975;
Vitaliano and Vitaliano, 1975); science has not yet
provided archaeology with the answer to this problem (cf.
Hédérvari, 1971; Rapp and Cook, 1973).

What is clear is that Mycenaean sway in the Aegean
replaced Minoan power: perhaps Minoan cultural ambiance
had little to do with political unity; perhaps Mycenaean
supremacy was an influence loosely exerted over a federation of autonomous states; perhaps the islands knew little
immediate difference – but the orientation of Aegean life
had changed.

Archaeological evidence indicates that Rhodes had become
an important trading station of the maritime Mycenaean
empire.   But the importance of Rhodes has perhaps been
overestimated.   It has been suggested that Rhodes had an
independent foreign policy and was a power familiar to
the Hittites.   Hittite documents of the fourteenth and
thirteenth centuries refer to Akhkhijawā more manageably
transliterated and pronounced as Ahhijawā, which – despite
philological objections – is generally taken to be
'Αχαιϝία, Achaia.   (Millawanda, generally identified with
Miletos, also occurs.)   A persuasive case for equating
Ahhijawā with Rhodian Ialysos can be made (Page, 1959).
However, when archaeological evidence and the evidence of
Homer is added to that of the Hittite documents, Mycenae
seems a stronger contender (Huxley, 1960).   While it is
unlikely that the question will ever be solved decisively,
the opinion of some Near Eastern experts that Ahhijawā
should not be placed in the Greek world at all but in
north-western Anatolia must induce caution (Mellaart,
1958, p.22 n.151; cf. review article, Houwink ten Cate,
1973).

Caution is again indicated by the evidence relating to
local pottery manufacture in Rhodes between about 1400 and
1150 BC (pottery of the LMIII and LHIII groups).   The
technique of detection of trace elements by optical
emission spectroscopy makes it possible to determine the
provenance of pottery by analysing small samples and
isolating composition types.   This is a valuable method,
as subjective discrimination is made difficult by the
uniformity in form and style characteristic of pottery of
this period.   Analysis of Rhodian pottery indicates that
50 per cent was of local manufacture, 50 per cent imported
from the Peloponnese – a surprisingly high proportion of
imported ware (Catling, Richards and Blin-Stoyle, 1963;
cf. Catling, 1970).   This finding tends to suggest that
the island was not important enough for Ahhijawā.   The
dominance of the Peloponnesian pottery group in all the
areas examined indicates close contact of the parent
Mycenae with centres everywhere.

The Homeric epics supplement the findings of the
archaeologist concerned with the Bronze Age, and are
peculiarly important as the earliest Greek written source

available. Whatever view is taken about the date of final
composition and transmission of the poems, it is clear
that the subject matter (and, to a large extent, the
expression of it) is drawn from many centuries of oral
tradition. The poems incorporate detail about the Bronze
Age - Early, Middle and Late - known from archaeological
finds to be authentic, and apparent reminiscences of the
Dark Age, alongside anachronistic material about Iron Age
practices drawn from the poet's (or compiler's) own
experience of a much later period. The epics give
information about the part played by the eastern islands
in the Trojan expedition. The Catalogue of Ships, listing
Agamemnon's allies ('Il.' 2), which presents a picture of
the Bronze Age known to be accurate in part and felt to be
credible in general, has some surprises for us when it
comes to the islands. First, the northern islands, which
played so important a part in later Greek history, are
not mentioned at all, while the islands on the south-east
fringes of the Aegean do appear. (Miletos, on the coast
nearby, is on the Trojan side.) Rhodes sends nine ships,
with a son of Herakles as leader; Syme sends three and a
coalition led by Kos - Nisyros, Krapathos, Kos and the
'Kalydnan islands' - sends thirty, under a grandson of
Herakles. Krapathos stands for Karpathos by metathesis.
The identity of the 'Kalydnan islands' was debated by
Strabo (10.5.19). The expression may refer only to
Kalymnos (for the plural used idiomatically, cf. Athenai
and Thebai); if it is a true plural, it may refer to
Kalymnos, Pserimos, Telendos and possibly also Leros.
Even more surprising than the absence of the northern
islands is the relative unimportance of Rhodes: it
contributes few ships and islands later subject to Rhodes
are assigned to Kos (Nisyros, Karpathos, Kasos) or
independent (Syme). The insignificance of Rhodes in the
catalogue - added to the verdict of pottery experts on
the quantity of imported ware in the island - strongly
suggests that Rhodes cannot be Hittite Ahhijawā.

The sack of Troy is dated on archaeological evidence
to about 1200, not far from the dates estimated in
antiquity by Herodotos (1250) and by Eratosthenes (1183).
Pottery from Troy VIIa ('Homer's Troy') shows marked
similarities with that of Mycenaean sites on the Greek
mainland which were destroyed or abandoned around the same
time (Stubbings, CAH I3 pp.239-47). The cause of the
mainland disasters is obscure, masked by an archaeological
'Dark Age' of some three centuries following. The fall of
Mycenae and other Mycenaean strongholds had little immediate
impact on the islands. There was a population influx as
displaced people left the Greek peninsula in search of

safer homes overseas, but no destruction and no such
cultural break as is associated with the mainland and a
less protracted Dark Age (Desborough, 1964, p.30).

The comparative prosperity of the islands at the very
end of the Mycenaean period (LHIIIC, corresponding
approximately to the twelfth century) and their immunity
from destruction and collapse is marked. The desertion of
the great mainland strongholds has been attributed to
climatic change: extreme drought and consequent famine
leading to depopulation and flight from the mainland
centres to the east (Carpenter, 1966); but it is more
generally and more plausibly regarded as the result of
war, associated directly or indirectly with the Dorians.
Whether the Dorians actually destroyed the Mycenaean
palaces, or merely profited from destruction by others is
uncertain; as is the scale and timing of their arrival.
Literary sources record the coming of the Dorians as the
'return of the Herakleidai'; archaeologically the Dorians
are elusive.

In Homer's account of the forces accompanying Agamemnon
to Troy, the island contingents are led by descendants of
Herakles. Herakles was later the Dorian hero par
excellence, with the tribe of the Hylleis claiming descent
from his son Hyllos. His appearance here seems to imply
that the population of the islands at the time of the
Trojan War was already Dorian. The objection to this is
that Homer's picture in general is of a pre-Dorian Greece;
the Dorian invasion or return of the Herakleidai, according
to modern calculations, happened after the sack of Troy
(cf. D.S.1.5.1), and it was only some time after the
Dorians had occupied the Peloponnese that they swept across
the sea in a great colonizing movement to the islands.
Herakles' place in the Homeric genealogies is suggestive
of the presence of Dorians, but not conclusive: he was
never exclusively Dorian property and the exploits of
Herakles the man cover many regions of the Greek world.
However, other considerations point to an early Dorian
presence. The description of the Rhodians as 'arranged
in three groups' (655) and their island as 'inhabited in
three groups by tribes' (668) is striking. Line 655 has
been taken to refer simply to the three cities Lindos,
Ialysos and Kameiros (named in the next line), but it is
more difficult to dismiss line 668, which has a clear
reference to three 'phylai' or tribes ('kataphyladon').
The division into the three tribes Hylleis, Dymanes and
Pamphyloi was one of the most characteristic features of
Dorian communities throughout their history. When we add
to this the consideration that the tribes were generally
used in Dorian states as units for military organization,

it becomes significant that the islands send their ships
to Troy in multiples of three (nine from Rhodes, three
from Syme and thirty from the Koan coalition). It is
also significant that the verb used in 655 ('kosmein') is
elsewhere in the 'Iliad' a technical term of military
arrangement ('Il.'2.806, 3.1, 12.87, 14.379). This is not
the only Homeric evidence for the presence of Dorians in
the south Aegean. In the only passage where Homer
explicitly names Dorians, they are said to form part of
the mixed population of Crete, again with stress on three-
fold organization ('Od.'19.177; for the adjective,
'trichaikes', cf. Merkelbach and West, 1967, p.233; for
Dorians in Crete, Willetts, 1962, pp.131-7). Strabo
states that Dorians in east Crete came from Thessaly,
from the country previously called Doris (10.4.75). The
name Doris was also given to the Gulf of Kos (Ptol.'Geog.'
5.2.8; cf. Fraser and Bean, 1954, p.70 n.1). Thessaly is
an area of crucial importance in the early Greek world,
Iolkos (modern Volos) in particular being a key-point in
Greek prehistory. There is a high concentration there of
Neolithic and Early Bronze Age remains (not yet fully
excavated) and to this area belong old and rich strata of
myth, in particular the Argonaut saga. Evidence for
connections between the islands and Thessaly is explored
in Chapter 7.
    It is easy to allege that the Odyssean description of
the population of Crete is interpolated and that the lines
which imply the presence of Dorians in Rhodes - or,
indeed, the whole section about the islands - are a late
accretion to the main body of the poems (Page, 1959). But
this is a violent and unnecessary expedient. There is no
need to abandon the Homeric record simply because we
cannot fully understand it. It is of some importance that
the settlement pattern in the islands in the Late Bronze
Age exactly fits Homer's account of their habitation
(Hope Simpson and Lazenby, 1962, 1970a, 1973). Diodoros'
account of these events, while agreeing in general with
Homer's, does not mention Karpathos: this may be a chance
or careless omission, but it is possible rather that he
is using a tradition independent of Homer, the separate
existence of which would lend some support to the Homeric
version (D.S.5.54.1). Strabo's objections to the presence
of Dorians in Homer in the passage where he attempts an
exegesis of the catalogue are as cogent as those of modern
commentators; no more, no less (Str.14.2.6). The most
convincing argument against interpolation lies in the lack
of answers to the questions why, when and by whom the
passage might have been added. Dorian intervention in
the text of Homer, as transmitted to us, was slight. There

was a tradition that Lykourgos - the Spartan lawgiver,
a very shadowy figure - brought the poems to the Greek
mainland, but there is little contamination in them to
support this; in any case, such a person would have scant
interest in glorifying the islands. Only Rhodes among
the islands was later powerful enough to wish to foist a
change into the catalogue - and a Rhodian interpolator
would certainly not have given his island such an
ignominious place, contributing a mere nine ships. The
fact that Rhodes contributes so few ships and that islands
later in the Rhodian orbit are either assigned to Kos or
independent indicates that this is not a case of Rhodian
tampering with the text. Later (in the Hellenistic
period) Kos annexed only Kalymnos: the very unexpectedness
of its supremacy here has the ring of truth.

Is it credible then that the islands were populated by
Dorians at this early date? Material culture cannot help
us here: the remains from the islands are thoroughly
Minoan or Mycenaean in character, without a trace even of
the alleged earlier population of Karians and Leleges
(Hdt.1.171; Th.1.4.8; cf.Chapter 4). But there is no
single archaeological feature which can be definitely
assigned to the Dorians, and it may be that the best
description of them at this time is as a Greek ethnic
group, whose main peculiarity distinguishing them from
other Greek ethnic groups was their tribal system. The
dialect which developed later was a further differentiation, but a differentiation which was fully evolved after,
not before, they were ensconced in the areas which became
their domain. (It is now generally believed that the
Greek dialects developed in the Greek peninsula, the older
view being that they were brought by successive 'waves' of
settlers speaking different dialects. Disagreement remains
as to when dialectal differences crystallized and as to what
areas were populated by speakers of 'proto-Doric', etc.
(summary, Birchall and Crossland, 1973, p.343).)

It is not doubted that there were Dorians on the fringes
of the Mycenaean world before its collapse, and it is now
believed that the Dorians came in a series of forays,
gradually infiltrating the peninsula, rather than in a
single sudden dramatic influx; or even that they were
present alongside the Mycenaeans in the Peloponnese as a
subject population (Chadwick, 1976; Hooker, 1977; cf.
Dietrich, 1974, pp.262-4). Ancient traditions gave
different routes for the 'return of the Herakleidai', and
one of these was by sea, from Thessaly to a point near
Argos. It seems probable that there was an earlier movement of Dorians from Thessaly to the south Aegean. The
early presence of Dorians in Crete, attested by Homer in

a completely different context, lends much support to this
contention, as does, cumulatively, the evidence of
connections between the islands (especially Kos) and
Thessaly; and the myths associating Herakles with the area.
Had Homer placed Dorians in the north of the Aegean rather
than in Crete and Rhodes, areas where they later settled,
his account might, paradoxically, have encountered less
scepticism, as anachronism would not have been immediately
suspected.

After their striking cultural prominence in the late
Mycenaean period, the islands yield no remains for at
least a century (c.1050-950). This Dark Age is gradually
becoming less dark, but the break, as elsewhere in Greece,
is none the less complete (Snodgrass, 1971). Probably
some areas of Greece suffered a period of complete depopulation, while, in others, communities struggled on,
leading an isolated and impoverished existence. When
material culture re-emerges and contacts between communities are re-established, it is in the context of broad
changes in settlement areas, in artefacts and in craft
techniques. Greece has passed from the Bronze Age to the
Iron Age, from the world of the Mycenaeans to that of the
emerging city-states. Yet this nascent culture sprang
from Bronze Age roots. Traditions of the glorious past
survived orally, to be enshrined in the Homeric epics;
the Greek language survived, though the script used by
the Mycenaean bureaucracy was lost (see Chapter 4);
religious ideas survived (see Chapter 7). In material
objects, too, continuity is apparent. Protogeometric
pottery is very different in spirit from Mycenaean vases,
yet uses some of the same motifs; archaeologists are often
unable to determine whether isolated finds of striped
sherds are Mycenaean or archaic. A continuous evolution
in pottery styles is demonstrated by the heterogeneous
grave-goods from a tomb of the Serraglio cemetery in Kos,
where Mycenaean vases of the fourteenth century are re-
utilized alongside protogeometric pots, made some four
centuries later, and only the expert can assign dates to
the finds (Snodgrass, 1971, illust. p.75).

The islands became populous again with the Dorian sweep
overseas from the Peloponnese in the eighth century.
Settlers came to Thera from Sparta (with Minyans also in
the group); to Melos also from Sparta; to Rhodes from
Argos and the Argolid, also to Karpathos and Kasos; to
Astypalaia from Megara or Epidauros; to Kos from Epidauros;
to Kalymnos and Nisyros from Kos; to Syme from Argos,
Sparta, Kaunos and Rhodes (Hdt.7.99; Th.5.84.2; D.S.5.53-4;
Str.8.3.19, 10.5.1, 14.2.6; IG IV 2, 147). According to
Herodotos, Thera was founded in the first generation after

the arrival of the Dorians in the Peloponnese (Hdt.4.148);
in the fifth century, the Melians believed that their state
had existed for 700 years (Th.5.112). Melos and Thera seem
to have preserved shadowy memories of an early movement of
population to their area, just as Kos had a folk tradition
of connections with Thessaly. The earliest geometric
pottery found on Melos and Thera implies an eighth-century
date for the main arrivals, fitting the broad pattern of
movement at this time from the mainland to the Aegean and
the East.

Traditions of an early Rhodian thalassocracy are probably
exaggerated. Kastor of Rhodes who wrote a history of sea-
powers (quoted by Eusebios from a lost book of Diodoros)
had an interest in giving Rhodes prominence in his work,
which in any case seems an uncritical schematic list, with
thalassocracies - Rhodes, Phrygia, Cyprus, etc. - succeeding one another like kings in an accession list (FGH II
250). Trade certainly flourished, as is demonstrated by
finds of Rhodian objects overseas and of imported goods -
gold, ivory, faience - in Rhodes (Dunbabin, 1948, 1957;
Boardman, 1964, pp.81, 84, 89, 95, 111; Austin, 1970,
pp.50-1 n.2 and p.52 n.2). Under foreign influence,
goldsmiths set up workshops in Rhodes. Melos meantime
became the centre of the seventh-century gem-working and
jewellery craft.

Strabo's assertion that long before the first Olympiad
(776 BC) the Rhodians had sailed to Spain and Italy,
founding colonies in the West (Str.14.2.10; cf.3.4.8,
6.1.14, critically treated by Jeffery, 1976, p.195;
accepted with reference to Mycenaean settlement by
Pugliese Carratelli, 1958b) probably refers to later events.
A rapid population expansion led to the foundation of
colonies from the islands. Around 690, Lindos founded
Phaselis in Lykia and joined Crete in sending colonists to
Gela in Sicily. Some sixty years later, Kyrene in Libya
was founded by Thera on the injunction of Apollo
(Hdt.4.150-9; Meiggs and Lewis, 1969, pp.5-9 no.5 = SEG 9
(1938-44) no.3). That Rhodians joined in this settlement
was stated in antiquity and is rendered plausible by finds
on the north African coast of late seventh-century Rhodian
pottery (Xenagoras, FGH II 240 F10; Boardman and Hayes,
1966, p.41; cf.Seltman, 1955, p.82). That Rhodian
individuals travelled as mercenaries to Egypt, serving
under Psammetichos (probably Psammetichos II, 594-589) is
known from an inscription of Abu-Symbel (graffiti
impudently scratched on the legs of one of the famous
giant statues) with the names of men from Kolophon, Teos
and Rhodes (SIG 1 = SGDI 5261).

Evidence for island institutions in the archaic period

is scanty, but the pattern is kingship followed by a
hereditary aristocracy (Th.1.13; Arist.'Pol.'1290b). The
three towns of Rhodes were autonomous, each with its own
sovereign, its own territory and its own coinage.
Kleoboulos, who ruled Lindos in the first half of the
sixth century, is a little less shadowy than most archaic
rulers. His political and military leadership was long
remembered: the Lindian Chronicle records an expedition
to Lykia and a dedication to Athena. He may have been
associated with the inception of the coinage, first
issued by Lindos around this time. Kleoboulos was later
regarded as one of the seven sages (a variable group, but
most commonly Kleoboulos with Bias of Priene, Chilon of
Sparta, Periander of Corinth, Pittakos of Mitylene, Solon
of Athens and Thales of Miletos), and is the sort of
figure around whom stories accumulate and to whom maxims
are attributed (cf. Chapter 5). In the same way, riddles
are associated with the name of his 'daughter' Kleoboulina
(West, 1972, II pp.50-1).

From Herodotos, we know of the sixth-century power
struggles in the East, and the rise of the successive
empires of Lydia and Persia. Lydia was content to remain
a continental power; the Persians were ambitious to extend
their sway to the islands of the Aegean and ultimately -
partly because of Athens' provocation in encouraging the
Greeks in the East to resist - to the Greek mainland
itself.

The Greek cities of the Asiatic coast which had been
annexed to the Persian Empire by Cyrus' general Harpagos
made a bid for freedom in the 'Ionian Revolt' of 499.
This the Persians suppressed after a struggle lasting some
six years. Ionian Miletos led the revolt, and the battle
which saw its end was fought at Lade, just offshore. In
this situation, Greek drew closer to Greek, but not Dorian
to Ionian. Athens sent twenty ships to help the eastern
Greeks; Sparta merely registered a protest (Hdt.5.99.1,
1.52.3). The Dorian communities near at hand kept a
prudent or an enforced silence. Herodotos' account of the
débâcle at Lade in 494 makes no mention of contingents
from the Dorian islands. According to the Lindian
Chronicle, the entire population of Rhodes was thrown into
a panic by the arrival of the Persian fleet, under
Dareios, and took refuge at defensible points, such as
Lindos. There, only providential rain helped the Rhodians
to resist siege and come to terms with the Persians (cf.
Burn, 1962, pp.210-11 and p.218, additional note 1, dating
these events to 494). The strategic importance of Rhodes
to any power with pretensions to dominate the Aegean is
shown by the attention Polykrates, tyrant of Samos, paid

to the island; it was a significant outpost of his domain,
held by his son, who was known as 'Polykrates of Rhodes'
(Bowra, 1961, pp.249-50). Politic gifts were made to the
shrine of Athena at Lindos by an admiral of Dareios; also
by King Amasis of Egypt, allied with Kroisos of Lydia
(Hdt.3.47.2).

Kos was certainly under Persian sway, apparently as a
free dependency under King Kadmos, son of Skyphes, whose
family was much trusted by the Persians. Kadmos abdicated
power in favour of a more democratic régime - perhaps
under the pressure of popular movements against 'tyranny'
at the time - and left for the West, where he continued
to lead an eventful life (Hdt.1.163-4, with How and Wells,
ed.; cf. Burn, 1962, pp.309-10). By 480, the Karian
rulers, satellites of the Persian court, were in control
of several of the islands. Nisyros, Kos and Kalymnos,
together with Halikarnassos led by Artemisia, contributed
five ships to the Persian fleet which fought at the battle
of Salamis. At the same time, Melos with Siphnos and
Seriphos was on the other side. Melos contributed two
pentekonters (smaller and slower than triremes, but a
useful backup to a fighting fleet) and Siphnos and
Seriphos one each to the Greek side at Artemision. The
same three islands contributed four pentekonters for
Salamis (Hdt.7.99.2, 8.87-8, 8.46.4, 8.48).

The island states probably felt very vulnerable,
situated so close to the Asiatic power bloc, and caught
in the crossfire of the wars. The scanty evidence for
their activities at this time suggests that they kept
quiet as far as possible, hoping that a token contribution
to one side or the other might be taken as sufficient
support or forgiven as slight opposition by the eventual
victor.

Herodotos' full account of the fortunes of Kadmos
contrasts with his silence on the involvement and attitudes
of the islanders generally. Individuals, like communities,
doubtless felt unsure of their position. Timokreon of
Ialysos was one Rhodian who threw in his lot with the
Persians and later regretted it. Timokreon left Rhodes
for the Persian court, then, when events proved he had
backed the wrong side, tried to get back to Ialysos with
the help of the Athenian general Themistokles. Themistokles
failed him, perhaps because of a counter-bribe from
Timokreon's enemies, and left Timokreon a very embittered
man (Ath.10.415f; Plu.'Them'21.2; cf. Meiggs, 1972, p.414,
endnote 2). The personal feud of Timokreon with
Themistokles and Simonides (the latter perhaps for no
better reason than that he was Themistokles' friend)
coloured his whole literary output as a lyric poet (cf.
Chapter 5).

Perhaps a similar mistaken assessment of military probabilities lay behind events in the life of the daughter of Agetorides of Kos, who left the Persian camp - with the story that she had been forcibly carried off to be the mistress of Dareios' nephew Pharandates - after the Greeks emerged victorious at Plataia. This Koan girl was more fortunate than Timokreon, and was granted a safe conduct to Aigina (Hdt.9.76; cf. Paus.3.4.9). With hindsight, no Greek - unless unhappily compromised by Medism - would own to any sympathy with the Persians. The correspondence asking Hippokrates to go to Persia and containing Hippokrates' refusal, on the grounds that the Persians were barbarians and enemies of the Greeks, is a late fabrication, but it aptly reflects the anti-Persian sentiments prevailing after the repulse ('Ep.'1-9; cf. Plu.'Cato' 23.3).

After the defeat of the Persians, Ionia and the islands were free. Aischylos includes Rhodes among Greek cities which threw off the Persian yoke after Salamis (A.'Pers.' 891). Athens, taking the credit for Greece's victory, expected gratitude, in the form of loyalty to a new league formed to keep the Persian menace under control; and ultimately, both loyalty and material tribute to herself (Meiggs, 1972, pp.459-64; but cf. Rawson, 1969, pp.15-16 on the Dorian contribution at Plataia). The basis of the league was Ionian (Th.1.95.1); the Athenians set up its treasury and nominal headquarters at Delos, supposed birthplace and important cult centre of Apollo. This move was calculated to win the loyalty of all Greeks. The Delian festival was a great Ionian gathering, but Apollo was also an honoured Dorian god (cf. Chapter 8). However, Apollo was not worshipped with the title 'Delian' at Melos or Thera and this may be a significant factor in later events. Melos and Thera differ from the other Dorian islands in geographical position, furthest west of the group, and in their antecedents, as colonies of Sparta. Resulting differences in cults and attitudes may account for differences in the part they played in fifth-century history.

The islands off the Asiatic coast were founder members of the Delian League and remained loyal for many decades: at the start of the Peloponnesian War the Athenian allies included 'the Karian coast and the Dorians neighbouring the Karians' (Th.2.9.4). In the lists of tribute the southern offshore islands were included in the 'Karian' group: Astypalaia, Chalke, Kalymnos, Karpathos (as four separate contributors), Kasos, Kos, Rhodes (three separate contributors) and Syme. Islands later dependent on Rhodes were assessed independently by Athens, as were certain places on the mainland opposite, later in the 'Rhodian Peraia'. At the same time, Nisyros - like Leros - was placed in the 'Ionian' group.

There are some indications that Kos shared in the growing dissatisfaction in the Aegean with Athens' conduct of the League and appropriation of its resources. Between the years 449 and 446 - precisely the time when masons began to erect the Parthenon - Kos either failed to meet her assessed contribution of five talents (a large sum, indicative of the island's prosperity) or paid it in instalments. There are some signs of Koan recalcitrance against Athens' fiat, probably shortly before 445, that no allies should issue their own silver coins, but that all should employ Attic coins, weights and measures (Seltman, 1955, pp.148-50; Jenkins, 1972, pp.90-1; Meiggs, 1972, pp.168-70). Rhodes too was restive under Athens' demands: the title of a lost speech of Antiphon, 'On the Tribute of Lindos', indicates that Lindos had appealed against her assessment. In 440, unrest in the islands was quelled by a show of force against Samos, when Athenian troops under Pericles and Sophocles met a force led by the philosopher Melissos.

By 443, all notable islands of the Aegean were members of the League, with the significant exceptions of Melos and Thera. Then Thera appears in the tribute quota lists of (probably) 429 and (certainly) 428. It seems that Melos and Thera had been subjected to pressure and that, while Thera yielded, Melos resisted, professing neutrality but in fact giving active support to the Spartan war effort. In 426, Athens sent a punitive force against Melos. Melos refused battle, and the contingents withdrew after ravaging the land. The tribute assessment of 425 demanded from Melos fifteen talents - a huge sum expressive of Athens' anger and frustration. (For comparison, it may be noted that in 434, Kasos and ten other cities together were assessed at under three and a half talents.) In 416, events came to a head. Athens now despatched a strong naval force to subdue Melos. When the people refused to surrender, the Athenian troops killed the men and carried the women and children off as slaves. The island then became an Attic 'cleruchy' or settlement but was restored to Melians, surviving in exile, by the Spartan Lysander in 404 (Th.3.91.1-3, 5.84-116; Plu.'Alc.'5; cf. Meiggs, 1972, pp.250, 314, 321-2, 385-90; Seltman, 1955, pp.174, 176).

In 415, Athens sent out a massive expedition against Sicily, opening a new front in the war. To this Rhodes contributed two pentekonters (Th.6.43). It is remarkable that the Rhodians made any contribution, the Sicilian Dorians being their kin; however, its unimpressive size

suggests a reluctance to be involved at all. The
failure of the Sicilian enterprise left Athens vulnerable
and gave disaffected states an opportunity to secede.
Rhodes revolted, and became for a time a naval base for
the Peloponnesians. Her new affiliations did not protect
her from sporadic Athenian raids. Kos was even more
unfortunate, being in the course of a single decade badly
ravaged by both Athens and Sparta; the island suffered a
serious earthquake in 413/412 and the Spartans took
advantage of its weakened state to invade; Kos then
vacillated in her loyalties before following Rhodes in
backing Sparta; as a result, an Athenian force under
Alkibiades subjected it to severe reprisals (Th.8.44, 55,
108; D.S.13.42.3; cf. IC pp.xlix-li).

These interstate events had an impact on internal
politics. In 409/408, the Rhodians concentrated their
resources by synoecism, forming the new city of Rhodes
on the eastern promontory of the island where the modern
capital still stands (D.S.13.75.1; cf. Moggi, 1976,
pp.213-26). Rhodes now presented a more concerted military
front to the outside world. Also, this site was
strategically placed to command the shipping routes and
from its foundation dated Rhodes' commercial prosperity.
In 366, Kos followed the lead of Rhodes in synoecism,
creating a new city in the east of the island, and
relegating the old towns to 'demes', or districts
(Str.14.2.19; D.S.15.76.2; cf. Craik, 1967; Moggi, 1976).
Kos too rapidly prospered, as inscriptions and a prolific
coinage indicate.

Rhodes, Kos and Nisyros yet again changed sides in the
protracted confrontation between Athens and Sparta in 394,
leaving the Spartan alliance after the victory of the
Athenian admiral Konon at Knidos. Konon's conquests
extended to Melos, where he set up a naval base.
Repercussions of these events on individuals are recorded.
Dorieus of Ialysos was a man of strong Spartan sympathies
who left Rhodes, then allied with Athens, for Thourioi.
He returned to his country after the Sicilian Expedition
and helped to consolidate Rhodes' revolt against Athens.
Caught by an Athenian squadron in 407, he could expect no
quarter; but was unexpectedly pardoned because of his fine
athletic record of victories at Olympia and the Panathenaia
(cf. Harris, 1964, p.124). Paradoxically, Dorieus escaped
death at the hands of the Athenians only to meet it at
those of the Spartans with whom he was ideologically in
sympathy. He happened to be in the Peloponnese at the
time of the Rhodian defection to Athens from Sparta in 394
and was killed as a scapegoat (Paus.6.7.1-7; X.'Hell.'
1.1.2-4, 1.5.19; D.S.13.38.5, 14.84.3; D.Chr.31.126).

A renewed upsurge of pro-Athenian sentiment led to the
foundation in 378 of a further Athenian alliance. This
was shortlived, though the Athenians fought hard to retain
their allies. Rhodes and Kos, with several other states,
seceded and won independence after defeating Athens in the
'Social War' around the middle of the decade 360-350,
thanks to the aid of Mausolos of Karia (D.15.314). Karia's
encouragement was not disinterested, and before long
Rhodes and Kos were in an oppressive stranglehold,
appealing to Athens for help against Karian despotism. In
the debate following this request, Rhodes was championed
by Demosthenes, who made an impassioned appeal to the
people not to bear a grudge against Rhodes for her recent
revolt against Athens, but to intervene and restore
democratic institutions on the island (D.15.3-4, 21):

> Mausolos, who was the architect and inciter of these
> events, while claiming to be a friend of the Rhodian
> people, will be exposed as the despoiler of their
> freedom; those who set themselves up as their allies,
> the Chians and Byzantines, will be exposed as failing
> to help them in their misfortunes; while you, whom
> they feared, will alone of all peoples be the occasion
> of their security....
> If anyone says that the Rhodians deserve their
> plight, this is not the time to gloat over them....

Athens was unpersuaded by Demosthenes' quixotic oratory.
In the peroration of his speech 'On the Peace', delivered
some five years later, in 346, Demosthenes reminded the
citizens (D.5.25):

> We allow the Karian to take possession of the islands,
> Chios, Rhodes and Kos.

Rhodes and Kos had regained their freedom by 339, when
they went with Chios, as independent allies, to the
assistance of Byzantium, besieged by Philip of Macedon.
Athens too went to the rescue of the city, and found
herself fighting - successfully, as it turned out - on
the same side as the islands against the new menace from
Macedon. On succeeding his father Philip in 336,
Alexander soon embarked on his meteoric career of conquest.
In 334, he came to the south Aegean coast and captured
Halikarnassos, though the garrison in the citadel held
out for a time. When this garrison was ultimately taken,
all the cities of the region, and also Thera, went over
to Alexander (Arr.'An.'2.5.7). The fortunes of Kos were
then to undergo some rapid changes: Memnon, a Rhodian who
was a naval commander in the service of the king of Persia,
recovered Kos for his master; it was retaken by Alexander's
generals soon afterwards. Macedon had now established its
sway in this region and could look further east.

After the death of Alexander in 323, Kos and Rhodes
became embroiled in the power struggles of Alexander's
generals. According to Diodoros (D.S.20.81.3):

Alexander ... honouring Rhodes above all cities
deposited there the testament disposing of his whole
realm;

but this is doubtful (cf. PA II p.947 n.16 on the
'historically tendentious items in the Testament'). Rhodes
and Kos passed to Ptolemy, Alexander's general who had
been appointed governor of Egypt. It was on Kos that
Ptolemy's wife Berenike gave birth to a son - later Ptolemy
Philadelphos - in 309. However, as battles raged between
those ambitious to increase their share of Alexander's
realms, Ptolemy lost his command in the Aegean after a
major defeat at Cyprus, against Demetrios, the son of
Antigonos (of Macedon). Demetrios' supreme naval
commander was a Koan, Pleistias (D.S.20.50.4). Antigonos
now hoped that Rhodes would feel bound to co-operate with
him in his attack on Ptolemy. Rhodes, however, refused
and Demetrios - surnamed 'Poliorketes', the Besieger -
laid siege to the island. This siege, which lasted a
year (305/304), is one of the most famous of all time; it
caught the imagination of many later writers (D.S.20.81-100;
Plu.'Demetr'.20.5-22.4; App.'BC'4.67). The stability of
the Rhodian state (which had the confidence to arm its
slaves in its defence), the loyalty and courage of the
people and of resident foreigners (such as the painter
Protogenes, who calmly continued with his work in the
suburbs) are celebrated. The activities of the besiegers
are also chronicled, with descriptions of the vast numbers
of men in the attack (including a gang of pirates serving
as mercenaries, no doubt hoping for a personal revenge on
the Rhodians), and of the technology applied to the
construction of ever more powerful and terrifying siege
machinery. Rhodes won through - helped at a crucial point
by gifts of food supplies from Egypt and elsewhere - and
gained favourable terms, including the right to remain
neutral in war between Antigonos and Ptolemy; also the
siege engines, left behind as a grim souvenir. With
some enterprise, the Rhodians used the scrap metal to
finance the erection of a landmark, and perhaps also as
scaffolding, in the construction of the Kolossos at the
harbour mouth (see Gabriel, 1932). The commission for
the sculpture went to a local man, Chares of Lindos.

Rhodes had won the respect of the world, and went from
strength to strength. Rhodian foreign policy was one of
armed neutrality (Plb.30.5.8), avoiding firm alignment
with any other power (cf. CAH VII p.822, on the belief,
previously widespread, but now regarded as mistaken, that

there was a fourth-century alliance between Rhodes and
Rome). Through time, Rhodes annexed a large part of the
mainland opposite (the 'Peraia') as well as several of
the islands, to her own territory. These regions were
benevolently administered as demes, incorporated in the
Rhodian state, or, in the case of later additions, as
subject territory (see Fraser and Bean, 1954, for the
fortunes of Chalke, Karpathos, Kasos, Nisyros, Syme and
Telos). Rhodes was a power to be reckoned with, building
up a strong fleet, gaining a reputation for honourable
dealings, suppressing piracy and policing the seas,
consolidating her trade contacts. Rhodes' fiscal strength
and influence is shown in loans made to Argos and Priene
early in the third century and in the adoption by many
far-flung cities of the Rhodian standard for silver coins
at this time (cf. RR I p.71, II p.877 n.69); her naval
strength is apparent in inscriptions honouring Rhodian
admirals overseas (e.g. SIG 455, Delos); her diplomatic
reputation is evident from her role as arbitrator in such
international disputes as a territorial wrangle between
Priene and Samos, c.240. Kos had some share in all this
prosperity and prestige: the Koan legal system was
recommended to a new town by Antigonos (SIG 344; cf.
RR II p.875 n.64). Of the other islands at this time, we
hear little. Thera remained a Ptolemaic possession and was
used as an Aegean naval base.

The third century is dominated by the power struggles
of the families of Alexander's generals who inherited his
conquests - the Ptolemies of Egypt, Seleukids of Syria
and Antigonids of Macedon - with, on the sidelines, the
rulers of small independent states. At best the equilibrium between these powers was uneasy. Antigonos Gonatas
gained mastery of the Aegean in a crucial engagement near
Kos, probably in 258 (but the date is much disputed, opinion
ranging from as early as 265 to as late as 245: see RR II
p.931 n.26), when his allies - which included Rhodes -
defeated the combined forces of Egypt - which included
Kos. By the peace then concluded, Ptolemy was allowed to
keep Thera, but little else. Rhodes suffered a serious
earthquake in the decade 230-220, probably in the year
227. This overthrew the giant Kolossos and almost
flattened the city itself. Gifts of grain and cash flowed
in from all the great powers; and in a few years Rhodes
had recovered her position (Plb.5.88.1-90.8; cf. Casson,
1954).

In 220, Byzantium decided to impose a tax on all ships
passing the Hellespont, a crucial trade-route with exports
including cattle, salt fish, wax and - especially - grain,
and with imports of oil and wine (Plb.4.38-52, 3.2.5;

cf. Phillipson, 1911, p.380). This move was clearly
inimical to the common interests of the Greek states and
had far-reaching implications as to the legitimacy of
states' levying tolls in their territorial waters. It was
Rhodes which intervened, making Byzantium retract (Plb.
4.52.4-5):

> Treaties were made, that with the Rhodians being in
> simple terms, to this effect: 'The Byzantines are to
> levy no tolls on ships sailing to the Pontos; the
> Rhodians and their allies, on this condition, will be
> at peace with the Byzantines.

Rhodes' protectorate over the Aegean and beyond is further
seen in assistance rendered Sinope at this time: Rhodes
sent financial help, provisions and weapons to prevent
annexation by Mithridates (Plb.4.56.1; cf. RR II p.1077
n.23).

The year 220 BC (the 140th Olympiad) was taken by
Polybios (1.5) as a starting-point in his account of

> how ... in less than fifty-three years almost all
> regions of the inhabited world have fallen under the
> single sway of the Romans....

Documentation of the events of the following centuries is
full, complex and often conflicting in the pages of
Polybios, Appian, Dio, Livy and other historians; their
accounts can be supplemented by the evidence of many
inscriptions set up by the Greek states. Only a brief
summary, skirting contentious questions, can be given
here.

Rome's involvement with the East was precipitated by
the actions of Philip V of Macedon. Philip's alliance
with Rome's enemy Hannibal had both military and diplomatic consequences: sporadic fighting between Macedon and
Rome ('the first Macedonian War') and Rome's counter-
alliance with Pergamum and with the Aitolian League (a
confederation of states in central Greece). Peace was
concluded between the Aitolians and Philip in 205.
Thereupon Philip turned his attention to the Aegean and
in particular to an attempt to undermine Rhodes' power at
sea. Philip incited Crete to war with Rhodes and Kos
(the 'Cretan War' of SIG 569; cf. RR II p.746 n.36, p.914
n.141), contrived to destroy part of the Rhodian arsenal
and ravaged the Peraia. Rhodes met this provocation by
forming an alliance against Philip, with Pergamum,
Byzantium, Chios and other states. This alliance inflicted
some losses on Philip's forces, but was unable to press
its advantage home decisively. It was to Rome that Rhodes
now (201) sent envoys, complaining of Philip's conduct,
and relaying news - perhaps merely a rumour, or even a
fabrication - of a compact between Philip and the Seleukid

king Antiochos III, planning acts of aggression and aggrandizement. After some debate, the Romans first simply sent orders to Philip not to molest the Rhodians (App.'Mac.'4; cf. Livy 31.2.1; Plb.16.24.3); then, when this ultimatum was repudiated, determined on a second war with Macedon. In 199 the Romans landed in Epeiros; in 198 the consul T. Quinctius Flamininus defeated Philip's forces at Kynoskephalai. Flamininus had Greece in his power, but elected to restore its freedom. Amid great jubilation, a settlement was proclaimed at the Isthmian games of 196 (App.'Mac.'9.4; cf. D.S. 18.16):

> The Roman people and Senate, with their general Flamininus, having defeated the Macedonians and King Philip, leave Greece free from garrisons, and from levies, to enjoy its own customs and laws.

Rome was again drawn into conflict in the East when Antiochos III, although checked by the Rhodian navy from seizing Samos and some Karian cities (Livy 33.20.11; cf. RR II p.946 n.49), invaded Greece. Rome was assisted in the war against Antiochos by Pergamum (under Eumenes II) and Rhodes (cf. D.C.18.4). Rhodian admirals were much in demand, and not all served on the Roman side: Appian ('Syr.' 22-5) records a contretemps between Pausimachos (commanding a Rhodian fleet for the Romans) and Polyxenidas (a commander under Antiochos). Eudamos, who commanded another Rhodian contingent, also faced his compatriot Polyxenidas in naval engagements. After a decisive battle in 190, Antiochos surrendered on crippling terms, ceding to Rome all his dominion in Asia Minor. Rome divided these lands between Rhodes and Pergamum, Rhodes receiving Lykia and much of Karia (as far as the river Maiander). The Rhodians were delighted initially with the success of their plea to the Roman senate that the Greeks in Asia Minor be free (Plb.21.22.7):

> To their state, this seemed the finest thing and that most worthy of Rome, that the Greeks in Asia should have their freedom and gain that autonomy which is dearest to all mankind.

(Cf. Plb.21.43, 30.5.12; App.'Syr.'44; 'Mith.'62; Livy 37.54). However, Rhodes did not hold these new possessions for long (D.Chr.31.48; App.'Syr.'44.)

When the 'third Macedonian War' broke out between Rome and Perseus (Philip's son) in 172, Rhodes and Kos were politically torn, each side having its advocates. Pergamum, as before, helped Rome; but relations between Rhodes and Pergamum were strained at this time (App.'Mac.'4). The Rhodians first offered some ships to the Romans, but later, when the pro-Perseus party gained the ascendant, retracted, proposing themselves as mediators instead (Plb.27.7-8).

Rhodian envoys went to Rome, but were ignominiously kept
waiting for a hearing till the victory of L. Aemilius
Paulus over Perseus at Pydna made the purpose of the
delegation superfluous and its position embarrassing.
Further envoys hurried to Rome to avert reprisals and -
belatedly - seek an alliance (D.S.20.68; Plb.29.10, 19).
In revenge, Rome now stripped Rhodes of her possessions
in Karia and Lykia and declared Delos a free port (cf.
RR II pp.954-6 nn.67-8; Finley, 1973, pp.130-1). Rhodes
continued to protest, and finally won an alliance with
Rome in 164. Her trade and position as a transit port had
been badly hit by Delos' new prosperity, with a huge loss
of revenues from tolls and harbour charges, but succeeded
in making a partial recovery (Plb.30.31).

     The inexorable march of Roman power continued. After
the capture and sack of Corinth by Mummius in 146, Greece
became the Roman province of Achaia. Thirteen years later,
when Attalos III of Pergamum died without an heir, he
bequeathed his kingdom to Rome, and the province of Asia
came into being. Soon, however, a new power was in the
ascendant, and further Roman wars in the East loomed.
Mithridates VI of Pontos (120-63) who had already extended
the boundaries of his kingdom to the north, began to look
covetously at the Roman protectorate to the south.
Astypalaia meantime achieved a new position of privilege:
in 105, the island became a 'civitas foederata', a free
ally of Rome, and thereafter retained its independence as
a Roman naval base (IGRR IV 1028; cf. Jones, 1937, p.63;
CAH IX p.464). Mithridates overran the Roman province of
Asia, then turned his attention to Rhodes, which he
besieged in 88 BC. Rhodes had previously maintained good
relations with Mithridates, but, forced to choose between
Mithridates and Rome, chose Rome (Cic.'Verr.'2.65, 159).
Mithridates, like Demetrios Poliorketes, brought all the
resources of new military technology to bear on Rhodes;
but, like Demetrios, was forced to give up the siege
(App.'BC'4.67; 'Mith.'24-7; IG XII 1, 730; cf. RR II
p.1104 n.40). Kos while assisting Roman refugees, also
welcomed Mithridates. The Koans had been entrusted with
the safe keeping of the young prince of the Ptolemaic
family, and with royal fortunes of cash and valuables.
Both child and riches they handed over to Mithridates
(App.'Mith.'23, 115; 'BC'1.102).

     Mithridates exploited the undercurrent of hatred and
resentment felt against the Romans by the people of Asia.
In 88, he ordered the massacre of Romans and others from
Italy living in Asia Minor; and readily secured popular
co-operation in inflicting brutal atrocities. Kaunos,
among other communities, carried these out. Rhodes and

Kos sheltered Italian refugees; these included L. Cassius, the proconsul of Asia. When Rome finally defeated Mithridates in this 'first Mithridatic war', Sulla simultaneously punished Kaunos for the bloodshed and rewarded Rhodes for its loyalty by handing Kaunos over to Rhodian rule. Sulla also inscribed Rhodes as an ally of the Roman people (App.'Mith.'23-4, 61; Tac.'Ann.'4.14; Cic.'Q.Fr.'1.1.11.33).

Although powerful enough to maintain supremacy in her own waters, and to repel the siege of Mithridates, Rhodes had never fully recovered her naval presence abroad after the humiliations inflicted by Rome in 168. Piracy, earlier suppressed by the efficient action of the Rhodian navy, had become rife in the Aegean (cf. RR II p.1160 n.9). In 69, the harbour of Delos was devastated in an audacious piratical raid; this and other acts of provocation forced Rome to intervene. Pompey, sent east with massive resources of manpower and ships, swiftly suppressed the menace. Rhodes had contributed ships to Pompey's operation, and was permitted the rare privilege of fiscal independence. In 61, Pompey returned to Rome and was accorded a sumptuous triumphal reception (in which he wore a robe belonging to Alexander, from the Ptolemaic treasures deposited in Kos).

In the war between Caesar and Pompey, Rhodes - with Cyprus, Crete and other islands - sent help to Pompey at Pharsalos (50 BC); but Pompey's forces were routed. Pompey fled to Egypt, where he was murdered shortly afterwards (App.'BC'2.71, 83). Caesar was now assisted by Rhodian vessels in his campaigns of 48. Rhodes was further caught in Roman power-struggles by the activities of a mercenary fleet from the island, which assisted Dolabella against his rival Cassius: the later argument that the ships had been intended as 'escorts', not 'allies', cut little ice (App.'BC'4.60, 61). After the assassination of Caesar on the Ides of March 44, Cassius had his revenge on Rhodes, demanding payment of a huge financial settlement. Some Rhodians were eager to fight over the issue (App.'BC'4.66); but a deputation led by the philosopher Archelaos went to Rome to plead for mercy. Appian gives a highly coloured rhetorical account of the speeches exchanged between Cassius, who had been brought up and educated in Rhodes, and Archelaos, who had been his teacher. After an indecisive sea-battle at Myndos, Rhodes was besieged. This time the city fell, probably by treachery, and was mercilessly sacked and plundered. Cassius proceeded to confiscate all Rhodian wealth, both public moneys and private fortunes, sparing only a single sculpture representing Helios (D.C.47.33; D.Chr.31.86). A Roman

garrison was left on the island (App.'BC'4.74). After
Antony defeated Cassius at Philippi, Rhodes rebelled.
Antony's celebrated involvement with Cleopatra led to his
estrangement from Octavian, who had fought with him at
Philippi, and ultimately to the battle of Actium, with
the deaths soon afterwards of Antony and Cleopatra. The
way was now clear for Octavian's ascendancy. In 27 BC,
he assumed the title 'Augustus' and became the first
Roman Emperor. The elevation of Octavian had political
repercussions in Kos. The tyrant Nikias, who had seized
power some eight years before, was now deposed (Bowersock,
1965, pp.45-6; cf. Syme, 1961, pp.25-8).

Under the Empire, the fortunes of Rhodes and Kos
fluctuated: 'Rhodiis libertas adempta saepe aut firmata'
(Tac.'Ann.'12.58). The vicissitudes of the islands, with
spells of freedom alternating with periods of Roman rule,
are well documented, although the chronology is uncertain
(cf. RR II p.1406 n.24, pp.1427-9 nn.9-10).

Rhodes still had a high reputation. In the first
century AD, Dio wrote an oration protesting against the
current failure to grant appropriate honours to illustrious
benefactors, and in particular against the parsimonious
practice of utilizing existing statues, merely changing
the inscription. Among the considerations he adduces are
(D.Chr.31.40):

> The reputation and the size of your city allows nothing
> which happens in it to go unnoticed, so that many
> people take exception, if Rhodes seems to go wrong in
> any way.

Dio also remarks on the civic pride of the Rhodians
(ibid.146) and on the thoroughly Hellenic character and
dignity of the people (162-3). Some sixty years later,
Aelius Aristeides (to whom the spurious 'Rhodiakos',
mentioned in Chapter 1, is also attributed) wrote an
address to Rhodes, eulogizing and flattering the island
(Aristid.22.45), while recommending 'homonoia', political
unity, with a scarcely veiled hint at Roman exploitation
of disunity: 'You will run the risk of being deprived of
this pretended freedom.'

Tiberius, who later succeeded Augustus as emperor,
chose Rhodes as his place of exile from Rome, 6 BC - AD 2;
perhaps the most celebrated of the island's many visitors,
he made use of his stay to attend classes in philosophy,
and to dabble in astrology (cf. Bowersock, 1965, pp.77,
133-4). Rhodes long remained an attractive tourist resort
(cf. Luc.'Am.'7-8; Philostr.'VA'21-3; X.'Eph.'5.11-12), a
welcoming haven for men banished into exile from Rome
(cf. RR II p.958 n.74) and a flourishing intellectual
and cultural centre.

Part II
Achievements

4 Language and Script

As observed in the previous chapter, archaeological
evidence suggests that the Late Neolithic and the Early
Bronze Age were characterized by a uniformity of material
culture throughout the Aegean region. There is good
reason, from the evidence of place-names, to suppose that
the early rapport between the islands and Asia Minor
extended to language. A very wide linguistic continuum
is evinced in a substratum of place-names: it embraces
an area from the Iberian peninsula in the west to the
Caucasus in the east, from the Balkans in the north to
Italy in the south (Devoto, 1972).
  Since the pioneer work of Kretschmer (1896), it has
been recognized that many words used in Greek are of alien
origin. In particular, certain place-names of Greece are
betrayed as non-Greek by their suffixes. The most typical
non-Greek formation is in -ss- or -nth- (of which -nd-
seems to be an Anatolian variant); -rn-, -mn- and -nt-
are also significant. (Hester, 1957, after a statistical
analysis of the proportion of open syllables in the roots
of supposedly non-Greek place-names with that in those
demonstrably Greek, and a comparison with English and
Maori place-names in New Zealand, reached the persuasive
conclusion that the suffixes listed are significant, and
of a common linguistic group; but not those in -1-, -m-,
-n-, -r- and -s-.) Such names occur in our area as names
both of islands (Kalymnos) and of places in them (Lindos,
Kamyndos and Brigindara in Rhodes; Halasarna in Kos).
Rhodes, which had a month Sminthos and festival Sminthia,
was given the name Sminthe, if we may associate two
traditions about Orestes' travels after his matricide:
that he went to Rhodes, and that he went to the island -
otherwise unidentified - of Sminthe (Apollod.'Epit.'6.27;
Hyg.'F'120). The Greeks were aware that some such names
had a foreign ring: it was said that the dried figs of the

Brigindara region were 'barbarian' in name, though 'Attic'
in the enjoyment they gave (Lynkeus ap. Ath.14.652d; on
the variant forms Brikindara, Brygindara, etc., see
Cunningham, ed., 1971, on Herod.2.57).

It was long ago shown that there is a thick cluster
of non-Greek names around Early Bronze Age sites in
Greece (Haley and Blegen, 1928). Although it can be
argued that non-Greek need not imply pre-Greek, and that
a later diffusion of the place-names is a possibility
(Gomme, ed. Thucydides, 1945, I pp.97-8; cf. Mellaart,
1958), it is more commonly believed that the distribution
of the place-names (with the same name occurring in Greek
lands and in the depths of Asia Minor) and their early
appearance (in the Linear B texts of 1400 BC) indicates
that the people who first used them had come from Anatolia
to Greece by the middle of the second millennium. Of the
few names known for townships on Thera in historical times,
none has the typical non-Greek formation common in the
eastern islands. As place-names - with places - of Bronze
Age Thera were lost in the cataclysmic destruction of
around 1500, this may indicate that non-Greek elements
elsewhere are genuinely early, rather than coming from
late influences and contacts. Of the many different names
allegedly given to the islands, at least some suggest
linguistic change (cf. Dossin, 1972, on Anaphe; Halliday,
1913, on Meropis for Kos).

Another difficulty, perhaps more insidious than that of
possible later diffusion of the names, arises from the
common use of a non-Greek suffix preceded by a recognizable
Greek root, as in Pyranthos (on the Karian coast), incorporating 'pyr', 'fire' or 'pyra', 'funeral pyre'; and
Ophioussa (an old name for Rhodes), based on 'ophis',
'snake'.

While some believe that the people of the place-names
were pre-Indo-European as well as pre-Greek, most regard
their language as Indo-European. It is easier to isolate
non-Greek elements in place-names than to identify the
language, or reconstruct the linguistic group, to which
they belong. One line of approach starts from the
suffixes. As -assas or -assis is known to be a possessive
in Luwian (an Indo-European language akin to Hittite),
-ss- names may be associated with this tongue (Mellaart,
1958). Again, -andas may simply be Indo-European -want,
'belonging to'. Another line of approach concentrates on
the roots. An early attempt (Fick, 1905) to assign the
names to particular languages on the basis of their
alleged etymology, disregarding suffixes completely, was
highly speculative; however, Fick's collection of names
is still useful, and in many ways his was a pioneer study.

More recent work has sought to isolate - or even reconstruct - a linguistic substratum in Greek. This non-Greek, but Indo-European, substratum is sometimes called 'Pelasgic' or 'Thraco-Pelasgic', after the Pelasgoi, a prehistoric people of whom traces remained in classical Thrace (Kretschmer, 1925, followed by Carnoy and others, cf. Carnoy, 1960). It may, however, be mistaken to look for particular peoples with distinctive cultures and distinct languages at this period, among the ancestors of later peoples and the precursors of later languages, and it is perhaps best to use the general term 'Aegean' or 'Anatolian' for the people of the place-names while admitting agnosticism about the intermediate stages between their language and Greek ('Aegean' - Beattie, 1961; 'Anatolian' - Dow, 1960; useful review articles are Hester, 1968; Crossland, 1973; Renfrew, 1973a and b; a good general survey is Sakellariou, 1974; on the agnostic standpoint, cf. Severyns, 1960, pp.39-47).

Much attention has been paid to non-Greek place-names, scarcely any to the names of characters in myths. But myths do provide incidental linguistic information, valuable because unselfconscious, in the names given to persons as well as places. On the whole, this corroborates the evidence of place-names for the early linguistic situation: for instance, -mn- and -nth- appear in Thamneus and Phalanthos, figures in Rhodian myths which can be related to events of the Bronze Age (see Chapter 7).

Archaeological evidence, discussed in Chapter 3, can tell us nothing about linguistic change or admixture. It is very rarely that a neat identification of the archaeologist's people, described by their material remains, and the philologist's people, identified by their speech, may be made. It has often been suggested that the arrival of Greek-speakers in Greece was associated with the appearance there of grey 'Minyan' ware around 2000 BC (Palmer, 1965); but this link is now sceptically viewed (Crossland, CAH I3 p.850; also 1973). There are similar difficulties in putting other groups with linguistic affinities - such as the Karians - in an archaeological context (cf. Chapter 3). The problems of effecting a synthesis between different types of evidence, which allow different types of conclusions and demand differing expertise, are formidable, and at times aggravated by mutual distrust or hostility between scholars following different disciplines (cf. Wainwright, 1962, for an account of the similar difficulties facing the historian concerned with Dark Age Britain). However, for the pre-literate period, the silent testimony of archaeology, the eloquent but ambiguous evidence of myths and such indirect

information as is afforded by place-names are alone
available as a basis for conjecture about the linguistic
and indeed historical situation.

The advent of writing in Greece solves some problems
and creates others: early writing is not historically
informative and questions relating to the decipherment
of the scripts are highly controversial. Minoan Crete
used first a pictographic then syllabic scripts. Of the
latter, Linear A, as yet undeciphered, but with Luwian
most canvassed as a possible key, has been discovered
outside Crete, at Phylakopi on Melos (Renfrew, 1977);
Linear B has been found, written on clay tablets dating
from around 1400, not only in Crete, but also on the
mainland at Pylos, Mycenae and Thebes. Linear B was in
1952 deciphered as Greek amid a scholarly furore in which
acclaim and disbelief were mingled (Ventris and Chadwick,
1953).

A plausible case has since been made that the Linear
B texts are neither entirely in Greek nor entirely in some
other language; but contain several languages of which
Greek is one (Levin, 1964; 1972). It might seem prima
facie unlikely that different languages should coexist in
writing; but according to Homer, Crete was polyglot, with
a heterogeneous population, comprising Achaians,
Eteokretans, Kydones, Dorians and Pelasgoi ('Od.'19.175-7;
cf. Willetts, 1962, pp.131-6). This lends credence to the
view that, by the end of the Bronze Age, Greek was the
dominant language in the south Aegean area, but was not
the only language spoken or written.

An unknown language, as yet undeciphered, was used in
some inscriptions of Crete as late as the third century
BC. This language, written in the Greek alphabet, is
conventionally given the name 'Eteokretan' from the
Homeric passage detailing the population of Crete. The
group Eteokarpathioi, known from inscriptions of Karpathos,
is generally believed to represent a similar substratum of
'aborigines' in the population, possibly retaining a
language other than Greek. However, there is no evidence
for the survival of a separate language in Karpathos, and
the prefix Eteo- ('true') need not imply linguistic
isolation. In a poem set in Hellenistic Kos, Eteokoos
seems to mean 'honest Koan' (Herod.6.65). Again, the
Eteokarpathioi might be a group similar to the Athenian
Eteoboutadai, a family with closely guarded cult privileges
(D.21.182; cf. Harp.s.v.). As deme or state membership
was a requirement for eligibility for many cults, the
ethnic Eteokarpathioi is as readily explicable in such
terms as is the patronymic Eteoboutadai. That Lemnos of
the seventh or sixth century still had a pocket of non-

Greek speech is apparent from an inscription written in a
language as yet undeciphered, but believed to be akin to
Etruscan.

Even within the Aegean basin, then, these pockets of
non-Hellenic speech persisted to a remarkably late date.
This tended to happen on islands - Lemnos and Crete
certainly, Karpathos possibly - where communities away
from the main town and harbour could be very isolated.
(Similarly, Cyprus continued to use its own peculiar
syllabary - a pre-alphabetic script - until the third
century BC.)

The Greeks were always conscious of the presence of
'barbarians', non-Greek speakers, on the fringes of their
world. The people of Thrace to the north of the Greek
peninsula and all the peoples - Phrygians, Lydians,
Lykians, Karians - of the vast Asiatic landmass to the
east of the Greek coastal settlements spoke unintelligible
tongues. The Persians, who came to dominate much of this
eastern region, were to the Greeks of the classical period
the 'barbarians' par excellence. Herodotos came to the
conclusion, on the basis of contemporary survivals, that
the speech of the Pelasgoi was 'barbarian' (Hdt.1.57.2;
cf. Thomson, 1954, pp.171-7). Homer describes the Karians
as 'barbarian in speech' ('Il.'2.867). Educated Greeks
were aware of the influence of alien elements on the
formation of their language. Plato's Sokrates refers to
the existence of 'barbarian' words in the current speech,
and Attic in particular borrowed from outside (Pl.'Cra.'
409e; [X.]'Ath.'2.7). The survival of two names 'divine'
and 'human' for certain things perhaps indicates linguistic
admixture.

According to Thucydides, Minos drove the Karians from
the islands; according to Herodotos, he made them his
subjects. The Karians are archaeologically elusive, and
are later most famous as pirates, adventurers and
mercenary soldiers, or as hired mourners (Hdt.1.171 sqq.;
cf. 7.99; Th.1.4.8, with Gomme, ed., 1945, I pp.106-8;
Pl.'Lg.'800e; Str.14.2.27; cf. Thomson, 1954, pp.166-71;
Cook, CAH III, Part 2, pp.790-6). Myths give oblique
corroboration of a prehistoric Karian presence in the
islands (see Chapter 7). Traces in place-names point in
the same direction. Several place-names of mainland Karia
are echoed in the islands: the island Syme and Karian
Symaithos; Ladarma in Rhodes and Karian Lade. Also,
Karpathos and Karis, an old name for Kos, may be of Karian
derivation (but Carnoy, 1960, p.322 suggests that Karpathos
comes from an Indo-European root, ger-b-, 'île, élévation
en mer Égée').

Halikarnassos, the coastal town just across the strait

from Kos, remained Karian for centuries. At the time of
the Persian Wars, the Karian Queen Artemisia was in control
of several of the islands, and in the Athenian tribute
lists the area called Karian embraced several offshore
islands also (cf. Chapter 3). A Karian presence continued
to spill over into the islands from the Asiatic hinterland.
Unintelligible graffiti from Kalymnos seem to be Karian
(Jeffery, 1961, p.354). That there was a Karian minority
present in the island population is shown by such names
as that of Imasaolla in an epitaph of the late sixth
century at Lindos (IG XII 1, 887; cf. Robert, 1963). In
literature, too, Karian elements crept in. Timokreon of
Rhodes, writing lyric poetry in the early fifth century,
is said to have used a 'Karian fable'. The fables of
Aesop circulated against just this Asiatic Greek background
and the tenth letter in the collection attributed to
Aischines, originating in Hellenistic Rhodes, is a later
offshoot of the same tradition.

The islands in the south-east Aegean were on the Greek
side in the Trojan War and, as is argued in the previous
chapter, had a Dorian (though perhaps not Doric-speaking)
population at this time. After the fall of Mycenae, the
islands had an influx of population from the Peloponnese;
then in the eighth century came the main arrival of Dorian
settlers.

Population movement from the Greek mainland to the
islands and the Asiatic coast, in waves and in sporadic
migration, formed three distinct Aegean zones. Dorians
from the Peloponnese brought Doric speech with them and
a resulting dialect 'bridge' spanned the south Aegean
from the Peloponnesian mother cities Argos, Megara,
Epidauros and Sparta to the islands, then on to Knidos on
the Asiatic coast. Immediately to the north was another
'bridge' of Ionic from Attica and Euboia, embracing such
islands as Samos and crossing to the coastal region
around Miletos. To the north again was Aiolic, running
from Thessaly and Boiotia through Lesbos to north-western
Asia Minor.

The main philological classification of the dialects
has conventionally been into East Greek and West Greek.
East Greek comprises Aiolic, Ionic and Attic (the dialect
of Athens and environs), also Arcado-Cyprian, a primitive
dialect shared by Arkadia, isolated by its mountainous
situation and Cyprus, isolated by its distant position,
which seems closest to the Mycenaean Greek of Linear B.
West Greek comprises Doric and North-west Greek, spoken
in Phokis and neighbouring regions. This classification
of the dialects is based on the evidence of inscriptions,
which are at all periods closer to everyday speech than

is the language of literature; in any case, not all
dialects are represented in extant literature.

It was an axiom of Greek popular tradition that the
alphabet reached Greece from the Semitic world (Hdt.
5.58-61), and a term meaning simply 'Phoenician' (sc.
writing) was used as an ordinary description of 'letters'
(SIG 38.37 from Teos; on cognate terms in a Cretan
inscription of c.500 BC, cf. Edwards and Edwards, 1974,
with Jeffery and Morpurgo-Davies, 1970). Kadmos was often
named by Greek writers as the liaison between Greece and
Phoenicia, who brought the art of writing to Greece. This
is a good illustration of myths' preservation but confused
presentation of historical facts. The scripts used in
Bronze Age Greece - in the time of 'Kadmos' - were
syllabic. The adoption of the alphabet belongs to a much
later date, perhaps mid-eighth century (but see Naveh,
1973, on the possibility of an earlier date). The belief
that Kadmos brought writing to Greece may have arisen from
the conflation of two traditions, each true in itself but
properly relating to different periods: that Thebes, a
city supposedly founded by Kadmos the Phoenician, had
possessed a (syllabic) script in the remote past, and that
the Greek alphabet was derived from the Semitic script.

That the Greek alphabet was indeed modelled on the north
Semitic script is clear from resemblances in letter-forms,
letter-values and letter-names. But the common Phoenician
blueprint was modified and adapted by different regions in
different ways. The Greek language itself imposed certain
changes in letter-values; others resulted from the needs
of particular dialects. Letter-forms as well as letter-
values show change and variation from one area to another.
Despite this great regional diversity, broad resemblances
between the early scripts suggest that the alphabet was
taken over in one place and subsequently spread over the
Greek world, rather than that there was a simultaneous
slow infiltration of the script in several areas.

The place of the original adoption and centre for
ensuing diffusion of the script - if in Greece and not,
as many opine, in the Semitic world - may well have been
one of the islands. Rhodes in particular has a strong
claim to consideration. The position of Rhodes with her
hospitable harbours led to contacts over a wide area;
the island was a natural stopping point for ships bound
for destinations in Greece from the East and vice versa.
Cyprus, similarly well placed, has frequently been
canvassed (cf. the suggestion of Carpenter, 1938, p.125,
that the alphabet was 'invented' by a Rhodian living in
Cyprus, and then spread to Crete, Thera and Corinth) and
Crete is another strong contender (Raubitschek, 1970).

Euboia too has its supporters (cf. Johnston, 1975).
It is likely that the alphabet was first transmitted
to a community with a sizeable Semitic element settled
among its population, rather than through sporadic trade
contacts (although, of course, the latter might lead to
the former). The adoption of a script suggests leisurely
relations, rather than brief meetings for business,
intellectual curiosity rather than pragmatic demands, the
wish to make records rather than the need to facilitate
ephemeral communications. Rhodes seems to satisfy the
requirement of having Phoenicians in its population.
Myths tell of Phoenicians in Rhodes: Kadmos made a
dedication (of an inscribed object) to Athena, and his
companions were ancestors of the priests of Poseidon at
Ialysos; Phalanthos the 'Phoenician' (and he certainly
has a non-Greek name, with its -nth- suffix) led the
forces defending Achaia, possibly also at Ialysos, against
siege (cf. Chapter 7). Archaeology can show some
Phoenician artefacts to bolster Rhodes' claim, but these
could come from transient contacts; the apparent eastern
influence on such art-forms as ivory-working is more
significant. Thera, Melos and Anaphe had traditions of
Phoenician settlement, seeming to reflect Bronze Age
contacts rather than influence of the archaic period, for
which there is no archaeological evidence. Crete, by
contrast, lacks tales of Phoenician settlement, but
archaeology points to eighth-century contacts. Karpathos,
lying between Crete and Rhodes, has yielded no early
inscriptions which might help settle the question of
priority between the two. For Kos too, the archaic
period is blank.
   Early inscriptions from our area come from Rhodes and
Thera - and they are among the earliest known from any
part of Greece. (It is, however, possible that the Theran
rock inscriptions seem older than they are, primitive
features being retained in this isolated community.) The
dominant epichoric script of Rhodes is strikingly different
from that of the islands further west, where Crete, Thera,
Melos, Anaphe and Sikinos form a more or less homogeneous
group, and is different also from that of Halikarnassos,
which resembles its Ionian neighbours to the east (on the
diversity between Ialysos and Kameiros, see Johnston,
1975). These differences may be summed up in the terms
'eastern', 'western', 'southern', with their colour-coding
of blue, red and green, which were introduced by Kirchhoff,
1877, and have since been widely used despite their
limitations. Whereas Rhodian Kameiros used a script of
the red 'western' type (with Ψ representing the sound chi
and X or ΧΣ xi), Halikarnassos was pure blue, with an

'eastern' usage which prevailed also at Ialysos (Ψ psi and X chi) and the other islands mentioned above were green or 'southern' (without the letters Φ, X and Ψ at all). Also, of the two mutually exclusive forms of the sibilant, Rhodes used sigma ς, Σ) and the other islands san (M).

As the variations in the epichoric scripts of the Dorian islands clearly demonstrate, dialect is not the only factor operating on script. Similar variations are apparent in the scripts used by the Dorians of the Peloponnese, where the states around the Isthmos form a more or less homogeneous group, using the sibilant san, not sigma, and the same unusual form (B) for the vowel sound 'e', but Lakonia is different, using sigma. While the distribution of the dialects reflects the movements of population from the Greek mainland to the islands, the distribution of the scripts does not: evidently, the alphabet was adopted after these movements took place. There is little indication in scripts of continued contact between colony and mother city, although some similarities are apparent: fragmentary inscriptions from Kalymnos of the early seventh century show affinities with Argos (Jeffery, 1961, pp.353-4), and the Rhodian script has resemblances with that of the eastern Argolid. Whatever complex processes affected the spread of the alphabet in Greece, colonial contact was not a significant one. Naturally, however, a colony founded after the advent of literacy would follow the practice of its mother city, as Kyrene of Thera and - with certain modifications - Gela of Lindos (Jeffery, 1961, pp.319, 272).

Differences in the local scripts of Greece gradually faded out, and the Ionic 'eastern' script was universally adopted. Most states show Ionic letters (H for long 'e'; Ω for long 'o'; Ψ as psi and X as chi) becoming predominant in the course of the fifth century. At Athens, the final adoption of this script for official documents was formally ratified by a decree proposed by Archeinos in the archonship of Eukleides, 403/402 BC. In other places, the changeover was less clear cut.

A glance at archaic inscriptions is a salutary reminder of the difficulties faced by early writers, using a script not yet fully developed to the clearest expression of the sounds of Greek and not consistent - though no doubt mutually intelligible - over even a small area. The poems of Peisandros of Rhodian Kameiros and Panyassis of Halikarnassos (seventh-century contemporaries) would look very different from each other, and both would certainly look very strange to us if we could see them in the authors' autographs. The process of transmission of texts eliminated such differences at an early stage. Literary texts, because of their intrinsic and perennial appeal, were preserved by conscious design and rewritten in new forms over the centuries, whereas inscriptions, of limited and usually transient interest, survived by chance if at all, and in their original format.

Of dialect too, as observed above, inscriptions give a clear record. Literary works are subject to tampering, with the reinterpretation of successive generations of scribes and the assimilation of unusual forms to standard usage, or of other dialects to Attic, more familiar to copyists. Also, literature is selfconscious and a writer's choice of dialect is affected by complex influences, whereas inscriptions naturally reflect the contemporary local speech. In state decrees this may take an idealized form, but in informal private records - such as dedications, epitaphs or graffiti with the names of people (often earliest of all inscriptions from a region) - there is little overlay on the vernacular. A partial exception must be made of verse epigrams commissioned for gravestones or dedications: in a more artificial literary format, these are not necessarily composed by local residents. The writers commissioned to supply such verses might adapt the dialect to the patron or adhere to literary conventions.

The most striking feature of the Doric dialects of the islands - as of the local scripts - is their great variation (see Buck, 1955, nos 100-5, Rhodes; 108, Kos; 109-13, Thera; 114, Melos). Divergences in vocabulary are particularly marked. Titles of magistrates and terminology of sacrificial rites are well documented (cf. Chapter 9). Here, local civic pride may lie behind individuality of expression in peculiar terms. It is more surprising to find Rhodes using a unique word for 'tomb' in the sixth century, and Kos with its own word rather later (Rhodian 'lescha', Buck, 1955, no.101 = IG XII 1, 709; Koan 'thekaion', IC 155-61). The Dorian settlers brought the Doric speech of their home states to the islands (on a striking echo in Melos of Peloponnesian usage, cf. Buck, 1955, p.45); but there it proceeded to develop on independent lines. Similarly, the influence of Rhodian colonists on the dialect of Sicily was shortlived, with the assimilation and integration of the dialects of different settlers and the formation of a uniform Sicilian Doric (Bartonek, 1973).

Local differences in dialect must have been a serious obstacle to free communication between members of the Greek states. The dialects, though mutually intelligible, were superficially very different. Aristophanes' parodies of Boiotian, Megarian and Lakonian demonstrate both the differences between these dialects and Attic, and

the fact that these differences rendered the speakers of
alien dialects outlandish and ridiculous to the average
Athenian. Educated Greeks may have been less prejudiced:
Plato allows a Theban an expletive from his patois
('Phd.'62a). Parodies of dialects in fourth century
comedy show that regional differences were still marked.
Boiotian in particular produced a stock response,
apparently implying gluttony. Doctors in comedy conventionally spoke in Doric, probably with the implication
of Koan origins (e.g. Men.'Aspis' 439-64).

The linguistic situation was one of fundamental
underlying unity, with striking superficial divergences.
And this situation exacerbated tensions between the
Greek states. Herodotos' words, attributed to Athens
after the Persian Wars (8.144.2):

The Greek people, alike in descent and in speech,
having in common temples and festivals of the gods
and like-mannered customs

epitomize a grandiloquent statement of an ideal. In fact,
such pan-Hellenic aspirations were sporadic and the
superficial differences more often obscured the underlying
unity. While the Greeks felt themselves to be unique and
through their shared speech distinctly separate from all
other peoples - 'barbarians' - this consciousness was
always precarious and often forgotten through regional
parochialism. Tensions between Ionian and Dorian,
possibly reaching back to conflicts of Mycenaean times,
are marked in Greek political, cultural and religious
institutions throughout the classical period.

Herodotos' idealistic stress on the ethnic and
linguistic unity of the Greek people is perhaps a product
of his early environment. The people of Halikarnassos,
his home town, were originally Dorians, like those of
offshore Kos and the other neighbouring islands, but by
the time of Herodotos they had adopted the 'eastern' script
and Ionic dialect; a remarkable divergence between ethnic
origins and linguistic practice. Halikarnassos' adoption
of Ionic, the dialect of its northern neighbours, is an
extreme case of the interpenetration of different dialects.
But no community at any time was free from some adultera-
tion of its local dialect by extraneous elements. A 'pure'
Greek dialect scarcely exists, save as a philological
abstraction. Even in the archaic and classical periods,
the eradication of local peculiarities had begun.

The Doric of the islands incorporated forms used by
their Ionic speaking neighbours. Already in the fifth
century, coins from Rhodian Ialysos bear 'Ιελυσιόν (Ionic)
as an alternative legend to 'Ιαλυσιόν (Doric). From the
fifth century onwards, Attic exerted a profound influence

on all other dialects through the political hegemony and cultural dominance of Athens. A long sacrificial calendar from fourth-century Kos provides a good example of modified Doric (Buck, 1955, no.108 = IC 37). Here, Attic and Doric forms are found side by side: ἱερεύς and ἱαρεύς, οἱ and τοι, εἱ and αἱ. (Buck, 1955, p.106, notes that εἴ κα is often found, with εἱ replacing αἱ but the retention of Doric κά rather than adoption of Attic ἄν.) A similar mixture may be seen in the Theran Testament of Epikteta (Thumb, 1909, p.135) and in a short inscription also from Thera dedicating land to the 'Mother of the gods' (Buck, 1955, no.112 = IG XII 3, 436 = SIG 1032), where Doric θύσοντι and Attic φέρουσιν coexist.

The Macedonian conquests which swept the Greek world dealt the deathblow to the independent development of local dialects, though these persisted for a time. In particular, the Rhodian infinitive in -μειν long remained current. Attic was adopted as the official medium of communication at the Macedonian court and, through its use by army, administration and business became the basis of the 'koine' or common language, which ultimately embraced all Greek speaking communities.

As the local dialects became assimilated to common Greek, an antiquarian interest in them grew. In the late fourth to early third century, Simias of Rhodes wrote on the Cretan dialect (cf. Chapter 5); about a century later, Klearchos commented on similarities between Rhodian and Sicilian vocabulary (Ath.1.49f = FGH II 327); in the second century, Moschos of Syracuse was an expert on the dialect of Rhodes (Ath.11.485e); Eukrates, of unknown date, also took an interest in Rhodian dialect words (FGH III 514) as did Kleitarchos (Ath.15.666c, 701a). Works with such titles as 'Glossai', or 'Etymologia' were in circulation (Ath.1.49f).

With the advent of the Romans, the Greek language accommodated a range of Latin words, simply transliterated. A Koan inscription, with a relief of a gladiator, bears the legend, 'He was permitted to leave the "ludus" ("sport")'. A 'familia' of gladiators occurs in another (IC 138; 141; cf. NS 562; Robert, 1940, p.39). While Romans learned Greek and became bilingual, Latin infiltrated the Greek vernacular (cf. Degrassi, 1941).

In the following chapters of Part II, the contribution to Greek literature and thought of writers from the islands is examined. As none of those wrote in pure Doric, local literature bears little relation to local speech. In the main, a writer's choice of dialect was dictated or influenced by literary conventions.

Epic was the oldest literary genre; rooted in the
Bronze Age, it germinated in the Dark Age and flowered
in the eighth century. Homer stands alone at the
culmination of a long line of oral poets; to us alone
because contemporary or near-contemporary epic is lost,
and to the ancients alone in the uniqueness of his genius
and achievement (Hdt.2.117, 4.32; Arist.'Po.' passim).
The artificial Homeric dialect, based on Aiolic and
Arcado-Cyprian, with an Ionic colouring, became, together
with the hexameter, the hallmark of the epic style. By
700 BC, with the advent of literacy, other poems were
being set down. Among these was the 'Herakleia' of
Peisandros of Kameiros. A single couplet surviving amid
the wreckage of meagre citations in later writers runs
(Kinkel, 1877, fr.7):
    For him at Thermopylai the grey-eyed goddess Athena
    created warm baths at the sea-shore.
The diction is Homeric, with a conventional formulaic
epithet applied to Athena, and a common epic expression
(παρὰ ῥηγμῖνι θαλάσσης) used for the sea-shore. But it
is known that the poem had Doricizing elements, as an
ancient critic remarks that Peisandros used Doric αἐ
for 'always' (fr.11).
    Lyric poetry, as it evolved in the seventh and sixth
centuries, had two strands of development: for choral
performance or for a solo singer. In general, choral
lyric is less personal in content and feeling than monody.
For choral lyric, the Doric dialect became the accepted
literary medium, largely because of the prominence of
Sparta - with Alkman and other poets - in the evolution
of the art-form. A modified Doric - not the vernacular
of any one locality, but an idealized Doric with some
epic admixture - is employed by the Boiotian Pindar and
the Ionian Simonides for this genre; also by the Attic
dramatists for the choral odes of tragedy and comedy.
Monody, by contrast, was often written in the poet's own
dialect - as it was by Sappho in the Aiolic of her native
Lesbos. (But Terpander of Lesbos, associated also with
Sparta, adopted Doric.) The split between those regions
with a predilection for choral lyric and those where
monody flourished is in part simply geographical. In
part, however, it reflects the different social conditions,
political aspirations and temperamental characteristics
of Dorians, for whom the group performance and extrovert
themes of choral lyric had an appeal, and the more
individualistic Ionians (cf. Kirkwood, 1974, pp.21-2 and,
for a contrary view, Will, 1956, p.25). But lyric poetry
is the most chameleon-like of genres.
    Timokreon of Rhodes was a highly idiosyncratic writer

of choral lyric, using its conventional triadic structure
to express the alien theme of private emotion. The
language, too, is mixed, with vivid colloquial expressions
alongside rather stilted literary ones, and the occasional
slide into the Rhodian patois (see PMG p.375; Kirkwood,
1974, p.278 n.6). The poems of Timokreon in fifth-century
Rhodes foreshadow in some respects those of Herodas,
writing two centuries later, in (probably) Kos and
Alexandria. The mimes of Herodas, with bawdy stories
couched in an artificial archaic Ionic diction interspersed
with an occasional Doric form, show the same tension
between form and content and the same experimentation with
linguistic admixture which typify Timokreon's style.
Although neither was a comic poet proper (the Suda mentions
a 'comedy' by Timokreon, but this is usually interpreted
as meaning a vituperative attack on Themistokles; Herodas'
mimes were not written for stage performance either), both
mark points in the long and lively tradition of Dorian
farce, which had its greatest native exponents in Sicily
or south Italy and which exerted a profound, albeit elusive,
influence on the Attic stage. West Greek comedy seems to
have reached heights in the early fifth century and again
around 300 BC - in the lifetimes of Timokreon and Herodas
respectively. In the earlier period, Epicharmos, whose
family may have originated in Kos (D.L. 8.7; Suda;
sceptically viewed by Pickard-Cambridge, rev. Webster, 1962,
p.236) was the most important playwright; in the later,
the 'hilarotragoidiai' of Rhinthon and others were popular.
Fragments of this comedy show that it parodied Euripides
in the local Doric dialect.

     In the third century, Theokritos gave Doric a new
literary lease of life by the invention of pastoral poetry.
Using the dialect of Sicily and Kos as a basis, he grafted
on many extraneous elements to create his own sophisticated
artificial diction. Theokritos' choice of Doric may have
stemmed partly from a feeling of local patriotism, the
sort of consciousness which motivated contemporary
historians to write about the past of their locality rather
than about wider political issues; or again partly from
Dorian 'nationalism', aiming to preserve a dying dialect
from complete extinction under the advance of the 'koine';
or again to an Alexandrine fondness for the recondite -
which Doric had now become. There can be no doubt that
poets and compilers of glossaries interacted at this time.
Theokritos, skilled in his manipulation of literary Doric,
was capable of tongue-in-cheek mockery of Doric speakers:
in his poem 'Adoniazousai', set in Alexandria, people
conversing in the crowd attract attention because of
their broad accents. (Similarly, Anaxandrides from Rhodes

put Doric-speaking characters on the Attic comic stage
(FAC II p.48 fr.9).)

The attitude of sophisticated poets to the dialects
was complex at this time. Lyric was a flexible genre,
allowing great change and variation, made still more
elastic by such innovations as those of Theokritos.
Kallimachos, equally at home in Aiolic, Ionic and Doric,
prided himself on his virtuosity (cf. PA II p.1050 n.244).
Yet epic and drama still imposed their traditional
limitations, and authors voluntarily complied with these.

As there is less reason for a prose writer than for
a poet to adopt an alien dialect or affect an artificial
diction, the history of this aspect of Greek prose writing
is less complex. The earliest prose writers were Ionians,
and Ionic was established as the accepted prose medium
by the sixth century. Herodotos naturally followed the
example of Hekataios and other Milesian chroniclers in
using Ionic, however different his style from theirs.
An Ionic flavour crept into the prose of the Attic
historian Thucydides, because of these precedents. But
in the fourth century, when Athens was the centre of
literary activity - with the philosophy of Plato, with
the oratory of Demosthenes and his contemporaries, and
with history represented by Xenophon, the Attic dialect
finally and completely triumphed.

An important body of early prose is associated with
Kos: the Hippokratic Corpus. Here, all the treatises are
written in Ionic, despite their probable origin in Dorian
Kos or Knidos. Hippokrates and his followers were
strongly influenced by the traditions of Ionian Miletos
and Aelian's explanation that Hippokrates used Ionic
'because of Demokritos' is in essence correct ('VH' 4.20).
There was, by contrast, little Doric prose. Pythagoras,
at the centre of the west Greek scientific movement, was
an Ionian from Samos who settled in Italy around 530 BC.
Pythagoras himself left no writings, and soon became
almost a legendary figure (Hdt.2.81, 4.95). To Aristotle
in the fourth century, who refers to 'the Pythagoreans'
or 'mathematicians' rather than to 'Pythagoras', he is
clearly very nebulous ('Met.'985b23, etc.). The
Pythagorean movement had considerable appeal to Dorians
(cf. Croiset and Croiset, 1914, II p.519) and favoured
Doric in its maxims, all later attributed to the founder.
(Perhaps Doric was affected in aphorisms because of the
celebrated Lakonic wit and brevity of the Spartans.)
However, the Greeks of the West did not establish the
practice of writing sustained prose in Doric. Antiochos,
writing in the sixth century, is known to have used Ionic;
and many scientists or philosophers, like Empedokles,

chose in any case to write in verse. Sophron's prose
mimes, written in Doric in the fifth century, represent
a casual and ephemeral art-form.

Menander depicts a fake doctor, summoned to a 'case'
in Athens, talking broad Doric ('Aspis' 439-64). This
particular masquerade is farce, but similar parodies are
unlikely to be completely untrue to life (Gomme and
Sandbach, ed. 1973, p.93 list parallels). It seems,
therefore, that, despite the Ionic of the Hippokratic
treatises, doctors from Kos or Sicily did not necessarily
use this dialect in conversations with their patients.
It would be rash to suppose that instruction and
professional discussion in the Koan medical school were
conducted exclusively in any one dialect.

In the third century, Archimedes elected to use
Sicilian Doric to expound his elegant mathematics. Perhaps
the west Greek world had not yet yielded to the pervasive
spread of the 'koine'; perhaps, rather, Archimedes chose
this oblique way to assert an affinity with the Pythagoreans
represented for us by such fragmentary remains as the
writings of Archytas and Philolaos.

Two analogies may be made by way of conclusion. An
uneducated islander of the fifth to fourth century,
accustomed to Doric, might react to spoken Attic or Ionic
much as his modern counterpart, accustomed to demotic
Greek, would react to spoken 'katharevousa' forms. He
would be familiar with alien dialects from communications
sent to his country by other states, but would be un-
accustomed to hearing them spoken. Or the position of
Doric, language of choral lyric and informal communication,
and Ionic, language of prose and formal exchange, may be
compared to the position of Scots vis-à-vis English in
present-day Scotland. Despite a lively literary revival,
there is a lack of expository prose written in Scots.
Also, twentieth-century writers of Lallans are comparable
with Theokritos and his contemporaries who affected
'hyper-Dorisms' in that their poems are not immediately
comprehensible to Scots speakers but are written for a
minority public: as in the third century BC, there is an
interaction between poets and compilers of dictionaries.

5   Literature

Greek literature is often loosely equated with the
literature of classical Athens. But no genre of literature
was peculiarly indigenous to Attica. Epic was heavily
influenced by the Near East, had its genesis in Ionia and
came late to the mainland. Choral lyric had Dorian roots
and, even in its developed form, use of the Doric dialect
persisted as a literary convention; its greatest
practitioners were the Boiotian Pindar and Bakchylides
from the island of Keos. The great Athenian dramatists
wrote the lyrics of their plays in Doric. Neither tragedy
nor comedy - the pride of the artistic achievement of
fifth-century Athens - was free from Dorian influences in
its early development. Of the historians, Thucydides was
indeed thoroughly Athenian (though he did have a Thracian
father and affected Ionic idiom in his prose); Herodotos,
whose outlook was cosmopolitan, came from Halikarnassos
and settled in Thourioi; Hekataios, the predecessor of
both, lived in Miletos. Philosophy too had its origins
in the Milesian spirit of enquiry. Later, the sophists -
Gorgias, Protagoras and others - who unwittingly supplied
the impetus for the philosophical developments of Sokrates
and Plato, were all foreigners. Aristotle, though spending
many years living and teaching in Athens, came originally
from remote Thracian Chalkidike, and had family connections
with Euboia, where he died. Even Attic oratory was
conditioned by the non-Attic sophists' formative influence
on rhetorical expression and ideas. Most of the orators
were themselves Athenians; but Lysias, often regarded as
writing the 'purest' Attic, was a metic of Sicilian
extraction. Thus, in its greatest era, Athens distilled
influences from all over the Greek-speaking world.
    After the great flowering of Attic culture in the fifth
and fourth centuries, there was a shift to other centres.
The courts of Alexander's successors - the Antigonids in

Macedon, Seleukids in Antioch and above all Ptolemies
in Alexandria - attracted circles of poets and intellectuals, while similar côteries flourished also at Pergamum
under the Attalid dynasty, especially in the second
century, and in Sicily. Athens remained a centre for
philosophical and rhetorical schools - rivalled here by
Rhodes - but in creative literature her charge was spent.

Athens, then, contributed little to the literary
movements of the archaic or the Hellenistic period, and
Attic literature of the fifth and fourth centuries is
largely derived from and bound up with forms and ideas
originating in other regions. This is nevertheless
regarded as the mainstream of Greek literary tradition
because it was in classical Athens that these ideas
received their finest artistic expression and reached
their fullest intellectual development; and also - a
reason which is less often noticed - because from that
place and of that period the best works have been
preserved. (In the case of Euripides, a comparison may
be made between ten plays which were selected, probably
in the second century AD, for special study and a random
group of nine others which survived by chance - apparently
part of a collection arranged alphabetically by titles
(cf. Barrett, ed. E.'Hipp.', 1963, pp.50-3). Here, few
would quarrel seriously with the ancient selector's
critical judgment). For other places and other times the
process of transmission has been more random.

The famous saying of the Athenian politician Themistokles
to a man from the insignificant islet of Seriphos
(Plu.'Them.'18; cf. Pl.'R' 329e):

'Had I come from Seriphos I should not have been
famous; nor would you had you been an Athenian'
might be extended to literature of the islands, with the
argument that another provenance would not have enhanced
its quality or ensured its survival. However, the loss
over the centuries of so much Greek literature - indeed,
of the bulk of it - makes assessment of what has survived,
and of the contribution to this of a particular region,
difficult. A reminder that great tracts of Greek
literature are lost, and that our understanding of what
survives may any day need modification in the light of
new finds comes from such discoveries as that of Kenyon
at the end of last century of the mimes of Herodas on
papyrus of the second century AD. With this discovery,
a shadowy literary figure suddenly acquired substance.
Many writers are known - as Herodas had been - only by
name or repute, and many others only from short citations
or comment with paraphrase in later authors. These later
authors, often commentators, grammarians, or compilers of

anthologies, choose excerpts for reasons of their own,
which seldom have anything to do with aesthetic appeal
or literary merit. Those who make such quotations are
more interested in recherché diction, unusual sentiments,
pithy expression or in content of a particular kind (food
and drink in the case of Athenaios, whose assiduous but
one-sided researches give a curious impression of a
stomach-orientated literature), than in the general tenor
of a work. And so our knowledge is unrepresentative as
well as partial. We are almost entirely dependent on
such quotations for information about early verse:
archaic lyric poetry is a wreck of which only chance
flotsam and jetsam has been found.

For Hellenistic verse, the situation is more favourable,
with works surviving in their entirety. Writers in the
islands at this time were in a good position to secure
the 'publication', circulation and preservation of their
work. Rhodes and Kos had strong links with Ptolemaic
Alexandria which had a monopoly of the production of
papyrus, where royal patronage fostered a lively literary
ambiance and where the existence of a library encouraged
the idea of writing for posterity. The Alexandrian
connection accounts for the preservation of Hellenistic
Rhodian verse, when the contemporary poetry of Crete
(Rhianos, Dosiadas) disappeared; Alexandrian interest in
Aratos' 'Phainomena', written in Macedon, secured its
survival, when the work of Antagoras, the official
Macedonian court poet, was lost. It is a trick of history
that the thoroughly Alexandrian Apollonios is remembered
as 'Rhodian', whereas the name of Antagoras, his
contemporary who also wrote epic and who came originally
from Rhodes, is almost completely forgotten. The paradox
does, however, highlight the position of Rhodes in Greek
letters at this time.

In philosophy too, Rhodes attracted intellectuals from
overseas to settle and sent her own citizens abroad.
Strabo lists among prominent Rhodian philosophers both
native Rhodians and immigrants (Str.14.2.13). Of the
extensive philosophical and historical prose of the
region little has survived, in striking contrast with the
voluminous Hippokratic Corpus.

The contribution of the Dorian islands to Greek
literature depends in part on their Dorian origins, in
part on their geographical position on the fringes of
Ionian Asia Minor, at times on their attractive scenery
and climate (which drew exiles, like Aischines, and other
immigrants to the region) and at times on their involvement
with external political powers offering patronage to
writers. Of these, the most significant factor is

patronage, which had operated earlier also, but assumed
a new importance in the Hellenistic period. (Even in
classical drama, the genre ostensibly least subject to
patronage, its effects are apparent: Aischylos died in
Sicily, Euripides in Macedon and Sophokles' refusal to
leave Athens except on state service was regarded as
unusual.) Pindar's ode for Diagoras of Rhodes ('0'7) and
Theokritos' encomium of Ptolemy Philadelphos, with its
Koan background (Idyll 17) show one side of the coin;
conversely, the Melian Melanippides and the Rhodian
Antagoras were lost to the region when they left for
Macedon.

The potentially stifling effect of patronage was
offset by the social mobility and intellectual interchange
it allowed writers - largely denied to their readership.
Patronage lies behind the vital cosmopolitanism to be
found in much of Greek literature, though the parochial
insularity endemic in popular attitudes was never
completely eradicated: just as superficial differences
in dialect were often allowed to mask the underlying unity
of the Greek people, so in their literature regional and
ethnic prejudices often obtrude.

As observed in the previous chapter, epic is the oldest
literary genre. In the fifth century, Herodotos accepts
the historicity of Hesiod and Homer, but acknowledges
controversy about their date and their place in the
development of Greek verse (Hdt.2.53.2-3):

> I believe that Homer and Hesiod precede us in time
> by 400 years and no more. These are the poets who
> created a theogony for the Greeks, gave the gods their
> titles, assigned their prerogatives and spheres and
> outlined their natures. Poets who are said to have
> preceded these men lived later, in my view.

The other poets hinted at by Herodotos are generally
taken to be the nebulous Orpheus and Mousaios; perhaps
rather such epic poets as Eumelos of Corinth, Arkteinos
of Miletos or Peisandros of Rhodes, now known only from
meagre fragmentary remains, are intended. According to
the Souda, some critics regarded Peisandros of Rhodes as
earlier than Hesiod; and in the commemorative epigram of
Theokritos Peisandros is described as 'pratos', perhaps
'earliest' rather than 'foremost', of verse-writers.

On Homer, the Souda comments:

> He has been claimed by various authorities as a
> native of Smyrna, Chios, Kolophon, Ios, Kyme, Kenchreai
> in the Troad, Lydia, Athens, Ithaka, Cyprus, Salamis,
> Knossos, Mycenae, Egypt, Thessaly, Italy, Loukania,
> Gryneia, Rome and Rhodes.

Most of these claims are demonstrably implausible; that
of Rhodes is certainly so, in view of the Aeolic-Ionic
character of Homeric diction. However, familiarity with
the myths of the Trojan War is apparent in early Rhodian
art (Davison, 1961, p.234 and pl.28). Chios has the
strongest claim to Homer ('h.Ap'.169-73; Semonides fr.29;
cf. AP 16.293-9). Hesiod is less elusive, giving the
autobiographical information that he lived at Askra in
Boiotia, where his father had brought the family from
Aiolian Kyme ('Op.'633-40).
     Early hexameter verse shows strong influence from the
East. The hexameter itself, a metre not naturally suited
to the Greek language, which falls more readily into
iambic or trochaic rhythms, may have been adopted from
the traditional verse of another tongue (cf. Arist.'Po.'
1449b25). The subject matter of Hesiod's 'Theogony' has
close affinities with the myths of Near Eastern peoples
(West, ed., 1966, pp.19-31). The Homeric epics show a
surer familiarity with the seaboard of Asia Minor than
with continental Greece. Also, the epics were commonly
said to have been 'brought' to the mainland: to Athens
by Peisistratos (or other figures of political and social
prominence), to Sparta by Lykourgos (Plu.'Lyc.'3-4;
cf. Str.10.4.19; [Pl.]'Hipparch.'228b).
     Homer gives us glimpses of many stories, relating to
a wide area of the Greek world, subordinate or subsidiary
to his main theme and therefore not elaborated: the
history of Thebes under the ill-starred Oidipous, the
exploits of Herakles, the expedition of the Argonauts are
incidentally and allusively mentioned (e.g. on Herakles,
'Il.'2.653-80, 5.392-7, 638-42, 8.363-8, 11.690-3, 15.28,
18.117-19, 19.95-136, 20.144-8; 'Od.'11.269, 21.22-30).
Itinerant singers of songs and tellers of tales ensured
the dissemination of genealogical traditions and accounts
of heroic deeds, kept alive by the descendants of
Mycenaean minstrels through the Dark Age, over a wide
area, though it was in Ionia that came the first main
confluence of the poetic stream.
     The achievement of Homer, moulding age-old tales into
a unified artistic whole, gave a new direction to the
bardic traditions; further poems were soon composed. The
advent of literacy, with the adoption of the Semitic
script, secured the preservation of this new art-form,
created from the oral poetry of the past. Also, prevailing
political and social conditions, with a leisured aristocratic society, encouraged the review of past glories.
And as the city-state emerged, the spirit of chauvinistic
competition, so persistent in Greece, came into being; it
became imperative for each state to keep its end up in a

parade of heroic traditions. The organization of state
festivals, forums for athletic, musical and literary
display, fomented these aspirations. Conditions were
ideal for epic poetry to flourish.

States vied with one another to consolidate their
records of Bronze Age splendour - or, in some cases, to
compensate for the lack of it. Here, the Dorians were in
an embarrassing position: they had played a significant
part (whatever its nature) in the collapse of the Bronze
Age culture so eloquently sung in epic traditions. Yet
many poets from Dorian communities appear in the forefront
of the new wave of epic. It would be very interesting to
know whether such poets as Eumelos of Corinth and Kinaithon
of Sparta were members of the ruling classes or came from
the subservient population. If it could be determined
whether early Peloponnesian epic is an attempt of 'serfs'
to reassert themselves or of their overlords to rehabili-
tate themselves, much light would be cast on the vexed
question of the role played by the Dorians in the fall of
Mycenaean civilization. But it is impossible in the case
of meagre fragments to detect the existence, far less
reconstruct the content, of any unbroken folk traditions
from the past. And the universal use of the same artificial epic diction by poets of all regions and all
dialect affiliations renders the personality and background
of the individual poet inscrutable.

Dorians scarcely occur in Homer. Different states
adopted different expedients to make good the Dorian
deficiency in subject matter. Eumelos of Corinth
ingeniously identified Corinth, insignificant in Homer,
with Ephyre, which had splendid heroic traditions (Huxley,
1969, p.61). More commonly, poets of Dorian states
concentrated on the cycle of stories associated with
Herakles, whose exploits conveniently embraced most
regions, and who was increasingly claimed by the Dorians
as their champion and progenitor. (Similarly, epics on
Theseus and the city's glorious past became popular later
in Athens.) In the forefront on the Herakles theme are
two poets of Rhodes - Peisinous of Lindos, a very shadowy
figure, and Peisandros of Kameiros, who has slightly more
substance (Kinkel, 1877, pp.248-53; Huxley, 1969, pp.100-5;
Galinsky, 1972, Chapters 1 and 2).

Peisandros was highly esteemed in antiquity, and in
the time of Theokritos was honoured with an epigram as
'foremost' (or 'earliest') 'versifier of the old days'
(Theoc.'Ep.'22). Possibly there was a revival of interest
in Peisandros because the Ptolemaic house regarded
Herakles as an ancestor. But Peisandros' fame must have
rested on literary merits as well as political considera-

tions, for there was much competition on his theme:
Aristotle remarks on the plethora of poems about Herakles,
noting that unity of plot is not ensured by having a
single hero (Arist.'Po.'1451a19; cf. Craik, 1970).

Peisandros' epic shows the insinuation of references
to his Rhodian background, and some traces of allegory.
The couplet (fr.7)

For him at Thermopylai the grey-eyed goddess Athena
created warm baths at the sea-shore

may be an oblique reference to the warm springs at Rhodian
Thermydrai, where Herakles was honoured (Apollod.2.5.11).
And the cup of Helios received by Herakles from Okeanos
(Panyassis has the same story, with the substitution of
Nereus for Okeanos) for his journey to the far west may
be a poetic representation of the seafaring exploits of
early Rhodes, with their hero helped by the gods of the
sea (fr.5; Panyassis fr.7). However, in the main, the
exploits of the hero were probably depicted in a straightforward non-rationalizing spirit, as Herakles in lion-skin
and club (first given him by Peisandros and adopted by
vase-painters, who found useful such a ready means of
identifying their subject) faced up to such fabulous
dangers as an encounter with the many-headed Hydra
(Souda; Eratosth.'Cat.'12; Paus.2.37.4). This approach
forms a marked contrast to the rationalizations of myths
attempted somewhat later by the Milesian writer Hekataios
(FGH I 1, 19, etc.).

Lyric poetry, short pieces sung to musical accompaniment,
most commonly of a lyre, is a genre with its roots in the
convivial atmosphere of Mycenaean palace society. Frescoes
(notably one from the throne room at Pylos) depict
musicians playing the lyre; Homer mentions both solo
singers with lyre accompaniment entertaining at banquets
and also choirs, chanting dirges and other types of song.
However, the earliest written examples from the archaic
period seem to represent a revival, with a movement away
from epic, rather than a direct tradition from the heroic
age.

Choral lyric impinges on traditional folk-songs and
often involves the community. On many occasions, sad or
happy - funerals, weddings, celebrations of religious
festivals or of personal successes - a choir with a leader
would perform a song, imbued with old, well-established
conventional elements, but given a new slant by poet or
performers. Monody, by contrast, is often highly
individual in content. Artificial or spontaneous,
commissioned by the wealthy or improvised by the populace,
lyric poetry had many facets.

Kleoboulos, the sixth-century Lindian ruler, was famed
for his verse as well as for his statesmanship. Authenticity, however, presents a problem. An epitaph in
hexameters expressing the literary conceit that the
memorial will last as long as there are trees, sun, moon,
rivers and sea is criticized by Simonides:

for everything is weaker than the gods; and stone even
men's hand can break

giving its author firmly as 'Kleoboulos dweller in Lindos';
according to Diogenes Laertius it was merely 'said by
some' to be the work of Kleoboulos (AP 7.153; Simon.fr.48d;
Pl.'Phdr.'264d; cf. Bowra, 1961, pp.370-1; Jeffery, 1976,
pp.198-9). The attribution to Kleoboulos of a song sung
by children in spring is certainly suspect. The song –
with 'birds' begging gifts – is clearly of a traditional,
typically anonymous character. Such mendicant folk-songs
may be readily parallelled in Greece (most closely in
songs sung by Koronistai, collecting for Korone, the
daughter of Apollo turned into a crow) and elsewhere
(Ath.8.360c = PMG 848; cf. Smyth, 1900, pp.507-8;
FGH III 526 and 533; cf. Parke, 1977, p.76).

Timokreon of Ialysos, politician manqué, athlete and
poet, was a lyric writer as deeply embroiled in events of
the fifth century as Kleoboulos in those of the sixth
(PMG pp.375-8; Ath.10.415f; cf. Bowra, 1961, pp.349-58;
Kirkwood, 1974, pp.182-5). Plutarch gives an account of
his 'outrageous' and 'extravagant' censure of Themistokles,
and his subsequent gloating over Themistokles' discomfiture
(Plu.'Them.'21.4; cf. Meiggs, 1972, p.414):

While you praise Pausanias, or you Xanthippos, or you
Leotychidas, I praise Aristeides, the best man of all
who came from holy Athens; for Leto loathed Themistokles,
liar, rogue, traitor, who was induced by filthy money
not to restore his friend Timokreon to his native
Ialysos. He took three talents of silver and sailed
off to his ruin, restoring some exiles unjustly,
expelling some, murdering others. Tainted by money,
he acted the host at the Isthmos, absurdly, providing
meats which were cold. People ate them and prayed
that no good fortune would come to Themistokles.

Themistokles retaliated by proxy with Simonides' vituperative epitaph – scarcely for a real tomb (AP 7.348):

Great drunkard, glutton and slanderer, here I lie,
Timokreon of Rhodes.

Timokreon and Simonides exemplify recurrent Greek traits.
Two centuries later, Apollonios and Kallimachos conducted
a bitter feud, again partly in Rhodes, through literary
channels. There are parallels in Athens too: Aristophanic
comedy attacked individuals openly; and in the fourth

century, when private vendettas were conducted through
litigation, before the interested gaze of jury and
spectators, forensic speeches were written up for circulation.

The dithyramb, a type of choral ode originating in cult-
hymns to Dionysos, was an art-form with widespread popular
appeal, which showed a lively development over a long
period of time, and was strongly Dorian in many of its
phases. Tradition recorded that Arion produced dithyrambs
at Corinth around 600 BC; dithyrambs were already performed
at Sikyon in the time of the tyrant Kleisthenes, about
600-570; it was from Hermione in the Argolid that Lasos,
credited with the institution of dithyrambic contests at
Athens in the late sixth century, originated (Arion –
Hdt.1.23; Sikyon – Hdt.5.67; cf. Ath.14.629a, Bakchiadas
also of Sikyon; Lasos – Hdt.7.6.3; Souda; see Pickard-
Cambridge, rev. Webster, 1962, pp.1-59 for a comprehensive
treatment). Pratinas of Phlious, traditionally associated
rather with satyr drama, invoked Dionysos in a song of
revelry, almost certainly a dithyramb, with the words
(Pratinas fr.1 = Ath.14.617f; cf. Souda):
     Listen to my Dorian dance.
     In Aristotle's day, a Dorian claim to be the originators
of drama was made, bolstered by spurious linguistic arguments (Arist.'Po.'1448a29). In the case of tragedy, the
Dorian claim to priority is not without foundation if it
is the case that tragedy stemmed from 'those who led off
the dithyramb' or indeed that it once had a satyric
character (Arist.'Po.'1449a11, 20; cf. Pickard-Cambridge,
rev. Webster, 1962, pp.89-97 and Else, 1965, on this
complex question). In the case of comedy, plays were
written and staged in Syracuse by Epicharmos and Phormis
as early as, if not earlier than, the first Attic comedies
(but see Breitholz, 1960, for a sceptical view of Dorian
origins) and there is some evidence for an early connection
of comedy with Megara (cf. MacDowell, ed. Ar.'V',1971, on l.
57). The silent testimony of vase-painting and of terra-
cotta statuettes suggests that pre-mimetic dance was
widespread in the seventh and sixth centuries – at Lindos,
Crete, Cyprus and elsewhere in the East as well as at
Corinth and Athens on the mainland (Pickard-Cambridge,
rev. Webster, 1962, pp.301-11; cf. Webster, 1956, p.157).
From artistic representations, it is difficult to determine
the boundary between masked dance, or singing revelry, and
dramatic performance. The earliest clear evidence (though
not all regard it as clear; cf. Dover, 1972, p.220) of an
activity approaching comic drama comes from a vase of
early sixth-century Corinth.

As already noted, the Attic dramatists used Doric for
the lyric songs of their plays. It is possible that the
iambic metre of dialogue is somehow related to the
Syracusan tradition of 'iambistai' singing and carrying
phallic objects in honour of Dionysos (Ath.5.181c). It
was, however, in Athens that drama reached the climax
of its development. Although neither tragedy nor comedy
was an indigenous Attic growth from elements peculiar to
Athens, only Athens achieved the metamorphosis and fusion
of these elements, with the elevation of mimetic dance
and of the rudimentary dramatic interchange universally
present in group song into great art-forms. In Athens,
there was a continuous mutual influence between dithyramb,
tragedy and satyric drama, which drew on the common stock
of myths for their themes.

Aischylos, who in a few decades changed the character
of the new genre tragedy, and Melanippides of Melos, who
made sweeping and influential modifications of the old
dithyramb, were contemporaries of the Rhodian Timokreon
and his adversaries Themistokles and Simonides. (For
Melanippides, see PMG pp.392-5, nos 757-66; Pickard-
Cambridge, rev. Webster, 1962, pp.39-42.) It is now
generally agreed that there was only one Melanippides,
though the Souda gives two, grandfather and grandson.
Melanippides was victorious at Athens in 494 (Marm.Par.
A47) and died at the court of Perdikkas of Macedon some
time after 454. (For the name Melanippides, cf. Hdt.
5.67.)

Fragments of Melanippides' works 'Danaides', 'Marsyas'
and 'Persephone' are extant (fr.2D, 'Marsyas'):

Athena threw the instrument [the flute] away with
her holy hand and said, 'Go, ugly thing, distortion
of my person. I do not countenance such baseness'.

Several fragments show a penchant for onomatopoetic
jingles and an interest in the type of pseudo-etymology
popular with the sophists - such as linking Acheron with
'ache', 'distress', and Oineus with 'oinos', 'wine'
(frr.3, 5). However, verbal play of this kind was not
new in Greek literature, and such 'nomen omen' allusions
abound. Also, such 'derivations' are peculiarly prone
to be quoted by later writers (Athenaios does in fact
attribute the Oineus-'oinos' association to Nikander of
Kolophon, Ath.1.35a) and they may not have been so very
common in Melanippides' work.

In antiquity, Melanippides was regarded as the supreme
practitioner of dithyramb, just as Homer was of epic, or
Sophokles of tragedy (X.'Mem.'1.4.3). Melanippides'
creative originality, not much apparent in the extant
fragments, was apparently expended on the introduction of

'anabolai' (variously interpreted as lyric solos,
musical preludes or melodic changes) into dithyramb
(Arist.'Rhet.'1409b; cf. 'Pr.'918b). Melanippides'
innovations did not go uncriticized, especially by the
comic poets, who were in general hostile to dithyramb, or
at least found it good for a laugh.

The proverbial expression, 'more stupid than a dithyramb', hints at the tendency in dithyramb for intellectual
content to give way before emotional impact (Schol.Ar.
'Av.'1393). The music came to swamp and stultify the
words. In the absence of any musical scores, it is
impossible to be sure that this was a bad thing. We do
know, however, that dithyrambs were traditionally written
in the Phrygian mode, strident, flamboyant and excited;
also that the flute was the accompanying instrument, while
the lyre remained conventional in cult-songs to Apollo
(Arist.'Pol.'1341-2).

Diagoras resembled Melanippides in that he came from
Melos, wrote dithyrambs and other lyric poems, and spent
some time in Athens. (On Diagoras, see PMG pp.382-3, nos
738-9; Jacoby, 1959; Woodbury, 1965; Guthrie, 1969, III
pp.235-7; Dover, 1976.) However, Diagoras was much more
celebrated, in his own time and later, for his atheistic
beliefs than for his verse. It is tantalizing that we
have fragments of his poems, but none of his prose
treatise 'Apopyrgizontes' or 'Phrygian Discourses'
(probably alternative titles for the same work). It is
even more tantalizing that the poems, so far from evincing
atheism, seem redolent of a rather conventional piety.
Anecdotes told of Diagoras suggest a defiant profanity,
or harmless persiflage, rather than a philosophical stance
like that of such sophists as Protagoras. It was said,
for instance, that he once used a statue of Herakles as
firewood, urging the hero to perform a thirteenth labour
and cook the lentils.   However, according to the orator
Lysias, Diagoras' offence was in words, not deeds, and
it was later said that Protagoras shared in effect the
beliefs of Diagoras of Melos, but was less outspoken about
them (Lys.6.17; VS II 80 A23).

Diagoras, whether or not he can be counted a 'sophist',
was clearly on the fringes of the sophistic movement, which
was gathering momentum against the background of Athens'
political supremacy. The sophists, itinerant teachers of
rhetoric, were typically foreigners exploiting the ready
market for their skills among the affluent citizens of
democratic Athens. The sophists provide an analogue to
the contemporary dithyrambic poets. While the latter
wrote vacuous verse, the former affected a meretricious
manner in prose writing; while music took over from meaning

in poetry, the sonorous affected language of prose
obscured the ideas expressed.

Diagoras remains an elusive figure. Little is certain
except that he came from Melos, wrote rather indifferent
verse, was expelled from Athens soon before the production
of 'Birds' in 414, where Aristophanes implies a recent
prosecution, for impiety of a kind now obscure but then
notorious enough to warrant jokes at his expense on the
comic stage (Ar.'Av.'1072-8; 'Nu.'830).   Tradition does
not record how long Diagoras had spent in Athens before
his expulsion, or where he went afterwards. His homeland Melos had (in 416) been brutally subjugated for
adopting an independent stand in the politics of the
Aegean, and refusing affiliation with Athenian aggrandizement (see Chapter 3). It may be wondered whether Diagoras,
persona non grata in Athens, would be permitted to join
the Athenian settlers on his native island, and whether
the timing of the prosecution is coincidental. It is not
hard to imagine why the Athenians might have felt
uncomfortable in his company.

Philoxenos of Kythera (436/435-380/379), who worked in
Athens and also visited the court of Dionysios of Syracuse,
may be added to Melanippides and Diagoras as a further
notable dithyrambic poet from the Dorian islands (cf.
Arist.'Pol.'1342b9). In the fifth and fourth centuries,
the most successful practitioners of dithyramb, and music
generally, were non-Athenians (Plu.'Mor.'348b). But they
came to Athens, the most prestigious centre for drama and
music - as Olympia was for athletics - to perform and
compete.

While poets from all over the Greek world achieved fame
with lyric compositions, fifth-century drama was dominated
by Athenians. Foreigners could apply to produce plays,
but Ion of Chios, a contemporary of Sophokles, was almost
the only outsider to make his mark with tragedies composed
for Attic festivals; he also wrote dithyrambs and a book
of memoirs. Neophron of Sikyon, Alkimenes of Megara,
Phanostratos of Halikarnassos and Melanthios of Rhodes
are all post-classical, as is patently L. Marius Antiochus
from Corinth; and of these only the first had much stature
(TrGF 15, 19, 201, 192, 303; on the date of Neophron, and
his alleged influence on Euripides' 'Medea', see Page, ed.,
1938, pp.xxx-xxxvi).

The versatility of fifth-century tragedians is
impressive. They had to compose choreographed lyrics for
the chorus as well as dialogue in iambic verse for the
characters; their plots were based on myths but usually
aimed to give the story a new twist; staging was circum-

scribed by limits on realism, and characterization too
had certain constricting limits. Also, they produced
their own plays. None of this need have deterred
prospective foreign participants; but in addition tragedy
very often had a pronounced patriotic tone. The eponymous
archon, who decided which groups of plays should be
eligible to compete at the festivals, perhaps based his
choice on political as well as other criteria: this may
account for the preponderance of local writers, eulogizing
Athens overtly or obliquely.

Comedy demanded a similar virtuosity, though the subject
matter of its plots was less restricted. Our view of
fifth-century comedy depends on Aristophanes, who eclipsed
his rivals and whose work is for us represented by eleven
extant plays. Here, it was even more difficult for
foreigners to break in, as contemporary local affairs and
personalities were popular themes and the Lenaïa, the main
festival for comedy, was not even attended by foreigners.
However, in the fourth century, there was a change of
direction. Dramatists turned for their themes from public
life and prominent figures to mythological burlesque, then
to private concerns and domestic situations. This change,
already discernible in the last two extant plays of
Aristophanes ('Ekklesiazousai', 392 and 'Ploutos', 388)
has much to do with the defeat of Athens in the
Peloponnesian War and her ensuing loss of confidence and
political direction. It is not a coincidence that, of the
earlier plays of Aristophanes, that which has least
contemporary colour is 'Birds', produced in the aftermath
of the disastrous Athenian expedition against Sicily.
The ancient view that ridicule of public figures was
dropped through fear of reprisals from a powerful oligarchy
puts too much stress on transient conditions, too little
on general trends of the age (cf. FAC I pp.572-3).

Foreigners now had the opportunity to present comedies
in Athens. One of the first aliens to make an impact was
Anaxandrides from Kameiros, described as a picturesque
figure - tall and good looking, wearing his hair long and
dressing in purple and gold (Chamaileon ap. Ath.9.374b;
for Anaxandrides, see FAC II pp.42-81). Anaxandrides'
contemporary Antiphanes, a prolific comic poet, was also
of foreign origin and possibly also from Rhodes; but the
biographical data conflict (Souda).

Aristophanes died in, or a little before, 385;
Anaxandrides' first victory at Athens came in 376. The
gap is only a decade, whereas a real gulf in time and
spirit separates Aristophanic 'Old' Comedy from the 'New'
Comedy of Menander (who put on his first play in 321) and
his contemporaries. Of Anaxandrides and other poets of

the 'Middle' Comedy, enough has survived - though in the
unsatisfactory form of titles of plays and short citations
(some eighty in the case of Anaxandrides) - to show that
the change came gradually.

By the time of Menander, the chorus had declined to
such an extent that it simply provided entr'actes without
direct relevance to the play; plots were now based on
coincidence within family and marital relationships
(replacing the typical Aristophanic dream-like sequence
in a fantasy world); gross jokes about sex and bowels
had vanished, as had direct.ridicule of politicians.
New Comedy is, none the less, a direct descendant of Old:
there is some domestic comedy in Aristophanes (for instance,
the sketch of the relationship of Strepsiades with his
sophisticated wife and spendthrift son in the opening of
'Clouds') and there is some political comment in Menander
and his contemporaries (cf. Webster, 1970, pp.37-56;
Gomme and Sandbach, ed. Menander, 1973, p.24 n.1).

Fourth-century comedy also owed much to fifth-century
tragedy, especially to Euripides (as was recognized
already by Satyros, writing a brief biography of Euripides
in the third century). Anaxandrides was credited by the
Souda with the introduction on stage of love-affairs and
the seduction of girls - themes so prominent in later
comedy. Aristophanes had countenanced a seduction in
'Kokalos', a late play staged for him by one of his sons
('Vita'). Euripides had forestalled both comic poets.
In 'Ion', the seduction, indeed rape, of Kreousa by Apollo
is crucial to the plot, though it precedes the action of
the play by many years; the lost 'Antigone' was apparently
based on the love-affair between Antigone and her cousin
Haimon. At the end of the fifth century, tragedians led
by Euripides were experimenting with the introduction of
humorous elements into tragedy (cf. Craik, 1979); by the
end of the fourth, comic poets were borrowing techniques,
such as the management of recognition scenes, from the
tragic stage. Tragedy and comedy were written by different
poets for different occasions, and acted by different
actors competing for different prizes. But a rapprochement
of the genres is apparent.

Myth is the crossing-point between tragedy and comedy,
as it is between tragedy and satyric drama, or tragedy and
dithyramb. The genres were at their closest in the early
decades of the fourth century, when mythological burlesque
was popular with comic poets. Anaxandrides wrote plays
with such titles as 'Herakles', 'Helen', 'Nereus'.
Anaxandrides' 'komoidotragoidia' (FAC II p.54, fr.25) well
expresses the approach of comedy to tragedy, as does the
term 'hilarotragoidia' ('cheerful tragedy') applied to the

tragic parodies written by Rhinthon of Tarentum at the
end of the fourth century. As titles of Epicharmos' plays
suggest a marked fondness for mythological themes, it
seems that burlesque was long popular in Sicily and
southern Italy. However, it would be wrong to overstress
the affinities of Attic Middle Comedy of the early fourth
century with the comedy current in the Greek West at an
earlier and later period. In Attica, too, mythological
themes had been used earlier - for instance, by Kratinos
in 'Odysseis' and Aristophanes in 'Aiolosikon' (cf. Dover,
1972, p.218): this latent trend is developed in Middle
Comedy. Other popular themes to be seen in Anaxandrides
were based on contemporary 'types' of character ('The Bad
Woman', 'Pious People') or occupations ('Painters',
'Huntsmen').

Aristotle, writing about the middle of the century,
regarded 'recognition' and 'reversal' as hallmarks of
tragedy. These are present in classical tragedy, but are
even more important in New Comedy - a development he
apparently did not envisage. Aristotle seems to have
viewed Aristophanes with some distaste, but to have
approved more of his own contemporaries. Anaxandrides'
work is several times cited with approbation (cf. Else,
1957, p.311). Anaxandrides enjoyed a general popularity
in his day. In 375, two of his plays were accepted for
production in Athens. In 311, 'The Treasure' was revived.
Later, however, he was less admired; there is no evidence
of a Latin adaptation of any of his plays.

The following quotations are fairly typical of the
fragments of Anaxandrides which have survived; they also
illustrate the type of material commonly excerpted by
later writers. The first is a maxim preserved in Stobaios'
anthology; the second, with food as its subject, comes
from Athenaios; the third, also from Athenaios, alludes
to notable fourth-century prostitutes in an exchange
between an Attic and a Doric speaker (Stob.2.1.3 = FAC
II pp.54-5,fr.21; Ath.14.654f = FAC II pp.56-7, fr.30;
Ath.13.570d = FAC II pp.48-9, fr.9).

From 'The Basketbearer': 'We are all fools before God,
and we know nothing.'
From 'Nereus': 'The first to discover a great choice
head of greyfish, inviting the knife, and the shapely
splendid tunny, and other foodstuffs from the salt sea -
Nereus - rules over all this region.'

From 'Dotage': Ath.   'Do you know Lais from Corinth?'
Cor.   'Aye, hired by the day.' (reading τὰν ἀμεραῖαν:
codd. την ημεριον)
Ath.   'She had a friend Anteia.'
Cor.   'I had fun wi' her an' a'.'
Ath.   'By God, Lagiske was still a beauty then, and
Theolyte was really good-looking and nice, and "Basil"
showed the first signs of being a stunner.'

Aristotle inaugurated the serious study of the theory of
drama at a time of peculiar interest in its practice.
Drama, especially comedy, was on the upswing as popular
entertainment. The theatre at Athens was rebuilt around
330, and other towns to construct new theatres include
Epidauros and Megalopolis. Gradually, drama became for
writers and performers (musicians as well as actors) an
international profession. Inscriptional records – most
full from Athens, Delos and Delphi – have a cosmopolitan
character. Akesios from Rhodes, who performed at Delos
in 279 BC, is only one of the many itinerant players
(O'Connor, 1908, p.78; cf. Sifakis, 1967, pp.148-52).
Writers too took their plays to any receptive audience
(cf. Sifakis, 1967, pp.24-30). Comic poets of Dorian
origin producing at the Lenaia in Athens include Anaxilas
and Damoxenos.

Around this time, organized guilds of Dionysiac
artists, actors and musicians, came into being (Pickard-
Cambridge, rev. Gould and Lewis, 1968, pp.281-2). These
theatrical guilds – the Athenian, the Isthmian and, later,
the Ionian-Hellespontine – maintained an independent
existence, with mutual rivalry for the monopoly of
festivals or the patronage of kings, until the time of
Augustus, when a world-wide organization was formed.
Inscriptions from the islands show the Hellespontine guild
active in the region. Because a Koan inscription records
privileges granted by Sulla to the guild, it has been
suggested that Kos was for a time its headquarters (Segre,
1938a; but see Sherk, 1966 for a contrary view). The
picture is complicated by the activities of smaller
troupes: at Rhodes, there were three separate companies
performing in the third century (cf. Pickard-Cambridge,
rev. Gould and Lewis, 1968, p.294 n.6; p.296 n.3; p.303

n.6 for 'technitai' in Kos and Rhodes). It is clear from
inscriptions that the Koan Dionysia, which became, like
the Asklepieia with its musical and athletic contests, an
international festival, incorporated competitions for
dithyramb and comedy (cf. Herzog, 1903, p.198). Most of
the small islands too had their own local theatres (cf.
Jacopi, 1932, pp.171-2 for Astypalaia).

As well as the mainstream activity of writing full-
scale comedy for performance by professional artists at
the top dramatic festivals, there was a great undercurrent
of which we have only occasional glimpses. It seems that,
when comedy evolved in fifth-century Athens, the pre-
dramatic mimetic activity of many communities continued
underground, making an occasional resurgence. It is a
salutary reminder that seemingly 'primitive' elements in
a culture are not necessarily early to read Aristotle's
statement that in his day phallic performances were common
in many areas (Arist.'Po.'1449a11). The names of people
involved in this casual art-form, which provided lively
ephemeral entertainment, especially popular perhaps in
places without a major dramatic festival of their own, are
seldom preserved. An exception is Antheas of Lindos, who
'composed comedies and many other literary creations of
this kind, which he led among the "phallophoroi" who
accompanied him.' He also 'continuously made merry by
day and night' and, on a more sober note, 'invented the
art of composition with compound words' (Ath.10.445a-b).
This innovation in diction seems to be of the type
commended by Aristotle in the 'Poetics' (Arist.'Po.'
1457a32).

The mimes of Herodas give a fuller insight into this
para-dramatic undertow. (The form Herondas, found Ath.
3.86b, is Boiotian and Herodas of other sources, notably
citations in Stobaios, is preferable. For Herodas, see
the editions of Headlam, 1922, and, especially, Cunningham,
1971). Herodas' work falls in the decade 270-260; he
evidently spent time in Kos, which he uses as a poetic
setting, but need not have been Koan by origin (Cunningham,
ed., 1971, p.2). In elevating folk-tradition into a
literary form, Herodas probably owes much to the prose
mimes of Sophron of Syracuse, a mid-fifth-century writer
of whom very little has survived; in verse and language,
he uses an amalgam of current forms.

The mimes encapsulate comic scenes and characters in
small compass. Herodas gives a series of vivid vignettes
depicting life and manners of his day; such characters as
slaves, brothel-keepers and cobblers are his stock-in-
trade. Sex is a prominent theme and the crudely explicit
humour is heightened by the incongruity between realistic

content and high-flown expression. The poems were
probably recited privately: it is unlikely that they were
performed before a wide audience.

Poem 2 is set in a Koan lawcourt and 4 in an Asklepieion
which may be that of Kos (but see Cunningham, 1966 for
counter-arguments; cf. Oliver, 1934). Poem 6, with a
domestic setting, is more typical in location. In this
mime, Metro visits her friend Koritto, to enquire where
Koritto has procured a particularly fine specimen of a
prized commodity; 'the subject is the use and supply of
leather penes for female masturbation' (Cunningham, ed.,
1971, p.160; cf. commentary on 7). This theme allows the
exploitation of the idea, common in comedy and elsewhere
in Greek literature (written by men) that women have
voracious sexual appetites (cf. Dover, 1974, p.101).
Other topics probably derived from comedy are that slaves
are lazy and lacking in initiative (1-11) and that
borrowing neighbours are a nuisance (82-4). In the
following passage (58-73), Koritto praises her clever
shoemaker, with his lucrative sideline in erotica:

'This fellow comes from Chios or Erythrai - I don't
know which. He is bald and small; you will say he is
exactly like Prexinos, as like as two peas in a pod -
however, when he talks, you will know it is Kerdon
and not Prexinos. He works at home, doing business
stealthily, for every door now shudders at the taxman;
but he is a true Koan in his workmanship. You will
fancy you see the handicraft of Athena herself, not
of Kerdon. As for me - he brought a pair with him,
Metro - when I saw them, my eyes started. Men cannot
make theirs - I'll say it, since we're alone - so
erect. And not only that, they were smooth as a
dream, and the lacings were wool instead of thongs.
You may search for a cobbler kinder to women, but
you won't find one.'

Of formal comedy written after the time of Menander,
very little has survived, while tragedy had largely become
ossified into repeat performances of the fifth-century
'classics'. The strong political colouring of Attic drama
of the fifth century had gradually faded in the decades
of the fourth, but left a residue. Of Athens, we know
that the comedies of Menander were imbued with local
colour, typically set in the city, though showing
familiarity with other regions ('Eunuch' shows knowledge
of Rhodes and Samos; cf. the suggestion of Webster, 1974,
p.14 that 'Misoumenos' was set in Rhodes, possibly for
production there); the plays reflect the social environment
of the prosperous urban bourgeoisie and one, 'Aspis',
assumes familiarity with the complexities of the Attic laws

of inheritance. In the provinces too, the community was
heavily involved in the administration of musical and
dramatic contests staged in local theatres. It was
frequently at theatrical festivals of Dionysos that state
edicts were proclaimed to the assembled populace. Formal
dramatic production continued to be essentially a civic
activity, sponsored by the community for the community.

However, the character of the local community was
undergoing tremendous change. Alexander had taken the
world by storm, and his conquests put an end to insularity
in political, religious and intellectual life. With the
passing of the inward-looking city-state and the growth of
wider power blocs, dominated from royal courts, patriotism
and local affairs, though still of interest to the
untravelled majority, no longer absorbed the literary
élite. And so, while drama, with its element of display
and competition, had a wide popular appeal, and continued
to be written, performed and enjoyed, it was not put into
literary circulation.

Intellectuals turned to a new kind of poetry. Hellenistic
poetry, like Hellenistic religion, is more personal in
character than that of the classical period. Personal
emotion, real or assumed, and private experience, actual
or invented, take on a new prominence. The almost total
loss of non-dramatic verse of the fourth century inhibits
analysis of the process of change, and it is pertinent to
recall that many elements regarded as typically Hellenistic
(such as erudite diction and arcane allusiveness in content)
had been present to some degree in Greek literature all
along; but the new wave gathered momentum around 300 BC.

Rhodes and Kos now enter a phase of great cultural
vitality, and the record of island achievements at this
time is a facet of the wider history of Alexandrian
civilization. In the following account, 'Alexandrian' is
used of the place, 'Alexandrine' of the period. Philitas
of Kos and Simias of Rhodes had a seminal influence on
later literature. They in turn had been influenced by the
work of poets and thinkers now lost, and possibly, through
Eudemos, by Peripatetic ideas. The intellectual richness
of the east Aegean and the coast of Asia Minor is
demonstrated by the numbers of talented men from this
area gravitating to Alexandria: Samos contributed
Asklepiades and Hedylos; Kolophon sent Antimachos and
Hermesianax; Ephesos was the original home of Zenodotos,
the first official librarian.

The islands, especially Kos, continued to have an
independent cultural existence, conducive to the realiza-
tion of the potential of local writers (who might then

emigrate in search of a public or a patron) and also
rendering the area attractive to intellectuals who wished
to shelter under the Ptolemaic umbrella, but not to live
in the city. The islands were sufficiently distant to
permit a certain detachment in their residents, and had a
valued political independence; Herodas remarks (2.26-7)
on 'that autonomy of yours on which you pride yourselves'.

It was in Kos that Berenike, wife of Ptolemy (who
declared himself Ptolemy I a few years later) gave birth
to her son (later Ptolemy II, Philadelphos) in 308. It
is easy to see why the island was chosen for the confine-
ment: obstetrics was a special study of the Koan and
Knidian medical schools. In a small community, the
Ptolemies would readily become acquainted with prominent
local residents, of whom one was the poet Philitas. When
his son was growing up, Ptolemy appointed Philitas to the
post of tutor; this began the scholar-poet tradition so
influential at Alexandria. (Str.14.2.19 calls Philitas
'poet and critical writer'; cf. 17.3.22 on Kallimachos,
'poet and grammarian'. For Philitas - not Philetas,
Coll.Alex.p.90 - see Coll.Alex.pp.90-6; Kuchenmüller,
1928; Pfeiffer, 1968, pp.88-93.) The links between
creative writing and literary criticism were stronger now
than at any other time or place in antiquity. Poets
served their apprenticeship as Homeric scholars, and
those in charge of the library were simultaneously writers.

Philitas' work is known to us largely at second hand,
through his immense influence on others. Theokritos
regarded Philitas, with Asklepiades, as his master in
style (7.39); later generations linked him with Kallimachos; Ovid identified him simply as 'Cous poeta'
(Ov.'AA'3.329). Of his critical work, we know of a
commentary on Homer (which probably influenced Zenodotos,
allegedly his pupil) and of a collection of rare words,
with explanations, perhaps the glossary used and cited by
Athenaios (11.467c, etc.). His multifarious creative
writing survives only in scanty fragments, found mainly
in Stobaios' anthology. The following three quotations
represent three very different kinds of poem, but are too
truncated to give an adequate impression of Philitas'
versatility (Stob.51.3 = fr.6, Coll.Alex. p.92; Stob.
40.11 = fr.1, Coll.Alex. p.90; Stob.56.10 = fr.12, Coll.
Alex. p.93).

From a short epic in hexameters, 'Hermes':
I accomplished the journey to Hades, the road where
traffic is one-way only.
From a narrative elegy, 'Demeter':
Now I ever brood, and a further new trouble is added.
There is no respite in sight from my misery.

From a collection of epigrams:
> I do not weep for you, dearest of friends; for you
> knew much happiness; but God sent you, in turn, a
> share of unhappiness.

That Philitas was originally most famous for his love-
poems (now completely lost), dedicated to Bittis, is
implied by Hermesianax (Ath.13.598f = Hermesianax fr.7.75-8,
Coll.Alex. pp.98-105):
> You know the poet of whom the Koans, citizens of
> Eurypylos, erected a bronze statue, singing of agile
> Bittis under a plane-tree: Philitas, worn out through
> unremitting debate and discussion.

This echoes Philitas' own epitaph (Ath.9.401e, cf. 12.522b):
> Stranger, I am Philitas. The deceitful word and
> puzzling over riddles at night were the death of me
> (reading καὶ νυκτῶν Kaibel; not καὶ νυκτῶν A).

Perhaps Philitas' studies sapped his vitality and cut
short his life. But epitaphs can be written only by the
living, and the mention of riddles seems a wry joke
(cf. Ath.10.452f on riddles and Dromeas of Kos). Features
of Philitas' verse which recur in his successors' are a
liking for recherché diction (e.g. the verb ἀέξεται in fr.1;
cf. Ath.9.383b), an interest in myth with a special liking
for unusual or piquant aspects, and a preference for short
poems on personal themes.

Simias presents many parallels to Philitas, living at
about the same time (late fourth to early third century),
in Rhodes to Philitas' Kos; and having the same combination
of interests in philology and narrative poetry based on
myths (see Coll.Alex. pp.109-20; HE I pp.511-16; Fraenkel,
1915). Simias too was a prolific writer, of whose work
little has survived: the Souda mentions three books of
glosses and four books of miscellaneous poems.

Examples of Simias' glosses cited by Athenaios suggest
an interest in Homer, early lyric and the dialect of Crete
(7.327e, 11.472e, 11.479a, 15.677b, c). Simias' verse
included epigrams and hymns to the gods, typified by an
allusive style; in one (Fraenkel fr.14, but on the text
see Coll.Alex. p.114, fr.17), Herakles is obliquely
addressed,
> Hail, lord, blessed companion of sacred Hebe.

A thirteen line fragment of a hymn to Apollo in hexameters
gives the impression of writing for cognoscenti, with a
direct 'lift' of an expression from a Pindaric ode (cf.
line 2 with Pi.'P'10.31) and of a learned diction, using
recondite adjectives given meanings apparently based on
current Homeric criticism; also of a tendency to explore
the picturesque byways of mythical tradition (Tz.'H'7.693 =
Fraenkel fr.1; Coll.Alex. p.109, fr.1):

I came through the rich land of the distant Hyperboreans,
with whom once upon a time Perseus, king and hero,
dined, and where the Massagetai who mount swift horses
live, putting their trust in far-shooting bows, and by
the wondrous stream of ever-flowing Kaspasos, which
brings eternal water to the divine ocean. I reached
the islands dark with green firs, covered with tall-
fronded reeds. I observed the multitudinous race of
dog-men, over whose shapely shoulders the head of a
dog grows, strong with powerful jaws. Their voice is
like dogs' howling, and they know nothing of the
articulate speech of other mortals.

Simias is today remembered best for his 'pattern-poems',
poems with lines of uneven length forming the shape of an
object. These are 'fun' poems, pop art of their day, but
may have had a serious origin, suggested by the practice
of inscribing objects dedicated to a deity. Of three
extant - Axe, Wings, Egg - that on Wings (sc. those of
Love) may be quoted (Fraenkel fr.20; Coll.Alex.p.116,
fr.24):

Look at me, lord of deep-bosomed Earth, who unseated Akmon's son
And do not tremble if though tiny I have a luxuriant beard
For I was born long ago, when Necessity ruled
And to her yielded, with baleful hearts,
All creatures, all which moved
Through the air.
From Chaos
Not of Aphrodite the child,
Swift of flight, and of Ares, am I,
For I have never ruled by force, but by gentle persuasion
Earth yields to me, and the depths of the sea, and the brazen heaven:
I have removed their ancient sceptre and set ordinances for the gods.

Theokritos, like his contemporary Herodas, demonstrates
the international character of Greek culture in the third
century. (On Theokritos, see the editions of Gow, 1950,
revised 1952, and Dover, 1971; cf. Lawall, 1967.) Born
in Syracuse, he spent time in Kos and Alexandria. The
duration of Theokritos' stay in Kos is not known, and the
questions of how much of his work was written there, and
how far his poems are coloured by Koan allusion are controversial. The suggestion of one ancient commentator that
he visited Kos while en route for Alexandria is probably
just a guess (Schol.Idyll 7 Arg.). Modern conjecture that
his family might have originated in Kos, but left for

Syracuse in the time of Timoleon is equally without firm
foundation (CAH VII p.277). Theokritos' literary contacts
embrace people from a wide region: Nikias of Miletos, a
doctor who had probably trained in Kos, and who himself
wrote occasional verse (HE I pp.149-51 and II pp.428-34)
and Dosiadas of Crete (probably 'Lykidas' of Idyll 7) may
be singled out for mention; there are affinities too with
the Rhodian Simias and Kallimachos writing in Alexandria.
    Idyll 7 is set in Kos and shows familiarity with several
places in the island, though its main setting is a quiet
farm, where an informal harvest festival is to be celebrated
(cf. Chapter 1). Idyll 17 gives some prominence to Kos,
although the poem was probably written in Alexandria, as
it betrays direct court patronage. In this encomium of
Ptolemy Philadelphos, Theokritos shows a combination of
political tact and literary artistry in manipulating a
traditional form for his purposes (cf. Cairns, 1972,
pp.100-12). The poem accurately reflects the religious
spirit of the age: Herakles is envisaged as the ancestor
of Ptolemy - and of Alexander, the details of the
genealogy being wisely left unspecified (26-7); Ptolemy
is a Zeus among men (1-4) and equal in honour to the gods
(14-18); the birth on Kos of Ptolemy is compared to that
on Delos of Apollo (66-70).
    The background of Koan topography and myth in Idyll 7
is directly related to the setting of the poem; in Idyll
17, Kos has an obvious relevance as birthplace of
Philadelphos. Perhaps a more significant, because unselfconscious, indication of Theokritos' familiarity with
Kos is that the natural history of the poems seems to fit
the south Aegean better than any other locality (Lindsell,
1936). Just as Homer's references to birds and animals
suggest he was more familiar with the islands and coastal
Asia Minor than with the Greek mainland, so Theokritos'
plants put him in an Aegean, not a Sicilian, setting.
Also, in Idyll 1 a ferry man is gratuitously given the
epithet 'Kalydnian' (line 57):
    In return for it (a fine cup), I paid the Kalydnian
    ferry man a goat and a huge cheese, from white milk.
As the most common ferry journey for someone living in
Kos would be to Kalymnos, this may be a small pointer to
Theokritos' place of residence at the time of composition
of the poem.
    Theokritos' reputation has long rested on his being
the originator of pastoral poetry. But he was versatile,
and would merit a place in the histories of Greek
literature for his epigrams alone. Those on famous poets
are clever pastiche, outstanding specimens even in this
age of the epigram. He also wrote short 'epic' pieces.

The extant poems show a mastery of traditional skills,
drawing elements from mime (dramatic presentation and
realistic effects) and folk-song (telling use of
repetition); but this is combined with striking innovatory
ability (especially in language), culminating in the
creation of a new genre.

   Erinna may most appropriately be placed here, despite
the Souda's statement that she was a contemporary of
Sappho. This assertion was probably based simply on
coincidence in sex and subject matter. (On Erinna, see
HE I pp.97-8; II pp.281-4; Bowra, 1936, pp.325-42.)
Erinna's work shows affinities rather with Theokritos in
language - basically, Doric with epic elements. Erinna's
place of origin is given as Tenos or Telos (St.Byz.,
Souda); on linguistic and other grounds, the latter is
more probable. Erinna seems to belong with the Koan
group of poets. A poem on Erinna by Asklepiades of Samos,
the most celebrated of the Alexandrine epigrammatists,
has a programmatic note, suggestive of a preface to a
'first edition' (AP 7.11):
   This is the sweet work of Erinna....
Erinna's epigrams won a place in anthologies, but her fame
today, as in antiquity, rests on her epyllion, 'The
Distaff', written in memory of her friend Baukis. This
may be seen, from a papyrus fragment sixty lines in
length, as well as from ancient quotations, to have had
a poignant personal note conspicuous even in verse of the
period.

Early Alexandria drew much talent from the regions of
Greece and attracted able and enterprising men in
literature as in other fields. A generation later, people
born in the city or its environs began to make their mark.
The epic poet Apollonios, writer of the 'Argonautika',
the only Hellenistic epic to survive intact, is one of
those. Apollonios spent much, perhaps most, of his life
in the capital, where he held the post of librarian. But
in later sources, he is always known as Apollonios of
Rhodes. Controversy surrounds the chronology and events
of Apollonios' life, and the question of interaction with
his contemporaries, especially Kallimachos, complicates
the issue. (The ancient sources conflict; these are two
'Vitae', Souda and also POxy 1241, the list of librarians,
where the existence of another Apollonios, the Eidographer,
adds to the chronological confusions. For a succinct
account of the controversy, see PA I pp.330-3 and 749-54.)
   A full discussion of the complex reasons for, and the
probable timing of, Apollonios' departure for Rhodes is
unnecessary here. Briefly, 245 is the most probable date

for his leaving Alexandria, and it is unlikely that he ever went back; his motives may have been as much personal as professional. Relations with Kallimachos, who was older than Apollonios (perhaps his teacher, as the biographers say, but the tracing of master-pupil relationships is a favourite pastime in ancient biography, seen in the statement, Soph.'Vita'4, the Sophokles 'learned' tragedy from Aischylos) were strained. Jealousy on Kallimachos' part because Apollonios won the post of librarian which had eluded his own grasp and differences of opinion on literary methods possibly exacerbated a touchy situation.

The biographical tradition records that Apollonios left after the first version of the 'Argonautika' was ill received in Alexandria, and adds that the second version was successful in Rhodes. References in the scholia to a 'proekdosis' ('previous issue') (Vian and Delage, ed., 1974, p.xxi and n.3) lend some support to the biographers' account of events. (The process of 'publication' was not, of course, standardized. There was probably no author's release of a major collection by Theokritos, for instance. But with a large-scale poem, there is prima facie more likelihood of a single major issue than with a series of shorter pieces. Publication, in the sense of the irrevocable release of work to a possibly hostile reaction certainly took place: in the second century, the Rhodian historian Zenon apologized to Polybios for his inability to take account of the latter's criticisms, explaining that his book had already been issued (Plb.16.20.7).) Pique at an unenthusiastic reception of his magnum opus, allied with literary isolationism and a feeling of alienation from the mainstream of contemporary composition in elegant short poems may well have prompted Apollonios to look for a retreat.

However, the literary aims and methods of Apollonios do not seem markedly different from those of his contemporaries. He wrote epigrams in the current fashion and proved himself adept in the conventional literary and scholarly activity of his day. We know of critical writings on Archilochos (Ath.10.451d) and Hesiod, as well as a treatise on Homer, entitled 'Against Zenodotos'; probably a semi-polemical tract dealing with points of detail. Apollonios' poems on the foundation of cities - including pieces on Rhodes and Knidos - show the same interest in early history and myth as permeates much Alexandrine verse (Coll.Alex. pp.4-8). Also, many episodes in the 'Argonautika' are miniature epyllia, set pieces in the Kallimachean fashion.

Interaction between Apollonios and Theokritos is

apparent in theme and treatment of several of these
episodes (e.g., the Herakles and Hylas incident, 1.1187-
1357, cf. Theoc.13;   the boxing match of Polydeukes and
Amykos, 2.1-97, cf. Theoc.22).   The question of priority
cannot be definitely settled.   However, the elaborate
treatment of events peripheral to his main theme suggests
that Apollonios is the borrower (but see Dover, ed. Theoc.,
1971, p.181).   Resemblances between Apollonios and
Kallimachos are even more striking, again not only in
theme but in treatment and phraseology (e.g. the visit of
the Argonauts to Anaphe and the aetiological account of
the cult of Apollo Aigletes there, 4.1711-30, cf. Call.
fr.7).   In this case, Apollonios seems to be deeply in
the other poet's debt, to an extent approaching wholesale
plagiarism (PA I pp.638-40, 751).

The long epic poem was apparently not popular in
Alexandria itself, though it flourished elsewhere.
(Perhaps, like drama, epic appealed less to the new
intelligentsia than to the general populace.)   Scholia on
Apollonios refer to other 'Argonautika';   Rhianos of
Crete produced an epic 'Herakleia' in fourteen books
(which makes the proportions of Apollonios' 'Argonautika',
with four, seem modest) and a work 'Thessalika', which
presumably covered some of the same ground as Apollonios'
description of the departure of the Argonauts from
Thessaly;   also, a little earlier, Antagoras had written
his 'Thebaid'.   The early epic poet Peisandros was
accorded formal honours at this time.

The 'Argonautika' itself seems to display a fusion of
the traditional epic form with Alexandrine literary
conventions.   The catalogue, a conventional epic feature,
is an opportunity for mythological excursus and display
of geographical knowledge.   The details of the journey
and, especially, the return of the sailors are similarly
deployed: in Book 4 the river systems of Europe and the
topography of the Aegean are laid before the reader.
Apollonios' familiarity with the geographical exploration
of his age comes from recently issued treatises of such
writers as Timagetas (whose name may be Rhodian or Koan,
PA II p.885 n.76).   Anthropological detail occasionally
obtrudes, as in the description of the practice of
couvade (2.1011-14).

There is extended elaborate description in the Homeric
manner, with mythological detail incorporated in the
contemporary fashion (1.721-67, describing a garment made
by Pallas).   Apollonios, though often allusive, is seldom
deliberately obscure;   for instance, Dionysos is readily
identified as 'son of Zeus, from Nysa' (4.1134).   When a
god is mentioned, there is a traditional list of cult-places

(1.307-9, 536-7, 3.1240-4);   alongside this there is
frequent aetiology of cult practices (2.928-9). Similes
are drawn, as in Homer, from natural phenomena, but also
from human situations, often with fine psychological
insight (1.774).

The description of Medea's emotions is particularly
telling. Her passion is conventionally termed 'ate'
(4.62, 449; cf. Helen's in Homer) and it is aroused by
the gods (4.413, by Eros as their agent, in the common
literary convention). But Medea's makeup is complex,
and internal motivation is provided: her magic powers
are allied with human fears and a human need for
'kedemones' (4.50-3, 91; cf. 360, 1036-41). Her
ultimate marriage with Jason, bitter-sweet because
precipitately celebrated, prompts the generalization
that human pleasure is never unalloyed (4.1165-7). In
other relationships too - Medea with her relatives, Eros
with his mother Aphrodite, Alkinoos with his wife Arete -
comes the same freshness of perception. This portrayal
of emotions with directness and without sentimentality is
one of the most striking features of the poem. Apollonios'
virtuosity, with learned display of antiquarian lore and
contemporary scholarship, makes the part scintillate, but
detracts from the impact of the whole. The 'Argonautika'
without Medea to unify its elements would have the air of
a series of Alexandrine pieces strung together.

If Apollonios, who settled in Rhodes, belongs to the
cultural history of Alexandria, Antagoras, who came from
Rhodes, was much involved in that of Athens and Macedon.
(Antagoras is Rhodian according to the heading of one of
his epigrams, AP 9.147 = HE I p.11; also according to
D.L.2.133 and the Aratos 'Vita'; cf. the error in the
epigram noted above, 1.3, where the bridge-builder
Xenokles, known to have been an Athenian of the deme
Sphettos, is described as Lindian, doubtless because a
knowledge of Antagoras' Rhodian origins was imported into
the passage.) The Macedonian court at Pella attracted
also Aratos, originally from Cilicia, whose 'Phainomena'
was immediately popular (soon circulating in Alexandria,
as literary echoes show) and also long influential.
Another overseas visitor to Macedon was Bion of Borysthenes,
who had the reputation of being such a compelling speaker
that he could hold the attention even of Rhodian sailors.

It was around 276 that Antagoras went to Macedon from
Athens, on the invitation of Antigonos Gonatas, probably
to become official court poet (cf. Webster, 1964, p.21).
In Athens, Antagoras was friendly with the philosophers
of the Academy. (It may be conjectured that his original
departure from Rhodes, which by this time had become a

Peripatetic centre, was prompted by sympathy for the rival
school.)   Antagoras wrote an epitaph for the leading
Academics Polemon and Krates (AP.7.103 = HE I p.11);   also
a hexamter 'Hymn to Love' (of which seven lines survive):
its topic reflects one of the continuing interests of the
Academy, expressed earlier in Plato's 'Symposion' and
'Phaidros'.   Antagoras' choice of the Theban myths as a
theme for his long epic may indicate a deliberate reaction
against Dorian trends, which favoured the exploits of
Herakles - narrated, for instance, by the contemporary
Cretan writer, Rhianos.

    After the abundant and diverse crop of verse in the
third century, Greek poetry declined.   Poetasters from
the islands, as from elsewhere, wrote on conventional
themes.   The epigram in particular had a long vogue.   In
the early years of the first century, Meleager, an
immigrant to Kos from Syria, compiled an anthology of
epigrams, known as the 'Garland of Meleager', which was
ultimately incorporated in the Palatine Anthology, a
definitive collection made in the tenth century AD.
Meleager himself was a poet of some stature, as well as
a Cynic philosopher and a linguist fluent in Syrian,
Phoenician and Greek (cf. HE p.xiv;   Webster, 1964,
Chapter 9).   Rhodians of unknown date represented in the
Palatine Anthology are Aristodikos, Dionysios of Ialysos
and Xenokritos (7.473, 189, 291).   Other poems make
reference to Rhodian legend (8.220), scenic beauty (16.49)
or artefacts (16.82).

In prose, as in verse, the first creative impulse came to
the Greek mainland from the East.   The first prose
treatise was believed to have been the 'Theologia' of
Pherekydes of Syros (cf. West, 1971).   The first great
intellectual centre in Greek lands was that of seventh-
to sixth-century Miletos.   Miletos at this time was a
sea-power with wide trading contacts.   Such an alliance
of maritime supremacy and cultural leadership is a
recurrent phenomenon in the Aegean, foreshadowed in
Minoan Crete and seen in Periklean Athens, Hellenistic
Rhodes and also (somewhat later) Pergamum.   Power at sea
brought with it wide contacts and awareness of cultural
trends, then a confidence to synthesize and innovate.
The thinkers and writers of Miletos embraced a formidable
range of topics and ideas.   Philosophy, history, cosmology
and medicine were all investigated;   few later Greek
writers are not in their debt, directly or indirectly.
    The growth to prominence of the school of medicine in
Kos owed much to the Milesian activity, and all the
treatises in the Hippokratic Corpus are written in the

Ionic dialect. Hippokrates was an almost exact contemporary of Sokrates in Athens - of the same generation as
the sophists and the 'impious' Diagoras of Melos. Ancient
biographers alleged that Hippokrates was influenced by
Gorgias of Leontinoi, Prodikos of Keos and Demokritos of
Abdera.

Relations of Hippokrates with the sophists Gorgias and
Prodikos can be neither proved nor disproved. No Greek
prose writer of the latter half of the fifth century
could have been unaware of Gorgias' rhetorical teaching
(persuasion by carefully constructed sentences full of
balance and sonority) and Prodikos' linguistic activities
(typically differentiation between synonyms), but there
is little in the Hippokratic Corpus to suggest a direct
personal influence. The style of the most polished works
in the Corpus recalls both Herodotos and Thucydides;
Herodotos in diction - Ionic with a poetic texture - and
Thucydides in style, economical and aphoristic but lucid.
Effective use of terse description is made in the
'Epidemiai'. In the case-history of a death from puerperal
fever, a first sentence of thirteen words (five conveying
an address) tells that it was a first birth and a difficult
one; that the child was a boy and that fever quickly
supervened. A day-by-day outline of the course of the
illness ends baldly ('Epid.'3.12 = Littré III pp.62-6):
'Age about seventeen years.'

But the treatises vary in style and, clearly, in
intention and authorship. Among the most rhetorical are
those on 'Fractures' and 'Joints', which Galen attributed
to Hippokrates' grandfather, and which are full of such
stylistic devices as anaphora and chiasmic arrangement of
balanced clauses. Other treatises in format and stance,
rather than style, seem aligned with the prose of the
sophists: in particular, 'On the Art' has the air of a
rhetorical pamphlet, written perhaps as an exercise. In
this debate on whether cures are effected by medical
attention or by chance, arguments and response are given in
the sophistic fashion, as ('Art' 5): 'The man who alleges
the opposite will then say.'

Much of the Corpus, in its technical vocabulary,
whether neologisms or everyday words given a specialized
meaning, reflects the background of Ionian philosophical
writing rather than overt sophistic influence. However,
even if we dismiss direct relations of Hippokrates with
Gorgias and Prodikos as an invention of the biographers
(always prone to make suggestions about meetings between
writers known to have been contemporaries) and note that
most of the treatises of the Corpus are rhetorically
restrained, it cannot be denied that there· is some

influence, in the sense that all Greek prose, from the mid-fifth century onwards, was influenced by the sophists.

The sophists of the fifth century paved the way for the great upsurge of professional oratory and speech-writing in fourth-century Athens. As foreigners, men of ambition and ability leaving their various home states for lucrative careers in Athens, they were unable to participate directly in Athenian civic or forensic activities. Their pupils, however, did so.

The turn of other regions to have their 'sophists' was to come. With the rise of Macedon in the fourth century, a feud conducted in the law courts developed between the hawkish Demosthenes, who inveighed against the tide of events, and Aischines, aligned with a policy of appease-ment. The protracted series of prosecutions in which Demosthenes and Aischines conducted their dispute came to an end with Aischines' ignominious defeat in the Ktesiphon case of 330, and his withdrawal from Athens. He chose Rhodes as a place of retreat, and lived out his life as a professional sophist, or teacher of rhetoric. (Evidence for the life of Aischines comes from the Souda, two 'Vitae' and Plu.'Dem.'24.)

Lysias, who did not become a teacher, was also loosely styled a sophist (D.59.21); Aischines himself casually refers to Sokrates as a sophist (Aeschin.1.173); Poseidonios too was so described (Souda, Str.14.2.13). The term sophist was originally neutral, or even compli-mentary, in tone, but gradually acquired a pejorative sense. The distinction between 'sophistes', 'rhetor' and 'philosophos' was not so widely recognized as Plato would have us believe. (Cf. Sidgwick, 1872 and 1873 on the running battle, centring on the use of these terms, between Plato and Isokrates; also Guthrie, 1969, III pp.27-34.)

Aischines was a cultivated man of wide literary interests (apparent in the exceptionally telling use made of quotation in the three extant speeches), an ex-actor with a grasp of practical rhetorical expertise. He mentions Anaxandrides, with whom he was probably acquainted: they had the theatre and their travels between Rhodes and Athens in common. That such a person chose to settle in Rhodes speaks for the cultural vitality of the island, and its potential for future development. It was said that Aischines founded the Rhodian school of rhetoric, later so famous and influential; and certainly Rhodes did emerge into prominence in such studies around this time. Aischines was sixty when he left Athens, but - when one recalls the longevity of Isokrates and Sophokles (for instance) - the possibility that he had many years of life yet before him cannot be discounted.

The death of Aristotle in 322 indirectly accelerated
the growth in Rhodes of philosophical and rhetorical
studies. Since the foundation of Plato's Academy (where
Aristotle himself had begun his career) and, later, of
Aristotle's Lyceum, these had been centred in Athens.
Two of Aristotle's most distinguished pupils were
islanders: Theophrastos from Lesbos and Eudemos from
Rhodes (on Eudemos, see Wehrli, 1969a). These two men,
superior to the others in 'intellect and industry'
(Gellius 'Noctes Atticae' 13.5 = fr.5) were rivals to
succeed Aristotle as head of the Peripatetic school in
Athens. When Theophrastos was preferred - according to
Gellius' anecdote chosen by Aristotle himself on the
dubious, if tactful, grounds that Lesbian wine was better
than Rhodian - Eudemos went back to Rhodes and opened a
school of his own there. (This is the most likely
interpretation of evidence for his life and work, more
tenuous than one might wish; see Bulmer-Thomas, DSB IV
pp.460-5.) This event was of decisive importance for
the future intellectual development of Rhodes. It was
probably Eudemos who pioneered the collection of a library
in Rhodes; his influence pervades the thought of later
writers of Rhodes and Alexandria; his school attracted
distinguished scholars and able pupils.
    Aischines left Athens in 330; Eudemos in or soon
after 322. If these two men - both 'sophists' in the
popular sense of the word - met in Rhodes and discussed
fourth-century politics, they probably found themselves
in general agreement. Aischines' exile was directly
occasioned by the persuasive effect on Athenian jurors of
Demosthenes' anti-Macedonian harangues; Eudemos had seen
Aristotle exiled for similar reasons. Aristotle, in his
old age, was forced to leave Athens and retreat to
Euboia. The pretext for the expulsion was a charge of
impiety - Athens' traditional weapon against undesirables -
but the real reason was a new upsurge of feeling against
Macedon following the death of Alexander, whose tutor
Aristotle had long ago been, and with whom he was still
popularly associated.
    One of Aristotle's gifts was the ability to delegate
research to his pupils and to foster its execution; on
this depended his grandiose scheme to edit a compendium
of world knowledge. In this encyclopaedic plan,
Theophrastos wrote on physics and Eudemos on mathematics
(not Aristotle's own forte). Theophrastos and Eudemos -
perhaps inevitably, as Aristotle's immediate successors -
were not great original thinkers; their interests lay in
consolidation rather than further advance. Their specialist
interests too were close. In addition to his work on

arithmetic, geometry and astronomy (represented by frr.
133-49 which suggest influence on later mathematicians),
Eudemos wrote, like Theophrastos, on physics (frr.31-123).
This work paraphrases Aristotle's own treatise 'Physics',
sometimes simply quoting word for word; he explains some
difficulties, but never expresses disagreement. Eudemos
wrote also on zoology (frr.125-32) and theology (fr.150).

The 'Eudemian Ethics' in the Aristotelian corpus takes
its name from Eudemos. While it has been suggested that
Eudemos was the author of the treatise, most regard him,
rather, as its editor. The view that the title of the
treatise conveys a dedication to Eudemos possibly arose
from a belief that the 'Nikomachean Ethics' was dedicated
in paternal exhortation by Aristotle to his son Nikomachos.
As such dedications, common among later philosophers, are
unknown for this time, Nikomachos, like Eudemos, was
probably the editor.

It is tempting to identify the Eudemos mentioned in
the Lindian Chronicle as author of a book on Lindos with
the Peripatetic, but there are no firm grounds for the
identification (cf. FGH III 524). Aristotle did write
accounts of the constitutions of several Greek states,
among them Rhodes, although the 'Athenaion Politeia',
discovered last century in a papyrus text, is the only
one extant. The 'Politics' shows clear signs of an
interest in Rhodes (1271b37, 1302b23, 1302b33, 1304b28).
It is likely that Eudemos was involved in this work to some
extent, at the very least as an adviser and source of
information. A rather shadowy Peripatetic figure,
associated with Eudemos, possibly his nephew, is Pasikles
of Rhodes (see Brink, PW XVIII.2.2061).

Throughout the third century - when the poets Herodas,
Theokritos and Apollonios were attracted to the region -
Rhodes continued to exert a strong pull on Peripatetic
philosophers. Rhodes offered a second chance to lead a
school for those who failed to achieve headship of the
Athenian Lyceum. Strabo lists among prominent Rhodian
philosophers both Praxiphanes, who according to other
evidence came from Mitylene in Lesbos - the conflicting
testimony is best reconciled by supposing that he came
from Lesbos but (after studying under Theophrastos in
Athens) settled in Rhodes to write and teach - and
Hieronymos, a native Rhodian who became a prominent
member of the Peripatetic establishment in Athens (Str.
14.2.13; on Praxiphanes, see Brink, 1946; Wehrli, 1969c;
on Hieronymos, Wehrli, 1969b).

Both Praxiphanes and Hieronymos belong in the middle
of the third century. The chronological evidence for
Praxiphanes rests on relations with Theophrastos (friendly)

and with Kallimachos (hostile);   also on a rather bald
honorary inscription from Delos (IG XI 4, 613 = Wehrli
fr.4). For Hieronymos, contemporary with the Athenian
thinkers Lykon and Arkesilaos, probable dates are
c.290-230.

Praxiphanes specialized in literary studies, one of
the traditional Peripatetic interests, inaugurated by
Aristotle. Aristotle's own work 'On Poets' is lost and
the (incomplete) 'Poetics' remains in many ways enigmatic.
Many of his successors wrote treatises on similar subjects
around this time or rather later; unfortunately very
little of these has survived. Praxiphanes' treatise on
poetry had a piquant scenario: a dialogue between Plato,
on a visit to Isokrates' country house, and his host
(D.L.3.8 = fr.11). Later sources describe Praxiphanes as
a grammarian, sometimes as the first grammarian (frr.8-10).
Apparently he differentiated between parts of speech
(foreshadowing Dionysios Thrax, who later worked in Rhodes),
as well as offering glosses of obscure words (fr.21,
following the trend inaugurated by Simias and Philitas).
The nexus of philological activity which sprang up at this
time is complex. Simias and Philitas may have been
stimulated by critical ideas brought from Athens by
Eudemos; Praxiphanes was subject to the dual influence of
the scholar-poet approach and of Peripatetic thinking.
Scholars and philosophers interacted, not always amicably.
Praxiphanes and Kallimachos were at loggerheads.
Kallimachos wrote a polemical tract against Praxiphanes
and in his verse took issue with 'Telchines', Rhodian
adversaries who, according to a scholiast, included
Praxiphanes (frr.15, 16; cf. Brink, 1946).

Hieronymos too made some contribution to the history of
literature. Fragments of his work on the poets show
unimpressive corrections of Aristotle on points of detail:
for example, he stated that it was Empedokles' daughter,
not his sister, who burned some of his works (D.L.8.57 =
fr.30). Hieronymos was used as a source by later
biographers, and is quoted by the writer of the Sophokles
'Vita' on Sophokles' piety. Many of the extant fragments
show a gossipy preoccupation with writers' personal lives
and especially their sexual proclivities: the love-lives
of Sophokles and Euripides are the subject of such comment
(frr.35, 36). This interest in biographical detail is
a facet of the typically Hellenistic cult of the
individual. With a psychological awareness which reflects
the same trend, Hieronymos also wrote philosophical essays
on such themes as anger, drunkenness, education - a genre
which had a great vogue later, especially with the Stoics -
and wrote extensively on ethics.

Aristotle had left a rich legacy of work to be continued or checked, in scientific fields as well as in philosophy, rhetoric or literary criticism. Both Praxiphanes in Rhodes and Hieronymos in Athens made their mark in the 'arts' rather than the 'sciences' and evidently had access to libraries. Aristotle had amassed a large collection of books, which he bequeathed to his successor Theophrastos (see D.L.5.11-16 for the will of Aristotle; Str.13.1.54 concurs that he left his library to Theophrastos). It seems that this library subsequently passed as a personal possession from one head to the next, symbolizing the ideals of the polymath Aristotle: the heart of the school lay in this tangible reminder of its founder, rather than in common views or aspirations of its members from one generation to the next. Perhaps it was fitting that this should be so for the Peripatetics, who valued the tradition of the memoir as a foundation for research or summary of conclusions; whereas, for the Academy, founded by Plato, who distrusted the written word, continuity had a more intangible basis.

The Alexandrian library had the biggest collection of books in the ancient world, but many lesser collections had preceded it, coexisted with it or were founded in emulation of it. It has been conjectured that the survival of the Hippokratic Corpus in its present form may be due to its having constituted the library of the Koan medical school; collected in one place, carefully maintained by a group of people who valued its content, then removed to the great book collection of Alexandria at a later date, possibly by Praxagoras in the third century. One source of Alexandrian book buying was Rhodes, which had become a centre of the Hellenistic book-trade, no doubt supplying local as well as foreign collectors (Ath.1.3b; cf. PA I p.325 and II p.481 n.148). The existence of book collections in Rhodes can be inferred from the erudition of writers who made their home there - unless we suppose that these men had prodigious memories, or were constantly commuting to other centres. It is extremely probable that Eudemos set up a library to assist him in his researches and his pupils in their studies, aiming at the kind of comprehensive collection made in Athens by Aristotle.

Rhodes certainly had an excellent library by the second century. The Lindian Chronicle, set up in 99 BC, provides indirect evidence. When it was decreed that the record be made, one Timachidas son of Agesitimos was given a month to collect data from official documents and literary sources, with the clear implication that these were available locally. In the Chronicle, some care is taken

over references to sources, and the names of over twenty
writers are recorded. More direct evidence for a Rhodian
library comes from a broken inscription of the second or
first century (NS 11), which lists authors and book titles
and is probably part of an official catalogue (although
some suspect, rather, that it is a list of donations).
That all the treatises mentioned are essays on politics,
one of the prevailing Peripatetic interests, is consistent
with the conjecture that the Peripatetics had been
instrumental in building up the collection. A library is
explicitly mentioned in a related inscription of around
the same date (NS 4; on the date - originally believed
to be second century AD - content and relation to NS 11,
see Segre, 1935 and 1936a; Robert, 1935; also Powell
and Barber, 1929). A list of donations of books and
money to a library occurs in a further inscription of
around the same period, found in Rhodes, but persuasively
assigned to Kos by Robert (1935, p.424: [l'inscription]
'doit avoir sa place dans le recueil, depuis si longtemps
annoncé, des inscriptions de Kos, si jamais ce Corpus
voit enfin le jour'; on Koan library facilities, cf.
Herzog, 1922, a German translation of an inscription not
yet published; on ancient libraries in general,
Burzachechi, 1963). The main state libraries of Rhodes
and Kos were probably located in the gymnasium, a public
building of sufficient size to accommodate the books, and
with staff numerous enough to act as curators; there,
the collection would be readily accessible to the ephebes
undergoing an intensive educational programme and to
others interested. (Gymnasia, like many temples, were
administered by state officials at civic expense for the
benefit of the general populace.)

Many traits of Hellenistic literature can be seen as
the direct result of a more general availability of books.
Where texts had obscurities, commentators tried to
elucidate them by annotation, especially by glosses;
where several versions were available, attempts were made
to lay down a definitive one. Besides formal scholarly
processes - and often with the same practitioners - an
incidental display of learning typifies Hellenistic
verse. The prevalence of erudite excursus, whether
exploring arcane myths with aetiological ingenuity or
deploying familiarity with the latest geographical
discoveries, derives from access to a comprehensive
collection of books, old and new.

Myth and history are peculiarly pervasive elements,
which appear as the subject of digressions in all types
of poem, are prominent in epic and absolutely central to
the theme of verse on the foundation ('ktisis') of cities.

In part, this is due to new attitudes to local history.
The sweeping political changes of the third century
resulted in a nostalgic awareness of the past. While
contemporary linguistic change prompted an interest in
disappearing local dialects, the slide into insignificance
of small states awoke interest in myth, especially local
myths and legends and especially in states - such as
Rhodes - which had successfully preserved their independence. The foundation of Alexandria, a city without a
history, which could not immediately engage the corporate
loyalty of its inhabitants, and where there was little
sense of patriotism, made other places examine their
traditions with renewed fervour.

Local chroniclers, who aimed to set down a complete
record of their area, represent an important new direction
in prose-writing. Makareus of Kos in the third century
and the many Rhodian chroniclers, of whom Polyzelos,
Gorgon and Zenon are best known - because they were
subsequently utilized by Polybios and Diodoros - show
these trends. Of the many Rhodian historians mentioned
in the Lindian Chronicle, all but two, writing about
Lindos at an unknown date, are known to have written after
the foundation of Rhodes in 408 and before 99, when the
record was compiled, many of them in the second century.
Because of its political importance and economic prosperity,
Rhodes interested foreign as well as local commentators.
However, most of the historians are local writers,
presenting antiquarian lore coloured by patriotic feeling.
The title of Ergias' work, 'On my Homeland', is indicative
of its tone.   The bias extended to contemporary history,
according to Polybios, who accused Zenon of distorting
the account of the sea-battle of Lade and minimizing
Rhodian losses (Plb.16.14.1-15.8).

The desire to record past achievements was one reason
for the commissioning of the Lindian Chronicle itself.
The output of Timachidas, who was compiler of this record,
includes also a collection of glosses, a commentary on
the dramatists and a creative work, entitled 'Deipnon'.

Later in the first century, Kastor of Rhodes issued an
ambitious compilation in six books, aiming to establish a
comparative chronological scheme, with a parallel format
of Oriental, Greek and Roman history, from earliest times
till Pompey's expedition to Asia Minor in 61/60. It
seems that Kastor, like his compatriots, was prone to
distort the record for Rhodes' greater glory. Such
schemes are a far cry from the discursive, wide-ranging
world-histories also popular at this time (one of
Poseidonios' projects aimed to complete that begun by
Polybios); however, historians drew material from the

chroniclers - as earlier, Hekataios and other Milesians
of the sixth and fifth centuries, models for Kastor and
his contemporaries, had influenced Herodotos and
Thucydides.

Biography flourished in the second century. In origin,
this is an offshoot of the Peripatetic memoir (as may be
clearly seen in the work of Hieronymos, discussed above),
given a new emphasis by the current interest in the
individual and in human behaviour. Sotion wrote biographical studies in Alexandria; Antisthenes and
Sosikrates in Rhodes. Antisthenes - who is probably the
priest of Helios, Antisthenes son of Architimos, named
in an inscription - is variously described as a historian
(by Diogenes Laertius; also Polybios links him with
Zenon) and as a Peripatetic philosopher (by Phlegon).
(On Antisthenes, see FGH III 508; Plb.14.14.15; IG XII
1, 63.) Antisthenes' 'History of Philosophers' treated,
among others, Thales, Herakleitos and Demokritos, with a
wealth of anecdotal material. A work with the same title
was issued by Sosikrates, again with the interest in
personalia, not in philosophical development. (On
Sosikrates, author also of 'Kretika', a work on Crete, see
FGH III 461; IG XII 1, 49 and 890. The existence of
mutual interest between Crete and Rhodes is further
demonstrated by the book on Rhodes written by the Cretan
Epimenides, FGH III 457.)

An interest in personalia shows itself also in the
circulation of spurious letters, purporting to be written
by great men of the past. The composition of such
communications may have been set as an exercise in schools
of rhetoric. Two collections are relevant here: the
correspondence attributed to Aischines, and the exchanges
included in the Hippokratic Corpus.

The twelve letters which have come down under the
name of Aischines were in all probability composed in
Rhodes. A recurrent misapprehension on the part of the
writer is that Aischines' exile from Athens was enforced,
not self-imposed: he is likened to such figures as the
ostracized Themistokles (2.2, 7.1, etc.; cf. Schwegler,
1913; Martin and de Budé, ed., 1952, II p.122). The
misconception is not a conclusive indication that the
letters are spurious. Speakers in the Attic lawcourts
often alleged that they were fighting for their lives, or
their citizenship, when they were doing no such thing, and
Aischines might well have indulged retrospectively in a
similar rhetorical hyperbole about his exile. Linguistic
considerations do, however, clinch the case against
genuineness. A Rhodian origin for the letters is likely,
as the first nine purport to deal with Aischines' settling

in Rhodes.   (The topographical detail, nevertheless, is
not impressive: for example, a beach is called simply
'The Sands', 9.1.)   The subjects are: his journey from
Peiraieus (1), his reception and the regulation of his
business affairs (4, 9), a letter of introduction for a
Rhodian to a friend in Athens (6), his receiving visitors
from Athens (8) and intervention in personal relationships
between his relatives and others there (2);   the third
letter consists of reflections on exile addressed to the
'boule' and 'demos', while the seventh is an appeal for
reinstatement.   Letters 11 and 12 are a kind of apologia
for his career: they seem to have been added to 1-9 by
a different, but not much later, writer.   The tenth letter
is entirely different in kind from the others, in that it
lacks any 'autobiographical' touch, and narrates the story
of an amorous adventure of one Kimon, told by a companion
in mock disapproval;   it seems a chance stray insertion
from a collection of stories.

The Hippokratic series contains a request that
Hippokrates should go to Persia and Hippokrates' refusal
to do so;   an Attic decree honouring Hippokrates for his
visit to Athens at the time of the plague of 429;   and a
correspondence relating to Demokritos.   This last,
comprising letters from the people of Abdera, from
Hippokrates and from Demokritos has an extraordinary
subject: Hippokrates is called by the town of Abdera to
treat Demokritos, who is believed to be in the grip of
'madness', but who turns out to be engrossed in 'labour
for virtue'.   The relevant letters are 10-21 and 23;
letter 22, misplaced in this series, is addressed to
Hippokrates' son Thessalos, urging him to apply himself
to his mathematics.   The writer ingeniously aims at an
illusion of authenticity by reference to Kos (11) and to
certain Hippokratic writings (19).   The letters are highly
rhetorical in style, full of sententiousness, paradox and
antithesis, as well as in content, with a tendency to
debate topics peripheral to the issue (in 11, the
impropriety of acting for monetary reward).   Demokritos'
letter to Hippokrates begins with a generalization:
> I believe that the study of philosophy is sister and
> cohabitant of medicine;   for philosophy delivers the
> mind from passion and medicine removes diseases from
> the body.

It then proceeds to a run-down of the parts of the body on
a remarkably unsophisticated level:
> The two nostrils, apt at breathing, lie between and
> near the eyes.

Clearly, Demokritos never wrote in this vein.   The letters

are palpable forgeries, but are of interest as a reflection
of the content and style of rhetorical teaching.

In its advance as an international centre for research and
teaching in rhetoric, philosophy and science, Rhodes was
well placed to attract visitors travelling between
Alexandria, Pergamum, Athens and, of increasing importance,
Rome. Its economic prosperity and internal stability
added powerfully to its attractions in the second and
first century. As political conditions deteriorated in
second-century Alexandria, with frequent riots and
administrative troubles disturbing the peace of the capital,
Rhodes by contrast drew scholars from abroad looking for
a combination of research facilities and a quiet working
environment. Then, in the first century, as the Seleukid
rule disintegrated in political anarchy, the islands
provided a haven for immigrants from the East.
    As a naval power in her own right, Rhodes could play
off Macedon and Egypt in their rivalry for control of the
islands and - for a time at least - look fearlessly at
the advancing power of Rome. In 168, Rhodes made serious
military and diplomatic misjudgments, which alienated
Rome and brought economic reprisals (see Chapter 3). This
was a grave blow to the prestige and naval strength of
Rhodes; but internally the island was stable and
intellectual life flourished. In this same decade, a
prominent immigrant from the East was Hipparchos the
astronomer, from Bithynia (see Chapter 6).
    Meantime, long before the conquest of Greece brought a
deep penetration of Greek culture into Roman life, the
hellenizing process had begun in Italy. In the second
century, Plautus and Terence had adapted the plays of
Menander for the Roman stage; in the earlier half of the
first century, Lucretius had put into verse the philosophy
of Epicurus, based on the ideas of the atomists Demokritos
and Leukippos. Greek culture was transmitted through
diplomatic and social exchange, as well as through an
influx of Greeks taken prisoner in Rome's wars in the
East.
    After the Roman victory at Pydna, hundreds of Greeks
were taken to Rome for trial on the charge of opposition
to Roman sovereignty. The prisoners of war included many
educated men, and a steady infiltration of Greek ideas
into Italy resulted. Among the Greeks who went to Rome
at this time was the historian Polybios, who became tutor
in the household of Aemilius Paulus. The influence of
Polybios on the young Scipio was considerable. Panaitios
of Rhodes was later a member of the same entourage. It
was frequented also by Poseidonios, who came originally

from Apamea in Syria, but who had studied with Panaitios
in Rhodes and become a Rhodian citizen. According to one
writer, Scipio took his Greek mentors with him even on
military campaigns (Velleius Paterculus 1.13.3).

In 159, Krates of Pergamum visited Rome as ambassador,
and in 155 the visit of Karneades, Kritolaos and Diogenes -
three philosophers representing different schools - created
a sensation. According to Plutarch ('Cato'22.3):

    Roman youths abandoned their other pleasures and
    pursuits, and raved about philosophy.

Despite the narrow nationalism of some men of this
generation, of whom Cato (234-149) is the best-known
representative, with his repudiation of the influence of
Greek philosophy on prominent Romans and his stern
chauvinism extending to a preference for Italian methods
of viticulture over Greek, the process was now irreversible.
Paradoxically, it was Cato who argued against the proposal
that military action be taken against Rhodes in 168. Even
Cato had Greek slaves: however, he did not entrust his
son's education to them, preferring to supervise it
personally (Plu.'Cato'20.3; cf. 21.1). Also, although
he knew Greek, he did not deign to use it when in Greece,
but insisted on the services of an interpreter.

By the time of the late Republic, all Romans of
intelligence and sensitivity were aware of the towering
cultural achievements of the Greeks, not only in science
and philosophy, but in literature, music and the visual
arts. If it was philosophy which made most impact on the
Romans, this was perhaps because of a special affinity
felt by the Roman temperament for Stoicism. Also the
social climate, which viewed the possession of Greek
slaves or attachment of Greek hangers-on, as a status
symbol, and which prized attendance at Greek schools of
rhetoric, favoured the introduction into wealthy households of Greek attitudes and values: that is, Stoicism
arrived first as a way of life and then as a philosophy
(cf. Luc.'Merc.Cond.'4, 25).

Already in the decade 90-80 BC, the rhetorician Molon
made two visits from Rhodes to Rome, where Cicero became
one of his pupils ('Att.'2.1.9; 'Brut.'90.312). Cicero,
who studied in Rhodes around 79-77, regarded Rhodes and
Athens as the foremost intellectual centres in Greece
(Cic.'Or.'8.25). Pompey added to the fame of Rhodes
by his stay in the island - making a detour for the
visit - and by his friendship and respect for Poseidonios
(Plu.'Pomp.'42.5; cf. Anderson, 1963, p.60). Cicero makes
no secret of his admiration for Panaitios, 'homo in
primis ingenuus et gravis' and of his use of Panaitios'
work as a model for 'De Officiis' (see 3.7). Poseidonios

too was admired by Cicero;   this respect may not have been
mutual if there is truth in the story that Poseidonios
declined to write a memorial of Cicero's political career.
Poseidonios did, however, compliment Cicero on his prose
style ('Att'.2.1.2; cf. 'Tusc.Disp.'2.61; 'de fin.'1.6).

Of all Greek philosophers who influenced the Romans,
Panaitios and Poseidonios are most prominent: it was
through Cicero - and therefore through these men - that
Stoicism spread at Rome. Both Panaitios and Poseidonios
have a strong Rhodian background, the former a native
Rhodian (son of Nikagoras and adopted son of Euphranoridas)
and the latter an immigrant who was thoroughly accepted in
his adoptive country, serving as 'prytanis' and acting as
state envoy to Rome in 87 BC, following Mithridates' siege
of the island (Ath.6.252e; Str.14.12.13; Plu.'Mar.'45).
(On Panaitios, see van Straaten, 1962; Tatakis, 1931;
on Poseidonios, Edelstein and Kidd, 1972; Laffranque,
1964.)

Strabo gives Panaitios pride of place in his list of
Rhodian intellectuals; he was respected, admired and
followed both at home and abroad. Many fellow-Rhodians
are named as his pupils, including Stratokles, who wrote
a history of the Stoa, Hekaton and Platon (Index Stoicorum,
Pap.Herc.1018 preserves an extract of Stratokles). The
travels of Panaitios were extensive (described as 'perpetua
peregrinatio' by Cicero), yet he remained loyal to Rhodes,
declining the honour of Athenian citizenship on the grounds
that 'the moderate man needs only one country' (fr.27).
He did, however, once hold the office of 'hieropoios' in
Athens, at the Ptolemaia (fr.28). Panaitios' activity
at Athens was not his only experience of religious office,
as he held the priesthood of Poseidon Hippios in his
native Lindos for a year. In addition, his father and
several other members of his family had been priests of
Athena at Lindos (fr.4).

Panaitios' philosophical interests extended beyond his
specialist studies of ethical questions. He was not a
conventional Stoic. Perhaps because of this, he is
sometimes called the first eclectic, breaking down barriers
and eliminating sharp contrasts between the different
schools of thought prevailing at the time (Academy, Lyceum,
Stoics, Epicureans; also the movement Cynicism). It may
be that the schools had always been aware of common ground,
but a trend towards open eclecticism now gathered momentum.
It was natural that, in an age of focus on the individual,
the personal impact of the various philosophies on different individuals should engage interest.

Modern estimate of Panaitios' work is bedevilled by
lack of direct evidence: second-hand paraphrase and comment

dominate the 'fragments'.   But his influence was undoubtedly seminal, and, through Poseidonios and other
pupils, had a long history in western thought. It also,
through Cicero and other prominent Romans, brought an
immediate rapprochment between philosophy and politics,
especially in the estimate and execution of social
obligations.

Like his teacher Panaitios, Poseidonios travelled
widely - beyond Rome to Gaul, Spain and North Africa -
everywhere collecting information, much of which he
contrived to record. Poseidonios firmly turned his back
on his Syrian origins, making scathing comments on the
luxury and slackness of the East. Reaction against his
early environment may in part account for his enthusiastic
embrace of Stoic austerity.

Poseidonios was the last of the great Greek polymath
philosophers, with interests in geography, ethnography,
oceanography, astronomy, mathematics, history, rhetoric
and logic. His own firmly held view that all branches of
knowledge were an integrated whole makes a distinction
here between philosophy and science seem inappropriate,
almost a betrayal. However, as it seems even more
inappropriate to squeeze this formidable figure into a
chapter on literature, a discussion of his scientific
work is postponed to the next chapter, where it joins
that of his predecessor Hipparchos and follower Geminos.

One of the Rhodian pupils of Poseidonios to achieve
fame and influence among his contemporaries was Hekaton.
Apparently his main interest was in ethics, in 'to
kathekon', 'duty' or 'appropriate action' in the sense
pioneered by Panaitios. Moral dilemmas, such as the
conflicting claims which might arise between the
interests of family and state, were explored in his work.

A younger contemporary of Poseidonios was the
Peripatetic philosopher Andronikos, who came originally
from Rhodes. Andronikos spent some time in Rome before
returning to Athens to lead the Peripatetic establishment
there, a position earned through assiduous editorial work
on the Aristotelian Corpus. He wrote a definitive
biography of Aristotle (including a transcript of his
will) and a long treatise discussing his work, with
particular regard to questions of chronology and authenticity. Andronikos evidently aimed to reintroduce
Aristotle's own writings to the Peripatos as 'set texts'
and in this seems to have succeeded. Certainly, his
influence on the form in which the works of Aristotle
were subsequently transmitted is very great. The editorial
work of Andronikos was probably effected in Rome, and
brought out after 43 BC. (As Cicero, interested in such

questions, does not allude to Andronikos' edition, it
probably came out after his death in that year.)   A
philosophical work, 'de Passionibus', circulating in
antiquity under Andronikos' name, is now generally
regarded as spurious;   also, an Andronikos who held
priestly office in Rome is probably not to be identified
with the philosopher (cf. Gercke, PW I 2164-7).

Andronikos had devoted his life to philosophical
stocktaking and to the preservation of traditions.   The
retrospective spirit apparent in his work may be seen in
that of other philosophers and scientists of the last
century BC and first AD.   Geminos' handbook on astronomy
is of just this character, as is that of Kleomedes.
Celsus' medical encyclopaedia, dating to Augustus' reign,
is of the same type.

A penchant for compilation is apparent also in the
work of Dionysios Thrax (c.170-90) on grammar.   Dionysios
(called Thrax because his father's name, Teres, was
Thracian) worked in Alexandria, Rhodes and Rome - the
places which drew all influential scholars of his day.
Dionysios' treatise, an ambitious attempt to give a
systematic account of the Greek language, has survived in
isolation;   but the name of one contemporary with the
same interests, Drakon, from Karian Stratonikea, is known
from the Souda.   Dionysios distinguished six parts of
'grammar', of which the noblest was literary criticism.
The literary aspect of Dionysios' study is often ignored.
It was probably given full play in the other commentaries
and treatises he wrote (Souda; FGH III 512).

Dionysios affords us one of our fullest glimpses of
the philological and rhetorical studies taught in Rhodes,
with its university (it approximated to this) patronized
by the affluent.   That Dionysios himself had no shortage
of wealthy pupils is apparent from an anecdote relating
that his students in Rhodes contributed money for a
costly antiquarian project, the reconstruction of the
precious 'cup of Nestor' described by Homer (Ath.11.489a).

The names of Apollonios Malakos and Apollonios Molon
who taught in Rhodes are frequently mentioned by Cicero
and others, but their work is not known at first hand
(Cic.'Or.'8.25;   'Brut.'15.31;   Quint.3.1.17;   cf. Wooten,
1975).   The main controversy in rhetorical studies was
now between 'Asianism' (ornate style with bombastic effect)
and Atticism (simple style aiming at brevity and clarity).
In Rhodes, a contribution was made to the debate by
Theodoros of Gadara, who taught Tiberius, later to become
the second Roman emperor, during his exile in the island.
Dio of Prusa, Aelius Aristeides and Lucian all - in their
different ways - pay tribute to the cultural vitality of

Rhodes (cf. Chapter 1).   Indeed in the first centuries of the Christian era, the island had come to be regarded as one of the final outposts of Hellenism.

6   Medicine and Science

MEDICINE

Generations of medical students have regarded the Koan
Hippokrates as 'father' of medicine. This stems partly
from the modern consciousness that the roots of western
civilization lie in ancient Greece - the same feeling
which makes Herodotos father of history, Thespis inventor
of tragedy, Pythagoras first of mathematicians and Thales
of natural philosophers. It is the result also of the
Greeks' own desire to name an originator of all human
activities, especially of all 'technai', crafts or skills
(cf. Kleingünther, 1933): traditionally, Prometheus
brought fire and associated technology, Palamedes
invented writing, Triptolemos initiated agriculture.
   Hippokrates, idealized founder of the medical
profession and exemplar of its virtues, is described in
one of the spurious letters preserved in the Hippokratic
Corpus as ('Ep.'2):
   distributing on all sides the aid of Asklepios, just
   as Triptolemos distributed the seeds of Demeter.
However, Hippokrates differs from other folk heroes and
'inventors' in that he was a real personage of the
classical period. The veneration accorded him shows that
even in the fifth century legends could be born.
   Sacrifices were performed to Hippokrates after his
death (Sor.'Vita'; 'Ep.'2; Plin.'HN'7.37; cf. Luc.
'Philops.'21, where a doctor with a private cult of
Hippokrates complains that the spirit of Hippokrates
upset things). A few other fifth-century figures attained
the same popular acclaim as Hippokrates. Alpheios and
Maron, the bravest men to fall at Thermopylai, were
honoured at Sparta; the Athenians who fell at Marathon
were worshipped; Sophokles was honoured with annual
sacrifices after his death (Paus.3.12.9, 1.32.4; Soph.
'Vita'17).

There had, of course, been doctors before the fifth
century: disease, accident and death were always there.
(Birth was more commonly the midwife's province, and even
in the Hippokratic Corpus normal birth is not much
discussed.)   But treatment of the sick was not allied
with study of medicine: practice and theory were not
associated.   Even after Hippokrates, the doctor proceeding
by purely empirical methods never disappeared from the
scene, but coexisted with more highly trained practitioners.
Before the fifth century, there was no specialization in
human anatomy, physiology and pathology: these vast
subjects were merely aspects of all natural history,
treated incidentally by early writers of philosophical
and scientific prose, whose works would not have attracted
the attention of the practical doctor even if they were
accessible to him.   The Hippokratic phenomenon, uniting
theoretical and practical medicine, was part of a contemporary intellectual movement, and belongs in a fifth-
century context.

Some contemporary or near-contemporary evidence for
the historical Hippokrates comes from Aristophanes and
Plato (Ar.'Th.'270-4;   Pl.'Prt.'311b, 'Phdr.'270c).   In
a passage of Aristophanes' 'Thesmophoriazousai' produced
in 411 an oath is sworn by the '"aither", home of Zeus',
then on the rejoinder, 'By what, rather than the community
of Hippokrates?' corrected to, 'Well, I swear by all the
gods together.'   This comic parody of the doctors' oath,
which begins:

I swear by Apollo the doctor, by Asklepios, by
Hygieia, by Panakeia and by all the gods and goddesses,
making them witness ...

suggests a general familiarity in Athens with Hippokratic
ideas and practices.

In Plato's 'Protagoras', Sokrates refers to the
activities of Hippokrates of Kos, the Asklepiad, as a
teacher of medicine, a famous doctor training pupils to
become doctors (compared to Polykleitos of Argos or
Pheidias of Athens, famous sculptors training others in
their profession).   In 'Phaidros', an analogy is drawn
between medicine and rhetoric, knowledge of the body and
knowledge of the soul.   The views of Hippokrates the
Asklepiad on the body are represented as analogous to
those of Plato on the soul: that to understand a part of
the soul or body it is necessary to understand the natural
structure of the whole of it.   The implication is that at
the time of the exchanges in the 'Protagoras' (late in
the decade 440-430) Hippokrates was a famous medical
teacher;   at the time of those in the 'Phaidros' (probably
before 415) recognized as an authoritative writer.

The date of composition of both 'Phaidros' and 'Protagoras' is much later than their dramatic date; and admittedly Plato is often anachronistic or careless in points unimportant for his main purpose. Indeed, it is arguable that Plato did not envisage an actual dramatic date; certainly it is often very difficult to establish one which is entirely in accord with the content of a dialogue. However, the attitude to Hippokrates as an established figure, recognized in his own day as prominent, perhaps pre-eminent, in his profession, fits information in the biographical sources.

Aristotle mentions Hippokrates in a passing analogy: just as the size of a state is irrelevant to its achievement, so ('Pol.'1326a15):

One would declare Hippokrates to be greater, not as a man but as a doctor, than someone who exceeded him in physical bulk

(not necessarily, as is often supposed, implying that Hippokrates was short).

The main biographical tradition for Hippokrates begins long after his lifetime. It is characteristically bedevilled by anecdote and by deductions or conjectures masquerading as known facts. There are four short 'Vitae' extant - three in Greek (one attributed to Soranos of Ephesos, a medical writer specializing in gynaecology who lived in the reigns of Trajan and Hadrian; one in the Souda; and one by Tzetzes, writing in the twelfth century) and one in Latin (in a twelfth century anonymous treatise entitled 'Yppocratis genus, vita, dogma'). Also important is a papyrus from the second century AD, which gives an extended account of early medicine (Soranos, ed. Ilberg, CMG 4.175.3-178.6; Souda s.v.; Tz.'H'7.944-89; Codex Bruxellensis 1342-50; Anonymus Londinensis no.1820P, for which see Jones, 1947; cf. in general Edelstein, PW suppl.VI.1290-1345 and Joly, DSB VI pp.418-31).

The data of these works are culled from a range of earlier writers. Those in the 'Anonymus Londinensis' are generally believed to be drawn from Menon, a pupil of Aristotle who contributed a history of medicine to Aristotle's 'encyclopaedia' (cf. Chapter 5); the earliest source named by the biographers is Eratosthenes, the Alexandrian astronomer of the mid third century (that is, already two centuries after Hippokrates). The 'Vitae' record many details which are miscellaneous, but not, on the whole, irreconcilable; and which may be taken as at least partially valid. They are unanimous that Hippokrates was an Asklepiad of Kos who travelled widely, and they name a number of contemporaries as his teachers.

The spurious epistles with colourful and elaborate

versions of some of the data found also in the biographers
may have been uncritically used as a source. Tradition
told of a trip to Persia (accepted in 'Yppocratis genus',
but not by Soranos or Tzetzes; the Souda records merely
an invitation to go); the letters provide a fictitious
text for the invitation and for Hippokrates' refusal to
accept, on the grounds of Greek patriotism (cf. Chapter 5).
There was a strong biographical tradition that it was at
Larissa in Thessaly that Hippokrates died; his grave,
between Larissa and Gyrton, was pointed out to later
generations of travellers: in this case, the letters
invent (or distort) a further connection with north Greece
through Demokritos of Thracian Abdera.

The text of the Attic decree, preserved among the
letters, honouring Hippokrates for his visit to Athens at
the time of the plague, is generally regarded as an
invention, and the visit itself apocryphal: perhaps a
forger found the neatness of a conjunction between the
greatest doctor of all time and the worst plague ever
recorded irresistible. Certainly, it is odd that
Thucydides, interested enough in medicine to give a full
account of the symptoms and progress of the disease, and
to touch on medical attempts to combat it, should fail to
mention Hippokrates' presence if it is a fact. However,
arguments from literary silence are dangerous, when there
is a possibility, as here, that new epigraphical evidence
might be found to confute them.

As noted above, one salient common feature of the
biographical tradition is the application to Hippokrates
of the term Asklepiad. In general usage, this term
'descendant of Asklepios' conveyed little more than
'doctor'. It was so used before the lifetime of Hippokrates
by Theognis, writing around the middle of the sixth century
(Thgn.432). Plato's references to Hippokrates have already
been discussed. In addition, in 'Republic', doctors are
designated with mild irony as 'the ingenious Asklepiadai'
and in 'Symposium', the doctor Eryximachos refers to 'our
ancestor Asklepios' who 'established our craft' ('R'405d,
'Smp.'186e). Kinship with notional descent from Asklepios
was important in the medical profession. A distinctive
and persistent feature of Greek medicine was that it ran
in families, father passing on his skill to son, generation
to generation. Many other occupations had the same basis,
sometimes with a similar feeling of exclusiveness: the
Spartan Talthybiadai, a family of heralds, and the Athenian
Eteoboutadai, a priestly group, are well-known examples
(Hdt.7.134.1; D.21.182).

Galen uses the term Asklepiadai more precisely, of the
Hippokratic School of which Hippokrates was the greatest

and Praxagoras the last representative (cf. PA II p.498 nn.15-17). The association ('koinon') of the Asklepiadai is mentioned in a fourth-century Delphic inscription, with the implication that the group is allied in kinship; the family ('genos') of the Asklepiadai of which Asklepios is founder ('archegetes') is mentioned in a Karian inscription of the second century (SEG 16.326; ASAA ns 23-4 (1961-2) p.587 no.16). That doctors form a cohesive group with its core in kinship is implied by the Koan calendar of sacrifices in the month Batromios to Zeus Polieus; doctors are recipients, along with 'descendants of Nestor' (Nestoridai), of special cuts of meat (IC 37.53-4; cf. HG 8A.18-19).

Genealogies in the biographical tradition make Hippokrates the literal descendant of Asklepios: seventeenth (Tzetzes) or nineteenth (Soranos) in a direct line. Hippokrates was described as an older contemporary of Sokrates (Gell.17.21); the birthdate allegedly established by Soranos of Kos from local records would make him somewhat younger (460 BC; Sokrates lived 469-399). The Hippokratic genealogies are evidently fabricated to accord with some such date for Hippokrates and an assumed date for Asklepios and his son Podaleirios. The chronology is based on a calculation of the time between the fall of Troy (typical ancient estimate, 1140 BC) and the birth of Hippokrates, with a division of this into the requisite number of generations. For instance, by allocating the date 1140 to Podaleirios and 460 to Hippokrates, and by allowing the duration of a generation to be forty years, one finds that Hippokrates is on inclusive reckoning nineteenth in the line from Asklepios.

Myth had it that Podaleirios was shipwrecked on the Karian coast, after the fall of Troy (Paus.3.26.10; St.Byz.). There, he first tended the king's daughter, injured in a fall from a roof; then married her and founded the city of Syrnos. Three branches of their family carried on the medical tradition in the area - in Rhodes, Kos and Knidos. That this tradition circulated as early as the fourth century is shown by a chapter-heading in the history of Theopompos of Chios, writing at that time (FGH II 115):

Concerning the physicians in Kos and Knidos; how they are called Asklepiadai, and how they first came from Syrnos.

However, in its details, the myth is certainly a late invention, as it is permeated with elements of folk-tale (gallant rescuer marries his princess) and of aetiology (the place-name Syrnos). The invention is of a piece with the bogus chronology. (On myths in general, cf. Chapter 7.)

The names given in the genealogies for Hippokrates'
immediate family are not suspect: father Herakleides,
grandfather Hippokrates, sons Thessalos and Drakon and a
daughter who married a doctor, Polybos. The names
Thessalos and Drakon occur at Kos (e.g. IC 10d35, 12.31).
The former reflects the island's early connections with
Thessaly, and may imply a connection of the bearer with
Asklepios, whose cult was probably of Thessalian origin.
There is some doubt about the accuracy of the Souda's
record of names for the three sons of Thessalos (Gorgias,
Hippokrates and Drakon) and of the statement that the
family were court doctors in Macedon. This is perhaps
no more than guesswork.

The 'teachers' of Hippokrates are named as, in medicine,
his father and Herodikos of Selymbria; more generally,
contacts with Gorgias, Prodikos and Demokritos are alleged.
It is most probable that Hippokrates did receive medical
instruction from his father and, in turn, give it to his
sons.   As already remarked, the Greek tradition of
family medicine was strong. Promises made in the
Hippokratic Oath - not, perhaps, formulated for all
practising doctors, but none the less summing up many
of the ideals of the profession in the fourth century
(cf. Phillips, 1973, p.116) - indicate that new recruits
who came from non-medical families to study medicine
entered into a quasi-filial relationship with their
teachers. The Oath contained the promise:

to regard the man who instructed me in this profession
('techne') on the same level as my parents; to share
my livelihood with him and, in case of need, to give
him in indigence a share of my goods; to consider his
issue equal to my brothers.

Herodikos of Selymbria, named as a teacher of Hippokrates,
is probably the famous gymnastic trainer mentioned by
Plato ('R'408d). The mention of the name shows a
recognition of the para-medical character of activities in
the gymnasium.

The possibility of a direct influence on Hippokrates
of the sophists Gorgias (Tzetzes) and Prodikos (Souda) was
discussed in the preceding chapter. Demokritos of Abdera
is a different, and more plausible, case both because of
the nature of his work (known, from fragments, to have
embraced biology, physiology and medicine) and because of
the evidence that the Abdera region was familiar to
Hippokrates, who died in north Greece; and familiar also
to the writer of the Hippokratic 'Epidemiai'. If Hippokrates
is indeed the author of this work, or even part of it, it
is very probable that the two men met.

The question of the nature and composition of the Corpus
as a whole must be considered here. The Hippokratic
Corpus, as transmitted in the best manuscripts, consists
of some sixty treatises; the same number again is almost
unanimously rejected as late. Since the edition of
Littré, 1839-61, there has been general agreement on the
basic corpus (cf. Phillips, 1973, pp.34-5). No one would
assert that all sixty are written by, or even contemporary
with, Hippokrates. One variant of the library theory
(cf. preceding chapter) holds that the Corpus was a
collection of books for use in the medical school, a
collection of which Hippokrates, in fact the first owner,
became the reputed author (Jones, 1945); this nucleus
was then subject to later accretions, both before and
after it reached Alexandria at some time in the third
century.

There is wide divergence of opinion as to which works,
if any, can be ascribed to Hippokrates. For this reason,
'Hippokrates' (in inverted commas) is henceforth used to
designate a Hippokratic writer. Scepticism has often been
expressed about the possibility of solving the problem of
authorship, and indeed the value of a solution could it
be found (cf. Edelstein, 1967, pp.133-44); on the whole
an agnostic viewpoint prevails (cf. Lloyd, 1975b; but
Joly, DSB, is more committed to faith in Hippokrates in
'Hippokrates'). There is an initial difficulty in
defining 'publication' or 'release' with reference to the
fifth century. Some treatises may have gone out for sale
to the general public, like the books of Anaxagoras
mentioned by Sokrates in Plato's 'Apology' (26e1); others
may have been in limited circulation among medical
students; others again may have been set down for the
writer's private use.

Because the works are not a literary expression of the
original investigations of one thinker, but rather set
down information reached by medical consensus, the authorship problem is not one of eliminating forgeries so much
as detecting collaboration and isolating later insertions
or revisions. This was already recognized by ancient
critics who attributed certain treatises of 'Hippokrates'
to the next or the preceding generation of Hippokrates'
family; for instance, according to Aristotle, it was
Polybos who wrote 'On the Nature of Man' ('HA'512b12).
A similar problem arises in attempts to isolate the
historical Pythagoras (because of the tendency to attribute
to the 'master' all subsequent discoveries or doctrines),
or to define the individual achievement of Aristotle (whose
works are more or less infiltrated with editorial contributions from his followers). The Attic orators too present

parallels: here again the problem is not so much to find
that a given speech is 'spurious' or 'authentic' as to
establish relative freedom from or proneness to intrusive
stylistic features (see Dover, 1968). Also, as in the
Lysianic Corpus, Speech XI is a synopsis of X and XV of
XIV, so in the Hippokratic Corpus there are some treatises
which summarize others: 'Leverage' consists of a précis
of 'Joints', with the addition of material from 'Fractures';
and the gynaecological treatise 'The Nature of Woman' is
a somewhat inaccurate summary of parts of 'Diseases of
Women'; while 'Prorrhetic I', 'Koan Prognoses' and
'Prognostic' are interrelated, as are 'The Sacred Disease'
and 'Airs, Waters, Places'.

Comment on 'Hippokrates'' style, with reference to the
question of authorship, has tended to centre on the
content and tenor of the works. Such close stylistic
analysis as has been used on the Lysianic Corpus (Dover,
1968) might prove a useful adjunct to those more subjective
general impressions. Unfortunately, there is, for the
Hippokratic Corpus, no treatise which is unanimously
regarded as being (all) by Hippokrates, in the way that
Lysias XII can be taken to be the work of Lysias.
Linguistic analysis of the dialect, with attention to the
intrusion of forms from the 'koine' is another avenue
worth exploration (cf. Jouanna, 1975; Mendoza, 1976).

The heterogeneous nature of the content of the Corpus
as a whole can be seen in miniature in the 'Aphorisms',
which contain a mixture of old wives' tales, rules of
thumb and obvious truisms permeated on the one hand with
magical or mystical notions and on the other with elements
of philosophical speculation (5.42, 5.6, 2.4):

A pregnant woman has a good colour if she is carrying
a male child, a bad colour if a female;
Those who are affected by tetanus die within four
days: if they survive those days, they recover;
Surfeit is not good, nor is hunger; nor anything
else which is in excess of the natural.

These occur alongside valid and acute observations on
pathology and physiology.

Many treatises seem reference books, or textbooks;
some of these factual works are carefully composed,
conveying technical information in an arresting style
('Fractures', 'Joints'); others again have the air of
jottings carelessly strung together. Some treatises deal
in general terms with human anatomy and physiology, with
preventive medicine and conservation of health by
attention to diet and environment, or with the ideal
conditions for the doctor's work and the importance of
hygiene. Among specialized works, embryology and

gynaecology are strongly represented; epilepsy is
discussed in 'On the Sacred Disease' (perhaps the best
known and most quoted of all the treatises); head wounds
are the subject of another study, written apparently for
ancient army surgeons.

Hippokrates was a Koan, but 'Hippokrates', the corporate
Hippokratic writer, cannot be entirely claimed for Kos.
There is evidence in the Corpus of academic disagreement
and debate between the school at Kos and that at neighbouring Knidos. It is generally agreed that some of the
works have a Knidian origin. The terms 'Koan prognoses'
and 'Knidian opinions', used in the Corpus, sum up the
fundamental difference in approach between Kos, stressing
prognosis, the desirability of foretelling the outcome of
an illness, and Knidos, stressing diagnosis, listing
symptoms, classifying diseases and establishing procedural
rules (see Lonie, 1965; however, Joly, DSB, argues that
the differences are not clear cut). Treatises generally
treated as Knidian include 'Affections', 'Internal
Affections', 'Diseases', 'Regimen in Acute Diseases' and
many of the gynaecological studies. According to mythical
traditions, the school at Knidos was just as old as that
at Kos. Euryphon, possibly the author of some of the
Hippokratic works, was its leading light. As will be
seen, 'Hippokrates' was influenced also by ideas emanating
from Sicily and south Italy.

'Hippokrates' very rarely mentions another writer by name,
and when he does so it is to disagree. He never admits
to using earlier writers, or gives any indication that
others have anticipated or influenced his views. However,
theorizing on general biological topics, as well as on
more specialized medical ones, was one of the many interests
of the 'pre-Sokratic' philosophers (to use the conventional,
if slightly misleading, title collectively applied to
earlier thinkers), and many passages in the Hippokratic
Corpus show affinities - unacknowledged, perhaps unrecognized - with their work. More or less direct influence
has been claimed for Alkmaion, Anaxagoras, Empedokles,
Herakleitos, Diogenes and Protagoras (see Longrigg, 1963
for a detailed discussion; also more generally, Gask,
1950).

In Greek terms, there is nothing unethical in
'Hippokrates'' failure to mention his predecessors, as
writers felt free to borrow ideas or even 'lift' phrases
and passages without reference to or acknowledgment of
their source. There was no objection either to the
repeated use by different writers of the same title: many
early treatises entitled simply 'On Nature' were in circu-

lation;   later philosophers gave unoriginal titles to
their essays;   Ion of Chios, like 'Hippokrates', produced
his 'Epidemiai', probably an autobiographical travel book
in his case.   (But some of these catch-all titles seem to
be labels, representing the content of a work, applied by
later critics for convenience of reference.)   It may be
remarked that if 'Hippokrates' is indebted to his
predecessors, later writers owe much to him.   The Corpus
is plundered by Plato, in the latter part of 'Timaios';
also by Aristotle writing on biological topics.

The spurious correspondence of Demokritos and Hippokrates was mentioned in the previous chapter. Demokritos'
home ground was certainly very familiar to the doctor, or
doctors, of the Hippokratic 'Epidemiai', with their north
Greek setting.   The seven books of the 'Epidemiai' seem
to fall into three groups (I and III; II, IV and VI;
V and VII) according to the doctor's main geographical
base, a grouping corroborated by textual considerations
(Littré V pp.10-13).   Doubts over the authorship of the
'Epidemiai' were expressed in antiquity;   Galen's view
was that some of the books were genuine Hippokrates, or
Hippokrates revised by Thessalos;   but that others (V and
VII in particular) were by another writer.

The 'Epidemiai' give a series of case-histories, set
against general background information about climate and
local conditions.   Many of the cases begin with the
patient's address - or rather, with a brief indication
of where he lived, in relation to such local landmarks
as shrines or the public water supply - perhaps a reminder
to reorientate the doctor, for whose own use the notes
seem to be made.   The prefatory remarks on local
conditions, of wider interest, may have been intended
for general circulation.   The town or country of residence
is usually specified.   From this, it is clear that the
doctor of I and III practised at Abdera in Thrace and on
Thasos, the island which lies off the coast there, though
he paid visits to other places: for example, Book III
contains six cases each from Abdera and Thasos (120, 122,
124, 128, 130, 136;   44, 102, 108, 112, 134, 142), two
from Larissa (118, 136) and one each from Kyzikos, on the
south coast of the Black Sea (140) and from Meliboia in
Magnesia, neighbouring Thessaly (146).   The doctor of II,
IV and VI again worked mainly in Thessaly and Thrace,
having a special connection with Perinthos to the north
of the Black Sea;   the doctor of V and VII treated
patients in Thessaly (Larissa is well represented), Thrace
and Macedon, but also travelled to Athens, the Peloponnese
and the islands.   Kos is mentioned only once in the
'Epidemiai':   the case of 'the sister of the man from Kos',

a woman who died of liver disease, is compared with similar cases. A Koan patient occurs elsewhere in the Corpus only in 'Prorrhetic I', Didymarchos, a case of 'phrenitis' ('Epid.'2.23 = Littré V p.94; 'Prorrh.'1.34 = Littré V p.518).

Fragments of Demokritos suggest particular coincidences with Hippokratic views in the field of embryology; for instance that the embryo was nourished in the womb by sucking ('Carn.'6 = Littré VIII p.592):

> The unborn child, pursing its lips, sucks and draws nourishment from the mother's womb.... The child is born with stools in its bowels, and excretes as soon as it is born.... Now, it would not have stools if it did not suck in the womb; nor would it know how to take the breast as soon as it is born, if it had not sucked already in the womb.

Similarly, in cardiology, 'Hippokrates' shares with Alkmaion the view that the brain was the seat of consciousness ('Morb.Sacr.'16 = Littré VI p.390; cf. Harris, 1973):

> For those reasons, I believe that the brain is the most powerful organ in the body. For if it is sound, it is our interpreter of the things which impinge on us from the atmosphere.... The eyes, ears, tongue, hands and feet act in accordance with the perception of the brain.... And as for understanding, the brain is the messenger.

But while 'Hippokrates' does not name Demokritos or Alkmaion, he does mention Empedokles and Melissos, in both cases implying that he is taking issue with current beliefs. The reference to Empedokles, who belonged to Akragas, on the south coast of Sicily, is a reminder of the important medical activity of the West. Herodotos (who nowhere mentions Hippokrates, his contemporary; or the medical school at Kos, neighbouring his native Halikarnassos) records that the foremost medical centre of the sixth century was at Kroton, on the south-east coast of Italy (Hdt.3.131.3).

The travels of the doctor Demokedes of Kroton to the courts of Dareios in Persia and Polykrates in Samos interested Herodotos. Kroton was the birthplace of Alkmaion, and it was there that Pythagoras spent much of his life. The influence of Pythagoreanism quietly infiltrated medical ethics and practice, though incurring some hostility from more 'scientific' doctors. 'Ancient Medicine', which attacks Empedokles explicitly, in passing, is arguably the vehicle for sustained implicit polemic against the Pythagorean Philolaos (Lloyd, 1963). However, the Hippokratic Oath is deeply imbued with Pythagorean

ideals and attitudes (Edelstein, 1967, pp.3-63). It is
uncertain at what date, or in what circumstances, the Oath
was given its definitive formulation, but its code met
with widespread and long-lasting general medical acceptance.
The rejection of abortion is a striking instance of
conformity with known Pythagorean principles.

Empedokles is cited by 'Hippokrates' as an example of
writers who think a study of the nature of man an essential
prerequisite for the study of medicine ('VM' 20 = Littré I
p.620):

> Some people, both doctors and thinkers ('sophistai'),
> allege it is not possible for anyone to understand
> medicine who does not understand what man is; but one
> who is properly to cure men must learn this. Their
> enquiry tends to philosophy - as Empedokles or others
> concerned with the nature of things have written about
> the fundamental nature of man, how he first began and
> how he was formed. But personally I consider that all
> those things said by thinker or doctor, or written,
> about the nature of things, belong less to the medical
> art than to the art of writing.

Empedokles is one of the most colourful figures in the
history of Greek thought (cf. the description of Dodds,
1951, p.146: 'magician and naturalist, poet and philosopher, preacher, healer and public counsellor'). His main
contribution to speculation on the 'nature of things' was
the theory of the four 'roots' or elements, which may have
its basis in Pythagorean ideas about number and opposites.
Empedokles put forward specialized theories also: his
ideas of respiration cited by Aristotle are a good illustration of his dazzling poetic technique, with polished
hexameters packed with simile, expressing abstruse thought
in abstruse terms (VS fr.100).

In criticizing Empedokles, 'Hippokrates' repudiates the
relevance of philosophical attitudes and literary artistry
to medical writing, in a plea for specialization, with
the recognition of medicine as an art in its own right.
'Hippokrates'' comment on Melissos (a Samian who led an
active military life as well as a contemplative one; cf.
Chapter 3 on the events of 441) is of a similar tenor.

In 'The Nature of Man' ('Nat.Hom.'1 = Littré VI p.32),
the remarks prefatory to a discussion of the humours
begin:

> He who is accustomed to listen to speakers on the
> nature of man beyond the point where this bears on
> medicine - well, the account which follows is not
> geared to him. For I do not say that man is all air,
> or fire, or water, or earth, or anything else that is
> not manifestly present in the human body.

Such theorists are then dismissed with the assertion that
their inability to agree on a single constituent substance
'justifies the theory of Melissos'. That is: because
those who believe that a single substance is paramount
cannot agree on which substance underlies all being, they
undermine their own position, and lend credence to such
theories as that of Melissos, who held that Being was an
eternal and unchanging unity.

In his criticism of Empedokles and in his comment on
Melissos, 'Hippokrates' takes issue with those who treat
medicine as a subject bound up with wider studies. The
intention is to detach medicine from the ambiance of
philosophy, and to establish the medical treatise as a
specialized genre, written by and for practising doctors.
This represents a fundamental new attitude in scientific
thought: the recognition of the possibility, or even
desirability, that knowledge be compartmentalized. Celsus'
comment that Hippokrates detached medicine from philosophy
('sapientia') makes this point. 'Hippokrates'' attitude
represents also a change in the practice of medicine, with
the arrival of a new generation of experts, who were not
content to treat their patients on a purely empirical
basis, who acquired their knowledge from books as well as
from personal contacts, and who recognized the value of
collaboration.

In the event, doctors were unable to sever the umbilical
cord which bound medicine to its parent philosophy (cf.
Lloyd, 1975a). Interaction between Hippokratic writers
and other thinkers of the fifth and fourth centuries is
apparent, for instance, in discussion of the 'techne' of
medicine, and its relation to other crafts. Medicine is
defined ('de Arte' 3 = Littré VI p.4): 'to relieve the
distress of the ill and alleviate the severity of illnesses'. The vocational character of medical training is
contrasted by Plato with the non-vocational education
offered by the sophists ('Prt.'311b-e and elsewhere; cf.
the argument that rhetoric is not a 'techne' at all, but
merely a knack, 'Grg.'463b, 'Phdr.'260e).

The Hippokratic Law makes some contribution to the
ongoing debate on the relative importance of natural
ability, instruction and practice in fostering achievement
in any 'techne': beginning with the uncompromising claim
that medicine is most glorious of all arts, it continues
with the assertion ('Lex'2 = Littré IV p.638) that it
requires 'natural ability, instruction, a suitable
location, teaching from childhood, application and time'.
The Law ends ('Lex'5):

   Things that are holy are revealed only to holy men. It
   is not right for profane people to learn them until they
   have been initiated into the rites of knowledge.

While medicine is a 'techne' and its practitioners have 'episteme', these practical or rational ideals are adulterated by semi-mystical notions borrowed perhaps from exclusive religious sects. The idea of initiation into the freemasonry of medicine may be a late development; but there are implications of an exclusive medical fellowship in the regular use of the term Asklepiadai; also in the phrase 'the community of Hippokrates', used by Hippokrates' younger contemporary Aristophanes.

The different strands of intellectual enquiry were never completely separated out: Aristotle, perhaps influenced by his father, a doctor, maintained an interest in observation of minute biological detail as well as in abstract metaphysics (and much else besides); Poseidonios recommended in theory, and personally adopted in practice, a synoptic global view of knowledge. In general terms, Hippokratic medicine is a particular offshoot of a widespread growth of interest in the physical world. In points of detail, also, as has been seen the Hippokratic treatises are influenced by earlier writers.

The ancient biographers - apart from the cursory reference to Demokritos - do not set Hippokrates in this context, but in a very different one. And it must be added that they are not alone in this. A strong tradition associated Hippokrates with the Asklepieion at Kos. Strabo tells us that Hippokrates studied the temple records; Varro, according to Pliny, wrote that he burned the records after taking a copy - a colourful story recorded also in the Tzetzes life and (though in a different version, related of the library at Knidos) in the Soranos life, where it is attributed to the medical writer Andreas (Str.14.2.19; cf. 8.6.15; 'HN'29.1). It may be asked if the story is pure invention, and if it is just a coincidence that the same small island had a great school of medicine and a great temple of Asklepios. Certainly, Hippokrates did not burn part of the temple; after such arson he would surely not have attained status in Kos during his lifetime, or have become a cult figure after his death.

The stories of a connection between Hippokrates and the Asklepieion seemed scotched once and for all when it was pointed out (Edelstein, PW suppl.VI) that archaeological evidence indicated that the cult of Asklepios was not introduced into Kos until the middle of the fourth century, a century after Hippokrates was born. However, the archaeological evidence is not clear cut (Robert, 1939). The town of Kos was founded only in 366/365. Asklepios was worshipped in the demes (Haleis, Halasarna, Isthmos) before this date. And, of course, one can never suppose

that the earliest reference to a god coincides with the
introduction of his cult to a community. A boustrophedon
inscription from Kalymnos mentions Panakeia; and it is
highly improbable that Panakeia (a minor deity associated
with Asklepios) was honoured in Kalymnos before Asklepios
in Kos. Also, Plato refers to Hippokrates as an Asklepiad,
and there are the regional myths about Podaleirios, son
of Asklepios - current at least as early as Theopompos,
born around 378 BC.

It is perfectly possible to argue that, even if
Asklepios was already worshipped in Kos in Hippokrates'
lifetime, Hippokratic medicine owed nothing to the
Asklepieion: to allow a connection between Hippokrates
and Asklepios, but not between 'Hippokrates' and the
Asklepieion. The development of healing shrines might
belong to a late stage in the cult of Asklepios (Pugliese
Carratelli, 1963-4). But it is evident from Aristophanes'
'Ploutos' produced in 388 that the Athenian Asklepieion,
established some thirty years earlier, effected cures by
that date, no doubt in imitation of practice elsewhere.

There was no discernible connection before Hippokrates
between Asklepieia (oldest centres at Trikka in Thessaly
and at Epidauros) and medical schools (early centres at
Kroton and Kyrene). The association found at Kos is
repeated in the second century AD at Pergamum, the birthplace of Galen and site of a great Asklepios temple.
There were no finds in the Koan Asklepieion suggestive of
a connection with Hippokrates: a few surgical instruments
were discovered, but so few as to appear dedicated objects,
not used in the shrine. Conversely, there is very little
in the Hippokratic Corpus to suggest a connection with the
Asklepieion. Asklepios' name occurs only in the Oath and
without any special exclusiveness: Asklepios is invoked
after Apollo and with all the other gods to witness the
oath. Asklepios is not among the gods to whom the patient
is recommended to pray in the case of particular dreams
('Salubr.'4.89 cf. 90 = Littré VI p.652):

in the case of good signs, to the Sun, to Zeus Ouranios,
Zeus Ktesios, Athena Ktesia, Hermes and Apollo; in
the case of the opposite, to the averter gods, to Earth
and the Heroes.
Further, medical treatment is given in a surgery or in
the patient's home, never in a temple.

In the innovation of setting down information previously
transmitted orally from father to son, 'Hippokrates' was
influenced, as already seen, by certain 'pre-Sokratic'
writers. If the Asklepieion already had a reputation as
a healing shrine, and if records of miracle cures, similar
to those found at Epidauros, existed at Kos, it would be

remarkable if Hippokrates and other Koan doctors
(collectively 'Hippokrates') did not read them, in
addition to literary sources. Temple archives constituted
the earliest Greek research centres. There is, however,
no evidence that the Koan shrine acquired this kind of
status. One of Herodotos' prime historical sources came
from the epigraphical records of Delphi, and of other
oracular shrines. It is not difficult to pick out from
Herodotos' narrative certain passages based on (or lifted
from) Delphic records. If 'Hippokrates' used such a
source, the tracks are very carefully covered, with a
guile alien to all we know of fifth-century literary and
scientific attitudes: there is, for instance, no lapse
into Doric, which would be the dialect of the records.
The inescapable conclusion is that records did not exist
on any great scale at this time, and were of insignificant
importance as a Hippokratic source.

There remains, however, the fact that practically
nothing is known of the young Hippokrates or of his early
work; and the related possibility that new evidence might
one day vindicate the ancient biographers, after all, or
at least show there is some truth in their stories. But
the rational art of the Corpus is the crystallization of
the thought and practice of centuries, rather than the
creation of something new out of temple procedure. Also,
after Hippokrates, temple medicine did not decline, but
became more and more popular.

The last sentence of the fourth Hippokratic treatise on
regimen ('Salubr.'4.93 = Littré VI p.662) runs:

> Following this advice, as it has been set down here,
> a man will lead a healthy life. In fact, I have
> discovered regimen, in so far as it is possible for a
> man to find it, with the help of the gods.

It has been suggested (Withington, 1921) that the phrase
'with the help of the gods', was the basis of Strabo's
assertion (14.2.19), 'They say that Hippokrates was
trained in the knowledge of regimen ('diaita') by the
votive offerings dedicated there (i.e. in the temple)'.
The phrase does not imply scrutiny of temple cures, but
is merely a pious addition to tone down a claim which
might seem boastful. A glance at the first sentence of
'Salubr.'1 shows the work introduced in similar terms of
modest confidence:

> If it appeared to me that any of those who have
> already written on human regimen directed towards
> health had throughout written with proper understanding
> all that it is possible for the human mind to grasp, it
> would have been enough for me, since others had
> completed the task, to recognize good work and use it,
> in so far as each point seemed to be applicable.

'Salubr.'4 is a work on the subject of dreams, generally
regarded as belonging to the late fifth century (but
Jaeger, 1945, III p.33, dates it later: to the mid fourth
century). It is an attempt to systematize the subjects of
dreams, to explain them and, above all, to use a patient's
dream experience as a basis for understanding and treating
his physical condition (cf. Dodds, 1951, p.119 and notes).
The treatise makes no forays into psychology or para-
psychology. There is a passing allusion to dreams of the
wish-fulfilment type (93):

> All a man's dreams about familiar objects indicate a
> yearning of the soul,

but more typical of the tone of the work is the statement
(88):

> All dreams which repeat in the ensuing night the day-
> time actions or thoughts of a man, and which represent
> them happening naturally ... these are good.

Dreams foretelling the future are dismissed as irrelevant
to the current investigations (87):

> All dreams which come from the gods and which foretell
> things which are going to happen, either to cities or
> to an individual ... there are people with a precise
> skill who interpret such dreams.

It comes as something of a surprise that this kind of
dream interpretation is described as a 'techne' and an
exact one too. (Some manuscripts omit the adjective.)
Perhaps this is a sop to public opinion - belief in such
dreams being widespread - or is intended to disarm
criticism from professional dream-interpreters, who might
feel doctors were poaching on their preserve. Like such
interpreters, the writer recommends prayer in certain
cases (88, 89, 90), but this is only part of his
prescription. His attitude to prayer is summed up in
the words (87):

> Prayer is proper and very good. But a man should
> help himself too, while calling on the gods.

The attempt to rationalize dreams on a purely
physiological basis is internally consistent and logical,
however fantastic the premises of this logic may be at
times. Great attention is paid to dreams about natural
phenomena, interpreted on the basis of a rather facile
symbolism. Astronomical dreams are particularly prominent.
Here it is as well to remember - before criticizing the
writer's ingenuousness or his patients' credulity - that
even professional astronomers were long in divorcing
astronomical observation from astrological interpretation
(cf. Chapter 6, 'Science', on Hipparchos). And if the
interpretations of astronomical dreams as having precise
physiological significance seem bizarre, or if it seems

unlikely that anyone would dream regularly about the sun and stars, one may yet point to the strict consistency of the theories as a virtue. It was this same consistency in interpretation in Freud's work of 1900 which carried such conviction. (One might perhaps be forgiven for arguing that Freud's determination to explain all dreams in terms of sexual symbolism is just as bizarre as the basic premises of 'Hippokrates' - or for wondering how many nineteenth-century Austrian girls in fact dreamt of serpents, horseriding, etc.)

One of the most interesting aspects of the fourth treatise on regimen is that it covers ground generally regarded as belonging to temple, not secular, medicine; that is, dreams. Some shrines of the healing gods were places of pilgrimage, where devotees flocked in the hope of a miracle cure, much as Catholics today go to Lourdes or Orthodox pilgrims to the shrine of the Panagia on Tenos. There is ample evidence for this activity in the temple records of Epidauros, in Aristophanes' 'Ploutos' (which shows that the practice was already current early in the fourth century) and, especially, in the 'Hieroi Logoi' of Aelius Aristeides, written in the second century AD. (For a revealing analysis of the particular case of Aristeides, see Festugière, 1954, pp.85-104.)

In later antiquity, an important part was played in this practice - often given the name 'incubation' - by dreams. The patient slept in the temple, hoping for an appearance of the god himself, to prescribe a course of treatment. There is an obvious difference in orientation in that the Hippokratic doctor used dream information as a basis for prescription, whereas the temple dream was itself the vehicle for a specific prescription; but there are striking similarities in the essence of the treatment meted out allegedly by Asklepios to Aelius Aristeides and in fact by 'Hippokrates' to his patients: diet, emetics, exercise and bathing. 'Hippokrates' offers reasons for his advice; Asklepios gives it categorically and often recommends more extreme doses, but the advice itself is much the same.

Perhaps the patients and their ailments were much the same. Aelius Aristeides is described in modern terms as a 'neurasthenic' or a 'neuropath' (Gask, 1950, p.9; Festugière, 1954, p.103); 'hypochondriac' might be the layman's choice of term. Similarly, one may conjecture that only someone extremely preoccupied with his health could consult a doctor about the significance of an astronomical dream. This is a different kind of medicine from the medicine of the 'Epidemiai', where the patients are critically ill. This is not to say that none of those

who sought help in the temples was ill. Probably, however,
their illnesses were typically of the chronic rather than
the critical variety. Where rational prognosis was
pessimistic, or a diagnosis could not be given, the
patient might have recourse to religious comfort and the
hope of a miracle cure (cf. Edelstein, 1967, pp.205-46).

Both the Asklepieion at Kos and its medical school
remained prominent for centuries. It seems that the two
institutions, with their different approaches but similar
interests, coexisted amicably. Doctors were probably on
average no more, or less, pious than their contemporaries,
any more than doctors today differ markedly from the rest
of the population in their religious beliefs. The writer
of the treatise on regimen gives prayer at least a
qualified recommendation. Nikias, Theokritos' friend,
carried out a daily ritual at a small private shrine of
Asklepios in his own home. (Theokritos composed an
epigram for a cedarwood image of Asklepios erected there:
AP 6.337 = HE I p.183.)   Galen described himself as
'servant of Asklepios' (for the term, cf. Peek, 1969, p.33
no.81a: epitaph of a doctor at Nisyros) - much as a
soldier might be designated 'devotee of Ares' or a
prostitute 'attendant of Aphrodite' (cf. Chapter 9 on
acolytes). One of the Hippokratic letters mentions an
annual procession made by doctors in honour of Asklepios
('Ep.'11). Doctors, 'Asklepiadai', maintained formal
connections with the cult of Asklepios without any direct
association with activities in the Asklepieion.

After 'Hippokrates', the nature of our evidence changes.
From the Corpus, we have a close-up doctor's view of
disease and of patients; from inscriptions (mostly later
in date), we have glimpses of the community's view of
doctors. However, before turning to the epigraphical
evidence, a brief account of the later development of
medical writing and teaching and of Kos' part in this, is
necessary.

Little medical writing of the Hellenistic and early
Roman period has survived intact; apart from a few 'late'
treatises attached to the Hippokratic Corpus. Most of
these are concerned with medical ethics and procedure
('Precepts', 'In the Surgery', 'Decorum') rather than
technical matters; but an exception is the work 'The
Heart', marked by close and accurate observations of the
function of this organ (cf. Harris, 1973, pp.83-5;
Lonie, 1965 on the dating question). The century or so
after Hippokrates' brilliance is very shadowy. The first
figure to emerge with any clarity from the mists is a

contemporary of Aristotle, Diokles from Euboian Karystos.
(The relative dates of Diokles and Aristotle and their
interaction with each other are fully discussed by Jaeger,
1963; cf. review Edelstein, 1967, pp.145-52; for other
views on the chronology cf. PA II p.500 n.29.)

One of Diokles' distinguished followers was Praxagoras
of Kos, who lived about 300 BC, the younger of two bearers
of the name, confused in later medical biography (Steckerl,
1958; Longrigg, DSB XI pp.127-8). Praxagoras apparently
developed a new theory of the humours and of the relationship between humours and diet. The influence of
Praxagoras on Hellenistic medicine is as pervasive as
that of Philitas on Hellenistic verse. Ideas from Kos
were developed and expressed in Alexandria. The great
doctors of Alexandria - Herophilos, Xenophon, Erasistratos -
all trained in Kos. Later - around the middle of the
third century - Philinos of Kos, working in Alexandria,
was the founder of the empirical school, in reaction
against over-dogmatic formal teaching of medicine, and in
tune with the philosophy of scepticism.

While Alexandria drew medical writers and academic
theorists, Kos maintained its pre-eminence as a training
centre for practical physicians. Knidos disappeared from
the scene, eclipsed not only by Kos, but by new foundations
at Alexandria, Antioch and elsewhere. It was only in the
second century AD that Kos was superseded by Ephesos and
Pergamum, the birthplace of Galen. With Galen's work -
twice as voluminous as the large Hippokratic Corpus -
ancient medicine is once more amply documented.

Patronage benefited doctors as well as writers. Already
in the sixth century Demokedes of Kroton worked at the
court of Polykrates of Samos, and at that of the Persian
king Dareios. At about the same time, Aineus of Kos
(perhaps a great-uncle of Hippokrates) was honoured in
Athens (see Phillips, 1973, pp.184-5). Menekrates of
Syracuse conducted himself with eccentric megalomania,
dressing as Zeus in purple cloak and golden crown while
arraying his attendants as minor gods: this may have
been a self-advertising gimmick to commend his services
as court doctor to Philip of Macedon. Koan doctors were
much in demand as personal physicians. Alexander was
attended on his Indian campaigns by a Koan (Arr.6.11.1).
And at the Alexandrian court medical men from Kos were
influential.

By the second century, Greek doctors were practising
in Rome, some as slaves, taken in Rome's wars in the
East, but some voluntarily, as free men. Cato deplored

their presence, exhorting his sons to distrust Greek
potions and to rely on his own homely panacea, cabbage
(Plu.'Cato'23.3);   but medical ideas from Greece
infiltrated Rome as surely as other aspects of Greek
culture. Asklepiades, originally from Bithynia, a
rhetorician who later adopted the medical profession for
which his name seems to destine him, played an important
part in this process. Under the emperors, Xenophon of
Kos was doctor to Claudius, and an influential figure at
court (Tac.'Ann.'12.61);   later, Galen became personal
physician to Marcus Aurelius.

'Graduates' of the Koan medical school travelled all
over Greece in the practice of their profession. (Perhaps
the term 'graduates' is misleading, as there is no
evidence that there was any set curriculum or any system
of examinations. The Oath suggests that each student
entered into a private and personal contract with his
tutor, not with an institution.) It is of these men,
many originating in Kos, where medicine was almost a
national profession, that we have glimpses in inscriptions.
(The epigraphical evidence was collected by Pohl, 1905,
discussed by Woodhead, 1952 and brought up to date with
great thoroughness by Cohn-Haft, 1956;   cf. also
Rostovtzeff, 1941, II pp.1088-94;   Peek, 1969, pp.38-40.)
In addition, the Doric speaking doctors of fourth-century
Attic comedy are probably to be regarded as Koans (cf.
Chapter 4).

Kos itself was well served by doctors. Decrees of
several Koan demes honouring the local doctor have been
found: of Aigele, Haleis, Isthmos and Kalymnos (for
detailed references, see Cohn-Haft, 1956, doc.nos 11, 12,
38, 60, 61). A third-century decree of the city honours
a physician, Xenotimos, son of Timoxenos, who helped out
when the public doctors were laid low by an epidemic of
'deadly diseases' (doc.no.13 = SIG 943). The term
'public doctors' ('iatroi damosieuontes') does not refer
to practitioners employed by a national health service
providing free medical care. (Cohn-Haft argues con-
vincingly against this view.) Rather, a chosen doctor
was paid a basic 'retainer' by a community to induce him
to stay and practise in its midst;   to this lump sum he
added the fees paid by his patients. A doctor might, and
sometimes did, waive his fees. Such disinterested
generosity is recommended in the Hippokratic 'Precepts'
and was put into practice by several doctors, for
instance, Pheidias of Rhodes, honoured at Athens in 304/
303 for giving free treatment (IG II/III 1.1.483). That
some doctors were very wealthy is evident from a Koan
inscription recording private donations made to a fund for

the construction of a fleet: the largest single sum
(4,000 drachmai) is given by a doctor, Philistos, and
another substantial contribution (500 drachmai) comes from
Hippokrates son of Thessalos, probably a descendant of the
great Hippokrates (IC 10b7-8, a51; cf. Cohn-Haft, pp.20-1
n.58).

Kos provided many communities with 'public doctors':
Iasos, Delphi, Delos, Halikarnassos and the Cretan cities
of Gortyn, Knossos and Aptera (for detailed references,
see Cohn-Haft doc.nos 10, 18, 19, 20, 31, 71;   also for
Halikarnassos IC 13;   cf. Robert, 1939).   The epigraphical
evidence from Gortyn indicates that requests for medical
practitioners, to be recruited from men who had trained in
Kos, were addressed to the state: it is recorded that the
people of Gortyn sent their request: that Hermias was
appointed and held the post for five years before returning
to Kos with a grateful Cretan escort.   One wonders how such
posts were filled - by a medical selection committee with
state representation is an obvious possibility.   (Herzog,
1931 argued, apparently on tenuous evidence, which has not
yet been fully published, that the state controlled the
career structure of the medical profession;   cf. Cohn-Haft,
p.63, for a sceptical treatment of this view.)

The duration of the doctor's stay in a locality varied.
Hermias' five years in Crete seems a fairly typical stint.
A popular doctor might be pressed to stay on, as was one
from Kasos, practising at Cretan Olous in the second
century (I Cret.I 249).   It was clearly regarded as
exceptional when Menokritos, a Samian, spent over twenty
years working at Brykous in Karpathos.   Menokritos is
honoured in a verbose second-century inscription, which
affords a typical example of the jerky syntax of epigraphical officialese (Cohn-Haft, doc.no.37 = IG XII 1, 1032;
the beginning and end are broken, and some of the body is
restored):

> Since Menokritos, son of Metrodoros, from Samos, having
> been in the public service for over twenty years, has
> continued assiduously and zealously tending everyone,
> and has shown himself irreproachable both in his
> professional skill and in his behaviour generally;
> since, when an epidemic of pestilence broke out and
> many victims were at risk of death - not only among the
> local people but also aliens in residence - by showing
> extreme assiduity and perseverance he was responsible
> for our survival (and before his contract with us, when
> he was living in Rhodes, he saved the lives of many of
> the demesmen whose condition had become dangerous,
> without accepting a fee;   and continued kindly and
> upright on his visits to everyone who lived in the

township): in order, then, that the deme Brykous show
that it is grateful and that it honours good doctors,
this proposal being passed, the deme has agreed: to
give praise to Menokritos son of Metrodoros from Samos
and to crown him with a golden crown and to announce at
the festival Asklepieia that, 'The deme Brykous gives
honour and crowns with a golden crown Menokritos son of
Metrodoros from Samos, for his professional skill and
his excellent qualities'.

After stating that Menokritos is to have the privilege of
attending all deme festivals, the remaining lines of the
inscription make the usual formal arrangements for the
ratification of the proposal, the recording of the honours
and the disbursing of public money for the crown and the
stone stele recording it. (On the ratification of a
deme's decree, see Francotte, 1964, pp.163-5.)

Doctors formed one of the most mobile groups in the
population, and were one of the most respected. While
they regarded themselves collectively as Asklepiadai, the
association was looser than that of the Dionysiac
'technitai'. However, they resembled actors - or philosophers, writers, artists and architects - in that they
travelled in exercising their skills. There is some
evidence that itinerant doctors augmented their income by
giving lectures (PA II p.526 n.159). Both Asklepiades and
Galen were rhetoricians as well as doctors. The content
of many of the Hippokratic works, dealing with preventive
medicine and the safeguarding of health, might well have
been aimed to appeal to a non-specialist as well as a
specialist public.

The evidence of inscriptions honouring public doctors
and of epitaphs which list their places of work is borne
out by the Hippokratic 'Epidemiai', which shows that a
professional career could embrace several far-flung
communities. Evidence of this kind, however, gives only
a partial picture of Greek medical care. The distinguished
foreigner who came as official doctor and who was highly
venerated by the local populace was the aristocrat of
his profession (the equivalent, perhaps, of a senior
consultant today). Such a man probably brought with him
at least one slave to assist him, perhaps also some pupils
learning the 'techne' and he may, in addition, have employed
local labour for menial tasks. Plato describes two
different kinds of medicine, practised by doctors or by
their assistants; the former theoretical, appropriate to
free patients and the latter empirical, for slaves ('Lg.'
720a-e; 858d). Assistants learning the 'techne' are
mentioned in the Corpus also (cf. Littré IX pp.201-2).
According to Aischines, one such apprentice abused his

position unscrupulously for purposes of prostitution
(Aeschin.1.40).

In addition to the entourage headed by the doctor and
his assistants, others practised medicine of a sort.
While the official doctors are known from the many
inscriptions honouring them, the unofficial undergrowth
of the profession was little publicized. 'Ancient
Medicine' makes the comment ('VM' 1 = Littré I p.560):

> Some practitioners are indifferent, others very
> superior. Now, if the art of medicine did not exist
> at all, and if no investigations and no discoveries
> had been made in the art, there would be no such
> distinction, but all would be equally inexperienced
> and ignorant in the art, and all aspects of the
> treatment of patients would be ruled by chance.

Similarly, elsewhere ('Morb.Sacr.'1 = Littré VI p.354 and
'Lex'1 = Littré IV p.639) 'Hippokrates' distinguishes true
doctors from charlatans.

It may be conjectured that in every sizeable ancient
community, from the fifth century onwards, there was a
wide range of medical attention available, from that of
the highly trained professional doctor - often not a local
man - to that of the untrained person with a reputation
for, or a knack of, giving the appropriate advice or
applying simple herbal remedies. (Cf. Temkin, 1953, making
a distinction between physician and 'leech'.)

The cases detailed in the 'Epidemiai' give the
impression that no one consulted a 'real' doctor unless
he was, or felt, desperately ill; perhaps only if he
wished to ask, 'Am I going to die?' rather than, 'What is
wrong?' 'Pronoia', foretelling the outcome of an illness,
was a desideratum in a doctor. One of the letters comments
cynically that if patients recover, the gods get the
credit; if they die, doctors are blamed. The doctor had
an obvious interest in predicting death (the outcome of
the majority of the cases detailed) in good time, to
forestall charges of incompetence or, at the least,
deficiency in prognostic skill.

Many people no doubt preferred to seek medical help
from a local man, whom they knew, rather than from the
unfamiliar state doctor; such local figures gave a
reassuring continuity of treatment. And self-treatment,
on the basis of such common-sense lore - or plausible
fallacy - as is contained in the Hippokratic 'Aphorisms'
was doubtless widespread. Religious healing too had its
undergrowth, in magic practices. Spells, incantations
and potions were peddled. Sacred and secular medicine
coexisted in their diverse forms in Kos for centuries, as
they did later in Pergamum. Within both, there was

tremendous variation in practice, from wonder-worker to
priest and from quack to medical specialist.

Kos is of fundamental importance in the history of
Greek medicine: as the early environment of Hippokrates
and background to 'Hippokrates'; as the site both of a
uniquely prestigious medical school which had a continuing
cachet because of the special relations enjoyed by Kos
with Alexandria, and the site too of the flourishing
Asklepieion. These two phenomena represent parallel
developments from the same impulse - a belief in the
importance of the individual, the belief which informed
so much of late Greek religion and philosophy.

SCIENCE

The more detailed latter part of this chapter is concerned
with activities of the second and first century, when
Hipparchos, Geminos and Poseidonios lived and worked in
Rhodes. The preliminary general survey is intended to
put these thinkers in chronological perspective and their
contribution to Greek 'science' in its intellectual context.
It may be remarked at the outset that - as in the case of
medicine - the Greek mainland will not figure largely in
this account.

To define 'science' in terms appropriate both to the
ancient and the modern world is not easy. The editors of
a very useful collection of extracts, 'A Source Book in
Greek Science' preface their work (Cohen and Drabkin,
1948, p.viii):
    it has seemed advisable to confine our material to
    that which would generally be regarded today as
    scientific in method, i.e., based, in principle, either
    on mathematics or on empirical verification.
The editors themselves acknowledge that this restriction
entails the exclusion of 'philosophic or speculative'
material; and that their criteria necessitate drawing a
rather artificial distinction, in the case of many Greek
writers, between science and 'pseudo science'; for
instance, between astronomy and astrology in Ptolemy. It
is aptly pointed out by Edelstein (1952, p.576) that:
    'pseudo science' ... theories ... which do not pass
    the muster of modern criticism, constitute in fact the
    greater part of the preserved material. To the Greeks
    they were just as scientific as those other views which
    happen to seem acceptable to the modern scientist
and (p.579) that:
    In fact, evaluating the tension between the various

tendencies within ancient science is one of the main
problems confronting the historian.

Similarly, Lloyd (1970, p.137) remarks that to Ptolemy
the distinction between astronomy and astrology was

not one between a scientific and a non-scientific, or
pseudo-scientific, study of the heavenly bodies, but
between an exact, and a merely conjectural, branch of
knowledge.

Of the two criteria applied to the material by Cohen
and Drabkin, the principle of a mathematical basis is
readily exemplifiable and justifiable, that of 'empirical
verification' opens up a wide and much discussed question.
It has often been asserted - and explained in social or
political terms - that the Greeks failed to make adequate
scientific observations, and to conduct controlled
experiments. It is indeed true that the principle of
amassing observable data as a basis for forming
conclusions, the principle of proceeding from many particular instances to one general theory was never systematically
followed; and that the early tendency to generalization,
to hazard unverified - often unverifiable - hypotheses
about the universal situation, without regard for detailed
cases, never completely disappeared. As Lloyd well puts
it (1970, p.141):

Experimentation was a corroborative, far more than a
heuristic, technique.

Thus, in the case of Aristotle's laws of motion (Lloyd,
1964, p.61):

The 'laws' of motion which Aristotle proposes are not
utterly at variance with experience: rather, they
are hasty generalizations based on superficial
observations.

In general, it may be found that there are (Wasserstein,
1962, p.63)

more or less rudimentary survivals of conventionalist
and axiomatic ... attitudes even in empirical
scientists.

However, a consideration of the utility or appropriate-
ness of experiment and observation in different disciplines
(cf. Lloyd, 1964) is essential. The ample material
presented by Cohen and Drabkin in their manual in itself
vindicates their twin criteria as giving a legitimate, if
partial, view; although, as will be seen, this chapter
takes a much broader view of 'science' than theirs.

Greek science - like Greek philosophy, Greek history
and to a large extent Greek medicine - had its origin in
the all-embracing 'historia' of sixth-century Ionia. As
already stressed in the chapters on literature and
medicine, early Greek thinkers were innocent of any

compartmentalization of knowledge. Strabo's words
(1.2.8), 'the first investigators and physicists, recorders
of myths', express their inherent diversity in apt, almost
untranslatable, terms. The separate compilations FGH and
VS reflect in their titles different aspects of these
figures, many of whom, however, resist this neat modern
pigeonholing. Hekataios, for instance, although not
included in VS, is arguably as much 'philosopher' as
'historian'. The persistent underlying tradition of
universal 'historia' accounts for the title given by
Pliny to his compendium of knowledge in the first century
AD.

As was seen in the previous chapter, the Hippokratic
writers were at pains to isolate the 'techne' of medicine,
distinguishing it from other practical skills ('technai'
of a para-medical character, such as dream-interpretation)
and detaching it from theoretical 'historia'. In this,
their success was only partial. Despite the stern
insistence in the Corpus on specialization, and on the
twin disciplines, both dependent on meticulous attention
to observed detail, of diagnosis and prognosis, in certain
areas philosophical theory took precedence over medical
practice and threatened to vitiate progress. The study
of pathology was based on the theory of the humours. And
physiology was seen in terms of an equilibrium of the
body in health subject to disturbance in illness. Galen,
who in the second century AD crystallized ancient medical
thought, with a strong dependence on Hippokrates, into a
definitive expression still influential in the middle
ages, was philosopher and rhetorician as well as medical
man.

Medicine is usually accorded a place in modern works on
Greek science, while other practical 'technai' - useful
arts, technology - are not. The vast documentation of
the Hippokratic Corpus contrasts with the silence of the
literature of the classical period on contemporary
pragmatic advance and achievements. It was generally
recognized that man's mastery of 'technai' furthered
control over his environment and the related progress of
civilization. Poetic expressions of this process are to
be found in Aeschylus ('PV' 447-506) and Sophokles
('Ant.'332-75); both dramatists include medicine in
their reckoning of 'technai' ('PV' 478-83, 'Ant.'364-5).
It was also generally recognized that many 'technai' came
to Greece from the East; this is reflected in the non-
Greek names of 'inventors' and in mythical traditions of
intermediaries, such as Kadmos (cf. Barnett, 1956).

Chapter 2, outlining the natural resources of the
islands, touched incidentally on the islanders' progressive
ability to exploit these. This progress depends on
'technai', foremost among them agriculture. Tools for
tilling the soil, then for treating foodstuffs, developed.
Equipment for hunting animals and catching fish, then for
the management of livestock, was discovered. Such
progress is charted by archaeologists from the remains of
prehistoric meals, gleaned from the poems of Homer and
Hesiod and reconstructed from the work of later writers.
(Xenophon, the fourth-century author of a prose treatise
on hunting, shows a leisured aristocratic attitude to a
sport, but incidentally gives information about later
developments in hunting gear and tackle.)

In arid regions, some management of the water-supply
was imperative, either by conduits to bring the available
water from the hills to the coast (where most of the
villages were situated), or by cisterns to collect rain-
water. On this, the most pressing human need, there is
a great silence in the literature. An inscription from
Kameiros records public subscription for improved water-
supply (Jacopi, 1932). The first known water tunnel was
one constructed on Samos in the sixth century: since
the technology existed for its construction, the likelihood is that it was applied elsewhere also (cf. Landels,
1978, p.40). Athenaios records (3.123d, citing the
'Island History' of Semos of Delos) that on Kimolos,

> chilling pits are constructed in summer, where they
> deposit jars full of warm water and draw them out
> again as cold as snow.

That such enterprise was shown by the inhabitants of
small, insignificant Kimolos suggests that similar simple
devices for refrigeration were in use elsewhere. (Kimolos
was famed as a source for fuller's earth; possibly pits
originally dug for the extraction of this were later
utilized as cold stores?)

Culinary expertise was allied with the preservation
and conservation of foodstuffs: drying fruit in the sun,
pickling fish in salt, extracting oil from olives, allowing
wine to mature. Clothing depended on tanning, weaving
and dyeing. Shelter - beyond the cave-dwelling level -
required tree-planting and timber-felling operations, or
stone quarrying. The skills of the islanders were
adequate not only for these day-to-day needs, but far
beyond, with 'useful arts' shading into 'technology'.

A considerable building technology lies behind the
erection of temples, often on a steep outcrop of rock,
with the transport of marble and limestone from quarry to
building site, the working of these raw materials and

their final elevation into a precise prearranged position.
Such skills are not the subject of comment in extant
literary sources. The erection of the Kolossos of Rhodes,
a bronze figure many times life size, which was stable
enough to withstand storms and gales for over fifty years
before collapsing in a violent earthquake, was an ambitious
and complex undertaking; but the statue was admired more
as a symbol of Rhodian power than as a technological feat.
Town-planners, such as the architect who laid out on a
grid plan the new city of Rhodes, founded by synoecism in
the last decade of the fifth century (possibly Hippodamos
who had been responsible for the plan of the Peiraieus
earlier in his career; but cf. Wycherley, 1962, p.17;
Ward-Perkins, 1974, pp.15-16 and fig.13) were admired for
the pleasing aspect of their creations, not for their
activity as civil engineers.

The Greeks - above all the Athenians and Rhodians -
were as skilled at shipbuilding as the Romans were in the
construction of roads and bridges. The famous fleet of
Hellenistic Rhodes was built in local shipyards (cf.
Casson, 1960, p.153). Smaller craft too plied between
the islands, or from village to village on the same
island: most habitation was on the coast and the sea-
route would be the normal one (cf. Casson, 1974, pp.66-72).
Transport overland lagged behind communications by sea
(as it still does in the more remote islands of Greece).

Skills in mining and metallurgy developed: silver was
mined (notably at Laureion in Attica and on the island
of Siphnos) and even small states struck their own coins.
In workshops all over Greece - typically manned by a free
owner and his family, assisted by their squad of slaves -
goods ranging from shields to musical instruments were
manufactured. The crafts of the potter, the sculptor and
the carpenter were all highly developed, as were
techniques of ivory-carving, gem-working, metal inlay
and other decorative arts. Like the supreme 'techne' of
medicine, humbler 'technai' were generally passed from
father to son. Expertise was acquired by listening and
looking, not by studying manuals. Craftsmen, however
skilled and mentally alert, were for the most part
illiterate, while the literate élite were uninterested
in or - at a later period - snobbish about manual work.

The anonymous writer of the Sophokles 'Vita' repudiated
the assertions of earlier biographers that Sophokles'
father had been a bronzesmith, carpenter or cutler,
offering as his own view, evidently formulated to endow
the family with respectability, the exoneration that
Sophillos had owned slaves active in such occupations.
Aristotle unselfconsciously described slaves as 'living

tools' ('EN' 1161b4). However, the reason traditionally
given for the failure of the Greeks to take an interest in
technology - the availability of slave labour to perform
routine tasks - is of very limited validity (cf. Edelstein,
1952, for a detailed refutation of this view, most
eloquently propounded by Farrington, 1944).

No one has accused the Romans, who also owned slaves,
of a lack of interest in technology. Indeed, the Greek
technological achievement, vis-à-vis the Roman, tends to
be underrated. It is often overlooked that the Greeks
laid the foundations on which the Romans built. It is
perhaps the silence in the literature which leads to this
somewhat distorted view: the artefacts have to stand as
their own record. (Cf. Cohen and Drabkin, 1948, p.182,
'It is to be remembered, however, that our best sources
for the technological applications are not literary but
archaeological'.)

Less tangible practical achievements were those in
time measurement. Rudimentary water-clocks, constructed
on the same principle as the egg-timer, were in use in
the Attic lawcourts of the fourth century. The sundial
was perfected in Alexandria in the first century BC (cf.
Dicks, 1970, p.174, expressing doubts on the validity of
the claim that Anaximander had achieved this already in
the sixth century). Greek states long used their own
individual, often idiosyncratic, calendar systems.
Attempts made by Meton, working in Athens in the mid fifth
century, to harmonize the lunar and solar year were
improved upon by later writers; but standardization was
slow to come.

The emergence of medicine as a 'techne' in its own
right was not immediately accompanied by the emergence
of other scientific fields. In part, this is because
there were no professional groups of scientific specialists
(in astronomy, physics, etc.) with the social prestige
and financial independence which doctors could command.
To doctors, their 'techne' was their livelihood; other
'scientists' were not following science for a living, but
had private means or other employment. This remained
true till the Hellenistic era, when royal patronage
brought about some change in the situation.

Like medicine, other 'sciences' began in sixth-century
Miletos; unlike doctors, other 'scientists' did not fight
to emancipate themselves from 'historia'. Scientific
'historia' began with Thales, regarded as pioneer and
innovator by Aristotle and Eudemos. Thales was a natural
philosopher in the sense that he theorized about the

nature, 'physis', of the universe, attempting to define
its primeval 'stuff', which he regarded as 'moisture'.
He was also a mathematician and astronomer, later credited,
probably undeservedly, with having predicted the solar
eclipse of 585 BC (cf. Dicks, 1970, p.43; also pp.174,
225 n.45, dismissing the alleged prediction as 'out of
the question').

Further attempts to isolate the essential underlying
material of the world led to a sceptical reaction against
this simplistic monism and to more metaphysical world
philosophies (cf. the comments of 'Hippokrates' on
Melissos, cited in the previous chapter). The ensuing
Eleatic position - enunciated by Parmenides - that Being
is a spherical unity, not susceptible to change, had a
great philosophical future, but was scarcely calculated
to advance scientific thought. Meantime, in the west
Greek world, Pythagoras and the Pythagoreans pursued
studies which combined geometry, number theory and
religious mysticism. Both Pythagoreans and Eleatics
exercised a profound influence on Plato (cf. Raven, 1948
and, in general, Lloyd, 1970, pp.16-49).

The fifth-century sophists abandoned theorizing about
natural phenomena, turning to human and social problems.
However, in promoting politics, ethics, rhetoric and
semantics they did not entirely abandon the sciences.
Astronomy and mathematics were part of the curriculum
taught by many sophists. Hippias prided himself on his
virtuosity, teaching mathematics, astronomy and music
as well as practical handicrafts (Pl.'Hp.Mi.'368a-e).
Conversely, Demokritos the 'atomist' of the fifth century
(whose theory has at first sight a deceptive modern air)
wrote on ethics, linguistics and painting as well as on
physiology (where, as was seen in the previous chapter,
his views influenced 'Hippokrates'), also on geography
and mathematics (cf. Guthrie, 1965, II p.388).

Plato, absorbed in ethics and metaphysics, stressed
also the educational importance of mathematics and
astronomy, in both 'Republic' and 'Laws'. Plato's own
interest in harmonics and astronomy lay in the construction of theoretical models, in an 'ideal' study rather
than one based on real observed phenomena ('R'528e etc.):
thus, it is assumed in 'Timaios' that the movement of the
planets is orderly, uniform and circular. Despite this
speculative bias, which has led to the charge that he was
'anti-physical' (Landels, 1978, p.187), Plato was ahead
of his time in two fundamental ideals: the scientific
concept that natural phenomena might be understood by the
application of mathematics, and the visionary political
idea of state support for research projects.

The belief in perfect circular motion of the heavenly
bodies died hard. Eudoxos, a younger contemporary of
Plato, propounded a complex astronomical system, explaining planetary motion in terms of concentric spheres.
(Neugebauer, 1957, p.152 questions the influence of Plato
on Eudoxos; for a detailed discussion, see Dicks, 1970,
pp.151-89.)

Meantime, something of an educational controversy
developed between Isokrates, who stressed the value of
literary teaching rooted in rhetoric, and Plato, who
advocated rather mathematics and astronomy. However,
this is far from a modern dichotomy between 'two cultures',
and Plato and Isokrates had much in common; in popular
parlance, the terms 'philosophos', 'sophistes' or 'rhetor'
were equally applicable to both (cf. Chapter 5).

Aristotle, originally a pupil of Plato, was more of a
'scientist' than his teacher. Aristotle reacted against
the more abstract metaphysical speculations of Plato -
in particular, the theory of the 'forms' - but maintained
an interest in ethical, literary and historical questions.
In astronomy, he adhered to the theory of perfect circular
motion, failing here to throw off philosophical pre-
conceptions (the circle being the 'perfect' shape, and
so alone appropriate to the heavens). Aristotle's own
forte was biology, where his descriptive studies,
especially in entomology, record minutely detailed
observations.

A treatise preserved in Aristotle's works ('Mechanika',
see Hett, ed., 1936) raises many general problems of
mechanics, in an attempt - rare in extant sources - to
reach an improved understanding of everyday physical
situations by applied mathematics. The questions posed
include that of why rowers in the middle of a ship
contribute most to its propulsion, why dentists find the
extraction of teeth easier with forceps than with fingers,
and why it is easier to maintain objects in motion than
to start them from rest.

Aristotle's work in the Lyceum benefited from the
benevolent interest of Alexander and of the Macedonian
court. The conquests and explorations of Alexander,
opening up vast tracts of the East to contact with the
Greek world, gave a new impetus to such studies as
geography, ethnology, botany and zoology. The Peripatetics
rose to this challenge with Aristotle's projected
encyclopaedia of world knowledge (cf. Chapter 5). Also,
there began, around this time, a more steady infiltration
into Greek thought of Babylonian ideas in mathematics and
astronomy.

When Alexandria, founded in 331, began to rival Athens

as an intellectual centre, there was some polarization
of scholarly interests. Specialization made a belated
appearance, and a new rigour featured in studies of all
kinds. Athens maintained its well-established philosophical traditions, while Alexandria developed critical
scholarship (editorial and philological work); also
mathematics and astronomy. Patronage assisted researchers
in both the arts and the sciences: leading specialists
in different fields were courted by monarchs seeking a
vicarious prestige from their achievements.

Royal support was not always entirely disinterested.
Developments in war technology stemmed from investment in
armaments research. Appian's accounts of the Mithridatic
and Syrian Wars contain descriptions of the various types
of siege-engines and war machinery used (for instance,
the 'sambuke', described 'Mith.'26; or the long-handled
braziers invented for naval warfare by Pausimachos of
Rhodes early in the second century, 'Syr.'24).

Alexandrian science drew on the accumulated expertise
of both Lyceum and Academy. It may be conjectured that
a more direct line of influence can be drawn from the new
Peripatetic foundation of Eudemos in Rhodes, and that
Eudemos' mathematical work shaped the later intellectual
life of the capital no less decisively than the philological and literary skills of Philitas or the medical
teaching of Praxagoras. It is very possible that Eudemos'
histories of mathematics and astronomy, in themselves
unoriginal descriptive works of synthesis, provided the
springboard for the original researches of the third
century, the golden age of Alexandrian science. Proklos,
writing a commentary on Euclid in the fifth century AD,
cites Eudemos, with Theaitetos, in the preface, evidently
regarding their collections of theorems as groundwork
for Euclid's definitive work.

Euclid (who seems to have gone to Alexandria in the
first wave of immigrants, perhaps around 300 BC) wrote
on optics and astronomy as well as on mathematics.
Aristarchos of Samos, famed as the first astronomer to
form the hypothesis that the earth orbited the sun, not
vice versa, also worked in Alexandria. (Aristarchos no
more 'anticipated' Copernicus than Demokritos did Dalton:
he offered some reasons for his view, but was far from
proposing a coherent and reasoned system.) Earlier,
Herakleides, a pupil of Aristotle, had argued that some
of the planets orbited the sun, without including the
earth among them. Later astronomers reverted to the
geocentric view of the universe. (See Edelstein, 1952,
pp.591-2, arguing against the view of Farrington, 1944,
that political or religious pressures and prejudices

militated against the adoption of a heliocentric system;
also Lloyd, 1973, pp.57-61.)

Archimedes of Syracuse probably spent some years in
Alexandria in the middle of the third century; certainly,
he was in correspondence with Alexandrian scientists. He
himself made spectacular advances in geometry and
mechanics. Around the same time, Eratosthenes made his
mark in astronomy and mathematical geography, as did
Apollonios (originally from Pamphylian Perge) in the
field of geometry, particularly conic sections. (See
Heath, 1921, II; PA I pp.399-422; also Lloyd, 1973,
pp.33-52.)

After the great flowering of genius in the third century,
Alexandria declined as a centre of scientific research.
To some extent this is attributable to the withdrawal
from scientists of Ptolemaic munificence, to some extent
it is due to a deterioration in local conditions - an
unsettled political situation with sporadic urban unrest.
The growth of rival establishments at Pergamum, Rhodes
and Smyrna is also a significant factor. Of these,
Rhodes rose to great heights in the second and first
centuries. The importance of Rhodes at this time is seen
incidentally in the regular practice of measuring
distances relative to Rhodes and Alexandria; and in
the use of its latitude and longitude as a frame of
reference. Dikaiarchos regarded the world as divisible
in two parts by a line of longitude passing through
Rhodes; Eratosthenes gave the island a similar prominence
(cf. Aujac, 1966, pp.190-200). Also, Mount Atabyros was
one of the first mountains of which the height was
measured.

It is against this background that Hipparchos settled
in Rhodes around 162. (On Hipparchos, see Manitius, ed.,
1894; Heath, 1921, II pp.253-60; Neugebauer, 1945,
1950; Dicks, 1960; also, more generally, Lloyd, 1973,
pp.67-72.) Hipparchos was born at Nikaia in Bithynia, a
Greek town on the south coast of the Black Sea, where he
began his work on astronomy and mathematics, work with a
wide sweep, embracing astrology and mathematical geography.
Such studies had long been prosecuted in the region:
Aristotle taught at Assos for several years in his youth,
Herakleides came from the Black Sea area and Eudoxos of
Knidos also worked there for a time.

Other intellectual centres - Antioch, Pergamum and
Smyrna - were nearer than Rhodes to Hipparchos' original
home, and it would be interesting to know what drew this
astronomer to Rhodes. The island presumably had some kind

of 'observatory', with rudimentary equipment and, at the least, 'sight lines' to attract Hipparchos in the first place. Hipparchos' work in Rhodes spans some forty years, 162 to 126: it encompasses observations made there in those years. There is some evidence of observational astronomy conducted also in Kos: Dositheos, in the time of Archimedes, worked there, according to Ptolemy ('Phas.', ed. Heiberg, II pp.66-7) and the astrological activity of Berossos (discussed below) presupposes observations.

Hipparchos is best known for his commentary, which is extant, on the 'Phainomena' of Aratos, also extant: a critical work on this important and influential poem. Many short citations from Hipparchos' other works, which are themselves lost, may be culled from such later writers as the geographer Strabo and the astronomer Ptolemy. The 'Phainomena', written about 276 BC at the Macedonian court of Antigonos Gonatas, was based on the work of Eudoxos of Knidos, of around a century earlier. Immediately popular and widely disseminated, the poem long continued to attract commentators, translators (including Cicero) and imitators (including Vergil, in 'Georgics').

Hipparchos' commentary, a critical assessment of Aratos' interpretation of Eudoxos' views, is dedicated to a friend and protégé, Aischrion, and, though clearly intended for general circulation, written in an epistolary format. Hipparchos begins (1.1):

It was with pleasure that I saw from your letter your perseverance in an inclination to study.... It is on the topics covered by Aratos in his 'Phainomena' that I have now set myself to write to you, expounding in full everything he says, well or ill. From this, all will be clear to you, especially your difficulties.

A little later, he explains (1.5):

I decided, for the sake of your wish to learn, and for the general benefit of others, to record the mistakes he seems to me to have made.

Hipparchos is conventionally designated 'the greatest astronomer of antiquity' (Heath, 1921, II p.253; cf. Neugebauer, 1956, p.292). But, on closer scrutiny, the assessment of his achievement is problematical, in relation to the work of predecessors to whom he is indebted, and of successors who used his records, notably Ptolemy, writing in the second century AD. Broadly speaking, Ptolemy is to Hipparchos as Galen is to Hippokrates: Ptolemy distilled ancient astronomical findings much as Galen distilled those of medicine. But, whereas the relationship between Hippokrates and Galen is well documented, in Galen's (extant) commentaries on (extant) Hippokratic writings, the extent of Ptolemy's debt to his predecessors is much less clear.

Hipparchos is generally credited with the discovery of
the precession of the equinoxes, or with work which led
directly to this discovery; but some have attributed this
rather to the Babylonian Kidenas (Kidinnu), some 250 years
earlier. (See Neugebauer, 1950 for a lucid account of the
problem, rejecting Babylonian priority; also Neugebauer,
1945.) The question of the date and extent of the
infiltration into Greece of eastern astronomical - and
astrological - lore is very open, and likely to remain so
in the future. The Babylonian Berossos, a predecessor of
Hipparchos, who settled in Kos around 270 BC, is often
described as a key figure in the process of transmission,
on the basis of the statement in Vitruvius ('de Arch.'
9.6.2; cf. Cumont, 1912, p.56; Neugebauer, 1957, p.157):
    It was Berossos who settled in the island state of
    Kos and was first to open a school of astrology there.
(Berossos also wrote on Babylonian history, dedicating
his work to Antiochos I.) Mutual interaction, perhaps
competition, between Greek and oriental astronomers
obscures the chronological picture. Indisputable Greek
influences on Hipparchos are those of Apollonios,
Timocharis and - especially - Eratosthenes, working in
Alexandria.

    Hipparchos also compiled a catalogue of fixed stars,
which was extensively used by Ptolemy in the 'Almagest'.
Here, much depends on one's assessment of Ptolemy's
originality and objectivity in using the earlier material,
which is lost and cannot be assessed in its own right.
Hipparchos' contribution to the improvement of the
instruments available for astronomical observations is
less controversial: he modified the 'dioptra', a
sighting and measuring rod, and possibly also utilized
an astrolabe (see Dicks, 1954; also Heath, 1921, II
p.256 and Lloyd, 1973, pp.67-9).

    In geography, Hipparchos' ideal was to establish, by
careful astronomical observation, 'klimata', narrow
belts of latitude within which such phenomena as the
length of the longest day and the height of the celestial
north pole were effectively the same. He himself
conducted observations and collected data towards the
construction of such a world model; his empirical
approach and willingness to collaborate are striking
features of this work. However, Hipparchos' ambitious
and visionary scheme was only very sketchily realized.
The interest in the world generated by the conquests and
explorations of the age persisted, but found its
expression in descriptive rather than mathematical terms
(cf. Dicks, 1960, pp.154-64 on fr.39).

    Hipparchos was extravagantly praised by Pliny ('HN'
2.26):

The same Hipparchos, who has never been highly
enough praised as the man who, more than any other,
demonstrated the kinship of the stars with humanity
and that our souls are part of the heavens, discovered
a new and different star, which came into existence in
his own day.

Strabo too is complimentary, remarking (1.2.1):

Since it is not worth while to have a philosophical
exchange with everybody, but it is desirable to do so
with Eratosthenes, Hipparchos, Poseidonios, Polybios
and other men of this calibre.

Strabo's choice of verb ('philosophein') is a reminder
that all kinds of intellectual activity - including
geography - might still be grouped under this general
head. Also, the achievements for which Pliny commends
Hipparchos are as much philosophical as scientific.
(It may be added that scientists still frequently couched
their works in verse, as Aratos did his 'Phainomena'.
Archimedes and Eratosthenes, no less than the pre-
Sokratic Empedokles, were poets of distinction; the
Roman Lucretius followed in their footsteps.)

Strabo couples Hipparchos with Poseidonios in a further
passage (8.1.1):

Others, contributing to the sphere of physics and
mathematics, added certain considerations of this
nature, such as Poseidonios and Hipparchos.

Hipparchos was in fact a contemporary of Panaitios, and
so a good deal older than Poseidonios; both are important
influences on Strabo.

Poseidonios was philosopher first and scientist second.
(On Poseidonios, see Edelstein and Kidd, 1972; Laffranque,
1964, with a useful bibliography, pp.549-60.) Prefacing
the edition of the fragments, Kidd remarks (p.xxi):

in deciding the order of the fragments I have reminded
myself that Poseidonios was first and foremost a Stoic
philosopher. So after some general fragments on the
divisions and content of philosophy, follow the three
great categories of Stoic philosophy: physics, ethics,
logic.

Fragments on scientific subjects are then arranged under
the heads of mathematics, mathematical geography, tides
and hydrology, seismology, geology and mineralogy,
geography; fragments on history and the history of
philosophy complete the collection.

The collection of fragments somewhat resembles a
cleverly stitched patchwork: the pieces are individually
interesting and make up a harmonious whole, but, inevitably,
give little impression of their purpose and import in
their original setting. The problem of reconstructing

Poseidonios' thought is peculiarly acute because, while
his influence is clearly apparent in those writers who
quote him directly, it seems, in addition, to lurk, half-
hidden, in many others (see Kidd, p.xiii).

Poseidonios not only wrote on widely diverse subjects,
but also accorded each a treatment of wide scope. Thus,
it is clear from Strabo's quotations that geography for
Poseidonios embraced the subject in all its aspects. It
is easy to see why Galen regarded Poseidonios as the
'most learned of the Stoics' (Edelstein and Kidd T84 =
'de placitis Hippocratis et Platonis' 8.652).

Poseidonios' theory of the tides may be singled out as
an example at once of his strength and his weakness; it
also illustrates a tendency endemic in Greek observational
science (Edelstein and Kidd F 218 and 219; cf. Sandbach,
1975, pp.131-2). At Gades (modern Cadiz), Poseidonios
observed that the ebb and flow of the tide was connected
with the waxing and waning of the moon, with the highest
tides at full and new moon, the lowest at half moon.
From this, he went on to theorize - mistakenly, on
insufficient evidence, wrongly interpreted - that there
was a similar yearly cycle, with peaks at the solstices
and lows at the equinoxes. In the connection between the
phases of the moon and the movements of the sea, he found
evidence of the unifying cosmic sympathy in which he
believed. Here, Poseidonios - like Hipparchos - was
relying on data collected by personal research, and
making a commendable scientific attempt to collate these
with the findings of other investigators, in this case,
the observations of Seleukos at the Red Sea. However,
the intellectual curiosity and swift insight of
Poseidonios exceed his patience in making and acumen in
interpreting observations. The general Greek tendency
to leap from objective facts to subjective theory is
also apparent.

In the first century, an age of easy travel, Athens,
Rhodes and Rome were the main centres of science and
scholarship. Geminos, an important mathematician and
astronomer of this era, worked, like Poseidonios (who was
possibly his teacher) in various regions. (On Geminos,
see Aujac, ed., 1975; also Heath, 1921, II pp.222-34
and Dicks, DSB V pp.344-7.) His work mentions Rome and
Alexandria as well as Rhodes; there is some reason to
believe it was written for a Roman public (Aujac, ed.,
1975, p.lxxxix). The name Geminos, Roman rather than
Greek, has led to speculation that he was a Roman
freedman or even a slave. His date is also uncertain;
some would put him in the first century AD, not the first
BC. At any rate, 100 BC to AD 100 are the outer limits,

as he abbreviated Poseidonios, and is himself mentioned
by Alexander of Aphrodisias (Aujac, ed., 1975, p.xix):
around 70 BC is generally held to be the most probable
date for his scientific activity.

Citations in Proklos and other late mathematical
writers provide evidence that Geminos wrote extensively,
and authoritatively, on mathematical studies. However,
it is his 'Introduction to Astronomy' which has survived
intact. Dealing with fundamental questions in astronomy
and mathematical geography, this may have been intended
for circulation among 'students'. Geminos' expository
style is limpid. For instance, the section on the moon
begins with a clear, brief statement of the salient
points, before proceeding to details (9.1):

The moon receives its light from the sun; for it
always has its bright part turned towards the sun.
There is also a very lucid account of the problems
encountered in Greek attempts to regulate the calendar,
correlating solar year with lunar month, combined with a
palmary explanation of the religious considerations
which rendered regulation a desideratum (8.6-7). When
Geminos expresses his disagreement with others' views,
whether the mistaken ideas of earlier astronomers (7.18,
on the rise of certain constellations) or the naive
notions of laymen (17.1, on weather forecasting by the
stars), it is in tones of quiet scientific reasonableness,
without undue polemic.

In the last century BC and the first AD, a retrospective
spirit can be discerned in the work of philosophers and
scientists, a half-conscious summing-up of past achievements at the start of a new era. Geminos' compilation is
one product of this ambiance; another is the medical
encyclopaedia of Celsus. The same spirit lives on in
Galen and Ptolemy.

The cultivated public of Rome now had the accumulated
scientific knowledge of Greece in its grasp. The main
bridge between Greece and Rome was probably Poseidonios,
with his outstanding ability to synthesize and summarize
Greek thought for Roman readers. In the immediately
following centuries under the Empire, we see a dissemination of Greek scientific knowledge, but little new
development. Philosophy, literature and - especially -
rhetoric were elaborated, but not science. Abstract
scientific endeavour had scant appeal for the practical
Romans (cf. Landels, 1978, p.186). Pure mathematics, a
favourite Greek study, declined, while medicine remained
popular and applied science and technology came into its
own.

Roman attitudes of the early empire may be seen in

Pliny's 'Natural History'. Erudite, much travelled, but
essentially uncritical, Pliny produced a work treating a
multitude of topics including cosmology, geography,
medicine, biology and mineralogy. In this, he used
Greek sources extensively, but added little, either in
information or in interpretation, to any of them.
Meantime, Rhodes, earlier the adopted home of Hipparchos
and Poseidonios, now offered hospitality to expatriate
Romans, and, trimming her sails to the wind, specialized
in the teaching of rhetoric.

Part III
Religion

7 Myths

In this chapter, myths are regarded as stories believed
to relate to the distant past, having gods as well as
humans as their subject; mythology as a grouping of these
stories into a more or less coherent scheme; legends as
mythical stories about a particular place or person;
folk-tales as fictional stories told for amusement or
edification.

Modern interest in myth has been considerable (see
Kirk, 1970 for a valuable balanced review of past work;
also 1972, 1974). However, the Greeks' own views have of
late been rather disregarded. The Greeks viewed their
myths (that is, what are generally now called 'myths')
simply as early history, a record of events in the remote
past, at a time when gods and men rubbed shoulders.
Herodotos makes a revealing distinction between the
thalassocracy of Minos and Polykrates' ambitions in
'human times'. Similarly, Demosthenes, having mentioned
an ancient tradition that the court of the Areopagos
was used to settle disputes in which the gods were
involved, continues, 'But these are ancient affairs;
other things happened later' (Hdt.3.122; D.23.66;
cf. Arist.'Po.'1451b15).

Myths were not, of course, universally accepted as
true and immutable: creative writers must always have
been conscious of manipulating mythical material,
sometimes drastically, for their own literary or dramatic
purposes (cf. Craik, 1979); critical writers - including
the historians - did not pass on the myths untouched, but
doctored them for greater verisimilitude. Herodotos and
Thucydides both prefaced their histories with surveys of
the remote past, based on myths; their predecessor
Hekataios explicitly said that myths were 'many and absurd'
and made some tentative attempts to rationalize them
(FGH I fr.1; cf. 19, 27). In addition, oral tradition

was constantly at work: current myths might be revamped,
or new ones invented, to gratify chauvinism or to explain
or justify particular practices, especially in cult and
ritual.

Strabo has a perspicacious discussion of myth (1.2.7-9),
stating that Homer expounds myths more accurately than
later writers;   that myth is utilized by poets, states
and lawgivers aware of its persuasive force;   that
mythology has won a place in the social and political
scheme of life as well as in the history of facts.   Strabo
shows himself aware of the essential character of Greek
myths (that is, history, which may be told more or less
accurately) and alive to their pervasive importance in
culture and society.

Modern interest in myth has lain partly in demonstrating
its universality, by amassing and analysing sociological
parallels from different parts of the world.   This aspect
of myth rarely concerns us here, apart from occasional
analogies with Near Eastern motifs: most local myths
have direct reference to local places, practices and
beliefs.   Another question, more germane to the present
enquiry, concerns the relationship between myth and ritual.

Some myths are patently connected with ritual;   others
may be suspected of having such connections;   still others
are clearly unconnected with cults.   Where a connection
does exist, it is often difficult to explain it fully.
To put the question crudely, the myth may be earlier than,
later than or contemporaneous with the foundation of the
cult or inception of the ritual with which it is associated.
In the first case, a cult may have been initiated as a
result of a prevailing local story (for example, a story
of combat between two deities, with the victor requiring
commemoration);   of the second, aetiological myths provide
an example (myths invented to explain or justify unusual
rituals, of which the true origin is unknown);   in the
third case, there is a parallelism between ritual act
and ritual words.   The part allegedly played by gods and
heroes in events can be seen in some cases as foreshadowing
later cult practices and beliefs, in others as indicative
of the type of story later ages thought it worth while to
invent and propagate.

However, to a large extent, the question of connections
and categorization remains hypothetical.   Information
about myths can rarely be dovetailed with information
about ritual.   The information comes from two entirely
different types of source: literary and inscriptional,
full and allusive (as even the local chroniclers seem
prolix alongside the baldness of inscriptions).   Also,
inexactitude about time and place is common.   More

important - the modern preoccupation with the nature of
the link between myth and religion would have seemed
strange to the Greeks. Naturally myths were often about
the gods, who took an active part in the events of the
remote past; naturally therefore they often reflected or
affected ritual practices. In general, the modern
dichotomy between sacred and secular was not felt to
exist (cf. Chapter 9).

The relationship between myth and history was always
complex and is often now inscrutable, but few would deny
that some relationship exists. It is in areas rich in
legend that the main Bronze Age settlements have been
uncovered (Nilsson, 1932, p.28). Even sceptics concede
that in many legends lies a kernel of historical truth,
while arguing that layers of fantastic accretion make
this irrecoverable. Ancient writers were themselves aware
that these layers existed; but whereas they relied on
pure reason to strip them off - to accept, adapt or
occasionally reject myths - we now have external aids in
this process. Our view of Bronze Age Greece is much
wider than was that of the Greeks of the classical period:
they relied perforce on the fitful illumination shed on
the past by legends, while we can check this traditional
material in the light of archaeology, with some help from
philology.

Study of the Bronze Age is primarily the province of
the archaeologist, and it would be rash to elevate
'evidence' from myth to take precedence over archaeological
data; that is why discussion of myths has been postponed
to this point, rather than included in Chapter 3. It is,
however, fair to review myths from different literary
sources, and check them against the picture presented by
archaeology. That is one purpose of the present chapter;
the other is to adumbrate the background against which the
cults developed.

Archaeological evidence imposes its own limitations:
it can tell us about the arrival (or invention) of new
artefacts or techniques, and about contacts between areas
of settlement - but little about the nature of these
contacts. Myths, on the other hand, do provide information
about the nature of contacts - friendly or hostile,
sporadic or intensive, short lived or long lasting - but
they may or may not reflect the truth. The names given
to characters and places in myths often help too to build
up a coherent picture of prehistoric communications.

Some myths are of more value than others as sources
for Greek prehistory. To some extent, this is due to
variation in the trustworthiness or acumen of the writers
recording them; but in addition to this, some kinds of

myths are immediately suspect as late inventions: myths
incorporating folk-tale motifs, myths which are transparent
patriotic distortions, some aetiological myths, myths
about people with 'significant' names. In genealogies -
while something can usually be salvaged - chronological
exactitude cannot be expected, and some names in the list
may be inventions. However, events and influences can
often be glimpsed in allegorical or symbolical representations; linguistic affinities and influences can be traced.
     Cult-titles, especially the unusual or unique, are
often explained by myths. Myths are of most value where
the cult-title is obliquely rather than directly explained,
where it is incidental to and not the focal point of a
story, where the aetiology is not blatant. Such cult-
titles often provide valuable clues to the origins and
early orientation of cults.
     The sources for the myths of the islands are diverse.
The Homeric evidence, already discussed in Chapter 3, will
concern us again later in this chapter. Early epic of the
islands on the subject of Herakles is almost completely
lost, and with it perhaps clues to odd features in the
cult of Herakles in Rhodes and Kos, or to the use of the
crab as emblem of Herakles on Koan coins (cf. Chapter 5).
Pindar's ode for Diagoras of Rhodes ('O'7) makes typically
extensive and idiosyncratic use of myth, including an
aetiological account of the cult of Athena at Lindos.
This too is discussed later in the chapter. Other sources
are Hellenistic or Roman. Lateness in a source does not
in itself entail unreliability. Particularly where local
traditions are being recorded, one cannot discount the
possibility of oral narrative surviving from the remote
past.
     The rash of Hellenistic compilations on local history
and antiquities (providing much material for Pausanias'
more wide-ranging work in the second century AD) has been
mentioned in connection with literary trends (Chapter 5).
Several wrote on specialized topics, including cult-
practices. The loss of the treatise on cult-titles
('Epikleseis') by Sokrates of Kos is particularly to be
regretted; one may conjecture that its scale was
comparable with the work of Apollodoros on Athenian cult-
titles, but the one extant excerpt conveys only the bizarre
information that, according to Sokrates, Dionysos invented
'spitted bread' (toast?) on campaigns (Ath.3.111b). The
names of many Rhodian antiquarians are known from the
Lindian Chronicle, itself an important source for the
myths of Rhodes. The first names in the list of dedications which purports to go back to remote antiquity are:
Lindos, the Telchines, Kadmos, Minos and Herakles. This

epigraphical document provides a corollary to the history
of Zenon, best known of the chroniclers because he was
used extensively by Diodoros writing about Rhodes.

Diodoros' version of the early history of Rhodes is the
most full ancient account extant. In what follows here,
Diodoros' account is used as a starting-point for a
discussion of myths in relation to history on the one
hand and to cults on the other; material from the other
islands is adduced where appropriate. It is difficult
to hold a high opinion of Diodoros' critical acumen and
selectiveness in his treatment of Rhodes: inconsistencies
suggest that he used his sources indiscriminately and
there is no indication that he suspected them of
patriotic prejudice. All is presented as historical fact.
But this ingenuousness may be an advantage: it is at
least as valuable to know what the Rhodian chroniclers
actually said as to have an ancient commentary on it.
Diodoros is insistent on the relative chronology of the
events he describes, prefacing the sections of his
narrative with such phrases as 'after this period'
(5.56.1, 57.3, 58.1, 58.2, 58.4, 59.1, 59.5). The events
may be summarized as follows: Rhodes was inhabited first
by the Telchines, then by the Heliadai, visited about
this time by Danaos and shortly afterwards by Kadmos,
then settled successively by Phorbas, son of Lapithes, by
Althaimenes from Crete and by Tlepolemos from Argos.
(The mention of Tlepolemos brings us down in time to the
Homeric record.)
    Strabo's statement that the Telchines made the scythe
of Kronos makes them ante-date the Olympian gods
(Str.14.2.7). In other stories, they are contemporary
with the young Zeus and Poseidon, or meet Aphrodite soon
after her genesis, as she journeys from Kythera to Cyprus.
Ancient writers are agreed on two things about the
Telchines, and these reflect probable conditions of the
Early Bronze Age. (Eusebios, for what it is worth,
placed their arrival in 1737 BC.)
    First, they were skilled craftsmen and metalworkers -
so skilled, indeed, as to have a reputation for 'sorcery'.
(With D.S.5.55.3 and Str.14.2.7, cf. the statement in
the Lindian Chronicle that the vessel dedicated by the
Telchines was of a material which 'no one could know'.)
It is possible that this reflects a folk-memory of a time
when skills in metalworking were being transmitted from
the Near East to Greece, and when the new craft of
metallurgy seemed like magic to those unfamiliar with its
techniques and even its raw materials. Rhodes, a stepping

stone in the transmission of this and other skills from
the Levant, is a natural place to find such a mythical
people; in other traditions, the Telchines are placed in
Crete and Cyprus, islands which have the same importance
as intermediary points. (Crete was hence called Telchinia,
St. Byz., just as Rhodes was known as Telchinis, Str.
14.2.7; Cyprus is their home, Paus.9.19.1; Crete,
Cyprus and Rhodes are all their domain, Nic.Dam.,FGH II
114.)

Second - according to implication rather than direct
statement - the Telchines were a seafaring people. This
may be deduced from their origin as children of Thalatta,
the name Halia given to their sister, who married
Poseidon, and from the story that the Telchines brought
up the young Poseidon, entrusted to them and to Kapheira,
daughter of Okeanos by Rhea. As noted in Chapter 3,
the prehistoric inhabitants of the Aegean were great
mariners.

In addition to the fact that the characteristics of
the mythical Telchines (skills in metalworking and seafaring) are plausible for an early Aegean people, it may
be that physical conditions of the Bronze Age are
reflected in these myths. The reason given for the
departure of the Telchines from Rhodes is that they
foresaw a coming flood. The great eruption at Thera in
about 1500 was probably preceded by a period of violent
seismic activity, affecting the whole region, and earthquakes may well have caused inundation of the islands by
tidal waves.

Similarly, myths of the battles of Poseidon, god of
earthquakes, may have arisen from a tradition of a series
of tremors in the remote past. Such myths attach not
only to Rhodes, where he supposedly fought with giants
who sprang up in the east of the island, and where he
buried his sons under the earth in fury after they had
been impelled by Aphrodite to sleep with their mother
Halia; but also to the islands Nisyros, said to be a
fragment of Kos hurled by Poseidon at the giant Polybotes;
and Karpathos, where the headlands Ephialteion and
Thoanteion were named after the giants Ephialtes and
Thoas (D.S.5.55.5, 7; Str.10.5.16; Apollod.1.62). Stories
of warring generations of gods are common features in
myths about the most remote past. Here there is some
confusion between Poseidon's enemies, the giants, and
his sons, who get the same treatment. It is suggestive
that Polybotes, his enemy, has a name the doublet of
Polyphemos, his son, the one-eyed Cyclops of the 'Odyssey';
both names mean 'much-shouting'. It may be relevant that
Poseidon was worshipped on Rhodes as Γυλαῖος, γυλός being

glossed by Hesychios as ἑτερόφθαλμος, 'one-eyed'.

The location in Rhodes of the myth of the birth and upbringing of Poseidon, entrusted by Rhea to the Telchines, closely parallels that in Crete of the birth and upbringing of Zeus, entrusted to the Kouretes. Among the cult-titles of Poseidon at Kameiros was Kyreteios, which must indicate connections with the Cretan Zeus. Strabo preserves a hint that the two stories were linked in antiquity:

> Some say that of the nine Telchines who lived in Rhodes
> those who accompanied Rhea to Crete and brought up Zeus
> there were given the name Kouretes

and he himself likens the Kouretes to such bands as Daktyloi and Telchines (Str.10.3.7, 19). The Cretan Daktyloi, like the Telchines, were skilled craftsmen, mentioned as workers in iron in the chronology of Thrasyllos (where the Telchines are not named).

There is parallelism too in the stories of their exploits: Poseidon battled against giants and Zeus was engaged in struggles against the Titans. A further coincidence is in Zeus' liaison in Crete with the nymph Himalia, whose name is suspiciously like that of Poseidon's Rhodian consort Halia (D.S.5.55.5; cf. Farnell, 1896, I p.47 on Zeus and Poseidon and see Paus.8.8.2 for a similar parallel, in Arkadia). Zeus Amalos, worshipped at Lindos, is another link in this chain of connections, if - as has been supposed - the title is connected with the goat Amaltheia, which suckled the young Zeus in Crete (IL 26; 'amalos' in Homer is applied to young animals, 'Il.'22.310; 'Od.' 20.14).

These resemblances in the myths of Zeus and Poseidon are unlikely to be fortuitous. Either we have rival stories, Rhodes attempting to compete with Crete, or - more probably - the two traditions are variants of the same story, doubtless of eastern origin, filtered through the different channels of Crete and Rhodes, and differentiated by the different divine names Zeus and Poseidon. This differentiation may be a later facet of the myth: some have argued that Poseidon originated as a particular manifestation of Zeus.

In Pindar's account, the island of Rhodes was created for Helios, who had been absent when the other gods received their spheres ('O'7; according to a scholiast, on line 54, the story is Pindar's own invention, though he attributes it to 'ancient tradition'). Pindar in effect telescopes Telchines and Heliadai: he attributes to the Heliadai the skill in craftsmanship which is usually associated with the Telchines, of whom he says nothing. Pindar tells of the marriage of Helios with the nymph Rhodos, the birth of seven sons, the Heliadai, and

then of three grandsons, Ialysos, Kameiros and Lindos.
In Pindar's genealogy, Rhodos is daughter of Poseidon and
Aphrodite;   in Diodoros of Poseidon and Halia and in
Apollodoros (as Rhode) of Poseidon and Amphitrite ('O'7.14;
D.S.5.55.4; Apollod.1.4.5). Lindos too is given differing
pedigrees: Strabo makes Lindos child of Danaos, and the
Lindian Chronicle makes Lindos precede the Telchines,
giving a local priority to the mythical state eponym. In
cult, Helios was regarded as 'archegos' or 'propator' of
the Rhodian people and, with Rhodos, received dedicatory
offerings.

Diodoros goes into more detail than Pindar: after the
cataclysm, the island was dried up by Helios (the physical
nature of the sun temporarily replacing the anthropomorphic
character), who married Rhodos, the only female child of
Poseidon and Halia and the only survivor among their seven
children. Rhodos and Helios in turn produced seven sons,
named as Ochimos, Kerkaphos, Makar, Aktis, Tenages, Triopas
and Kandalos; also a daughter, Elektryone. Seven, a
favourite number in folk-tale, is noticeably recurrent.

Diodoros continues his narrative with the departure from
Rhodes of four of the Heliadai, guilty of the murder of
their brother Tenages, leaving Ochimos and Kerkaphos behind.
The story is appropriate to the ethos of a later age:
exile following murder, especially of a relative, is a
common motif in legend and accords with heroic ideas of
vendetta and blood-guilt. The myth has evidently been
subject to accretion and elaboration, as the alleged
motive for the fratricide, envy, belongs to the literary
conventions of a later age (D.S.5.57.2). In this connection, it may be added that the marriage of Kydippe (later
Kyrbia), daughter of Ochimos and the nymph Hegetoria,
with her paternal uncle Kerkaphos is appropriate to the
social conditions of classical Athens, where such marriages
between close relatives - especially uncle and niece -
were sanctioned and even encouraged, with the object of
keeping property in the family. Plutarch tells the story
that Kydippe, betrothed to the hero Okridion, was obtained
in marriage by her uncle, who prevailed on the herald,
acting as intermediary, to bring her to him; hence,
heralds were forbidden entry to the Rhodian shrine of
Okridion (Plu.'Mor.'297 c-d).

The destinations of the Heliadai who left the island
are given as Lesbos (Makar), Kos (Kandalos), Egypt (Aktis,
who founded Heliopolis) and Karia (Triopas). The final
dispersal of the Heliadai, as of the Telchines, is
explained by Diodoros as due to a great flood. It may be
that this too can be related to the Theran catastrophe.
In support of this, it may be added that Diodoros regarded

the Heliadai as contemporary with the Athenian king
Kekrops, who is put by the Parian Marble in 1582. Of
course, this chronological evidence is tenuous, and
conclusions from it must be speculative, but it suggests
a tentative placing of the Heliadai in the middle of the
second millennium, around 1500 BC.

The account of Triopas colonizing Karia from Rhodes has
the air of a patriotic Rhodian invention. The evidence
is rather that most of the Dodekanese was at one time
inhabited by, or under the influence of, Karians (see
Chapters 3 and 4). Traditions of connections of Triopas
with Karia and Rhodes are persistent, but very confused
(cf. van Gelder, 1900, pp.33-9). The Triopian peninsula
on the coast of Asia Minor supposedly derived its name
from this hero, and Syme (according to Stephanos a Karian
island; cf. the place-name Symaithos in Karia) was
colonized by Triopas, accompanying Chthonios, son of
Poseidon (D.S.5.56.3-57.8; cf. Str.14.2.8). However,
Karia is sometimes given as his place of origin, not his
destination; Thessaly is further alleged as place of
origin (see below on connections between the islands,
especially Kos, and Thessaly).

Melos and Karia are linked in a story told by Plutarch
('Mor.'246d-247a; cf. Polyaen.8.64): after an expedition
of Nymphaios from the island to Karia, and settlement at
Kryassos, a Karian plot to kill the newcomers is foiled
by the Karian girl Kaphene, who has fallen in love with
Nymphaios. The story is permeated with elements of folk-
tale - love interest, trickery and betrayal - and
rendered suspect by such late elements as the oracle the
dictates of which are obeyed by the Melians (cf. below, on
the siege of Rhodian Achaia).

The claim of Diodoros' Rhodian sources that it was the
Telchinian Lykos who founded the temple of Apollo Lykeios
on the river Xanthos may be a chauvinistic representation
of the same kind as that of Triopas colonizing Karia
(D.S.5.56). Once again the evidence points to eastern
influence on Rhodes rather than the reverse process.
Early connections of Apollo with Lykia are clearly
attested, in the location of many important shrines in
that area, in the name of Apollo's mother Leto, equivalent
to Lykian 'lada', 'woman', and in the distinctive cult-
title Lykeios, whatever may be its initial significance.
A recurrent theme in Rhodian myth is of traffic between
Rhodes and Lykia, with the Telchines as intermediaries;
and the Apollo cult in Rhodes shows strong affinities with
the myths of the Telchines. It seems likely that distant
memories of Apollo's coming from the East to Greek lands
gave rise to these myths.

Diodoros records that there was an Apollo Telchinios at
Lindos, Hera Telchinia at Kameiros, Hera and the Nymphs
with this title at Ialysos. (The nymphs are a group
commonly associated with Apollo in cult, and particular
nymphs - Halia, Himalia, Rhodos, Syme - feature prominently
in accounts of the Telchines.) Athena Telchinia is also
recorded (Nic.Dam.,FGH II 114). Third-century epigraphical
evidence attests a cult of Apollo Mylantios at Kameiros.
Mylas is explained by Hesychios as one of the Telchines,
who was credited with the invention of the windmill;
protection and processing of the grain would be a natural
extension of the activities of Apollo as agrarian god.
Mylantia is also, however, given as a place-name of a
promontory in the territory of Kameiros (St.Byz.; cf.
Mylasa in Karia). Theoi Mylanteioi (gods of the windmill,
gods of the region Mylantia, or gods worshipped by Mylas)
are mentioned by lexicographers, and tentatively restored
in an inscription from the neighbourbood of Rhodos
(D.S.5.55.2; Hsch.s.v.Mylas; St.Byz.s.v.Mylantia and
Mylanteioi theoi).

The difficulty, in the case of the cult-title Mylantios,
of disentangling myth, place-name and semantics, is
repeated in many other cases. For instance, the common
title Lykeios may imply connections with the place Lykia,
with a mythical personage homonymous with the place, or
with 'lykos', 'wolf'. Again, the unusual Ixios, applied
to Apollo on Rhodes, presents similar questions. Is
Apollo Ixios simply Apollo worshipped at the place Ixos,
or does the place take its name from a title of Apollo?
What connection, if any, is there with mistletoe ('ixos'):
is Apollo Ixios a god of vegetation, or Ixos a place where
mistletoe flourished?

The cult-title Erethimios evinces another link,
involving Apollo, between Lykia and Rhodes. Strabo
mentions a Rhodian sanctuary of Apollo with the title
Erythibios, which he takes to mean 'protector from
mildew', and copious epigraphical evidence from Kameiros
confirms this literary testimony (Str.13.1.64). Inscriptions attest the importance of the cult, with an ample
temple personnel, a festival Erethimia and, in the
Hellenistic period, associations of Eretheibiazontes or
Erethimiazontes: the cult was not an insignificant
agrarian one, and had a long history, dating from the
fifth century (as the ruins of the temple suggest), or
even earlier, until the Roman period. (Some of these
inscriptions, the sanctuary and the neighbouring theatre
were discovered by Ross last century, and have now been
re-examined by Italian archaeologists: see Ross, 1840-5,
IV p.58; cf. II p.101; Newton, 1865, I p.238; Jacopi,

1929;   Kontorini, 1975b). Hesychios, however, glosses
Erethymios as a title of Apollo among the Lykians, with
a festival Erethymia.

Rhodian borrowing from the East is reflected further
in the names given to the Heliadai and the Telchines.
These are an amalgam of Greek names, some of the significant type (Aktis, 'ray of the sun', Makar, 'blessed one')
and of foreign names. In particular, the name Kapheira,
given to the daughter of Okeanos who helped the Telchines
bring up Poseidon, seems to mean simply 'Karian woman'
(cf. Kaphene in the story of Nymphaios from Melos) and
Kerkaphos - who is commemorated in inscriptions as father
of Lindos (IL 57, 274, 477) - is reminiscent of Karian
Gergas (Laumonier, 1958, p.677). The name Kandalos is
also of interest, as its -nd- formation is typical of
the alien substratum in the Greek language.

Makar, who here goes to Lesbos, is elsewhere Makareus
and gives his name to the 'Islands of the Blessed'
(D.S.5.81). It has been suggested that the name is
identical with Phoenician Melkarth. Meropis (described
by Theopompos as an imaginary land of wonders) was a
name given to Kos. In such terms as 'Islands of the
Blessed', 'Meropis' and 'Atlantis' may be seen folk
memories of a splendid Bronze Age past.

Strong traditions told of visits to Rhodes by Danaos, on
his way from Egypt to Argos, and of Kadmos, going from
Phoenicia to Thebes. There is a parallelism in the
stories: the daughters of Danaos founded the temple of
Athena at Lindos, while the priests of Poseidon at
Ialysos were descended from companions of Kadmos
(Apollod.2.1.4; D.S.5.58.1, 3; cf. Hdt.2.182;
Str.14.2.8; Lindian Chronicle III, citing Polyzelos as
source; on parallelism between Danaos and Kadmos, cf.
Thomson, 1949, p.379). There is no doubt about the
antiquity of Lindos as a cult-site: the unusual worship
practised there, without burnt sacrifice, was probably
taken over by the Dorians from earlier settlers, and
there are vestiges of a pre-Hellenic pillar-cult. Athena
is much associated with Rhodes in myth: on her birth,
Zeus showered gold on the Rhodians; Rhodes stood next to
Athens in the goddess' favour; Athena was the mother,
by Helios, of the Korybantes (a startling variation on her
usual status as a virgin goddess) (schol.Pi.'O'7; cf.
schol.A.R. 4.1310).

Islands to the west also had traditions of a visit by
Kadmos or Phoenician settlement. Kadmos stopped at Thera,
then called Kalliste, and built a temple to Poseidon and

Athena;   Anaphe was originally called Membliaros from
a son of Kadmos who remained in the area;   the early name
of Melos was Byblis, derived from its first inhabitants,
Phoenicians from Byblos (Hdt.4.147;   Paus.3.1.7;   schol.
Pi.'O'7;   St.Byz.s.v.Melos).

The linking in popular tradition of visits to Rhodes
by Kadmos and Danaos may be considered with information
set down in the Parian Marble.   The compiler places the
kings close in time, mentioning Rhodes in connection with
Danaos, but not in connection with Kadmos.   Kadmos'
arrival in Thebes is put in 1518 and Danaos' sacrifice on
Rhodes in 1510 (assigning a date 1255 and 1247 years
respectively before the archonship of Diognetos, 264/263).
There is no need to believe in a historical Kadmos,
founder of Thebes, or a historical Danaos with a bevy of
daughters to accept that there were contacts between the
continents at this period.   Egyptian documents of around
1365 BC refer to a people called 'Danuna', generally
identified as the Greeks, who are 'Danaoi' in Homer.
Also, the Theran frescoes provide striking evidence for
the presence of alien cultural elements in the Aegean by
around the middle of the second millennium (Marinatos,
1973;   cf. Poulianos, 1972;   Baumbach, 1973).   It is
arguable that the Kadmeioi were Phoenicians who reached
Greece by way of Crete some time in the Middle Minoan
period (Thomson, 1949, pp.376-7;   cf. Willetts, 1962,
p.157).

Another mythical traveller was Perseus, the son of
Danae (an exiled princess of the Danaid family), who
came from Ethiopia to Argos and Tiryns via the island of
Seriphos.   Among his most celebrated mythical exploits
were the beheading of the Gorgon and the rescue of
Andromeda, an Ethiopian princess, from a sea-monster.
Seriphos is the only island mentioned in literary
traditions of this myth, but there are vestiges in
several of the Dorian islands of an extended geographical
claim to Perseus.   The earliest coins of Astypalaia, like
those of Seriphos, bore the head of Perseus (Head, 1911,
pp.630-1).   Artemis Andromeda was worshipped at Lindos,
where a list of her priests was set up in the second
century.   Also from Lindos come plates, dating from the
early sixth century, bearing a Gorgon-headed Artemis
figure (cf. Webster, 1956, pp.129, 156).   And the islet
of Kasos took its name, according to one derivation, from
Kassiopeia, the mother of Andromeda.

Associated with Kadmos' prominence in Greek myths were
strong traditions of Phoenician influence in the Aegean,
preceding the Minoan hegemony (Th.1.8, etc.).   A difficulty
in analysing these is that in myths 'Phoenician' seems

often to represent 'Minoan' or 'Cretan'. (This is an
interpretation now regarded as old-fashioned, but surely
with some truth in it.) Perhaps the Minoan civilization
of Crete, being Anatolian in origin and orientation, was
thought of as eastern and so loosely as Phoenician by the
later Greek world.

Some traditions about the Heliadai imply that they are
Phoenicians, others suggest an identification with
Minoans. This identification was long ago briefly canvassed,
because of the skills attributed to the Heliadai by
ancient writers (Myres, 1930, pp.139-40). Other arguments
may be added. Diodoros' silence about Minos in connection
with Rhodes is in itself suspicious, suggesting that
traditions of the Cretan hegemony may be lurking in his
account in another guise. Legends of a Cretan thalassocracy
are among the most pervasive in Greek tradition, and the
legends are vindicated by archaeological finds of Minoan
settlements in the islands (Chapter 3).

Archaeological evidence shows that the main Minoan
settlement on Rhodes was located near Ialysos, by the
modern village Trianda. It was with Ialysos that the
Phoenician Kadmos was particularly associated. In addition,
Diodoros' account (based on Zenon) referring to Heliadai
coincides in one significant detail with a story in
Athenaios (derived from Ergias) relating to Phoenicians.
The place Achaia, near Ialysos, is common to both. In
Diodoros, Achaia is founded by Ochimos and Kerkaphos, the
Heliadai who remained behind in Rhodes, while in Athenaios
it is defended by Phoenicians under Phalanthos against a
vigorous and ultimately successful attack by Greeks under
Iphiklos (D.S.5.57.6; Ath.8.360e; cf. 6.262e). The
argument that the place would not have been given the name
Achaia unless by Greeks - even if valid - does not vitiate
the coincidence. Both Diodoros and Athenaios might refer
to the place by the name it had in late antiquity, as their
Rhodian sources, Zenon and Ergias, would presumably do.
(The place-name does occur in an inscription, probably of
the third century, IG XII 1, 677. Cf. schol.Pi.'O'7.34,
Δίδυμος δέ φησι καὶ τετάρτην εἶναι πόλιν τὴν νῦν 'Αχαίαν
καλουμένην where νῦν may be significant.

In its details, Athenaios' account of the siege of
Achaia is a network of folkloric motifs. The besiegers
are ultimately successful through a stratagem. Apprised
of oracles (in the form of riddles) given to Phalanthos
about the capture of the city, they use their knowledge
of these to alarm the defenders into the belief that their
end has come. There is also a love interest, with the
princess of the beleaguered city betrothed, through the
agency of a nurse, to the leader of the enemy.

162   Chapter 7

However, the central kernel of the story, with
Phalanthos (a 'Phoenician', with a name of the non-Greek
-nth- type) attacked by the Greek Iphiklos (bearing a name
given in Homer to a Thessalian hero, 'Il.'2.677, 705, 735)
may represent actual events of the Bronze Age, when
Minoans at Ialysos were ousted by Mycenaeans from the
mainland (cf. Chapter 3). The Rhodian myth of Iphiklos
and Phalanthos' daughter in the siege of Achaia closely
parallels the Cretan story of Theseus and Ariadne. Both
myths may be allegorical representations of mainland Greek
attempts to overthrow Minoan towns, with the difference
that on Rhodes Iphiklos was successful, whereas in Crete
Theseus was only partially so, taking Ariadne but not
Knossos.

The Nymphaios-Kaphene story mentioned above (where
Nymphaios is a significant Greek name, 'bridegroom' and
Kaphene is Karian) and the well-known Jason-Medea story
are also of this type, though here rationalization must
be sought in terms of Greek raids on Asiatics (cf. Hdt.
1.1-5). There is evidence of hostilities between Crete
and Karia in the record that Minos drove the Karians from
the islands or made them his subjects (Hdt.1.171; cf.
7.99; Th.1.4.8). Melos might well have been allied with
Crete in such enterprises: there was a strong Minoan
settlement at Phylakopi. The Phoenician traditions of
Melos and Anaphe have already been noted. In addition,
the small island Pholegandros, near Melos, supposedly
took its name from a son of Minos (St.Byz.).

It has been seen that in myths of the Heliadai,
Phoenician and Cretan elements are mingled. The same
combination is present in Diodoros' account of the
arrival in Rhodes from Crete of Althaimenes, son of
Katreus and grandson of Minos, who went into exile in
an attempt, inevitably unsuccessful in the event, to
frustrate an oracle that he would murder his father.
This is immediately reminiscent of the Oidipous myth,
which perhaps had a wider currency in the ancient world
than is generally supposed, and which may have been of
Egyptian origin (cf. Velikovsky, 1960).

Althaimenes founded the cult of Zeus Atabyrios on
Atabyros, the highest peak in Rhodes. Zeus Atabyrios
features on Rhodian coins; the cult, and also Althaimenes,
are recorded in inscriptions. Zeus Atabyrios was associated with the bull; bronze images of bulls have been
discovered on the mountain, and there was a popular belief
that bulls roared there at times of danger to Rhodes.
Here, the immediate origin of the cult is Crete, but its
ultimate source is Phoenicia, the home of Europa, seduced
by Zeus in the form of a bull. In addition, the name

Atabyros itself is probably Semitic, from the root
'tabor'. (On the myth and cult, see Pi.'O'7.87-8, with
schol.; St. Byz.; Apollod.3.2.1-2; cf. Cook, 1925, II
pp.922-5.)

In Diodoros' account, Rhodes was settled first by Phorbas,
son of Lapithes, then by Althaimenes from Crete, then by
Tlepolemos from Argos. In taking up the story of Phorbas
son of Lapithes, we return to Triopas, as these two
figures are associated in many versions of the myth; and
so to the Heliadai. In that part of his history which he
says is derived from Zenon, Diodoros tells of Phorbas son
of Lapithes, who freed Rhodes of a plague of serpents
(the old name Ophioussa, from 'ophis', 'snake' is related
to this mythical exploit); he came from Thessaly where
'he was spending time, looking for a land to settle'.
Diodoros himself gives two other versions of the myth:
that Phorbas, son of Lapithes, went to Elis and that
Triopas, son of Phorbas, went to Rhodes (D.S.5.58.4-5,
4.69.2-3, 4.58.7).
   The Rhodian historian Polyzelos includes the elements
of a storm at sea and a plague of snakes in his account
(FGH III 521). Dieuchidas includes much circumstantial
detail in his narrative: the companions of Triopas
quarrel after his death and separate, some going with
Phorbas to Ialysos and some with Phorbas' brother
Periergos to Kameiros; Periergos curses Phorbas (and
from 'ara', 'curse', the islands Araiai between Knidos
and Syme receive their name); Phorbas is shipwrecked
but swims, with his sister Parthenia, to Ialysos, where
they are received by Thamneus (Ath.6.262e).
   In some respects, the story of Phorbas, as told by
Dieuchidas (a fourth-century source) is reminiscent of
the myths of the Heliadai, as recorded by Diodoros (some
three centuries later). Common elements are the brothers'
quarrel, the name Triopas and, by implication, the sister's
name, Parthenia ('maiden') being equivalent to Elektryone
('unwed').
   In Diodoros, Lapithes is the name of the father of
Phorbas; the Lapiths are a pre-Greek people generally
located in Thessaly. Further, Triopas is named as the
father of Pelasgos, and the Pelasgoi, another pre-Greek
people, are known primarily in the north Aegean area, with
especial connections with Thessaly (cf. Thomson, 1949,
pp.171-7). Pelasgoi from Thessaly supposedly settled Kos
under the leadership of Merops, son of Triopas; Kalymnos
too and Knidos on the neighbouring coast had traditions
of Thessalian settlement (St.Byz.). Some proper names -

of places and of families ('gene') - common to both areas
suggest connections between Thessaly and the islands.
(Cf. IC pp.xiv-xv and Appendix F, for coincidences between
Kos and Thessaly.)

In one tradition, Phorbas was father of Tiphys, the
helmsman of the Argonauts. The Argonauts - from Thessaly -
are strongly associated in myth with Anaphe and Thera.
The story went that the island Anaphe appeared suddenly
from the sea (hence its name) at Apollo's instigation to
shelter the storm-tossed travellers, allowing them to
beach their ships (A.R.4.1716 sqq; Apollod.1.9.26). Thera
too was magically created in myth - from a clod of earth
given to one of the Argonauts, Euphemos, by the god of
Lake Tritonis, and dropped into the sea on their way home
(Apollod.1.9.26; A.R.4.1701; cf. Luce, 1969, pp.121-6).
Apollo was worshipped on both Anaphe and Thera as Aigletes,
and on Anaphe also as Asgelatas, with a festival Asgelaia.
Aetiological myth explained this as a reference to the
lightning flash on that night of storm. Sceptics may point
out that the title is appropriate enough to Apollo in his
role as sun-god (and, indeed, the noun 'aigle' is commonly
used in verse, of the radiance of the sun or moon); but
the association between Apollo and the sun, so common in
myth, was not a regular feature of the worship of Apollo.
Perhaps the myth was invented to explain the cult-title,
but the choice of the Argonauts, from Thessaly, as the
sailors in the story may still be significant.

The earliest diffusion of Apollo worship over Greek
lands cannot be reconstructed. While it is the consensus
of modern scholarship that Apollo came from the East, the
rival claims of a northern origin are still sometimes aired
(see Miller, 1939, pp.4-24). Apollo at Delphi had
connections with Thessaly (cf. Guthrie, 1950, p.81). The
islands lying off the Asiatic coast show clear eastern
influence in the cult of Apollo; the evidence from the
western islands suggests rather a movement of Apollo
worship from the north.

The visits of Herakles to Kos and Rhodes after the 'first
Trojan war' (the siege of Troy by Herakles in revenge for
King Laomedon's failure to give him the promised reward
for a favour) are mentioned by Homer as well as by writers
of late antiquity ('Il.'14.255, 15.28; Apollod.2.7.1;
Plu.'Mor.'304c-d; Cornutus C31; Ovid'Met.'7.363). In
Apollodoros' account, Herakles is taken for a pirate and
stoned; he then takes the city by night and kills King
Eurypylos, son of Astypalaia and Poseidon. (This fits
against a background of piratical raids, with the resulting

suspicion that any unexpected visitors must be pirates;
cf. Hom.'Od.'3.71-4.)

A connection is sometimes sought between these visits
and certain odd features in the cult of Herakles in the
islands. In particular the transvestite ritual at Koan
Antimachia, where the priest's attire included a 'mitra' as
headdress, may be traced to Herakles' taking refuge, when
hard-pressed in battle with the Koans, at the house of a
'Thracian' (i.e. slave?) woman and concealing himself
there in women's clothes. (It may be further conjectured
that there is a connection between this and the exclusion
in Kos of slaves from sacrifices to Hera, Herakles'
implacable enemy.) Koan bridegrooms also dressed as
women, a practice anthropologically parallelled, but in
Kos probably stemming from the Herakles cult, as Herakles
did have some connections with marriage rites.

In certain sacrifices to Herakles on Rhodes, Herakles
was roundly cursed by his own priest. Aetiological myths
account for this by telling that Herakles had killed and
devoured an ox seized from a Rhodian peasant, who meantime
stood by and reviled the hero; some versions add that the
ox was stolen to assuage Hyllos' hunger and some name the
peasant as Theiodamas. In addition, the legend of
Herakles and the Delphic tripod probably lies behind the
tripod motif on Koan coins.

The Homeric Catalogue of Ships gives the following
details about the leadership of the contingents from the
islands: the nine Rhodian ships are commanded by
Tlepolemos, son of Herakles, the three from Syme by
Nireus, son of Aglaia and Charops, and the thirty from the
other islands are commanded by the Koans Pheidippos and
Antiphos, sons of Thessalos, son of Herakles. These
Homeric genealogies fit well with the legendary accounts
of Herakles' activities: Herakles' son Tlepolemos of
Rhodes and his grandsons Pheidippos and Antiphos of Kos
fight against Laomedon's son Priam and grandson Hektor.
This fits with the traditional chronology too: Herakles
is generally put at the end of the fourteenth century,
and the sack of Troy is dated on archaeological evidence
to about 1250 (the time given by Herodotos, in fact) -
that is, about two generations later (Hdt.2.145.4; cf.
Pfister, 1961, p.32; Snodgrass, 1971, p.12). Herakles'
descendants would have an excellent motive for joining the
Greek expedition against Troy in the 'second Trojan War' -
pursuance of the earlier hostilities.

Homer gives an account of the arrival of Tlepolemos in
Rhodes from the mainland: he had accidentally killed his
father's uncle Likymnios, and so been forced into exile.
Tlepolemos met his death at Troy. Nireus' only distinction

is the dubious one of being the best-looking of the Greeks
at Troy, except Achilles, but a weakling. (It is a
deviation from the usual epic values to find personable
appearance divorced from valour.) The Koan leaders are
not mentioned elsewhere in the epics. Thessalos, the
name of their father, was a common Koan name later, given,
for instance, to one of Hippokrates' sons.

There are several hints in Homer of early connections
between the islands and Thessaly. (The term 'Thessaly'
is post-Homeric, but the area which was later so called
was known to Homer and contingents from it accompanied
Agamemnon to Troy.) The name Thessalos itself is at once
suggestive. In addition, Homer describes Kos as 'city of
Eurypylos': the same name, Eurypylos, is borne by a
Thessalian hero who sent forty ships on the expedition.
Further, another Thessalian hero bears the name Iphiklos,
the same as that given by Athenaios for the hero who
overthrew the 'Phoenician' Phalanthos at Ialysos ('Il'.
2.677, 705, 735; Ath.8.360e). The Homeric evidence is
in accord with the many traditional stories linking the
areas. The Homeric Catalogue seems to conflate the
traditions of Phorbas and of Tlepolemos: connections
with Thessaly are implicit in the record, yet Tlepolemos
is already in Rhodes.

About the period following the Trojan Wars myths are
reticent. A few legends relate to the return of the
Greek heroes from the sack of Troy: Menelaos stopped at
Rhodes, where dedications by his helmsman Kanopos to
Athena and Poseidon are recorded in the Lindian Chronicle,
and where there was a cult of Helen (Paus.3.19.9); when
Agamemnon stopped at Kalymnos, the complement of four of
his ships decided to stay there (D.S.5.54); Podaleirios
too settled in the region.

In the next generation Orestes son of Agamemnon in his
wanderings paid a visit to Rhodes. Possibly the gruesome
ritual of human sacrifice to Kronos, with a condemned
criminal as victim, which was carried out at the Rhodian
shrine of Artemis Aristoboule (Porph.'Abst.'2.54) has
some connection with the mythical travels of Orestes and
Iphigeneia. Human sacrifice was central in the Asiatic
cult of Artemis, with which - as is well known from
Euripides' 'IT' (cf. 'IA' 1524-5) - Iphigeneia had strong
mythical associations. The rites of Artemis Orthia
(whose name is often interpreted as having the same
meaning as Aristoboule, 'of good counsel') at Sparta are
a classical analogue: there, brutal floggings, sometimes
resulting in death, were a prominent feature of the cult.

The hero Tlepolemos, an 'archegetes' leading the Dorian
colonists from the Peloponnese to new homes in the islands,

belongs with Ioklos from Argos who colonized Karpathos
and Menestheus from Sparta who led men to Melos (D.S.5.54;
Str.14.2.6;   Apollod.6.15b;   Pi.'O'7).   The affinity of
the islands with their mother cities (Melos and Thera with
Sparta; Astypalaia, Kos and Nisyros with Epidauros;   Rhodes
and Karpathos with Argos) had certain far-reaching effects
on their cults, as will be seen in the following chapter.

8   Cults

This chapter begins with an outline of the sources of
information about the cults of the islands, then goes on
to a brief historical survey, indicating the main periods
of change in cult practices. After these preliminaries,
the main part of the chapter is devoted to a discussion
of the cults of the region. A full catalogue of deities,
with cult-titles, festivals and religious associations is
given in an appendix.

A glance at the epigraphical appendix will acquaint
the reader with the range of gods worshipped in the
islands. In general, island practice is analogous with
that of other Dorian regions. (On Greek cults and
festivals, see Farnell, 1896; Nilsson, 1906; Stengel,
1920; on those of Dorian regions, see, on Sparta, Wide,
1893; on Crete, Willetts, 1962; on Thera, Braun, 1932;
on Rhodes, van Gelder, 1900, pp.289-367 and Morelli, 1959;
for collections of inscriptions relating to cults, see
Prott and Ziehen, 1896 and 1906 = PLS and ZLS; Sokolowski,
1955 and 1962.)

The evidence for the cults of the islands is primarily
epigraphical, and from the Hellenistic or Roman periods.
There are disadvantages in the enforced reliance on such
sources. First, while inscriptions do provide unequivocal
evidence that a particular deity was worshipped in a
particular place at a more or less clearly definable time,
they tend to be bald in format and allusive in content,
laying down regulations for ritual practices in conventionally formulaic terms. Second, the lack of very early
material means that a cult can rarely be traced from its
origins, but is seen in a developed or even ossified
form. Myths often give indirect help here, as does
comparative material from the Peloponnese and elsewhere;
sometimes too inscriptions of the period following the
Koan and Rhodian synoecisms refer to the revival or

regularization of earlier practices. The general
conservatism of cult practice also palliates this
difficulty; but such conservatism cannot be taken for
granted: rather, it must be postulated with caution in
individual cases, and allowance made for a process of
gradual unobtrusive change.

Names of months, places and people are indirectly
informative. Many of the ancient month names, much
varied from one community to another, are connected with
deities or with their festivals, and reflect local cult
practice. Artamitios (Artemis), Iobakchios (Dionysos)
and Thesmophorios (Demeter) are typical examples (cf.
Bickerman, 1968, p.20 fig.2). To the present day, certain
Rhodian place-names evoke the ancient gods; for instance,
Damatria, a village near the site of ancient Ialysos.
Many of the names of men and women known from inscriptions
are 'theophoric', i.e. derived from divine names.

Temples tell, by their size, of the importance of the
cults based in them, and by dates of building or reconstruction reveal its history. For instance, it is known
that the cult of Asklepios continued at Rhodes well into
the first century AD, and in Kos into the second because
the state temples, destroyed in earthquakes, were then
repaired. Again, the shrine of Athena at Lindos is well
documented: Kleoboulos carried out extensive rebuilding
there in the sixth century (cf. D.L.1.89) and further
reconstruction was necessary in the fourth century, after
a fire at the site.

Indirect testimony comes also from coins, bearing
images or symbols of particular gods (cf. Kraay, 1976,
p.3). Apollo was dominant on the coins of Kalymnos,
Helios on those of post-synoecism Rhodes. Numismatic
practice did not always keep pace with religious change:
it was not until around the middle of the second century
that Asklepios replaced Herakles or his symbols (prominent
from the synoecism till c.200) on the coins of Kos (Head,
1911, p.633).

Artistic representations of the gods do not help much
in the study of cults. That aesthetic, not religious,
considerations motivated sculptors' choice of subject is
evident from the preponderance of Aphrodite figures. The
work of great sculptors and painters was displayed in the
shrines of Kos and Rhodes (cf. Chapter 1). Apelles'
Aphrodite, commissioned by the Koans, became his most
celebrated painting, and Praxiteles executed a statue of
the goddess for Kos. From Melos came the Aphrodite most
famous today, much visited in the Louvre.

There is scant information from literary sources to
supplement the evidence of inscriptions. As already

remarked, the Hippokratic Corpus tells us nothing of
Asklepios worship in Kos, despite the Koan origins of
Hippokrates and the common interests (if not attitudes)
of temple and secular medicine. However, some desultory
information of antiquarian interest can be culled from
the fragmentary remains of the writings of the local
chroniclers; titles of hymns and elegies hint at beliefs
and practices; lexicographers give useful brief notes
on some cult-titles. Pindar Olympian 7, Herodas Mime 4
and Theokritos Idyll 7 all give incidental information on
cults.

The previous chapter surveyed the remote past, which
cast long shadows on cult beliefs and practices. Lingering
influences from the early East, from Minoan Crete and from
the Mycenaean presence in the islands will be apparent in
this chapter (cf. Dietrich, 1970, 1974 and 1975). The
underlying homogeneity of Aegean lands in terms of material
culture and linguistic usage of the Bronze Age has already
been explored (Chapters 3 and 4). In religion too there
seems early universality, in the widespread veneration of
a Mother or Earth goddess of the type later visible in the
Asiatic Kybele and echoed in the Greek Ge or Rhea (cf.
S.'Ph.'391 sqq.; Pomeroy, 1975, pp.13-15). Indeed, it
has been argued that all Greek goddesses derive from this
one basic prototype (Persson, 1942). This view gains some
support from the prominence of 'potnia' in the Linear B
texts and the later application of this same adjective to
a wide range of Greek goddesses (cf. Guthrie, 1959, p.39).

Anatolian influence is apparent in traces of vegetation
cults. Tree-worship, or the veneration of trees as sacred
objects, is in general an eastern attitude, found in Greek
communities only in an attenuated form. That trees had an
important place in Minoan beliefs is evident from seal-
rings, depicting figures larger than life, probably
goddesses, with trees. The sacred grove was a feature of
some classical sites and in a few - notably the oracular
shrine of Zeus at Dodona - was peculiarly important. The
complexity of the question of revival or survival of
'primitive' elements in religion is highlighted by the
alleged existence, last century, of a sacred tree in the
mountains of Kos (Rouse, 1902, p.13 n.2). Nevertheless,
it does seem significant that cult-titles implying
associations with trees or vegetation are unusually
prominent in Rhodes (Apollo Erethimios; also Zeus
Eredimios according to Hesychios; Dionysos Epikarpios;
Zeus Endendros; Zeus Karpophoros; cf. Paus.3.19.9 on
Helen Dendritis) and Kos (Apollo Kyparissios; Athena
Alseia; Dionysos Skyllitas; Dionysos Thyllophoros); as
these islands are avenues for the transmission of cults

from the East. Similarly, primeval aspects of Zeus are
prominent in the islands: he is a sky and weather, rather
than a civic, deity. Also, in Rhodes, Zeus is associated
with the cult of the agrarian goddess Demeter.

Anatolian influence is seen too in traces of the cult
of the empty throne, which is Sumerian in origin, found
at Rhodes and Chalke (Cook, 1914, I pp.141-2; Laumonier,
1958, p.681 n.1). In the rocks of Chalke, an empty throne
is carved out, with a dedication to Zeus and Hekate. A
Rhodian rock inscription, over a similar throne, invokes
Hekate (as 'hiera soteira euekoos phosphoros Enodia'). Of
clear Minoan origin is the title Zeus Kronides Anax,
accompanied by the motif of the double-axe, at Rhodes.

Undoubtedly, however, the strongest formative influence
on the island cults came from the Dorian cities of the
Peloponnese, as the settlers brought with them Greek cults
in the forms which flourished in their mother cities. The
relative prominence of Apollo Pythios (derived from Argos)
or Apollo Karneios (from Sparta) reflects the islanders'
origins from these states. (Similarly, the Rhodians
subsequently carried the cult of Athana Lindia to their
own colonies - Gela and elsewhere.) Direct mainland
influence did not generally continue once the new
communities were formed. There is, however, one known
instance of continued cult contacts between Astypalaia
and Epidauros: a fourth-century inscription arranges
that offerings be made by the islanders at their mother
city (IG IV2 1, 47; cf. Graham, 1964, pp.163-4).

From the beginning, the Dorians adapted their own
cults to accommodate those they found flourishing in
their new homes. Rhodian Athana Lindia probably represents
a conflation of the Greek newcomer Athena with an ancient
local goddess Lindia: it is a plausible conjecture that
the Greeks left the nature of the pre-Hellenic cult of
Lindia undisturbed in their worship of Athena (in particular, continuing ritual without burnt sacrifice), while
introducing a Greek sacrificial cult on the lower slopes
of the Acropolis at Boukopion (Blinkenberg, 1941). Lindia
is adjectival in form, as is Kekoia, applied to Artemis
at the place Kekoia in Rhodes, and often taken to imply a
pre-Greek cult of a goddess Kekoia, fused with Artemis.
Apollo Maleatas, found at Thera and at many other places
in Greece is a similar case. A clearer instance of the
placing of names side by side, with the old taken over in
parenthesis beside the new, is Artemis Andromeda at
Lindos.

The tendency towards 'syncretism', to uniting unfamiliar
new religious elements with familiar old ones, is typical
of Greek religious practice; as is the straightforward

addition of new deities to an ever-expanding polytheistic
system. The cults brought from the mainland were not
only initially fused with local cults, but were subject
thereafter to a continuous process of infiltration and
accretion. This process frequently makes it difficult to
decide whether non-Greek cults are pre-Greek.

Continuing influences from the East, especially from
Karia, is evident in the offshore islands. Hekate Stratia
on Kos and Apollo Stratagios on Rhodes are reminiscent of
the Karian Stratioi. Other island cult-titles derive
from important cult centres in Asia Minor: Apollo was
worshipped on Kalymnos as Didymeus, from the oracular
shrine at Didyma, destroyed by the Persians but rebuilt by
Alexander the Great; Artemis Pergaia, from the great
shrine at Perge in Pamphylia, appears on Rhodes (third-
century Lindos and Rhodos) and travels as far west as
Thera. (It ought perhaps to be conceded as an instance
of influence from the Greek mainland that Hermes Kyllanios,
taking his title from Kyllene, a mountain in Arkadia,
appears in Kos.)

The effect of Cretan proximity on the cults of the
other Dorian islands is marked. The cult-title Delphinios,
found in an archaic inscription from Thera (where
Delphinios is also a month-name and the dolphin motif
occurs on early coins) and in a second-century dedication
to Apollo from Nisyros almost certainly comes from Crete,
where very early traces of it can be found (Willetts,
1962, pp.262-4; cf. Farnell, 1907, IV pp.145-8;
Swindler, 1913, pp.22-9). Sminthios too is a Cretan title
of Apollo (Swindler, 1913, pp.29-33). An inscription from
Lindos makes it clear that Dionysos was worshipped at the
Rhodian Sminthia, both at the new capital Rhodos and at
Lindos, where the ritual was an old one with its prescrip-
tions revised in the extant inscription. Possibly Apollo,
elsewhere Sminthios, was somehow associated with Dionysos
in this ritual; or, rather, it may be suggested that
Sminthios was a pre-Greek deity, in some places conflated
with the Greek Apollo, but at Rhodes with Dionysos (cf.,
on IG XII 1, 762 = ZLS 146, Nilsson, 1906, pp.307-8).
The worship of Artemis as Toxitis at Kos may stem from
Crete, where she had the title Toxia (Willetts, 1962,
p.275).

In cults - as in linguistic usage (cf. Chapter 4) -
adjacent regions interacted. And in cults - as with the
dialects - great regional diversity is apparent within a
framework of superficial uniformity. The same gods are
worshipped, but with shifting emphasis on one or another,
and with different cult-titles. Many Greek communities
have a shrine of the 'twelve gods', but closer inspection

reveals that not always the same twelve are intended
(cf., on Kos, Chambers, 1955). The occurrence of a
particular cult-title is often as significant as the
occurrence of the god to whom it is applied. The gods had
many different facets, and different places laid emphasis
on different aspects. The unusual or unique cult-title
can reveal much about the source of a cult. There is
further diversity in the cults peculiar to sections of
the island populace, to particular tribes, particular
demes and particular families.

   In Kos, a codification of state ritual practices was
undertaken after the synoecism of 366; in Rhodes too the
synoecism had had repercussions on cults. The situation
for Athens is similar, in that a code of state religion
compiled in the first years of the fourth century has
survived in part (Lys.30; Sokolowski, 1962, pp.27-31
no.10; cf. Parke, 1977, pp.14-15). The material which
has survived from these regions provides valuable contemporary documentation of the cults, on the brink of an era
of change.

   Gradually, religion became more personal in character.
While the Olympian gods were still worshipped at state
festivals, a new diffuseness is apparent around the
edges of state worship. Both Helios and Asklepios,
coming into prominence after the synoecisms of Rhodes
and Kos, were worshipped in conjunction with attendant
minor gods. This entourage replaces cult-titles,
strikingly absent from these late arrivals. The individual
might make his appeal, or dedication, to one of these
lesser deities - a practice foreshadowing the role of the
Saints in the Christian church. Hygieia, 'daughter' of
Asklepios, the personified abstraction 'good health',
became prominent at Kos (cf. Herod.4.4-5). Similarly,
all over the Greek world, Nike, 'victory', once merely
an attribute of Athena, became a power in her own right.
Tyche, 'fortune', was widely venerated also. The cult of
the local Demos, 'people', is another new phenomenon.

   Rhodes influenced the cults of neighbouring regions as
well as other aspects of their way of life. Cults of
Helios and of the eponymous nymph Rhodos appear in the
islands, while there is evidence from the mainland for
that of the Rhodian Demos (see Fraser and Bean, 1954,
pp.130-7). The cult of the Dea Roma and of the Demos of
the Romans, later widespread, is foreshadowed here.

   Similarly, the deification of the Roman emperors is
anticipated in the granting of honours by several Greek
communities to Alexander and his successors. That there
was a shrine of Alexander himself on Kos is known from
the chance observation of the botanist Nikander that the

plant ambrosia sprouted from the head of his statue (Ath.
15.684e). The Ptolemies were given divine honours at
Astypalaia and Thera, as well as Kos and Rhodes. The
names of festivals might be made to accommodate these new
elements, as in the Rhodian Alexandreia and Dionysia (cf.
Dionysia and Seleukeia at Erythrai, SIG 410, 412), and
the Theran association in the middle of the third century
of the Ptolemies with the games of Hermes and Herakles
(cf. PA I p.245). The procedure of conflation is
identical with that adopted earlier, as in the old Rhodian
festival of the Herakleia and Tlepolemaia. Monarchs liked
publicity and grandeur in the recognition accorded them;
hence the association with the greatest festivals.

Blurring of distinctions between human and divine is
relatively easy in a polytheistic system. The early
heroes - typically founders of states, such as Tlepolemos -
are the precursors of the Ptolemies and other deified
rulers; except that the heroes win immortality through
their own exertions, not through an accident of heredity.
A closer parallel is perhaps with Roman magistrates
granted such honours. An intermediate point is marked by
the fifth-century figures who were heroized (for instance
Hippokrates), and by the regular Hellenistic practice,
discussed later in this chapter, of heroizing the dead.

After Alexander had opened up new areas to communication with the Greek world, a lively traffic of ideas from
east to west and from Egypt northwards followed. Many
foreign gods now make their appearance in the islands,
Isis and Serapis foremost among them. In some cases,
identifications were made with the indigenous Greek
pantheon: Melqart with Herakles, Arsinoe with Aphrodite.
A dedication at Lindos to Ammon, Parammon and Hera
Ammonia illustrates the process of syncretism. Later,
Roman gods appear (ClRh 10 (1941) pp.208-9 and 210-13).

Greater mobility of population brought an influx of
foreigners into Kos and Rhodes (cf. Peek, 1969, pp.40-3).
Bilingual inscriptions attest this presence; for instance,
a dedication from Kos, in Greek and Nabataian (Levi della
Vida, 1938). Groups of foreigners resident in Greek
communities often formed religious associations for the
worship of their own gods. By an ensuing extension of
this practice, the Greek gods too were honoured by such
associations. (On religious associations in general, see
Foucart, 1873; Poland, 1909; on those in Rhodes, see
Pugliese Carratelli, 1939-40.)

Rhodes, with its thriving trade connections and
consequent cosmopolitan ambiance, had a particularly
large number of these groups, as did the Peiraieus,
another busy port. They proliferated especially at Lindos

and Rhodos, with fewer at Kameiros, always a more
isolated and agrarian community. Kos too had many
associations, through proximity to Rhodes and through its
medical school, which attracted visitors from abroad.
There were apparently no religious associations on
Kalymnos – which had an inhospitable harbour and tended
to be inward-looking – but several are known from
Astypalaia, Chalke, Melos, Nisyros and Thera.

Religious activities were the common basis of these
associations, but probably not always their predominant
concern. Mutual interest of one kind or another might be
the motivation. That Aphrodite and Dionysos were
especially popular patrons suggests a social and sexual
bond. Some associations restricted membership to one sex
(cf. PA I p.790 and II p.1101 n.532 on a possible Dorian
tendency to homosexuality; also, for a contrary view,
Dover, 1978, pp.185-96). In some cases, burial of members
was in the association's precincts (IC 155-9; KF 40-4;
NS 489-98). Societies of people practising the same
profession – for instance, guilds of actors – also came
to flourish at this time. Here, Asklepiadai (doctors)
are to be distinguished from Asklepiastai (worshippers of
Asklepios). In some ways, the phenomenon of religious
associations approximates to freemasonry in our own
society, especially in the exclusive atmosphere cultivated.

Names for religious societies vary. The most common
are 'thiasos', 'koinon', 'koineion' and 'synodos', with
such combinations as 'koinon' of the 'thiasos'. The term
'mystai' is typical of Dionysiac societies. Of less
specifically religious groups, 'synaristion', 'synedrion'
and 'systema' are found. Members of occupational guilds
are 'homotechnoi' or 'technitai'.

With the growth of personal religion, the fate of the
individual after death became a matter of concern. Greek
families had always revered their ancestors, remembering
them ceremonially on certain fixed occasions. But in
the Hellenistic period, a change came with the regular
heroization of the dead. The terms 'hero' and 'heroine'
are ubiquitous on Hellenistic tombstones, meaning simply
'the deceased', and the verb 'heroize' was in common use
on Thera. Probably all those 'heroes' were brought humble
offerings by their relicts. Significantly, words for
'altar' or 'shrine' are used for 'tomb' at this time
('bomos', IC 281, 325; 'abaton' IG XII 3, 453, 454,
1626).

Public heroization, by 'boule' and 'demos', as well as
private, by one's own family, was common. On Thera,
heroization inscriptions date from about 250 BC to Trajan's
reign, coexisting with the beginnings of Christianity on

the island. Nikias, tyrant of Kos in the first century
BC, was apparently heroized in his lifetime: inscriptions
were set up to him as 'hero', 'benefactor' and 'patriot',
for his 'safety.' (IC 76-80; KF 17-20).

An extension of heroization is the formal institution
of family cult-foundations by individuals. This practice
began in the islands and later spread to the mainland.
Pythokles' cult-foundation in Kos was dedicated to the
worship of Zeus and Athena, not to that of Pythokles, but
it is a pointer to things to come that the festival was
known as the Pythokleia (a festival still celebrated in
the middle of the first century AD). Participation was
open to all the citizens, though the priesthoods were
hereditary, restricted to the family of Pythokles. Later,
Diomedon set up in Kos a cult of Herakles as Diomedonteios,
a step nearer to founder-worship, although sacrifices were
made also to Dionysos, Aphrodite, Zeus Pasios and the
Moirai. In the case of Epikteta's foundation on Thera,
sacrifices were made only to the Muses and the founders.
In both these cases, membership was restricted to direct
descendants of the founders, Diomedon and Epikteta.
(With the foundations of Pythokles, IC 34, Diomedon,
IC 36 and Epikteta, IG XII 3, 330, cf. that of Poseidonios
at Halikarnassos, IBM 896; see Kamps, 1937.)

Under the Romans, priesthoods of many deities were
often concentrated in the hands of one man, who might
also be holding state office (cf. the following chapter).
This tendency may have induced a blurring of the identity
of deities in people's consciousness: it was alleged
that many did not distinguish between Apollo, Helios and
Dionysos in the first century AD (D.Chr.31.11). However,
this is merely a continuation of a trend, as certain
deities had always been closely associated in Greek
worship (cf. Schlesinger, 1931). Zeus and Athena were
worshipped in close conjunction at Kos, where the cult-
titles of the two are almost coincident. Again, a close
link is evident between Artemis, Hekate, Persephone and
Eilythuia: identical literary epithets and cult-titles
are applied to Artemis and Hekate in their chthonian
aspects and association with the moon. Thus, Artemis is
Selasphoros at Rhodes while Hekate is Phosphoros at
Thera ('light-bearing'). The Rhodian cult of Artemis had
similarities with that of Kore or Persephone (Souda s.v.
Asphodelos), while Artemis was linked in dedications with
Eilythuia, goddess of childbirth.

The longevity of the Greek cults is striking. Apollo
Pythios was still worshipped at Lindos in the third
century AD, when the Delphic oracle itself was in a
decline. In many cases, the cults owed their survival to

adaptability and syncretism. Worship of the deified Roman emperors was fused at Kos with that of Asklepios (the festival becoming the Sebasta Asklepieia) and on Kalymnos with that of Apollo, the most important local gods. (The expression 'consecrated together' occurs of Asklepios and the emperor at Kos, NS 443, and of Apollo and the emperor at Kalymnos, TC 109.)

In Dorian states generally, and in the islands too, Apollo was more important than Zeus. The main state god of Anaphe, Kalymnos and Thera, he had an important cult at Koan Halasarna, was worshipped before Asklepios in the precinct later famous as the Asklepieion, was prominent in Rhodes and also in Astypalaia, Karpathos, Pholegandros and Telos. (The expression 'tribe of Apollo' in a second-century inscription from Telos, IG XII 3, 38, is perhaps an oblique way of identifying the Dymanes, the tribe which particularly honoured Apollo, pace Hiller von Gaertringen ad loc.) Strabo records the existence of a precinct of Apollo on Chalke also (10.5.15). Evidence for Apollo is particularly full and early (cf. TC 98, sixth century) from Kalymnos, where he is Apollo Dalios or Kalymnios and regarded as 'prokathegemon', 'presiding' god, a title used of the main state deity elsewhere; for example, Asklepios on Kos and Artemis at Ephesos.

  Apollo had very diverse attributes, and was worshipped with a wide range of cult-titles. A rudimentary classification of those used in the islands might be into titles deriving from important cult centres (Dalios, Didymeus, Pythios); titles used in minor local cults (of Kamyndos, Megisteus, Pyxios); titles of Apollo as god of the countryside (Epimelidios, Erethimios, Karneios, Kyparissios, Lykeios, Mylantios); titles of Apollo as protector - at sea, in battle, from disease, from evil is general (Apotropaios, Delphinios, Loimios, Maleatas, Oulios, Pharmakios, Prostaterios, Soter, Stratagios). But this classification is indeed rudimentary: many titles fall into more than one category (Ixios and Lykeios, discussed in the previous chapter), many fall into none (Pedageitnyos, also a month name), and of many - perhaps the majority - the original meaning is uncertain, blurred by time (Karneios). Also, in many cases, etymology is irrelevant to developed cult-practice.

  There are many titles of uncertain derivation where further suggestions might be added to those already in circulation. For instance, it may be that Rhodian Epiknisios is derived from 'knisa', giving the meaning 'presiding over sacrifice'. Again, Maleatas, a title of

Apollo as healing god, often linked with Asklepios, may
originally have referred to Apollo as protector at sea:
of the many places called Malea, the most famous was the
cape, on the southern tip of the Peloponnesian peninsula,
notorious for its storms. Third, the Rhodian title
Petasitas, 'with a "petasos" type hat' suggests a
connection in cult with Hermes, often represented as
wearing this headgear. (See Morelli, 1959, for other
suggestions.)

In cult-titles can be seen faint traces of the paths
of the primary diffusion of Apollo worship to Greek lands,
and clearer marks of its subsequent development. As noted
in the previous chapter, Rhodian traditions point east,
through the mythical Telchines, whereas those of Thera and
Anaphe look north, through the Argonauts.

The direct influence of the Peloponnese is seen in the
titles Karneios and Pythios. Karneios, regarded by the
Greeks as a peculiarly Dorian title of Apollo, and
particularly associated with Sparta (Th.5.54.2; cf.
Paus.3.13.3), is important on Thera, where the festival
of the Karneia was organized in the sixth or early fifth
century by Agloteles, whose descendants held the priesthood of Apollo Karneios, and that of Asklepios, for many
generations (IG XII 3, suppl.1324, XII suppl. p.86;
cf. Nilsson, 1906, pp.125-6). Also, Apollo Maleatas,
worshipped at Sparta, is known only at Thera among the
Dorian islands. Apollo Pythios derived from Argos, is
much in evidence on Rhodes (cf. Tomlinson, 1972, p.205
on the cult in the Argolid; also Swindler, 1913,
pp.15-22 on possible Cretan influence). In Lindian
priest-lists, Apollo Pythios regularly comes second only
to Athana Lindia. At Kameiros, the regular sequence of
titles Apollo Pythios and Karneios reflects the lesser
importance of the latter; indeed, the priesthoods of the
two were combined in the third century. In Kos there is
early (fifth-century) evidence for a precinct of Apollo
Pythios (KF 36; cf. REG 15 (1902) p.90).

Apollo was worshipped with the cult-title 'Delian' on
Kos, Nisyros, Rhodes, Syme and Kalymnos, where Apollo
Dalios was the main state deity and his priest, the
'stephanephoros', was the state eponym (cf. Chapter 9;
also, Craik, 1969). On Melos and Thera, Apollo Dalios
was not honoured. Dalios is a month-name at Kos,
Kalymnos and Rhodes, whereas in Thera Delphinios - from
a Cretan cult-title of Apollo - is found. It is significant that the Dorian islands which did not honour Delian
Apollo in their local cults are precisely those which
refused loyalty to the fifth-century Delian League
(cf. Chapter 3).

The distinctive character of the island cults appears not only in idiosyncratic local cult-titles, but more signally in the deities they singled out for peculiar honour. Asklepios was the main god of Hellenistic Kos, Helios of Hellenistic Rhodes. It may be conjectured that the rise of both these 'outsiders' to a dominant position was assisted by the connections they had with Apollo, whose importance in Dorian states has already been remarked.

In myth, Asklepios was son of Apollo by a mortal mother, variously named as Koronis (Pi.'P'3; A.R.4.617; D.S.4.71.1) or as Arsinoe (Apollod.3.10.3). Originally – like other progeny of gods and women – a mortal, named in Homer as the father of Machaon and Podaleirios, the Greek physicians at Troy ('Il.'2.731-2), Asklepios came to be worshipped as a god, taking over one of his father's roles, that of divine healer. (See Farnell, 1921 and, especially, Edelstein and Edelstein, 1945.) A strong, though not unanimous, tradition placed the origins of Asklepios and his sons in Thessaly. The myth of Podaleirios' arrival in Karia and his activities there is of a piece with other legendary traditions linking the two regions.

In cult, as in myth, Apollo and Asklepios are closely linked. It was only very gradually that Asklepios appropriated the Koan shrine of Apollo Kyparissios, in the course of the fourth century, and the locality long retained its name Kyparissos (Hp.'Ep.'11; cf. Laumonier, 1958, pp.691-5). A Koan epigram of the fourth (or possibly fifth) century refers to Paianos of the grove, who may be either Apollo or Asklepios, in a time of transition. Paian or Paion was the name of the physician of the gods in Homer ('Il.'5.401; cf. 'Od.'4.232), and his name came to be applied, both as literary epithet and as cult-title, to healing gods; particularly Apollo and Asklepios, but also to other deities, for instance Zeus at Rhodes (Hsch.) and Athena at Athens (Paionia, Paus. 1.2.5).

The great mainland centres of the cult of Asklepios were Thessaly and Epidauros, each staking a claim to priority. While a firm solution to the question of the inception of the cult and of the interaction of different regions in its diffusion is elusive, it seems very likely that the cult at Kos was originally introduced from Thessaly, then grew to prominence under Epidaurian influence. The Rhodian cult was probably, in turn, an offshoot of the Koan, although here too Peloponnesian influence, from Argos, is a possibility (cf. Morelli, 1959, p.115).

In the islands, the cult is widespread, occurring not
only at Kos and Rhodes, but also Anaphe, Astypalaia, Chalke,
Karpathos, Melos, Syme and Thera (see the appendix for
details). Theran rock inscriptions on the one hand and
the find at Melos of an ornate collection-box, bearing a
head of Asklepios and a lid in the form of a coiled
snake, show both simple and sophisticated aspects of the
cult in existence. The curative hot springs of Melos
doubtless gave an impetus to the cult.

The entourage of minor deities related to Asklepios,
not much in evidence except at the main centres of
Asklepios worship, is found in Kos and the other islands.
These are Machaon, the son of Asklepios; Epione, his
wife; and the personified concepts Hygieia, Iaso and
Panakeia, described as his daughters. Cheiron, the
Thessalian centaur who shared medical lore with Asklepios,
also occurs. Surprisingly, there is no trace of
Podaleirios, who is intimately connected with the area in
myth, in the local cults, although Machaon, the other son
of Asklepios, who is associated in myth rather with the
Peloponnese, does feature. The Hemerideioi of a second-
century Rhodian dedication - to Asklepios, Hygieia and
the Hemerideioi - are these related deities collectively,
while the term Asklepioi in a Theran inscription (IG XII
3, suppl.1330) of the second century AD - 'the great gods,
hearkening Asklepioi of Hypata' - refers to Asklepios and
his family. Here, the final title, 'of Hypata' (a place
in Thessaly) is an interesting, if late, hint at
Thessalian connections.

In Kos, the cult of Asklepios was deeply entrenched
in the civic life of the community. State proclamations
were made at the annual Asklepieia, a festival which
attracted both pilgrims and competitors from all over
the Greek world; state decrees were placed in the
Asklepieion. The political advantages of the presence
of the shrine were guarded and exploited: religious and
diplomatic motives combined, for instance, in the asylum
granted Roman refugees from Mithridates (cf. Chapter 3).
Under the Empire, the site was recognized by Tiberius,
and honoured by Claudius, the latter influenced by his
Koan personal physician, Xenophon (Tac.'Ann.'4.14.2,
12.61.1-2).

The cult of Asklepios well illustrates the capacity of
Greek religion for change and adaptation. When the
ancient cult of Paian was merged with that of Apollo, the
superseded deity continued to exist adjectivally. Then
healing became a separate province, delegated to Apollo's
son, Asklepios, still sometimes known as Paian. It may
well have suited the religious hierarchy at Delphi to see

the rise of a new deity as an offshoot of the Apollo
cult, not in rivalry with it; rather than to countenance
a radical change in the nature of the oracular cult of
their god. At Athens - as at many other places - the cult
of Asklepios quickly gathered momentum. Introduced late
in the fifth century, it superseded the cult of Athena in
the Hellenistic period. Some accommodation of old to new
was achieved by the equation there of Athena with
Hygieia (cf. Parke, 1977, pp.47, 64). Cults and temples
of Asklepios (known at a late date in our area for Kos,
Rhodes and Thera) continued well into the Christian era,
and indeed posed a serious challenge to the nascent world
religion, Christianity (see Edelstein and Edelstein, 1945,
pp.132-8). Christianity met the challenge with St Luke,
a doctor especially honoured in places where Asklepios
had been important.

The connections of Helios the sun-god with Apollo are
more elusive than are those of Asklepios with his 'parent'.
The popular assimilation of the sun with Apollo ('Carm.
Pop.'12; cf. E.fr.781; Pl.'Lg.'946) is ultimately
canonized by the mythographers. However, literary
allusion and the content of myth does not coincide with
epigraphical evidence and practice in cult: the equation
of Apollo with Helios is not a feature of the cult of
Helios, nor indeed of Apollo. While Artemis is a lunar
goddess in both myth and cult, a solar character is not
apparent in Apollo cults. Thus, the epithet Phoibos
(generally held to refer to the sun's brightness) is a
purely literary term (as in IC 58), not a cult-title
(cf. Miller, 1939, pp.26-8).
    As 'helios' is Greek for 'sun', as well as denoting
Helios, the god of the sun, a certain ambivalence is
inherent in the term. Even in Rhodian myth, Helios is
not always fully anthropomorphized: for instance, a
great flood is said to be dried up by Helios (D.S.5.56.3).
As will be seen, a similar terminological haze surrounds
Hestia, the goddess of the 'hestia', 'hearth'.
    Sun worship was strikingly absent from formal Greek
religion, but the divinity of the sun was implicit in
popular belief. In Attic tragedy, characters call on
the sun as witness of terrestrial events, implying rather
than asserting its divinity (S.'Tr.'94 sqq., 'At.'100
sqq.) The ambivalence of the Athenian attitude to
worship of the sun may be illustrated from two passages
of Plato: in one, it is dismissed as peculiar to
'barbaroi' ('Cra.'397c), while in the other it is implied
that Anaxagoras' contention that the sun was not a god

was regarded as blasphemous ('Ap.'26d). Aristophanes,
like Plato, regarded sun worship as barbarian ('Pax'406-
13); yet, when it suited him, he would, like Sophokles,
represent it as a god ('Ec.'5). Rhodes was directly
mocked in a comedy, produced towards the end of the fifth
century in Athens, for its reverence of Helios (by
Lysippos).

Late introduction or elevation of the cult of Helios
is apparent in several other localities, although not on
the same scale as in Rhodes, the only Greek community to
make Helios its main god. There were early cults of
Helios in the Peloponnese (at Argos, Corinth, Sikyon and
in the Mount Taygetos region of Lakonia) and in Karia;
there are traces of them also in Crete. Doubtless,
Rhodian sun worship was part of the local religious
'undergrowth' before it became a cultured plant in the
late fifth century. Certainly, myth associated Helios
with Rhodes long before the synoecism: Pindar depicts
the island as his peculiar province, and Helios as a
divinity on a par with the Olympians ('O'7.60).

The choice of Helios as the patron god of the new
state was probably due to his connection in myth with
the island as a whole, 'father' of the three states
Lindos, Ialysos and Kameiros rather than peculiar to any
one of them, and so providing a new and neutral focus
for pan-Rhodian aspirations (see van Gelder, 1900, p.290).
The cult of Aphrodite Pandemos and Homonoia at Kos,
after the synoecism, is similar in intention (cf. below).

The cult of Helios at Rhodes - like that of Asklepios
at Kos - was promoted as a civic enterprise. The priest
of Helios was state eponym. Games, the Helieia (in
inscriptions designated Halieia, Haleia or Halia)
analogous with the Koan Asklepieia, were organized by
'agonothetes', gymnasiarch and special treasurer (SIG
1067). There, the religious processions, sacrifices and
competitions were attended by representatives from many
Greek states (App.'Mac.'11.4), temporarily (one supposes)
happy to forget that worship of the sun was appropriate
to barbarians. Rhodian ritual calendars prescribed the
sacrifices due to Helios: in Dalios, the sacrifice of a
cow by the 'demiorgos'; in Panormos, of three goats by
the 'hieropoioi'; in Hyakinthios of a kid.

A bizarre sacrifice to Helios of a team of horses
hurled into the sea is attributed to the Rhodians by the
scholar Festus, writing in the second century AD (s.v.
October equus). There are parallels from the Peloponnese
for such practices (Farnell, 1907, IV p.20). However,
the consensus of modern scholarship is that this rite
belonged to Poseidon worship on the island, and to the

festival Hippokathesia at Kameiros (see Morelli, 1959,
pp.98-9, for a summary of the evidence and of modern
views).

In the adjacent islands, Helios makes sporadic
appearance, through Rhodian influence. An inscription
from Saros refers to the Rhodian games; on Kos there
occurs an association of Heliastai. Also, finds on Kos
include a small shrine to Helios and Hemera ('day'), and
an altar dedicated to Helios and his 'theoi symbomioi'
('deities linked in worship').

Myths and genealogies strongly suggest that Poseidon
cults were of great antiquity in the islands. Poseidon
is entrenched in Rhodian myth as the father of the
eponymous nymph Rhodos; the Koan king Eurypylos was also
designated son of the god. Kadmos supposedly founded the
shrine of Poseidon at Ialysos, and built a temple on Thera
to Poseidon and Athena; the Rhodians founded a shrine
of Poseidon Asphaleios on Thera after the great eruption
there; dedications were made to Athena and Poseidon by
Kanopos, the helmsman of Menelaos.

A Bronze Age context for these myths has been adumbrated
in the previous chapter. That they belong to pre-Dorian
times seems confirmed by the pattern of Poseidon cults on
the mainland. Poseidon is not a Peloponnesian god, but
has strong Thessalian connections. The prominence of
Poseidon cults in the islands may provide further
confirmation of early contacts between this region and
Thessaly, though of course there is an allegorical element
present in cult as in myth: it is natural to find a god
of the sea honoured in island communities, and a god of
earthquakes propitiated in a seismic region.

The unusual cult-titles Gilaios and Kyreteios were
discussed in the previous chapter. Poseidon was also
worshipped as god of the sea (Pelagios, a common title,
found also, for instance, at Athens), or the straits
(Porthmios, the main god of Karpathos, a more uncommon
title) or rivers (hence the title Phytalmios, 'nourishing';
cf. Plu.'Mor.'675f). He was god of horses (Hippios at
Kos, Kameiros and Lindos; Hippotas at Thera) and god of
earthquakes (euphemistically Asphaleios, 'securer';
probably also intended in a Theran rock inscription
reading Gaiaochos, 'earth-holder', this being a title of
Poseidon at Sparta, Crete and elsewhere; cf. Paus.3.11.9;
Farnell, 1907, IV p.77). Political overtones are evident
in the cult of Poseidon in Kos: the god is linked in one
inscription with Kos and Rhodos and in another with
Asklepios, Aphrodite Pandemos and Hestia Tamias, deities
promoted after the synoecism.

In the Rhodian cults of Zeus, there are striking echoes
of early Crete, notably the cult-titles Amalos and
Atabyrios, discussed in the previous chapter, and the
designation Kronides Anax, which is accompanied by the
Minoan motif of the double-axe. Primeval aspects of Zeus
as a sky and weather god are prominent: for instance, as
god of thunder and lightning (Astrapatas or Astrapton,
Bronton, Keraunios and Kataibates). Also, Zeus was
invoked as Hyetios, god of rain, in times of prolonged
drought at Kos and Rhodes: an altar of Zeus Hyetios at
Argos is recorded by Pausanias, and the equivalent Ombrios
occurs elsewhere in Greece (Paus.2.19.7, 25.10; cf., in
general, Cook, 1925, II pp.722-858).

Drouthios, known as a title of Zeus at Kameiros of the
third century, is probably of direct Argive origin, with
the meaning 'strong' (Hsch.; Morelli, 1959, p.142).
Patroios, occurring at Kalymnos, is said to be a typically
Dorian title of Zeus (A.fr.162.3). Several of the titles
given to Zeus in the islands - as elsewhere - are
familiar as literary epithets: Hikesios, god of suppliants
(A.'Supp.'616; S.'Ph.'484; cf. Paus.1.20.7, 3.17.9) and
Ktesios, protector of property (A.'Supp.'445; cf. Harp.
s.v. are examples. Some titles are of a very conventional
type; for instance, Hypsistos, 'supreme', and Olympios,
'Olympian', the latter applied to Zeus in many places
far distant from Mount Olympos, including Sparta, Sicily
and Priene in Asia Minor (see Paus.3.12.11, 14.5; cf.
Wide, 1893, pp.9-10 for Sparta; Plb.9.27.9; IG XIV 7
for Sicily; IvPr. 28.30, 188.24 for Priene).

At Lindos, Zeus gradually came to be associated with
the great cult of Athena. His name began to accompany
that of Athena in inscriptions of the beginning of the
third century; a little later - probably around 280 -
the association became official (Blinkenberg, 1941).
Dedications, however, were still made most often to
Athena alone, the goddess retaining her popularity with
the people. In myth, Hera and Zeus are united in a
rather tempestuous marriage; in cult, Zeus is linked
with his daughter Athena rather than with his wife.
Zeus and Athena are frequently worshipped or invoked
together in their role of protectors of the state.

Athena is strikingly different from other Greek goddesses.
Aphrodite, Demeter, Hera and Hestia fit into the same
general pattern, arguably variations on the early Aegean
mother-goddess blueprint: all are concerned in some way
with food or fertility. Artemis fits this pattern to
some extent, although there is tension in her case: she

is the virgin goddess concerned with childbirth, the
huntress who protects wild animals. Athena, the
political goddess, is an exception, and the contention
that her origins lie in a Minoan-Mycenaean palace goddess
is widely accepted.

Cults of Athena were generally served by priests, not
priestesses, in a variation on the rule of priests for
male and priestesses for female deities. Women were
excluded from one of the Rhodian cults of Athena. But
elements alien to Athena and characteristic of other
goddesses do obtrude in some cases. That in Astypalaia
Athena had a priestess, not a priest, is attested by a
fourth-century dedication. In Kos, the sacrifice of a
pregnant ewe to Athena (a type of sacrifice often made
to Demeter) is suggestive. Also in Kos, Athena was
worshipped with the title Alseia ('of the grove'). The
mainstream of Athena worship is, however, political.

Athena, as protector of the state, ensured victory in
war and security in peace. Hence, she has the titles
Apotropaia ('averter' of evil), Areia (connected with
Ares, the war-god), Nike ('victory') and Soteira
('saviour'). Athena was also protector of the family
unit (Phratria), and of arts and crafts, as Hyperdexia
('clever') and Machanis ('contriver').

Polias is by far the most common cult title of Athena,
often worshipped in close conjunction with Zeus Polieus.
At Kameiros, the titles Athana Kameiras and Athana Polias
are interchangeable; so at Ialysos are Athana Ialysia
Polias and Athana of the town of Achaia. The towns on
Karpathos had independent cults in the same way:
Athana Polias is known at Arkaseia in the third century,
while Athana Lindia was worshipped at Potidaion. The
Athena in whose sanctuary is deposited a copy of the
prized decree concluding a defensive alliance between
mighty Rome and Astypalaia, 105 BC, is doubtless Polias.
Telos and Thera also worshipped Athena as Polias.

In the Koan sacrificial calendar for the month Batromios,
detailed provisions regulate the choice of a victim to be
sacrificed to Zeus Polieus, and govern the preliminaries
to the sacrifice (cf. Smith, 1973a). Zeus Polieus in
this ritual is closely associated with Hestia. A
sacrifice to Athena Polias is also mentioned, but briefly,
almost as an afterthought to the main ritual. Later
inscriptions indicate that at Kos, as elsewhere, Zeus
Polieus and Athena Polias came to be closely linked in
cult, sharing priests and sacrificial offerings.

Athena was the main deity of the separate Rhodian
townships before the synoecism, and remained important
locally long afterwards. Repairs to temples (Syme) and

statues (Melos) of Athena are recorded in the Hellenistic
period: while new cults were introduced, the old ones
were not forgotten, but revitalized.

Athena was, of course, the patron goddess of Athens.
As has been seen, the Athenians chose to emphasize the
pan-Hellenic cult of Apollo at Delos, rather than Athena,
to their fifth-century allies. There was, however, an
annual demand of the contribution of a cow for sacrifice
to Athena from the allies, as a symbolic gesture of
loyalty; it is not known how many of the islands complied.
Some traces of Athens' hegemony remain in the mention at
Kos of Athena 'caring for Athens' (i.e. Athenian Athena
Polias) and at Karpathos of the despatch of cypress wood
for the Athenian shrine. Later, the Panathenaistai of
Chalke seem to name their association through Athenian
influence.

Cults of Hestia are not widespread in the islands, but
are of some importance where they do occur: at Kos,
Rhodes and Thera. As goddess of the hearth, domestic as
well as ritual, Hestia seems to hold Hera's position as
protector of conjugal life. (A Koan ritual calendar,
ordaining cereal offerings to Hestia on the 'hestia',
'hearth', epitomizes the personification, IC 401.) In
ritual, Hestia seems at times to usurp Athena's position
alongside her father Zeus.

A common feature of Hestia cults in the islands is
the close link between Hestia and Zeus (Polieus at Kos,
Soter at Kameiros and Thera, or Teleios also at Kameiros).
At Kameiros, the eponymous 'demiorgos' holds the priesthood of Hestia and Zeus Teleios; Hestia occurs with
Zeus Soter in a dedication there. Altars are dedicated
to Hestia, in one case coupled with Zeus Soter, in
second-century Thera. At Kos, Hestia herself is Tamias,
bearing a title usually reserved for Zeus.

In the important state sacrifice to Zeus Polieus,
Hestia Tamias is, as remarked above, involved. After the
most elaborate preliminaries, an ox was selected for
sacrifice to Zeus, and the price of the beast was paid to
Hestia Tamias, that is, probably, to a special state fund
(cf. Farnell, 1909, V pp.349-50). The presence of Hestia
Tamias with Aphrodite Pandemos (embodiment of civic unity),
Homonoia ('concord') and Asklepios (the new state god) in
another Koan inscription is a further indication of
Hestia's political importance.

The persistent link between Hestia and Zeus is peculiarly
apparent in a Theran inscription commemorating Hestia
Boulaia Agrippina, mother of Caligula, and Zeus Boulaios

Germanikos Kaisar, his father. It is revealing that
Hestia, not Hera, is singled out for syncretism with the
Roman imperial family and given a marital relationship
with Zeus.

Hera had little importance in the islands, even in those
populated from the Argolid, her main cult centre on the
mainland (cf. Tomlinson, 1972, pp.203-4 for Argive Hera).
The earliest evidence for worship of Hera in our area is
a dedication made by a priestess of Hera at Astypalaia,
in the fourth or early third century. From Rhodes and
Thera, there is second-century evidence and from Kos
Roman material.
   Most of the cult-titles given to Hera in the islands
are conventional in type: Basileia ('queen'), applied
also to Aphrodite and other goddesses, Olympia ('Olympian')
and Ourania ('heavenly'). A more unusual collocation is
Argeia, Eleia, Basileia, applied to Hera in Roman Kos.
Eleia ('of the meadow') was a title of Hera in Cyprus
(Hsch.). The record of a priestess of Hera Dromaia at
Thera recalls the title Dromaios given Apollo, as patron
of racing, at Sparta and the festival Prodromia at Sikyon
(Paus.2.11.2). Connections with Apollo are perhaps
implicit also in the cult of Hera Telchinia, with the
nymphs, at Kameiros. (On Hera in conjunction with Apollo,
cf. Paus.3.11.9; Wide, 1893, p.25.)

Aphrodite was, according to the Souda, particularly
honoured in the islands (ἐνοικέτις τῶν νήσων ἡ
Ἀφροδίτη· ἐξαιρέτως γὰρ ἐν αὐταῖς ἐτιμᾶτο). However,
the available evidence suggests that the worship of
Aphrodite was neither of great importance nor of great
antiquity in the islands, despite their proximity to
Cyprus, the place of her genesis.
   The earliest evidence comes from the third century,
with the record of priests at Kameiros and a priestess
at Kos. There are indications of a growing popularity
after this period: Diomedon included sacrifices to
Aphrodite in initiating his cult-foundation; at Anaphe,
a small shrine of Aphrodite was established in the
sanctuary of Apollo Asgelatas. Also, many religious
associations made Aphrodite their patron (cf. Poland,
1909, p.190).
   The importance of Aphrodite Pandemos ('of all the
people') as a civic deity at Kos has already been remarked.
Pausanias records that the Athenian cult of Aphrodite
Pandemos was instituted by Theseus at the time of the

synoecism (Paus.1.22.3). Plato, however, contrasts
Aphrodite Pandemos with Aphrodite Ourania, as representing
a baser type of love, sensual, not intellectual, and other
Athenian evidence suggests that Aphrodite Pandemos was
popularly regarded as the goddess of courtesans (Pl.'Smp.'
181a). It is doubtful that the state cult ever had these
overtones, even when the supposed connection with Theseus
was forgotten. It seems that Kos after the synoecism -
like Athens after Theseus' measures - gave the goddess a
new political title. From this probably stems the
representation of a head of Aphrodite on a Koan coin of
the turn of the second and first century (Head, 1911,
pp.633-4).

Eudie ('calm'), a title given to Aphrodite by a
Rhodian association of female membership may, like
Pandemos, have political overtones (cf. PA I p.636).
However, the adjective is used especially of weather
conditions, and an alternative possibility is that in
this evidence, late as it is, we have a vestigial
survival of Aphrodite as nature goddess (cf. SBA (1911)
p.639, Cypriot inscription).

Other cult titles given to Aphrodite are of the
conventional courtesy type: Basileia ('queen'), Hypakoos
('hearkening' to prayer). Paphia (of Paphos, in Cyprus),
which is a common literary description of Aphrodite, is
also found, used by a Rhodian association.

The most famous Greek centre of the worship of Demeter
was at Eleusis in Attica; the most important Attic
festival of the goddess was the Thesmophoria. The place-
name Eleusis is found also on Thera (Ptol.'Geog.'3.15.25),
and the month-name Thesmophorios on Rhodes. Evidence for
the cult of Demeter, with or without her daughter Kore
(or in some cases for Kore alone) exists from most of
the islands. It seems that the cult was both old and
widespread.

Demeter, more than any other Greek goddess, typifies
the mother-earth figure, whose origins reach back into
pre-Hellenic times and of whom there are manifestations
in Minoan Crete (cf. Picard, 1927). A sacrifice shared
by Demeter and Ge ('Earth') in first-century Kalymnos
suggests the persistence in the island of a primeval
conception of the goddess.

In Thera, there was an archaic cult of Kore, named in
a rock inscription in the precinct of Apollo Karneios.
There too, a fourth-century inscription mentions a priesthood of Demeter and Kore; Kore appears alone on a third-
century altar and Demeter occurs without her daughter in

another inscription. At Astypalaia too, Kore appears
alone in dedications.

There is much evidence from fertile Kos for cults of
Demeter. Philitas wrote an elegy to the goddess;
Theokritos described agrarian festivities (the Thalysia)
in her honour. Epigraphical evidence details the appointment of a priestess of Demeter (see the following chapter)
and lists the appropriate sacrifices to be carried out in
the month Batromios. On Rhodes, the expression Damateres
was used of Demeter and Kore, and Zeus had the title
Damatrios.

Conventional cult-titles used of Demeter are Olympia
and Soteira ('saviour'), the latter used in a Koan cult
which excluded men, as did the Athenian Thesmophoria.
The title Thesmophoros is implied in the existence of a
Rhodian association of Thesmophoriastai. Theokritos'
Thalysia ('thelus', 'female') suggests a similar
exclusiveness. Late evidence from Kos shows a cult of
Demeter Karpophoros ('fruit-bearing'), linked with the
worship of the Roman emperor, illustrating the survival
of a primitive title with dilution or complete loss of
meaning. The title is a common one, known at Epidauros
(perhaps the source of the Koan usage) on the mainland,
at Paros and Lesbos in the Aegean and at several places,
including Ephesos, in Asia Minor.

Herakles' prominent place in the myths of Kos and Rhodes
was remarked in the previous chapter. Like Asklepios,
Herakles belonged in myth to the generation preceding
that of the heroes of the Trojan wars and, like Asklepios,
he was simultaneously honoured as a real ancestor (founder
of the early dynasties in Kos and Rhodes) and worshipped
as a hero-god. The difference between Herakles and such
heroes as Tlepolemos is one of degree rather than of
kind: thus, in the Lindian Chronicle, Herakles - like
many humans of heroic stature - makes dedications to the
goddess Athena at Lindos.

Much concerning the cults of Herakles in the islands
is obscure. Ancient mythographers essayed aetiological
accounts of the Rhodian practices in which Herakles was
cursed by his own priest. Modern consideration of the
question is inconclusive. Farnell despairingly dismissed
the custom as 'an eccentric freak' (1921, p.160) while
van Gelder offered the plausible, though unprovable,
suggestion that the ritual might have arisen through
hostility on the part of earlier inhabitants of Lindos
to the Dorian newcomers, and the replacing of bloodless
rites with animal sacrifice (1900, p.348; cf. Nilsson,

1906, pp.450-1 and Morelli, 1959, pp.148-9, with
bibliography to which Arnold, 1936 should be added).

Other puzzles centre on the transvestite ritual at
Antimachia (but perhaps this is less atypical than our
evidence, as always defective, suggests: cf. Dodds, ed.
E.'Ba.' 1960, on 453-9 for the universality of the
conception of the womanish god and effeminate priest);
and on the choice of the crab as symbol of Herakles for
depiction on Koan coins.

The Dorian tribe of the Hylleis, who claimed descent
from Hyllos, son of Herakles, worshipped Herakles with
special rites: a Koan inscription records a sacrifice
made by this tribe at the Herakleion in the area known as
Konisalos. Also in Kos, Apollo and Herakles were
worshipped together in an old ritual, eligibility for
which was a carefully guarded privilege of families at
Halasarna. The pattern of this Herakles festival involved
a sacrificial meal, a feature incorporated as a prominent
part of the new worship of Herakles Diomedonteios
instituted by Diomedon.

Many dedications to Herakles - and to Hermes, often
named with him - have been unearthed in the gymnasia
of Hellenistic cities, made by victors at the games, or
by gymnasiarchs and other officials. Associations of
Herakleistai or Herakleotai and of Hermaistai or
Hermaizontes were common.

Like Herakles, Hermes was a popular god. Worship of
Hermes was informal: there are no records of priests or
of temples, and most inscriptions naming him are dedicatory.
The patronage of Hermes extended over the day-to-day
activities of ordinary people, in the household, in the
gymnasium, in the market-place and on journeys (including
the last journey to the underworld).

Hermes Propylaios ('before the gates') at Kameiros and
Megiste was envisaged as protector of the people inside
the 'gates', as with the Hermes figure surmounting a
pillar, so common on the domestic scene. The mercantile
associations of the god can be seen in a dedication at
Lindos to Zeus Agoraios ('of the agora'), the Themites
('Right Ways') and Hermes; similarly, at Thera, the
Agoreioi are Hermes and Herakles. Hermes' connections
with death are evident in the record of a Koan sanctuary
of the Moirai ('Fates') together with Hermes Kyllanios
('of Kyllene', a mountain in Arkadia), Artemis Toxitis
('archer', referring perhaps to her shafts, bringing
death to mortals) and Olympian Zeus; also in a Lindian
dedication to Hermes Hagemon ('conductor' of the souls of
the dead).

The god Dionysos had to fight for his place in the Greek
pantheon. Myths incidentally touched on in Homer and
given extended treatment in later writers tell of battles
between Dionysos and recalcitrant Greek monarchs who
rashly repudiated him. Strong traditions placed the
origins of Dionysos in the East, in Phrygia or Lydia.
One view of his genesis is that the cult of a Greek
agrarian deity Dionysos was fused with that of the
orgiastic Lydian Bakchos (Otto, 1933). Other traditions
suggested a Thracian origin for Dionysiac worship. Like
Apollo, Dionysos may have reached Greece by two separate
routes: from the North, via Thrace and Delphi and also
from the East, via the Aegean islands. Crete and Naxos
laid strong claims to Dionysos in myth, while in cult
Delphi long retained a peculiar importance. Dionysos
belongs to a later stratum of myth than does Apollo,
being placed in the era of Kadmos (cf. Dodds, ed. E.'Ba.',
1960, p.xxi). But, if he is 'younger' than Apollo, he
was none the less established on the Greek mainland by
around 1400, being mentioned in the Linear B tablets;
that is to say, Dionysos was worshipped by the Greeks in
the heroic mortal lifetimes of Herakles and Asklepios.

Festivals of Dionysos in our region abound. Astypalaia,
Kos, Rhodes and Thera all had Dionysia (in Rhodes, later,
Alexandreia and Dionysia). Dionysos was also worshipped,
both at Lindos and Rhodos, in the festival Sminthia. On
Anaphe, the festival known as the Theodaisia was probably
Dionysiac (Hsch.Theodaisios: Dionysos; cf. the month
Theodaisios at Kos, Kalymnos and Rhodes). An association
attached to Anthister Pythochrestos in first-century Thera
may imply a festival Anthesteria (more usual in Ionian
states) there. The month Agrianios at Kos, Kalymnos and
Rhodes recalls the Argive Agriania, a festival of Dionysos.

At the Rhodian Dionysia, tragedy and comedy were
performed; at the Koan festival there is evidence for
comedy and dithyrambic poetry. At Astypalaia too,
dramatic competitions took place at the festival, in the
month Iobakchios. Dedications highlight the connections
of Dionysos with the performing arts: by a tragic poet
at Astypalaia and by a flautist at Kos (IC 58). Associations of Bakcheioi, Dionysiastai and 'technitai' of
Dionysos were formed, both locally and on an inter-state
basis, some vocational and others not.

Because of Dionysos' associations with the theatre, he
was often worshipped with the Muses and linked with
Apollo. At Kameiros, a priest of Dionysos performs
sacrifices to the Muses and Mnemosyne; in Kos, there
were processions to Dionysos and the Muses, while Apollo
and Dionysos are named together in a dedication. Dionysos

was patron also of the visual arts, and the Rhodian
temple of Dionysos was a repository of valuable art
treasures.

The festivals of Dionysos were great state occasions,
with sacrifice to the god a preliminary not only to the
dramatic and musical competitions, but also to the issue
of proclamations such as the announcement of honours
accorded public benefactors, made before the assemblage
of citizens and visiting foreigners. Because of this,
some political aspects crept into the Dionysiac cults.
This trend is reflected in the presence of Dionysos -
replacing Helios - on some late Rhodian coins. At Kos,
there was an altar to Dionysos in the Agora: in the
third century, one copy of a list of patriotic contributors
to a military fund was placed there, other copies going to
the theatre and the Asklepieion.

Titles of Dionysos in the islands reflect various
common aspects of his worship: Propoleos ('before the
city') and Kathegemon ('leader') are civic in character
(but see Dodds, ed. E.'Ba.', 1960, on 920-2 for another
view of Kathegemon, seen in more primitive terms);
Bakcheios is orgiastic, as is Trieterikos. Alongside
these, titles of Dionysos as a god of vegetation (the
aspect which led to his specific association with the
vine) are Epikarpios, Skyllitas and Thyllophoros.
Dionysos Thyllophoros was still important in Hellenistic
Kos, where the priesthood was offered for sale to a
female buyer (by contrast, Dionysos Skyllitas had a
priest): regulations for the payment for the priesthood,
installation of the priestess and appointment of an
acolyte are all detailed.

This rather summary treatment of the cults and festivals
of the main gods of the region (Apollo, Asklepios, Helios,
Poseidon, Zeus, Athena, Hestia, Hera, Aphrodite, Demeter,
Herakles, Hermes and Dionysos) has aimed to explore the
pattern of conservatism and change in local practices;
with the accommodation of established traditions into an
ever-changing cultural scene. Great regional diversity
is apparent in the islands, with different gods honoured,
under varying cult-titles, in communities linked by shared
geographical setting, common historical influences and
kindred origins and speech. This diversity - though
possibly exaggerated by the exiguous character of the
available sources - is deep-seated.

9   Administration

Aristotle, with his zeal for observation and classification, attempted to compartmentalize religion as one of the activities of the community, alongside fiscal, legal, military and other aspects of civic life ('Pol.'1322b 18-30):

> Another kind of administration ('epimeleia') is that concerned with the gods, exemplified by priests ('hiereis') and administrators ('epimeletai') of matters connected with the temples - the conservation of existing buildings and rebuilding of those which become dilapidated - also, of all other matters laid down in relation to the gods. It happens that this administration is in some places a single office, for instance, in small communities, but in others it comprises many offices, distinct from the priesthood, such as 'hieropoioi', 'naophylakes', treasurers ('tamiai') of the sacred revenues. Connected with this administration is the office appointed for all the state sacrifices, which the law puts not in the hands of priests, but of those who have a position of honour based on the state sacrificial hearth. Some places call these 'archontes', some 'basileis', some 'prytaneis'.

Two significant points emerge from the Aristotelian analysis. First, there is a persistent overlap between sacred and secular. This is apparent from the passage quoted, in the conduct of certain sacrifices by the state officials 'archontes', 'basileis' and 'prytaneis' and also in the administration of temple finance by special treasurers. Similarly, in the following section, it is state officials who are responsible for organization of Dionysiac and other festivals ('theoriai'). Earlier too (1321b39) there is evidence of fluidity in use of terms for officials of cult and state, when 'hieromnemones'

('sacred recorders') are not distinguished from
'mnemones' (recorders). The second point is that
different states use different titles for their officials
(1321b38, 1322b11, 1322b28; cf. 1322b25). It is clear
that, while communities had broadly similar administrative
requirements, and met these with broadly similar types of
organization, the terminology employed varied greatly from
one region to another.

The overlap between sacred and secular, which forced
itself on Aristotle's attention, was a consequence of the
integral part played by religion in the life of the
community. As remarked in the previous chapter, festivals
provided recreation and entertainment for the populace,
as well as a forum to impress visiting foreigners, while
the state sanctuaries were often used as repositories for
important records or strongrooms for public funds.
Naturally, therefore, the state was concerned that
festivals be properly conducted and that archivists and
treasurers carry out their work efficiently.

No firm lines of demarcation can be drawn between
state and cult officials, or between administrative and
ritual activities. It is much easier to make a distinction between personnel concerned with sanctuaries and
those concerned with festivals. In the passage quoted,
Aristotle is more interested in the former.

As will be seen in the course of this chapter, the
variation in terminology applied to their civic and
religious functionaries by the different Dorian islands
is no less marked and idiosyncratic than the divergences
they display in dialect (see Chapter 4) or in the usage
of cult-titles (see Chapter 8). Before examining the
other types of official mentioned by Aristotle and
isolating their regional equivalents, we turn first to
a study of the terms 'hiereus' (priest) and 'hiereia'
(priestess). In the ensuing discussion, the English
words 'priest' and 'priestess' are used only to translate
'hiereus' and 'hiereia'; similarly 'priesthood' is a
translation of 'hierosyne'. Reference to other officials
who might be called, broadly, 'priests' is by their Greek
title transliterated.

A preliminary point of some importance is that not all
deities had priests, and not all shrines had an attendant.
That there was a priest is certain only when the
expression 'priest of' occurs, as in many Rhodian
catalogues, or when we have a list of priests who held
office in a particular sanctuary. Dedications by a
priest to a god are not necessarily to the god he serves:
on Kos, a priest of Apollo dedicates a shrine to Hekate
(KF 217). The island of Karpathos shows little evidence

for priests. There is a list of those who have held the priesthood of the 'Samothracian gods', but no other gods are named in this way. Doubtless, however, in this instance Poseidon Porthmios the main god of the community had priests as well as the 'hieragogoi' mentioned in inscriptions.

Closely related deities, such as Zeus and Athena, or Asklepios and the minor gods of healing, often shared a priesthood. In such cults, the relative status of deities might differ at different periods. As observed in the previous chapter, Zeus gradually encroached on Athena's pre-eminence at Lindos, while on Kos Asklepios worship was originally a subsidiary part of the worship of Apollo and was ultimately fused with the cult of the deified Roman emperors. The priesthood of the cult of Asklepios, the emperor, all the gods and the Koan 'demos' (NS 443) is described in several different ways, implying differing degrees of syncretism: priest of the emperor and the 'demos' (NS 462); priest of the 'philosebastos demos' of the Koans (NS 446); priest of Asklepios Kaisar (IC 130, NS 464); priest of Asklepios Kaisar Sebastos, Hygieia and Epione; priest of Asklepios, Hygieia, Epione and the Sebastoi (AA 18 (1903) p.193).

Tenure of one priesthood did not preclude simultaneous or subsequent tenure of others (see, as a sample of the many instances at Rhodes, IG XII 1, 818, 820, 826, 831, 832; and cf. IC 125 for a Koan example). In such cases, it is generally impossible to determine whether the priesthoods were held concurrently or consecutively, but it is clear that the holding of several priesthoods at once, often with life tenure, had become much more common in the Roman period.

In some cults, the office of priest was hereditary; in others, priests entered office by a process of election, of lot or of purchase. In Thera, one family (with the predominant names Admetos, Aglophanes and Theokleidas) held the important priesthoods of Apollo Karneios and Asklepios from the sixth century BC till the early days of the Roman Empire. This family may have been descended from the early kingship, with a continuous tradition of religious power of royal origin (Hiller von Gaertringen, 1901; cf. Arist.'Pol.' 1290b on the Theran aristocracy). In Sparta, the kingship was long vested with religious as well as secular authority, and the constitution of Thera was influenced by that of her mother city in other respects (cf. Craik, 1969, on the Theran ephorate).

The priestly prerogatives of the descendants of Agloteles, who organized the sacrifices to Apollo Karneios, are analogous with the arrangements made in the family cult

foundations of Hellenistic times. When Pythokles
instituted the Pythokleia, with sacrifices to Zeus and
Athena, he arranged that there should be two priesthoods
(of Zeus and of Athena) descending through his two sons in
two lines of his family. This was a public cult, open to
all the citizens, like the other state games, not a private
one involving only Pythokles' family. Later, the associations of Diomedon on Kos and Epikteta on Thera restricted
membership to direct descendants of the founders:
illegitimate children were eligible for membership, but
debarred from holding office as priest or 'epimenios'.

In hereditary priesthoods, the priesthood was usually
passed on in a simple father-to-son sequence. Occasionally,
however, it descended by generations. An inscription from
Halikarnassos gives full documentation of this process in
the case of the priests of Poseidon, who claimed descent
from that god (SIG 1020). After the death of Telamon,
son of Poseidon and head of the list, his three sons were
priests in turn, followed by the two sons of the eldest
son and the son of the third son (the second being child-
less), before the priesthood devolved on the next generation. The family tree shows how the sequence began.

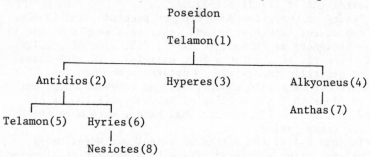

There is no record of dispute in the transmission within
the family of hereditary priesthoods, but occasionally the
office was voluntarily resigned, or delegated to the next
in line of succession. Tradition had it that the
philosopher Herakleitos refused to take up a priesthood
('office of king') which fell to him by inheritance, and
a similar example of a priest of Poseidon in Athens is
recorded by Plutarch (D.L.50.9.6; Plu.'Mor.'843f).

Sacral officials known to have entered office after
election are the 'hieragogoi' on Karpathos and also, on
Kos, the 'epimenioi' employed in the cult instituted by
Diomedon, where the priesthood proper was hereditary
(IG XII 1, 1035; Historia 7 (1933) pp.577-88, no.7;
IC 367.91 sqq; KF 221).

Lot was widely used in the Greek world as a means of

appointment. On Rhodes, the eponymous priest of Helios
was appointed annually by lot, and in the event of his
death during year of office his successor was appointed
by the same method (SER 5.38). On Astypalaia, a priest
of the 'patrioi theoi' honoured in an inscription of the
third or second century for his conscientious term of
office had been appointed by lot; probably, however,
from members of an association, not from the entire
community.

Naturally, eligibility for a cult was a prerequisite
for eligibility for the priesthood. A Koan inscription
which issued revised rules for the conduct of the cult of
Apollo and Herakles at Halasarna laid down that the
'napoiai' should check all those who handed in their
names as candidates for the priesthood, to be allocated
by lot, against the list of those entitled to participate.
A list of priests in this same cult sometimes names
Apollo or the 'demos' as incumbents, probably at times
when no one volunteered for the office (cf. the record
in D.57 of procedure in the cult of Herakles in the Attic
deme Halimous).

In certain cases, only members of a particular family
could hold a priesthood; another Koan inscription
records the appointment of a priest by descent but
simultaneously also by 'divine intimation', i.e. lot
(IC 103). Qualifications of a different kind were
specified in a third-century inscription dealing with
the appointment of a priestess of Demeter: the incumbent
was to be appointed by lot from volunteers prepared to
put up a fixed sum of money (IC 386 = SIG 1006 = ZLS 132).

It has been suggested that the inscription just
mentioned marks a point of transition between appointment
by lot, and sale of the office to the highest bidder
(ZLS p.330, noting that the presence of the candidates
at the drawing of lots is no longer obligatory and
suggesting that a greater laxity in procedure resulted
from the introduction of the financial requirement). In
the event of the introduction of fundamental change in
cult organization, a new set of regulations had to be
formulated. And so Koan inscriptions which state that
certain priesthoods are to be put up for sale incorporate
full instructions about the involvement of administrative
officials ('poletai', 'prostatai', 'strategoi', 'tamiai')
and about the procedure to be followed. There is
epigraphical evidence from Kos for the sale of the
priesthoods of Adrasteia and Nemesis, Aphrodite, Asklepios
and Hygieia, Demeter and also Dionysos Thyllophoros.
In neighbouring Halikarnassos, the priesthood of Artemis
Pergaia was open to purchase.

The practice of selling priesthoods of state cults became prevalent in Asia Minor and the islands off its coasts in the Hellenistic period, though it is found as early as the fifth century at Miletos. To account for the prevalence of the practice in the Asiatic region, it has been suggested that the sale of priesthoods became current in communities where the treasury was at a low ebb through financial losses incurred by the passage of Alexander and his troops through Asia Minor;   that it was an expedient to inject new revenues into the exchequer. It is then necessary to suppose that other communities, with less pressing fiscal problems, copied the custom, and also that it was retained when the crisis had passed (see Herbrecht, 1886; also Segre, 1937c and Sokolowski, 1957).

It may be, rather, that political and social pressures were constantly operating on the administration of cults. In the early aristocratic society, hereditary succession to office was probably the general rule, while a demo-cratic Greek community would appoint its priests - like many other office-bearers - by lot. Thus, in conservative Thera, the priesthood of Apollo Karneios remained the prerogative of one aristocratic family, while Rhodes, after the synoecism, employed lot to appoint successive priests in the newly inaugurated cult of Helios. Then, in the Hellenistic period, privilege again operated, this time the privilege of the nouveau riche: there resulted, on the one hand, the transition from lot (giving opportunity to all) to sale (restricted to the wealthy) and, on the other hand, an artificially created resurgence of hereditary transmission of priestly office as prominent families established their own exclusive cult founda-tions.

The qualifications required for holding a priesthood are rarely specified in inscriptions. State priests would naturally be citizens of free birth. Explicit mention of this is occasionally made; for instance, the Koan priestess who must choose a citizen as her 'under-priestess' is evidently herself of the citizen body. Physical health might be demanded. An age-limit was occasionally set; thus, the Koan priestess of Dionysos Thyllophoros had to be at least ten years of age (IC 27 = SIG 1012 = ZLS 133 = RP 17 (1940-1) pp.21 sqq.; cf. IC 30 = ZLS 135).

Certain priests were distinguished by their garb. A Koan inscription from the second century lays down that the priest of Nike wear white at all times except at the annual sacral procession, when he should wear a purple robe, gold rings and a crown of fresh leaves (Wilhelm,

1926, against Maiuri, NS p.150). The priest of Zeus wore
a special garment when presiding over the selection of an
ox for sacrifice (Wilamowitz, RM 52 (1897) p.188,
commenting on IC 37.10). As noted in the previous chapter,
the Koan priest of Herakles wore woman's dress on
ceremonial occasions.

Occasionally, the garb of worshippers was subject to
limitations. In the precinct of Apollo Oulios at Kos,
the wearing of a particular kind of garment - probably
black - was forbidden (Pugliese Carratelli, 1957b,
p.444, with Robert, REG 72 (1959) p.222; cf. Radke,
1936). Akin to these regulations about dress are
restrictions on certain kinds of food, forbidden either
categorically or for a set period to priest or worshipper:
lentils, cheese and goat-meat at one temple in Rhodes and
beans in another, probably that of Asklepios (IG XII 1,
789).

Sexual restrictions might be imposed on priests,
usually - at least in the Hellenistic period - for a
short time only, before an important sacrifice or
festival. In a Koan inscription, a 'hieropoios' chosen
by the priest to perform a sacrifice was forbidden to
have intercourse (with a woman or a man) on the preceding
night (IC 37 = SIG 1025 = PLS 5 = HG 1; IC 40 = PLS 8 =
HG 5). So far as is known, complete celibacy was not
practised by priests or priestesses in the islands.

Entry restrictions were imposed by certain sanctuaries.
Women were excluded from the cults of Zeus Amalos and of
Zeus Apotropaios and Athena Apotropaia at Lindos, while
slaves were debarred from the sanctuary of Herakles of
Kos. In another Koan shrine, freedom from recent contact
with a woman in childbirth, or with a corpse, and also
from sexual intercourse was a requirement (Fraser, 1953).
A shrine on Astypalaia prohibited entry to anyone not
'hagnos', 'pure', and another on Rhodes made the same
stipulation of 'purity'. Similarly, the Koan priest of
Nike was expected to be 'hagnos' in the way ordained for
all other priests (IG XII 3, 183 = SIG 980 = ZLS 123;
NS 441).

Ritual purity was negative rather than positive in
character, consisting primarily of the avoidance of
certain 'polluting' activites. In general, there was
stress on external observance of rules, rather than
inner state of mind, on physical condition, not moral
or spiritual qualities. Piety (as opposed to purity) was
never, it seems, laid down as a qualification for priesthood.

Doubtless the outward display of piety was valued,
nevertheless, as desirable for a priest in office.

Retired priests are commonly lauded in inscriptions for
their virtues of 'eusebeia', 'piety', 'sophrosyne',
'moderation' or simply 'arete', 'excellence'. There are
more inscriptions in praise of priestly piety from Anaphe
and, especially, Thera than elsewhere. It is possible
that these communities looked for high moral qualities
in their priests, but perhaps more likely that the
formula gained popularity there by a freak of chance,
and has no real significance. All the inscriptions which
commend piety are from the second century or later,
probably reflecting a new fashion in the terminology of
approbation. The expressions used in decrees, especially
honorary ones, did tend to become stereotyped, scarcely
varying from one individual to another (cf. IG XII 1,
831 and 832 from Lindos; XII 3, 247 from Anaphe; 513
from Thera; 1116 from Melos; NS 460 from Kos).
     The main work of a priest was to carry out the
appropriate sacrifices (EM 'hiereus', ὁ τὰς θυσίας ἀνα-
πέμπων τῷ θεῷ). Sacrifices are almost invariably
performed by the priest personally. At Rhodes, the
'hierothytes' or 'archierothytes', 'victim-sacrificer'
or 'chief-victim-sacrificer' might officiate (priest,
TCam.148, 151; 'hierothytes' IL 181, 182; 'archierothytes'
NSER 20). The title 'hierothytes' is typical of the
terminology used by Greek states in their administrative
practice, with its 'hiero-' prefix (which, in this case,
with '-thytes', is tautologous) and with local variation
in usage. The Rhodian 'hierothytes' performs sacrifices
but also presides over the 'hierothyteion', an administrative building. It seems that on Karpathos and Syme
the 'hierothytai' are a purely administrative board.
Apparently, in adopting the Rhodian term, these islands
ignore its underlying sacral connotation. (Historia 7
(1933) p.579, 'hierothytai' entertain benefactors of the
state to meals in the 'prytaneion' at Karpathos; cf.
IG XII 3, suppl.1270 for Syme). It is striking that
'hierothytai' appear most often in Dorian communities,
and especially in those which have connections with
Rhodes, in situation or by colonization (IG XIV, 290,
951, 952, Sicily; AE (1911) p.59, Peraia).
     The 'damiorgos' who makes sacrifices at Kameiros is
priest of Hestia and Zeus (TCam 152). Also at Kameiros,
sacrifices are offered by 'hieropoioi' (TCam 152, 155).
At Kos, one of the heralds is elected to act as 'sphageus'
of the animal to be offered to Zeus in the month Batromios.
This is the only known instance of 'sphageus' as a
sacrificial title, instead of denoting 'slayer',
'murderer' (E.'IT' 623; D.13.32, etc.). However, the
cognate terms 'sphage', 'sphagion' and 'sphagiazo' are

regularly used in sacrificial contexts, as 'sacrifice'
(noun), 'sacrificial victim' and 'sacrifice' (verb) (SIG
685.27). The interdependence of sacral activities and
other related spheres is evident in the delegation to a
herald of execution of this important Koan sacrifice (cf.
Aristeas 184 for the linking of 'hierokerykes' and
'thytai').

Preliminaries to the sacrifice, like the sacrifice
itself, were generally the concern of the priest. The
priest was responsible for offering prayers, pouring
libations, leading processions, ensuring that everything
required was ready for the due performance of the ritual
(IC 36 = SIG 1106 = ZLS 144 = HG 10; IC 37 = SIG 1025 =
PLS 5 = HG 1; IC 38 = SIG 1026 = PLS 6 = HG 2; IC 39 =
SIG 1027 = PLS 7 = HG 3; IC 386 = SIG 1006 = ZLS 132;
NS 441; IG XII suppl. 150; TC 31). In some cases, the
priest procured the sacrificial animal from money allocated
by the state or from cult funds. The Koan priest of Zeus
Polieus was personally responsible for selecting the
victim from a formidable herd of contenders (IC 36 and
37, with other references as above; 369 = ZLS 138;
IG XII 3, 30).

At the feasts which followed state sacrificial
offerings, priests received portions of honour ('gere')
from the roast meat. Frequently, a whole gigot was
allocated to the priest, that is, it may be supposed, to
his family, or his table at the banquet. The priest
often received the animal's hide also, doubtless for sale
to a tanner at a good price. The Koan sacrificial
calendar for Batromios gives minute details of the 'gere'
allocated to participants, including even the liver and
brains of the beast.

The priest or his authorized deputy had a monopoly of
performing sacrifices at his shrine (IC 27 = SIG 1012 =
ZLS 133; cf. ZLS 335). In certain cases, a charge was
levied for each sacrifice performed. In the case of
priesthoods put up for sale, a number of sacrifices might
be declared statutory, perhaps to attract purchasers by
the prospect of a guaranteed income (IC 29 = ZLS 139;
IC 369 = ZLS 138; KF 191 = SIG 1000 = ZLS 137).

The Koan priest of Nike received half of the money
paid into the sacred treasury by worshippers (NS 441).
Exemption from liability to perform state liturgies -
that is, to finance recurrent costly state enterprises,
military or cultural - was a privilege, tantamount in
modern terms to a tax concession, granted to certain
priests. Others again were entitled to take up a public
collection ('agermos') for themselves (IC 32 = ZLS 136;
IC 386.12; cf. SIG 1015, from Halikarnassos and ZLS 116,
from Samos).

All these varied provisions for the priest's material
welfare suggest that he was not actually paid for his
services, but derived many material advantages from his
office. Apart from these tangible benefits, priests
commanded a certain amount of prestige. Numerous honorary
inscriptions demonstrate this. The crown frequently
granted was a symbol of public recognition and respect.
Other rewards include grants of a commemorative statue,
a front seat at the games and subsidized meals in the
town buildings (ClRh 2 (1929) p.104 no.1). Lists of
holders of priesthoods were often compiled for the
information of posterity: of these, the longest and most
full is that of the priests of Athena at Lindos, embracing
incumbents of the office from the fourth century BC to
the third AD.

The duration of priestly office varied with type of
cult and means of appointment. Priests who inherited
office, whether in a closed family cult or in one
organized by the state, held it for the remainder of
their lives. The same applied to sold priesthoods, where
there might be an initiation ceremony to solemnize the
occasion (IC 27 = SIG 1012 = ZLS 133).

It was common too for priests to remain in office for
one year, probably because most cults celebrated their
main festival annually. Such priesthoods are those of
Apollo at Halasarna, of the Samothracian gods at
Karpathos and in Rhodes – among others – those of Athana
Lindia and Zeus Polieus at Lindos, of Athena and Zeus
Polieus at Ialysos and Kameiros; also that of Helios
(IC 367 = SIG 1023 = ZLS 130; KF 221; IG XII 1, 1034).
When priesthoods were held for a year, it was possible
for the same person to hold office more than once, either
for several years running or after a lapse of time.

The holding of many priesthoods concurrently and for
life became much more common in the Roman period. The
expression 'priest for life' is particularly common of
the priests of the Roman emperors (IC 92; 345 = SIG 804;
NS 462; 475; IG XII 3, 1116). These life-priests
frequently held other important positions in the
community. If a man was responsible for several priesthoods and also had state commitments, the ritual of
individual cults must have commanded little of his time
and attention. Apparently, there was less emphasis on
the meticulous execution of prescribed ritual of particular gods, more on the social and convivial aspects of the
religious life of the community.

The priest who presided over the ritual in the
sanctuary and, in particular, over sacrifice there, was
sometimes empowered to co-opt a colleague, who probably

deputized in case of the priest's illness or enforced absence. Examples of this practice from Kos are the appointment by the priestess of Asklepios and Hygieia of a priestess of Epione, the co-option by the priestess of Dionysos Thyllophoros of an 'under-priestess' and by another priest of his own 'nakoros' (IC 10; 27 = SIG 1012 = ZLS 133; 30 = ZLS 135).

As will be seen, large busy sanctuaries employed additional staff to relieve the priest of the more menial or routine tasks. Undoubtedly slaves also worked in temples, with tasks in cleaning and maintenance. There is some evidence - a dedication - for the title 'hierodoulos', 'sacral slave' in the region. It seems too that freed slaves might be placed in the service of a cult on the understanding that their descendants would carry on the same work (NS 451; IC 36 = SIG 1106 = ZLS 144 = HG 10; BSAA 40 (1953) p.36).

In the passage from the 'Politics' quoted at the beginning of this chapter, Aristotle cites, as examples of sacral offices distinct from the priesthood, those of 'hieropoios', 'naophylax' and 'tamias'. Such officials are known from our region, under those and other names.

'Hieropoioi' are mentioned in many inscriptions from Kos and Rhodes, typically officiating at processions and sacrifices (cf. Smith, 1972 and 1973b; Doermer, 1883, Part II.1.B; also the expression Antipho 6.45). Priests and 'hieropoioi' often act together, notably at Kameiros, where members of the college of 'hieropoioi', nearly always twelve in number, are regularly listed with the 'demiorgos', priest of Zeus Teleios and Hestia (IC 37 = SIG 1025 = PLS 5 = HG 1; 370, 383, 388; NS 441; TCam 17, 24, 27, 31, 38, 39, 40, 41, 43). 'Hieropoioi' served also among the personnel of the temple of Apollo Erethimios (IG XII 1, 694, 731). Dedications made by 'hieropoioi' are numerous (e.g. IC 370, 388, 406).

In one Koan inscription, the 'gere' of the 'hieropoioi' are shared with the 'thyaphoros', 'incense-bearer'. This is the only evidence for such an acolyte, but incense was probably regularly used, as dealers in incense were subject to a tax in Hellenistic Kos and one inscription records the dedication of a censer (IC 36.13 = SIG 1106 = ZLS 144 = HG 10; 37 = SIG 1025 = PLS 5 = HG 1; KF 191.15).

'Epimenioi', like 'hieropoioi', held appointment for particular sacrifices, perhaps originally, as the title implies, those celebrated at monthly intervals (cf. Hsch.). 'Epimenioi' are known in Kos as officials of tribe (IC 367 = SIG 1023 = ZLS 130), deme (HG 15) and association (IC 35, 382 = SIG 1107); the same title is employed for

functionaries in the cult foundations of the Koan
Diomedon and Theran Epikteta.

Aristotle's 'naophylakes', 'temple-guards', are similar
in character to Koan 'hierophylakes' and to the 'neopoiai'
found in many communities. At Kos, the 'hierophylakes'
are based in the treasury of Asklepios, where they take
charge of one of the keys, supervise the deposit of
money and assist with the account keeping. At Kameiros,
the 'hierophylakes' are an important committee, with their
own secretary and under-secretary, concerned with the
temple of Apollo Erethimios.

'Hierophylax', like 'hieragogos' (Karpathos) 'hierapolos'
(Telos), 'hierophantes' (Melos), 'hieropoios' (Astypalaia,
Kos and Rhodes) and 'hierothytes' (Rhodes) is a cult-term.
However, the 'hiero-' prefix does not in the Hellenistic
period invariably distinguish sacral from secular
officials, as was no doubt its original function. Dilution
of the sacral connotation of the prefix is more marked in
terms where the second half of the word may meaningfully
stand alone. Thus, as noted above, Aristotle's terminology
for record-keepers shows an awareness that 'mnemones' and
'hieromnemones' cannot be dissociated ('Pol.'1321b39).

The title 'hieromnemon' occurs at Thera in the prescript
to a record of manumissions, dated by the board of ephors
and the 'hieromnemon' (IG XII 3, 336; see Craik, 1969 and
for 'hieromnemon' as eponym cf. Plb.4.52, Byzantion and
SIG 1141, Issa). The 'hierothytai' in Karpathos and Syme
are purely administrative, resembling in their activities
'prytaneis' or 'prostatai' in other communities. The
Koan 'hierotamias' is a deme official, acting as archivist
and treasurer, while the 'hierokeryx' on Anaphe is the
state herald.

A common title for a priestly functionary, though one
not mentioned by Aristotle, is 'neokoros'. This is found
in our area at Kos, with a dedication by a 'neokoros'
to Isis Soteira (NS 449; see also Herod.4, which may be
set in Kos), Rhodes, where there are both 'neokoros' and
'under-"neokoros"' named in a dedication to Athane Nike
(IL 301) and at Thera (IG XII 3, 514).

There is slight evidence also for the related term
'zakoros' (NS 509, a third-century Koan epitaph; but see
AM(A) 51 (1926) p.10 for a reappraisal of this inscription). Ancient grammarians distinguished between
'neokoros' and 'zakoros' (see Reitzenstein, 1964, p.394,
quoting Philemon), but in fact the titles seem to be
applied to officials of similar status and activities:
in lists where both occur, the order is a matter of
indifference and the titles are at times interchanged.

'Neokoroi' are commonly found in temples of Asklepios;

there is evidence for the title at Epidauros (where the officials served also Apollo Maleatas, associated with Asklepios), Pergamum and Athens; also at the shrine of Amphiaraos at Oropos, where incubation was practised and dream oracles received (Ael.'NA'7.13, 9.33; Aristid.'Or.' 47.11, 48.29; IG IV 1, 393, 400, 401, 402; IG VII 235; cf. Festugière, 1954, pp.85-104).

'Neokoroi' occur also in other sanctuaries, with duties according to the local requirements. Delos was a great banking centre, and we find 'neokoroi' there as cashiers; Delphi dispensed manumissions, witnessed and filed by the 'neokoros' (BCH 14 (1890) pp.485 sqq.; SGDI I 2116.14). Plato regards the 'neokoroi' as temple police, responsible for law and order; epigraphical evidence from the island of Amorgos shows that in Plato's time 'neokoroi' were responsible there for the exclusion of foreigners from the shrine of Hera ('Lg.'759b; SIG 981.5; cf. 1157.78 from third-century Koropa).

In literary usage, 'neokoros' and 'zakoros', in common with other prevalent cult-titles, are applied metaphorically (Ath.13.590e; Luc.'Am.'48; Pl.'R'574d). A curious later development of this title is its application, in imperial times, to a city which has built a temple for the cult of the Roman emperor (OGIS 513; Pergamum under Caracalla is three times 'neokoros' of the emperors).

Aristotle's inclusion of treasurers as officials distinct from priests but involved in cult administration is readily justifiable. State decrees were regularly deposited in the main sanctuary of the community, duplicates occasionally being made for display in other regions (IC 10; IG XII 1, 1033). The expense of recording such decrees - that is, meeting the fees of the stonemason commissioned to execute the inscription - was generally met by the state, through its treasurer. Many inscriptions authorize the 'tamias' to disburse the necessary sums; sometimes a limit is set on expenditure, but more often no amount is specified. Responsibility for ensuring that a decree is recorded may also rest with the treasurer (IG XII 3, 167, 168, 170, 322; TC 9, 14, 17, 77, 112, 120), with another official ('prostatai', TC 36) or with the proposer of the decree (TC 30, 33, 34, 38, etc.).

A title commonly applied to the official in charge of recording decrees is 'epistates'. There is evidence for the title from Astypalaia (in the third century, an elected 'epistates' has an honorary decree inscribed and placed in the shrine of Asklepios, IG XII 3, 167), from Kos (in the third century, two elected 'epistatai' see that provisions for the cult of Demeter are recorded and

copies deposited in the temples of Demeter and Asklepios,
HG 8) and from Lindos (in the third century, an honorary
stele is placed in the shrine of Athena Polias by the
'epistatai' in office; in the first century, they give a
ruling on where in a shrine a stele be erected, SIG 340,
725). This title is also used in a general sense, of any
kind of supervisor, and in a specific sense, of an official
sent by a foreign power to a governed area; for instance,
by Rhodes to the Peraia and by the Ptolemies to Thera.

   'Poletai' (who issued contracts), 'strategoi' (civic
officials with fiscal responsibility), 'architektones'
(concerned with building operations) and 'trapezitai'
(public bankers) all had a certain degree of involvement
with the financial transactions carried out in connection
with the local cults. The presence of treasurers is
recorded in inscriptions which detail the regulations for
the sale of priesthoods; and in those which provide for
the payment into or disbursement from treasuries of sums
of money. The finances of state and sanctuary are in the
hands of a single board of treasurers at Astypalaia
(IG XII 3, 167).

   Aristotle concluded his list of officials involved in
religious administration with those concerned with state
sacrifices: 'archontes', 'basileis' and 'prytaneis'.
In our region, the 'prytaneis' of Astypalaia and Telos,
and the 'prostatai' who are their equivalents at Kos,
Kalymnos, Nisyros and Rhodes appear by virtue of their
office on various ceremonial occasions, and supervise
certain financial transactions. Among the privileges
of office was 'proedria', entitlement to a front seat at
state games. (On 'prostatai', see Schaefer, PW suppl.
IX.1290-1, noting that the title is typical of Rhodes,
its colonies and environs; Kos had 'prostatai' and yet
a 'prytaneion'.)

   Aristotle, as already noted, was not in the passage
quoted much interested in the administration of festivals.
He comments briefly (1323a1-4):

     In addition to this is the administration of athletic
     and Dionysiac contests and of any similar celebrations
     that happen to be held.

In our region, athletic festivals were organized by a
state 'agonothetes', or (in Thera) gymnasiarch. Dramatic
festivals were organized and financed by a 'choregos'.
At Lindos, this was a liturgy tenable by metics no less
than by citizens (IG XII 1, 762).

   In Hellenistic and, increasingly, in Roman times, the
feast which followed the procession, sacrifice and
athletic contests was generally regarded as the most
important part of the proceedings. Those who organized

the games often provided free meals for the populace; thus, the office of 'agonothetes' involved lavish expenditure but much honour (IC 131; IG XII 3, 218; 1119). Proclamations, often of honours conferred by the state, were made at festivals by the official state herald, or by the 'agonothetes' in person.

Deme and tribe cults - not mentioned by Aristotle - were administered in much the same way as those of the state, on a smaller scale. 'Neopoiai' and 'hierotamiai' of Koan demes are recorded: for instance, the 'neopoiai' of the deme Halasarna compile a list of those entitled to participate in the local cult of Apollo and Herakles by collecting names at the festival (IC 44). The demes had a demarch as their titular and administrative head.

At Kos, the title 'archeuon' is peculiar to tribal institutions (IC 367.87 = SIG 1023 = ZLS 130; 384). This rather unusual title occurs at Paphos, applied to a state official (OGIS 166). At Rhodes, the title 'phylarchos' is used (SER 19; the corresponding verb in a single late Koan inscription refers not to a tribal 'phylarchos', but to a Roman office).

Family cults, like associations formed to honour a particular god, had usually a committee of president, secretary and treasurer. Some unusual titles for such office-bearers occur; for instance, Epikteta's associa- tion was administered by 'epissophos', 'grammatophylax' and 'artyter'.

Aristotle made frequent use of the term 'epimeletes', 'administrator', responsible for certain types of 'epimeleia'. This word is a good example of the great fluidity in terminology relating to officials. Categories of 'epimeletai', ranging from the highest to the lowest echelons of power, from large organizations to small groups, are not easy to define. (For different attempts, see LSJ, where II.2 arguably should be related to II.5 and 6 and Oehler, PW VI.162-71 with a less schematic arrangement in three broad divisions, 'Staatsverwaltung', 'Kultus' and 'Staatlichen Unterabteilungen'.) 'Epimeletai' are often involved, directly or indirectly, in cult activities.

Just as the common title 'epimeletes' presents problems of interpretation, through its wide and varied range of applications, so do more unusual titles through a lack of parallels for their usage. The title 'therapeutas' at Thera (IG XII 3, 515) is probably sacral, as it is used of Aglophanes, son of Theokleidas, a member of the great priestly family of the island (pace LSJ, translating both 'therapeutas' and 'therapon' as worshipper; in support of a priestly 'therapeutas', it may be noted that Aristeides

groups 'therapeutai' with 'neokoroi' at Pergamum, 48.47).
On the other hand, the 'hyperetes' of the gods who
finances some building on Melos is unlikely to have held
a formal office, and the 'latris' of the Nymphs on Kos is
probably simply an afficionado of the arts (IG XII suppl.
165;   KF 163).

Much more space might be devoted here to the constitutional workings of the islands, fitting cult organization
into its civic framework. However, the existence of
pervasive local idiosyncrasies - with the use of the
same title given different applications, and the use of
a variety of titles for similar functions - inhibits the
formation of general conclusions. The titles given to
state eponyms in the islands illustrate their colourful
diversity: Astypalaia, Nisyros, Syme and Telos have
'demiourgoi', Kalymnos 'stephanephoros' (the local priest
of Apollo), Kos 'monarchos', Rhodes the priest of Helios
and Thera ephors (see Craik, 1969, for a full discussion
of these titles). Perhaps it is not surprising that even
Aristotle seems to flinch somewhat in his attempt to
systematize such data.

Appendix: Cult Titles

Note: For further detail and discussion (on Rhodes
only), see Morelli, 1959, in SCO, a periodical not widely
available in Britain.

1 THE OLYMPIANS

APHRODITE	An -	IG XII 3, 248 and suppl.p.279 = SIG 977 = ZLS 122
	As -	ALA 62 (1969) 44
	K -	IC 36 = SIG 1106 = ZLS 144 = HG 10; IC 369 = ZLS 138; NS 467; AR 10 (1907) 211; ClRh 9 (1938) 140; ASAA 25-6 (1963) 182
	Kl -	TC 114
	Rh -	Kam - TCam 17; 24; 27; 31; 38; 39; 40; 41; 43; 45; 50; 122
		Rho - IL 134; NS 12; SER 9
	Th -	IG XII 3, 1332
A. Basileia	Rh -	Rho - ASAA 1-2 (1942) 152
Eudie	K -	NS 495
Hypakoos	K -	NS 675
Pandamos	K -	IC 401 = PLS 10
(Paphia)	Rh -	Rho - ASAA 1-2 (1942) 165: Paphiastai
Aphrodeision	K -	IC 387; KF 191 = SIG 1000 = ZLS 137; HG 8, cf. AR 10 (1907) 404
Aphrodeisiastai	Ch -	IG XII 1, 962
	K -	IC 155; KF 40
	N -	IG XII 3, 104
	Rh -	L - IL 252; 391; ClRh 2 (1928) 211

		Rho - IG XII 1, 162; NS 18;
		34; 42; 43; ASAA 1-2 (1942) 151;
		152; 156; ClRh 2 (1928) 214
	S	- IG XII 3, 6
Aphrodeisia	Rh	- Rho - NS 34; SER 66a, c

APOLLO	An	- IG XII 3, 257; 258
	As	- IG XII 3, 185; ALA 62 (1969) 43;
		45
	K	- IC 40 = BCH 5 (1881) 220; 367 =
		SIG 1023, cf. KF p.139; 369;
		370; 372; KF 210; 221; Klio 2
		(1902) 320; 321; HZ 125 (1924)
		217 n.1; ClRh 2 (1928) 213
	Kl	- TC 31; 98; 99; 100; 101; 102;
		103; 104; 107; 151
	Kr	- IG XII 1, 977 = SIG 129
	Ph	- IG XII 3, 1057
	Rh	- Kam - TCamS 115a
		Rho - IG XII 3, 736 - SIG 1118
	T	- IG XII 3, 38
	Th	- IG XII 3, 356; 441; 463; 536
A. Aigletes	An	- IG XII 3, 259; 260
	Th	- IG XII 3, 412
Apotropaios	Rh	- Kam - TCam 119
Asgelatas	An	- IG XII 3, 248 and suppl.p.279 =
		SIG 977 = ZLS 122; 249 and XII
		suppl.p.83
Asgelaia	An	- ibid.
Dalios	K	- IC 40 = HG 5; IC 125; AA 18
		(1903) 10; RFIC 20 (1942) 8 (Kl);
		TC XIII (Kl); 'A.D.Kalymnas
		Medeon' IC 60
	Kl	- TC 52; 105; 106; 108; 109; 110;
		130; IC 60
	N	- IG XII 3, 92
	Rh	- Kam - TCam 50; 90
	S	- IG XII 3, 2
Delphinios	N	- AE (1913) 8
	Th	- IG XII 3, 537
Didymeus	Kl	- TC 69
Digenes	Rh	- Kam - TCam 7 = IG XII 1, 696; 47
Epiknisios	Rh	- Kam - TCam 120
Epimelidios	Rh	- Kam - TCam 135
Erethimios	Rh	- Ial - IG XII 1, 732; 733; 735;
		IL 441; 679; ClRh 2 (1928) 104;
		106; 107
		Kam - IG XII 1, 730 = SER 5b; SIG 724;
		SGDI 4135

Erethimiazontes,   Ial - IG XII 1, 734; NS 25; IL 384;
Eretheibiazontes   454; ASAA 2 (1916) 147; ASAA 1-2
                         (1942) 154; ClRh 2 (1928) 104;
                         105; 108
                   Kam - TCam 87
Erethimia   Ial - IG XII 1, 735; NS 18; ASAA 2
                         (1916) 147
Kalymnios   K - TC XXX (K1)
                   K1- TC 127B; 128B; 129B; 198; cf.145,
                       A.'Prokathegemon theos'
of Kamyndos   Rh - L - IL 282 = IG XII 1, 845; 294;
                           299c; 347; 349; 378; 398;
                           420b = IG XII 1, 830
Karneios   K - NS 460; 475; HG 4; SIG 928
                   Rh - Kam - TCam 7 = IG XII 1, 697;
                           31 = IG XII 1, 705; 38; 47
                           L - IL 282 = IG XII 1, 845;
                           294; 299c; 347; 349; 378b; 398;
                           420b = IG XII 1, 830
                   Th - IG XII 3, 508; 512 and XII
                           suppl.p.88; 513 and suppl.p.306;
                           514; 519 and XII suppl.p.88;
                           868; 869; 1294; 1406; 1407;
                           1408
Karneia   K - IC 38 = SIG 1026 = PLS 6 = HG 2
                   Th - IG XII 3, 336; 1324
Kyparissios   K - HG12; 15; cf. AA 20 (1905) 11
                           and RFIC 16 (1938) 194
Kyparissos   K - IC 43; cf. Hipp.'Ep.'11
Kyparisiotai   K - AA 20 (1905) 11
Lykeios   K1 - SGDI 3591
                   Th - IG XII 3, 551 (without A)
Maleatas   Th - IG XII 3, 372
Megisteus   Mg - SGDI 4330
Mylantios   Rh - Kam - TCam 15; 28; 30; 38
O(u)lios   K - PP 12 (1957) 443
                   Rh - L - IL 228; 282; 294; 299; 308b;
                             317; 347 = SIG 765; 131e;
                             349; 350; 378b; 398; 420b
Pedageitnyos   Rh - Kam - TCam 155
Petasitas   Rh - Kam - TCam 132
Pharmakios   Rh - Kam - TCam 90
Prostaterios   Ph - IG XII 3, 1057
Pythaeus,   An - IG XII 3, 268; 269; 270; 271
 Pythios   K - KF 36; 37; CRAI (1904) 164-73 =
                           SIG 398
                   Rh - Kam - TCam 7 = IG XII 1, 697;
                           17; 23; 27; 29; 30; 31 = IG XII
                           1, 705 = SGDI 4124; 35; 38; 39;
                           40; 41; 43; 44; 45; 46; 47; 50;
                           56

                                    L - IL 57; 61; 70; 84; 99; 102;
                                          103; 131; 136; 158; 159;
                                          167; 224; 228; 229; 232;
                                          247; 248; 251; 264; 270;
                                          282; 286; 293; 294; 299;
                                          300; 308; 317; 324; 343;
                                          347; 349; 360; 377; 378;
                                          420: 430; 462; 466; 488;
                                          cf. 195; 351; 448; 493;
                                          494; 657
                                    Rh - IG XII 1, 25; 57; 67;
                                          IL 134; SER 48; ClRh 2
                                          (1928) 211; BSAA 34 (1941)
                                          29
                                    S - IG XII 3, 1
                                    T - IG XII 3, 34; cf. 35
                                    Th - IG XII 3, 322; 1292
    Soter   K - HZ 125 (1924) 217 n.1
    Stephanephoros   Kl - TC 152; 153; 154; 166; 200
                                    Th - IG XII 3, 1346
    Stratagios   Rh - Rho - IG XII 1, 161
    Apolloniastai   K - NS 491
                                    Rh - L - IL 252
                                          Rho - IG XII 1, 163; NS 18

ARTEMIS   K - IC 372; KF 223; NS 460; HG 8;
                                          BSAA 40 (1953) 36
                                    Rh - Ial - IG XII 1, 732
                                          Kam - TCam 121
                                          Rho - IG XII 1, 57; NS 29; IL 697
                                    S - IG XII 3, 2
                                    Th - IG XII 3, 373; 381; 1326; 1327;
                                          1328; 1329
A. Andromeda   Rh - L - IL 22
   (Aristoboule)   Rh - Rho - ASAA 1-2 (1942) 151;
                                          Aristobouliastai
   Diktynna   As - SGDI 3475
   Einodia   Th - IG XII 3, 1328 (without A)
   Epekoos   Th - IG XII suppl.155
   (at) Kekoia   Rh - L - IL 91; 93; 100; 101; 106;
                                          111; 118; 131; 137; 150;
                                          157; 158; 159; 166; 168;
                                          194; 197; 219; 225; 227;
                                          231; 244; 245; 246; 248;
                                          250; 251; 260; 264; 282;
                                          283; 284; 285; 286; 287;
                                          293; 294; 299; 300; 308;
                                          311; 313; 317; 322; 324;

```
                              343; 344; 347 = SIG 765;
                              349; 351; 353; 360; 378;
                              384; 391; 408; 420 = IG XII 1,
                              830; 423; 424; 426; 427; 434;
                              437; 448; 449; 451; 462; 466;
                              479; 486; 488; 493; 494; 534;
                              565; 578; NSER 25; 26
  Kindyas           K  - NS 627
  Lochia            As - ALA 62 (1969) 44
  Pergaia           Rh - L - IL 384
                         Rho. - IG XII 1, 66 = SGDI 3802;
                         104 = SGDI 3842; ASAA 2 (1916)
                         137
                    Th - IG XII 3, 494 and suppl.p.306;
                         1350
  at Phagai         Rh - Ial - IL 680
  Selasphoros       Ph - IG XII 3, 1057 a, b
  Soteira           An - IG XII 3, 268; 269; 270; 271
                    M  - IG XII 3, 1671 (without A)
                    Th - IG XII 3, 414; 1328; 1350
  Thermia           Rh - Rho - IG XII 1, 24
  Toxitis           K  - NS 452
  Triodeitis        Th - IG XII 3, 1329


ELEITHYIA          As - IG XII 3, 192
                   Rh - L - IL 697


HEKATE             Ch - IG XII 1, 958
                   K  - IC 401 = PLS 10; AA 18 (1903)
                        191
                   Rh - Rho - SER 12
  Megale            K  - IC 40 = HG 5
  Phosphoros        Th - IG XII 3, 421
  Pontia            K  - KF 217; NS 475
  Propylaia         Rh - Kam - TCam 116; 119
  Soteira           K  - NS 676
  Stratia           K  - IC 370; 388


LETO               K  - IC 40 = HG 5; AA 20 (1903) 10
                   S  - IG XII 3, 2
  Artemeisiastai         ALA 62 (1969) 6
```

ASKLEPIOS   An - IG XII 3, 248 and suppl.p.279 =
SIG 977 = ZLS 122; 261

As - IG XII 3, 167 and XII suppl.p.79;
173; 186; 187; ALA 62 (1969) 45;
49

Ch - IG XII 1, 956

K - IC 14; 30 = ZLS 135; 31 = KF 110;
345 = SIG 804; 371; 401 = PLS 10;
402 = PLS 11; 406; 408; KF 1;
NS 460; 475; 628; HG 12; 14; 15;
AA 18 (1903) 10; ibid.193;
CRAI (1904) 164-73 = SIG 398;
RFIC 9 (1933) 365; ClRh 8 (1936)
242; RIA 6 (1938) 191; ClRh 10
(1940) 37; RFIC 20 (1942) 8

K1 - TC 155; 175; 176; 177

Kr - IG XII 1, 996

Ks - IG XII 1, 1041

M - IG XII 3, 1083 - 87

Rh - Kam - TCam 26; 27; 35; 38; 39;
41; 44; 45; 46; 47; 50; 56;
90

L - IG XII 1, 26; IL 174

Rho - IG XII 736 = SIG 1118;
IL 134; 442; 449; SER 248;
BSAA 34 (1941) 29-39; ASAA 2
(1916) 137

S - IG XII 3, 1

Th - IG XII 3, 515; 516; 865; 1330

A. Kaisar   K - IC 92; 130; NS 463; AA 18 (1903)
193; cf. NS 443

    Asklepiadai   K - NS 461

    Asklepiastai   Rh - Kam - TCam 78; 84; 87

L - IL 391; 392

Rho - IG XII 1, 162 = SIG 1114 =
SGDI 3843; 164; AE (1907)
215; AM 25 (1900) 109

S - IG XII 3, 6

    Asklepieia   K - IC 13; 14; 104 = SIG 1065;
KF 221; NS 462; HZ 125 (1924)
217; ClRh 10 (1940) 37; RFIC
20 (1942) 5-9; TC XIII

Kr - IG XII 1, 1032

Rh - Rho - NS 19

    Asklepieion   K - IC 8; 10; 13; HG 8

EPIONE   K - IC 30 = ZLS 135; 345 = SIG 804;
NS 460; 475; HG 14; 15; AA 18
(1903) 10; 193

HEMERIDEIOI   Rh - Rho - ASAA 2 (1916) 137

HYGIEIA   K - IC 30 = ZLS 135; 345 = SIG 804;
                          401 = PLS 10; 406; NS 460; 475;
                          HG 14; 15; AA 18 (1903) 10; 193
                     M - IG XII 3, 1084-7; IG XII
                          suppl. 164
                     Rh - L - IG XII 1, 26; IL 174
                          Rho - ASAA 2 (1916) 137
                     Th - IG XII 3, 1331

MACHAON   K - AA 18 (1903) 191

PAION   M - IG XII 3, 1088

PANAKEIA   Kl - TC 119
                     M - IG XII 3, 1088

ATHENA   As - IG XII 3, 173; 184 and XII suppl.
                     K - IC 125; 150
                     Kr - Historia 7 (1933) 577-88
                     M - IG XII 3, 1077; 1079; 1080
                     Rh - Kam - TCam 24; 26; 27; 29;
                          104; 109; 118
                     S - IG XII 3, suppl.1270
                     T - AE (1922) 44
                     Th - IG XII 3, 364; 411; 450b
A. Alseia   K - IC 55; NS 447
   Apotropaia   Rh - L - NSER 20a
   Athenon Medeose   K - IC 148
   Hyperdexia   Rh - Rho - IG XII 1, 22
   Lindia   Kr - IG XII 1, 998; 1033 = SIG 570
                     Rh - IL 1; 2; etc. (see Morelli, 1959)
   Machanis   K - IC 38 = SIG 1026 = PLS 6 = HG 2
   Nika   K - IC 43 = SIG 1028
                     Rh - L - IL 301
                          Rho - IG XII 1, 20; ClRh 2 (1928)
                          185
   Patria   An - IG XII 3, 262
   Phratria   Rh - Kam - TCam 127
                          L - IL 615

Polias	K - IC 37 = SIG 1025 = PLS 5 = HG 1;
	    IC 40 = PLS 8 = HG 5; IC 43 =
	    SIG 1028 = PLS 13 = HG 9; NS 460;
	    475

	Rh - Ial - IG XII 1, 786; IL 482; cf. 441; SER 54

	Kam - TCam 15; 17; 28; 30;
	        31 = IG XII 1, 705 = SGDI
	        4124; 35; 36; 37; 38; 39;
	        40; 41; 43; 44; 45; 46; 47;
	        48; 50; 61; 69; 84; 89; 148;
	        TCamS 50b; cf. IG XII 1, 786

	Rho - IG XII 1, 21 = SGDI 3766;
	        57; 61 = SGDI 3796; 62 =
	        SGDI 3797; IL 134; ClRh 2
	        (1928) 184; 186; 211

	T - IG XII 3, 40; AE (1922) 42
	Th - IG XII 3, 427; 495; 1362
Soteira	K - IC 34 = ZLS 131; NS 665
	Rh - Rho - ClRh 2 (1928) 184
Athanaistai	K - IC 157; 158; NS 490
	Rh - L - IL 252; 264; 300a; 391; 392a, b; 420a

	Rho - IG XII 1, 162 = SIG 1114 =
	        SGDI 3843; NS 28; 41; NSER 3;
	        ASAA 2 (1916) 139; ASAA 1-2
	        (1942) 151; 155; 166; PAAH
	        (1952) 560; ALA 62 (1969) 6

Panathenaistai	Ch - IG XII 1, 962
	Rho - NS 29
DEMETER AND KORE	As - IG XII 3, 197 (Ko); 198 (Ko)

	K - IC 37 = SIG 1025 = PLS 5 =
	    HG 1 (D); 56 (D?); 386 = SIG
	    1006 = ZLS 132 (D); KF 63
	    (D); 169 (K); HG 8 (D);
	    AA 16 (1901) 135 (D);
	    ASAA 8-9 (1925-6) 253 (D);
	    ClRh 5 (1931) 158 sqq. (D
	    and K); ClRh 9 (1938) 24 (D)

	K1 - TC 97 (D); 115 (D and Ko)

	Rh - Kam - IL 671 = SIG 1031 = TCam
	     156a (Damateres)
	     L - IL 181 (D?); 182 (D?);
	     183 (Damateres); 261 (D?)

	Rho - IG XII 1, 27 = SGDI 3769 (D);
	     28 = SGDI 3770 (D); 29 = SGDI
	     3771 (D and Ko)

	Th - IG XII 3, 355 (D); 417 (D); 418 and suppl.p.294 (D and K); suppl.n.1369 (Ko)
D. Karpophoros	K - NS 468a, b; cf. HZ 125 (1924) 239, n.1 on IC 411 and n.3; also ASAA 25-6 (1963) 182
	Rh - Rho - ClRh 2 (1928) 211 (D and Zeus: Karpophoroi)
Olympia	K - HG 8
Soteira	K - Ph W 1932.1011 sqq. (D and Ko)
Damatrion	K - IC 39
Kouriastai	Rh - Kam - TCam 84

HADES	Rh - ClRh 5 (1931) 186

DIONYSOS	As - IG XII 3, 190; 191; XII suppl. 150
	K - IC 10; 24; 43 = SIG 1028 = PLS 13 = HG 9; 58; KF 197; NS 439; RFIC 16 (1938) 253
	Kl - TC 116
	Kr - IG XII 1, 996
	M - IG XII 3, 1123
	N - IG XII 3, 164
	Rh - Ial - ClRh2 (1928) 185
	Kam - TCam 26; 27; 28; 29; 30; 38; 39; 40; 41; 45; 46; 56; 90; 151; 156; IL 678
	L - IL 109; 136 = IG XII 1, 809; 159; 166; 199; 224; 229; 264; 270; 282; 286; 293; 294; 299; 308; 327; 334; 343; 346; 347; 349; 378; 420; 430; 462; 486
	Rho - IG XII 1, 68; 309 = SGDI 3833; 369; 906 = SIG 1031 = SGDI 4231; IL 134; SIG 599 = SGDI 3758; SER 29; 42; ASAA 2 (1916) 139
	Th - IG XII 3, 419; 420; 468
D. Bakcheios,	K - IC 58
Bakchos	Rh - L - IL 449
	Rho - IG XII 1, 155 = SGDI 3836; REG 17 (1904) 204
Bakchiastai	K - NS 492
	Th - IG XII 3, 1296
Epikarpios	Rh - Kam - TCam 141

Kathegemon	K - RFIC 16 (1938) 253
	Rh - L - IL 264
Pro Poleos	Th - IG XII 3, 420; 522
Skyllitas	K - IC 37 = SIG 1025 = PLS 5 = HG 1
Smintheus	Rh - L - IG XII 3, 762 = SGDI 4155 =
	ZLS 146
Thyllophoros	K - IC 27 = SIG 1012 = ZLS 133;
	cf. RP (1940-1) 21
Trieterikos	M - IG XII 3, 1089
Dionysia	As - IG XII 3, 169; 170
	K - IC 5; 13; 14; 45; KF 13;
	TC XIII; XIV = RFIC 20 (1942) 8;
	9
	Kl - TC 64 = SIG 567
	N - ALA 62 (1969) 27
	Rh - TCam 106
	Th - IG XII 3, 322 and suppl.p.84
Dionysiastai	N - IG XII 3, 104
	Rh - L - IG XII 1, 937; IL 391; 392
	Rh - Rho - IG XII 1, 155 = SGDI 3836;
	161 - SGDI 3842; NS 46; ASAA 2
	(1916) 139
HELIOS	K - IC 64; AA 18 (1903) 191; AA 20
	(1905) 12
	Rh - See indices IG; IL; NS; SER;
	NSER; TCam; TCamS. Add: (Rho)
	SGDI 3756; 3767; ClRh 2 (1928)
	185; cf. Morricone (1952);
	Morelli (1959)
Heliadai	Rh - L - IL 292
Heliastai	K - NS 489
	Rh - L - IL 292
	Rho - NS 39; ASAA 1-2 (1942) 151
Helieia	Rh - See indices; add ClRh 2 (1928)
	188; 190; 210; PP 5 (1950) 76.
	Cf. Morelli (1959)
	Sr - IG XII 1, 1039
HERA	As - IG XII 3, 196; ALA 62 (1969) 44
	K - KF 198 (= PP 13 (1958) 418 sq.);
	RFIC 20 (1942) 5-8 (= TC XII)
	Rh - Ial - ClRh 2 (1928) 185
	Th - IG XII 3, 433
H. Ammonia	Rh - L - IL 77
Argeia Eleia	
Basileia	K - NS 475

Basileia	Rh – L – IG XII 1, 786 = TCam App.38
Dromaia	Th – IG XII 3, 513 and suppl.p.306
Olympia	Rh – Rho – ASAA 2 (1916) 137
Ourania	K – IC 62; TC XXXIII
Heraia	Kl – TC 205

HERAKLES	As – IG XII 3, 193
	K – IC 39 = SIG 1027 = PLS 7 = HG 3; IC 367 = SIG 1023 = ZLS 130; NS 448; RFIC 9 (1933) 365
	M – IG XII 3, 1090; 1091 and suppl. p.335
	Rh – Kam – TCam 31 = IG XII 1, 705 = SGDI 4124; 38; 90; 130 L – IL 2b; 132; 319 Rho – IG XII 1, 8; IL 134; ASAA 8-9 (1925-6) 321
	Th – IG XII 3, 331 and suppl.p.285; 339; 340; 390; 391 and suppl. p.292; 393; 431; 1314 = SIG 949
Herakleia	K – IC 367 = SIG 1023 = ZLS 130
	S – IG XII 3, suppl.1269; 1270
Herakleidai	K – NS 461
Herakleion	K – IC 39 = SIG 1027 = PLS 7 = HG 3
Herakleistai	Ch – IG XII 1, 963
Herakleotai	Rh – L – IL 391; 392 Rho – IG XII 1, 8; 36 = SGDI 3774; 158; 162 = SIG 1114 = SGDI 3843; IL 134; 482; NS 39; ASA 8-9 (1925-6) 321; 322; ClRh 2 (1928) 210
H. Diomedonteios	K – IC 36 = SIG 1106 = ZLS 144 = HG 10; cf. Nilsson, 1906, 451-2

HERMES	As – IG XII 3, 193
	K – KF 15; NS 448; 466
	Kl – TC 118
	M – IG XII 3, 1090; 1091 and suppl. p.335
	N – IG XII 3, 93
	Rh – L – IL 20; 496; NSER 21 Rho – SER 12
	Th – IG XII 3, 331 and suppl.p.285; 339; 340; 370; 390; 391 and suppl.p.292; 392; 394; 395; 396; 397; 1314 = SIG 949; 1352
H. Enagonios	Rh – Kam – TCamS 4

Hagemon   Rh - L - IL 184
Kyllanios   K - NS 452
Propylaios   Rh - Kam - TCam 116a
Stropheus   Th - IG XII 3, 1374 (without H.)
Hermaizontes,   K - IC 156 = SIG 1120
 Hermaistai   N - IG XII 3, 104
                   Rh - Kam - TCam 84; 159
                        L - IL 251; 656
                        Rho - IG XII 1, 101 = SGDI 3829;
                              157 = SGDI 3838; 162 = SGDI
                              3843; NS 42; NSER 3; ClRh 2
                              (1928) 203; ASAA 1-2 (1942)
                              151

HESTIA   Rh - Kam - See index TCam and TCamS
                        Rho - SER 10
                   Th - IG XII 3, 423; 1353; 1354; 1355;
                        1357; cf. 424
H. Boulaia   Th - IG XII 3, 1392
   Tamias   K - IC 37 = SIG 1025 = PLS 5 = HG 1;
                        IC 401 = PLS 10
   Hestiastai   Rh - Rho - IG XII 1, 162 = SIG 1114 =
                        SGDI 3843

POSEIDON   K - IC 401 = PLS 10; KF 191 =
                        SIG 1000 = ZLS 137; PhW (1932)
                        1011 sqq.; RFIC 20 (1942) 5-8
                   K1 - TC 116
                   M - IG XII 3, 1096
                   Rh - Kam - TCam 153; cf. TCam 114
                        L - IL 2B
                        Rho - IG XII 1, 739
                   T - IG XII 3, 37
                   Th - IG XII 3, 362; 441 and suppl.
                        1372
P. Argeios   N - IG XII 3, 103 = SIG 673
   Asphaleios   K - TC XXXIII
                   Rh - Kam - TCam 129
   Gaiaochos   Th - IG XII 3, 1371 (without P.)
   Gilaios   Rh - L - IG XII 1, 786
   Hippios   K - ClRh 8 (1936) 229
                   Rh - Kam - TCam 41; 45; 50; 90
                        L - IL 91; 127; 136; 158; 159;
                            167; 173; 223; 225a; 228;
                            282; 294; 299c; 347; 349;
                            378b; 398; 420; IG XII 1,
                            926 = SIG 725
                        Rho - BSAA 34 (1941) 29-39; IL 134

Hippotas	Th	- IG XII 3, 1372
Kyreteios	Rh	- Kam - TCam 31; 38; 41; 45; 50; 90
Pelagios	Th	- IG XII 3, 1347
Phytalmios	Rh	- Kam - TCam 137
		Rho - IG XII 1, 905 = SIG 1030 = PLS 23 = SGDI 4232
Porthmios	Kr	- IG XII 1, 1031; 1032; 1033 = SIG 570; 1035; 1036; Historia 7 (1933) 584
Poseidania	K	- IC 43 = SIG 1028 = PLS 13 = HG 9;
	Rh	- NS 18; TCam 63
Poseidaniastai	Rh	- Rho - IG XII 1, 162 = SIG 1114 = SGDI 3843; 164; ASAA 8-9 (1925-6) 322

ZEUS	Ch	- IG XII 1, 958
	K	- IC 43 = SIG 1028 = PLS 13 = HG 9; TC XII = RFIC 20 (1942) 5-8
	Kl	- TC 205
	M	- IG XII 3, 1075; 1092
	Rh	- L - IL 57; 342
	St	- IG XII 3 suppl.1280
	Th	- IG XII 3, 350-53; 424; 425; 426; 1313; 1317; 1318
Z. Agoraios	Rh	- L - IL 221; NSER 21
Amalos		L - IL 26
Apotropaios		L - NSER 20
Astrapatas		Kam - TCam 142
Astrapton	Th	- IG XII 3, 1359
Atabyrios	Rh	- Kam - Jacopi, 1928
		Rho - IG XII 1, 31 = SGDI 3772; SER 8
Atabyriastai, Diosatabyriastai	Rh	- L - IL 391, 392
		Rho - IG XII 1, 31 = SGDI 3772; 161 = SGDI 3842; SER 17; ASAA 1-2 (1942) 165
Boulaios	K	- PP 27 (1972) 182
	Th	- IG XII 3, 1393
Bronton	Th	- IG XII 3, 1359
Damatrios	Rh	- L - IL 183
Drouthios	Rh	- Kam - TCam 138
Hikesios	K	- IC 149; BSAA 40 (1953) 36
	Rh	- Rho - IG XII 1, 891
	Th	- IG XII 3, 404 (without Z.)
Hyetios	K	- TC XXXIII; IC 382
	Rh	- Kam - TCam 154
		Rho - ASAA 8-9 (1925-6) 321

Hyperdexios	Rh	- Rho - IG XII 1, 22
Hypsistos	K	- TC XXXIII; cf. IC 63
Karpophoros	Rh	- Rho - ClRh2 (1928) 211
Kataibates	M	- IG XII 3, 1093; 1094
	Th	- IG XII 3, 1360
Keraunios	Kl	- TC 69
	M	- IG XII suppl.165
Kronides Anax	Rh	- Rho - NS 13
Ktesios	An	- IG XII 3, 248 and suppl.p.279 = SIG 977 = ZLS 122 (without Z.)
Machaneus	K	- IC 38 = SIG 1026 = PLS 6 = HG 2
	Rh	- Kam - TCam 136
Meilichios	N	- IG XII 3, 95; 96; ClRh 2 (1928) 213
	Rh	- Kam - TCam 90
	Th	- IG XII 3, 1316 = SIG 1036
Diosmilichiastai	N	- IG XII 3, 104
Mesarkeios	Rh	- Kam - TCam 126; 127
Olympios	Rh	- Rho - ASAA 2 (1916) 137
	Th	- IG XII 3, 1345
Orlygios	Rh	- Ial - TCam App.38; SER 6
Pasios	K	- IC 36 = SIG 1106 = ZLS 144 = HG 10
Patrios	An	- IG XII 3, 262
Patroios	Kl	- TC 69
	Rh	- L - IG XII 1, 890 = SIG 931 = SGDI 4225; IL 648
Phatrios	K	- IC 150
Polieus	K	- IC 37 = SIG 1025 = PLS 5 = HG 1; 38 = SIG 1026 = PLS 6 = HG 2; IC 125; NS 460
	Rh	- Ial - ASAA 1-2 (1942) 155; SER 54
		Kam - TCam 15; 17; 28; 30; 31; 35; 36; 37; 38; 39; 40; 41; 43; 44; 45; 46; 47; 48; 50; 61; 69; 84; TCamS 50b
		L - IG XII 1, 21; 57; 61; ClRh 2 (1928) 184; 186; 211
	Th	- IG XII 3, 1362; cf. 363 (without Z.)
	T	- ALA 62 (1969) 23
Soter	As	- IG XII 3, 194
	K	- IC 34 = ZLS 131; IC 43 = SIG 1028 = PLS 13 = HG 9; NS 468; 496; 665; HZ 125 (1924) 239 n.3
	Kl	- TC 69
	Rh	- Kam - TCam 127; cf. 68
		L - IL 122

	Th - IG XII 3, 430; 1357; 1363; 1364; 1365; 1366
Diossoteriastai	Rh - Rho - IG XII 3, 139; 162 = SIG 1114 = SGDI 3843; IL 683; NS 28; ASAA 1-2 (1942) 151; 153; cf.148
Stoichaios	Rh - Kam - TCam 127
	Th - IG XII 3, 376 (without Z.)
Teleios	Rh - Kam - TCam 4, 62; 64; 67; 78; 80; 87; 124; TCam App 36; 37
Xenios	Th - IG XII 3, 428 (without Z.)
Diosxeniastai	Rh - Rho - IG XII 1, 161 = SGDI 3842

2   MINOR CULTS

Some minor gods are included in the main appendix: the gods of healing Epione, Hygieia and Machaon with Asklepios; Kore and Hades with Demeter; Eleithyia, Hekate and Leto with Artemis. Other deities fall into the following categories:

1 Olympian gods whose cult was undeveloped: Ares (N - IG XII 3, 103), cf. Enyalios (Rh - L - ClRh 9 (1938) 211); Hephaistos (Rh - Rho - ASAA 1-2 (1942) 151); The Twelve Gods (K - IC 38; 349; NS 432).

2 Gods of the old order: Rhea (K - IC 119; NS 450; 460; 475), cf. Ge (Th - IG XII 3, 374) and Meter theon (K - IC 402 = PLS 11 = IBM 339; Rh - Rho - IG XII 1, 162 = SIG 1114 = SGDI 3843; Th - IG XII 3, 436 = SIG 1032; 437-8).

3 Minor gods (Pan, Dioskouroi), heroes and nymphs (especially mythical ancestors): Alektrona (Rh - Ial - IG XII 1, 677 = SIG 338 = ZLS 145); Alka (Rh - Kam - TCam 147); Althaimenes (Rh - Kam - TCam 50; 90); Amphiaraos (K - IC 40 = PLS 8, cf. Farnell, 1921, 365); Amphilochos (Rh - Kam - TCam 139); Aristomenes (Rh - Ial - IG XII 1, 8); Brygindis (Rh - Kam - TCam App.32); Daiton (Rh - Rho - ASAA 30-3 (1952-4) 357 = SEG 15.513); Diktynna (As - IG XII 3, 189); Dioskouroi (Kl - TC 117; Th - IG XII 3, 422; XII 3 suppl.1351), cf. Anaxilea, IC 39, implying Anakes, contra Parke, 1977, p.173); Dousares (Ch - IG XII 1, 963); Kameiros (Rh - Kam - TCam 81b); Korybantes (Rh - Kam - TCam 90; Rh - Rho - IG XII 1, 8; PP 4 (1949) 73); Kos - K - KF 191 = SIG 1000 = ZLS 137; Lindos (Rh - L - IL 2; 57; 274; 282; 294; 299; 317; 347; 349; 378; 409; 477); Merops (K - NS 475; Historia 8 (1934) 432); Muses (K - NS 445); Nymphs (As - IG XII 3, 199; K - IC 44; KF 163; RIA 6 (1938) 191; Ks - IG XII 1, 1042; Rh - Kam - TCam 90; TCamS p.233; IL 456; Th - IG XII 3, 377-8 = ZLS 125-6; 439); Pan (Rh - Kam - TCam 57); Priapos (Th - IG XII 3, 421); Psithyros (Rh - L - IL 484); Rhodos

(K – KF 191 = SIG 1000 = ZLS 137; Rh – L – IL 140;
Rh – Rho – IG XII 1, 1 = SGDI 3749); Theoi Patroioi (Rh –
Rho – BSAA 40 (1953) 36; T – IG XII 3, 39).

4 Abstracts personified (merging into 3 in such cases
as Damos Rhodion, similar to Rhodos): Adrasteia and
Nemesis (K – IC 29 = ZLS 139; KF 9; cf. Rh – L – IL 644,
Nemesis alone); Agathe Tyche and Agathos Daimon (K – IC 57;
NS 494; Rh – Kam – TCam 134; 145; Rh – Rho – ASAA 2 (1916)
137); Damos Koion (K – NS 443); Damos Rhodion (Rh – L –
IL 438); Homonoia (K – IC 61; 401; Epigraphica 1 (1938)
9-16; Kl – TC 137B); Moira or Moirai (K – NS 452; Rh –
Kam – TCam 127; 128; Th – IG XII 3, 421); Muses (Rh – Ial –
IG XII 1, 680; Rh – Kam – TCam 38; 39; 44; 151; L – IL
134; BSAA 11 (1941) 29; ASAA 2 (1916) 139); Nike (K – NS
441; Rh – L – IL 2; 200; 252; 319; 418); Pheme (Rh – Kam –
TCam 131; 150); Tyche (N – IG XII 3, 97; Rh – Rho – IG
XII 1, 67; SER 11).

5 Foreign gods: Adonis (Rh – L – IL 656; Rh – Rho –
ASAA 1-2 (1942) 147; S – IG XII 3, 6); Ammon (Kr – Historia
7 (1933) 577; Rh – L – IL 77); Astarte (K – NS 496);
Atargatis (As – IG XII 3, 177; 188); Isis and Serapis
(As – IG XII 3, 200; Ch – IG XII 1, 957; K – NS 449; 475;
493; Kr – Historia 7 (1933) 577; Rh – Kam – TCam 30; 35;
38; 39; 40; 41; 43; 44; 45; 46; 50; 78; 84; 90; 157;
L – IL 131; 166; 167; 223; 224; 228; 229; 247; 248; 270;
282; 286; 293; 294; 299; 308; 317; 343; 344; 346; 347;
349; 378; 398; 420; 430; 449; 462; Rh – Rho – IG XII 1,
8; SER 11; S – IG XII 3, 1; 4; Th – IG XII 3, 443-5);
Minerva and Mars (K – ClRh 10 (1941) 208-9 and 210-13);
Roma (Rh – Rho – PP 4 (1949) 73; Samothracian Gods (Kr –
IG XII 1, 1034; S – IG XII 3, 6).

Abbreviations

(Excluding those of standard type, e.g. ancient authors and works as in LSJ.)

1 ISLANDS (IN APPENDIX)

An	Anaphe	Rh		Rhodes
As	Astypalaia		Ial	Ialysos
Ch	Chalke		Kam	Kameiros
K	Kos		L	Lindos
Kl	Kalymnos		Rho	Rhodos
Kr	Karpathos	S		Syme
Ks	Kasos	Sr		Saros
M	Melos	St		Seutloussa
Mg	Megiste	T		Telos
N	Nisyros	Th		Thera
Ph	Pholegandros			

2 EPIGRAPHICAL COLLECTIONS

HG   HERZOG, R.
(1928), 'Heilige Gesetze von Kos', APrA, Phil.-hist. Klasse, 6

IBM   NEWTON, C.T. et al.
(1874-1916), Ancient Greek Inscriptions in the British Museum, Oxford

IC   PATON, W.R. and HICKS, E.L.
(1891), The Inscriptions of Cos, Oxford

ICret   GUARDUCCI, M.
(1935-50), Inscriptiones Creticae, Rome

IL   BLINKENBERG, C.
(1941), Lindos. Fouilles et Recherches, II Inscriptions, Copenhagen

IvPr.	HILLER VON GAERTRINGEN, F.W.
	(1906), Die Inschriften von Priene
KF	HERZOG, R.
	(1899), Koische Forschungen und Funde, Leipzig
NS	MAIURI, A.
	(1925), Nuova Silloge epigrafica di Rodi e Cos, Firenze
NSER	PUGLIESE CARRATELLI, G.
	(1955-6), 'Nuovo Supplemento epigrafico rodio', ASAA, 17-18, 157-81
PLS and	PROTT, I. DE and ZIEHEN, L.
ZLS	(1896 and 1906), Leges Graecorum Sacrae e Titulis collectae, Leipzig
SER	PUGLIESE CARRATELLI, G.
	(1952-4), 'Supplemento epigrafico rodio', ASAA, 14-16, 247-316
TC	SEGRE, M.
	(1944-5), 'Tituli Calymnii', ASAA 6-7, 1-249
TCam	SEGRE, M and PUGLIESE CARRATELLI, G.
	(1949-51), 'Tituli Camirenses', ASAA, 12-13, 141-318
TCamS	PUGLIESE CARRATELLI, G.
	(1952-4), 'Tituli Camirenses, Supplementum', ASAA 14-16, 211-46

3 PERIODICALS

AA	Archäologischer Anzeiger
AAA	Athens Annals of Archaeology
ABSA	Annual of the British School at Athens
AC	L'Antiquité Classique
AD	Archaiologikon Deltion
ADAW	Abhandlungen der Deutschen Akademie de Wissenchaften zu Berlin
AE	Archaiologike Ephemeris
AHDO	Archives d'Histoire du Droit Oriental
AJA	American Journal of Archaeology
AJP	American Journal of Philology
ALA	Abhandlungen der sachsischen Akademie der Wissenschaften zu Leipzig
AM	Mitteilungen des Deutschen Archäologischen Instituts: (A) Athenische Abteilung; (I) Abteilung Istanbul
APrA	Abhandlungen der Preussischen Akademie·der Wissenschaften zu Berlin
AR	Archiv für Religionswissenschaft
ASAA	Annuario della Scuola Archeologica di Atene
BA	Bolletino d'Arte

BAGB	Bulletin de l'Association G. Budé
BCH	Bulletin de Correspondance Hellénique
BICS	Bulletin of the Institute of Classical Studies
BIHM	Bulletin of the Institute for the History of Medicine
BSAA	Bulletin de la Société d'Archéologie d'Alexandrie
CHJ	Cambridge Historical Journal
CJ	Classical Journal
CP	Classical Philology
CQ	Classical Quarterly
CRAI	Comptes rendus de l'Académie des Inscriptions et Belles-Lettres
CSCP	Cornell Studies in Classical Philology
ClRh	Clara Rhodos
EAE	To Ergon tes Archaiologikes Etaireias
GLO	Grecolatina et Orientalia
GR	Greece and Rome
HSCP	Harvard Studies in Classical Philology
HTR	Harvard Theological Review
HZ	Historische Zeitschrift
JAOS	Journal of the American Oriental Society
JBAA	Journal of the British Astronomical Association
JDAI	Jahrbuch des Deutschen Archäologischen Instituts
JEA	Journal of Egyptian Archaeology
JHI	Journal of the History of Ideas
JHS	Journal of Hellenic Studies
JNES	Journal of Near Eastern Studies
JOAI	Jahreshefte des Österreichischen Archäologischen Institutes in Wien
JP	Journal of Philology
MC	Mondo Classico
MH	Museum Helveticum
OA	Opuscula Archaeologica
PAAH	Praktika tes en Athenais Archaiologikes Etaireias
PBA	Proceedings of the British Academy
PCPS	Proceedings of the Cambridge Philological Society
PP	La Parola del Passato
PPS	Proceedings of the Prehistoric Society
PTRSL	Philosophical Transactions of the Royal Society of London
PhW	Philologische Wochenschrift
RBP	Revue Belge de Philologie
REG	Revue des Études Grecques
RFIC	Rivista di Filologia e di Istruzione Classica
RHA	Revue Hittite et Asianique
RIA	Rivista dell'Istituto Nazionale di Archeologia e Storia dell'Arte

RLi   Rendiconti dell'Accademia dei Lincei
RLo   Rendiconti dell'Istituto Lombardo
RM   Rheinisches Museum für Philologie
RP   Rendiconti della Pontificia Accademia di
         Archeologia
SBA   Sitzungsberichte der Preussischen Akademie der
         Wissenschaften zu Berlin, Phil.-hist. Klasse
SCO   Studi Classici e Orientali
TAPA   Transactions and Proceedings of the American
         Philological Association
UCPCP   University of California Publications in
         Classical Philology
ZN   Zeitschrift für Numismatik
ZPE   Zeitschrift für Papyrologie und Epigraphik

4   MISCELLANEOUS

BAMA   CROSSLAND, R.A. and BIRCHALL, A. (eds)
         (1973), Bronze Age Migrations in the Aegean,
         London
CAH   Cambridge Ancient History
CMG   (1908-   , in progress) Corpus Medicorum
         Graecorum, Leipzig
Coll.   POWELL, J.U.
 Alex.   (1925), Collectanea Alexandrina, Oxford
DSB   (1970-6), Dictionary of Scientific Biography,
         New York
FAC   EDMONDS, J.M.
         (1957-61), The Fragments of Attic Comedy,
         Leiden
FGH   JACOBY, F.
         (1923-), Die Fragmente der griechischen
         Historiker, Berlin
HE   GOW, A.S.F. and PAGE, D.L.
         (1965), The Greek Anthology. Hellenistic
         Epigrams, Cambridge
LSJ   LIDDELL, H.G. and SCOTT, R.
         (1940), A Greek-English Lexicon, 9th edn,
         revised by JONES, H.S., Oxford
n   note
no.   number
PA   FRASER, P.M.
         (1972), Ptolemaic Alexandria, Oxford
PMG   PAGE, D.L.
         (1962), Poetae Melici Graeci, Oxford
PW   PAULY-WISSOWA
         Realenzyklopädie der Klassischen Altertums-
         wissenschaft

RR	MAGIE, D.
	(1950), Roman Rule in Asia Minor, Princeton
TrGF	NAUCK, A.
	(1889), Tragicorum Graecorum Fragmenta, 2nd edn, Leipzig
VS	DIELS, H. and KRANZ, W.
	(1954), Die Fragmente der Vorsokratiker, 3rd edn, Berlin
WS	WACE, A.J.B. and STUBBINGS, F.H.
	(1961), A Companion to Homer, London

Bibliography

Note: For reasons of space, it has been necessary to
exclude many items. Works cited in 'Abbreviations' above
are excluded, as are editions of ancient authors (but not
collections of fragments), articles in CAH, PW, etc.
For a further list of articles in which inscriptions are
published or discussed, see, on Rhodes, SER pp.308-16,
NSER pp.179-80; on the other islands, bibliography in
Craik, 1965. In addition to all works mentioned in the
text of the book, I have listed those books and articles
I personally have found most interesting or useful.
However, a bibliography of this scope is bound to have
its idiosyncratic inclusions and omissions.

ALLEN, T.W.
(1921), The Homeric Catalogue of Ships, Oxford.
ANDERSON, W.S.
(1963), 'Pompey, his friends, and the literature of the
first century BC', UCPCP, 19, no.1, 1-88.
ARENA, R.
(1974), 'Per una interpretazione dei termini Meropes e
Chaoi', RLo, 108, 417-37.
ARNOLD, I.R.
(1936), 'Festivals of Rhodes', AJA, 40, 432-6.
ASHBURNER, W.
(1909), The Rhodian Sea-Law, Oxford.
ATKINSON, T.D. et al.
(1904), 'Excavations at Phylakopi in Melos', Society for
the Promotion of Hellenic Studies, suppl.4.
AUJAC, G.
(1966), Strabon et la science de son temps, Paris.
AUSTIN, M.
(1970), 'Greece and Egypt in the Archaic Age', PCPS suppl.2.

BARBER, R.
(1974), 'Phylakopi 1911 and the history of the later
Cycladic Bronze Age', ABSA, 69, 1-53.
BARNETT, R.D.
(1956), 'Ancient oriental influences on Archaic Greece',
212-38 in Studies presented to Hetty Goldman, New York.
BARTONEK, A.
(1973), 'Greek dialects of archaic Sicily', GLO, 5, 71-89.
BAUMBACH, L.
(1973), 'A fresco from Santorini', Akroterion, 18, 26-7.
BEAN, G.E. and COOK, J.M.
(1952), 'The Cnidia', ABSA, 48, 171-212.
(1955), 'The Halicarnassus peninsula', ABSA, 50, 85-171.
(1957), 'The Carian coast', ABSA, 52, 58-146.
BEATTIE, A.J.
(1961), 'Languages of the prehistoric Aegean', in WS,
311-24.
BENT, J.T.
(1885), The Cyclades, London.
BICKERMAN, E.J.
(1968), Chronology of the Ancient World, London.
BILIOTTI, E. and COTTRET, l'Abbé
(1881), L'Île de Rhodes, Rhodes.
BING, J.D.
(1971), 'Tarsus. A forgotten colony of Lindos', JNES, 30,
99-109.
BIRCHALL, A. and CROSSLAND, R.A.
(1973), 'Retrospect and prospect', in BAMA, 323-47.
BLINKENBERG, C.
(1915a), Die Lindische Tempelchronik neu bearbeitet, Bonn.
(1915b), 'Rhodische Urvölker', Hermes, 50, 270-303.
BLINKENBERG, C. and KINCH, K.F.
(1931; 1941), Lindos: Fouilles et Recherches, I Les petits
objets; II Inscriptions, Berlin and Copenhagen.
BOARDMAN, J.
(1964), The Greeks Overseas, Harmondsworth.
BOARDMAN, J. and HAYES, J.
(1966), Tocra: The Archaic Deposits, London.
BOSANQUET, R.C.
(1898), 'Excavations of the British School at Melos', JHS,
18, 60-80.
BOULANGER, A.
(1968), Aelius Aristide et la sophistique dans la province
d'Asie au IIe siècle de notre ère, Paris.
BOWERSOCK, G.W.
(1965), Augustus and the Greek World, Oxford.
(1969), Greek Sophists in the Roman Empire, Oxford
BOWRA, C.M.
(1936), 'Erinna's lament for Baucis', in Greek Poetry and

Life, Essays presented to Gilbert Murray, Oxford.
(1961), Greek Lyric Poetry, 2nd edn, Oxford.
BRANIGAN, K.
(1971), 'Cycladic figurines and their derivatives in Crete', ABSA, 66, 57-78.
BRAUN, J.A.
(1932), De Theraeorum rebus sacris, dissertation, Halle.
BREITHOLTZ, L.
(1960), Die Dorische Farce im griechischen Mütterland, Göteborg.
BRINK, K.O.
(1946), Callimachus and Aristotle: an enquiry into Callimachus' "pros Praxiphanen"', CQ, 40, 11-26.
BÜCHNER, G.
(1888), De Neocoria, dissertation, Göttingen.
BUCK, C.D.
(1955), The Greek Dialects, Chicago.
BURN, A.R.
(1930), Minoans, Philistines and Greeks, London and New York.
(1960), The Lyric Age of Greece, London.
(1962), Persia and the Greeks, London.
BURTON BROWN, T.
(1947), 'Prehistoric remains on Calymnus', JHS, 67, 128.
BURZACHECHI,M.
(1963), 'Ricerche epigrafiche sulle antiche biblioteche del mondo greco', RLi, 18, 75-96.
(1976), 'L'adozione dell'alfabeto nel mondo greco', PP, 31, 82-102.
CADOGAN, G., HARRISON, R.K. and STRONG, G.E.
(1972), 'Volcanic glass shards in Late Minoan I Crete', Antiquity, 46, 310-13.
CAIRNS, F.
(1972), Generic Composition in Greek and Roman Poetry, Edinburgh.
CANN, J.R. and RENFREW, C.
(1964), 'The characterization of obsidian and its application to the Mediterranean region', PPS, 30, 111-33.
CARNOY, A.
(1960), 'Les suffixes toponymiques pré-Grecs', AC, 29, 319-36.
CARPENTER, R.
(1938), 'Origin and diffusion of the Greek alphabet', AJA, 42, 125.
(1966), Discontinuity in Greek Civilization, Cambridge.
CARY, M.
(1949), The Geographic Background of Greek and Roman History, Oxford.

CASKEY, J.
(1962; 1964; 1966; 1971; 1972), 'Excavations in Keos',
Hesperia, 31, 263-83; 33, 314-35; 35, 363-76; 40, 359-96;
41, 357-401.
CASSON, L.
(1954), 'The grain trade of the Hellenistic world', TAPA,
85, 168-87.
(1960), The Ancient Mariners, London.
(1974), Travel in the Ancient World, London.
CATLING, H.W.
(1970), 'Analysis of pottery from the Mycenaean period',
PTRSL, A, 269, 175-8.
CATLING, H.W., RICHARDS, E.E. and BLIN-STOYLE, A.E.
(1963), 'Correlations between composition and provenance
of Mycenaean and Minoan pottery', ABSA, 58, 94-115.
CHADWICK, J.
(1956), 'The Greek dialects and Greek pre-history', GR,
3, 38-50.
(1976), 'Who were the Dorians?', PP, 31, 103-17.
CHAMBERS, M.H.
(1955), 'The twelve gods at Cos', HTR, 48, 153-4.
CHITTENDEN, J.
(1947), 'Some methods of research into the origin of Greek
deities', GR, 16, 97-107.
COHEN, M.R. and DRABKIN, I.E.
(1948), A Source Book in Greek Science, New York.
COHN-HAFT, L.
(1956), 'The public physicians of ancient Greece', Smith
College Studies in History, 42.
COLDSTREAM, J.N. and HUXLEY, G.L.
(1972), Kythera, London.
COLEMAN, J.E.
(1974), 'The chronology and interconnections of the
Cycladic islands in the Neolithic Period and the Early
Bronze Age', AJA, 278, 333-44.
COOK, A.B.
(1914-40), Zeus: a study in ancient religion, Cambridge.
COOK, R.M.
(1962), 'The Dorian invasion', PCPS, 8, 16-22.
CORBETT, P.E.
(1970), 'Greek temples and Greek worshippers', BICS, 17,
149-58.
CORDANO, F.
(1974), 'Rhodos prima del sinecismo e Rhodioi fondatori di
colonie', PP, 29, 179-81.
CRAIK, E.M.
(1965), Cult officials in the Dorian Islands of the Aegean,
M.Litt. dissertation, Cambridge.
(1967), 'Two notes on officials at Kos', PP, 22, 440-6.

(1969), 'Dating formulae in the Dorian islands', Maia, 21, 311-25.

(1970), 'Diplous Muthos', CQ, 20, 95-101.

(1979), 'Philoktetes: Sophoklean Melodrama', AC.

CROISET, A. and CROISET, M.

(1910-21), Histoire de la littérature grecque, 3rd edn, Paris.

CROSSLAND, R.A.

(1973), 'Linguistics and archaeology in Aegean prehistory', in BAMA, 5-15.

CUMONT, F.

(1912), Astrology and Religion among the Greeks and Romans, New York.

CUNNINGHAM, I.C.

(1966), 'Herodas 4', CQ, 16, 113-25.

DAVIES, J.C.

(1972), 'Some conflicting sources of Hippocratic theory', RM, 115, 308-10.

DAVISON, J.A.

(1961), 'The Homeric question', in WS, 234-65.

DAWKINS, R.M. and DROOP, J.F.

(1910-11), 'The excavations at Phylakopi in Melos', ABSA, 17, 10-22.

DEGRASSI, A.

(1941), 'Iscrizioni latine inedite di Coo', ClRh, 10, 201-13.

DESBOROUGH, V.R.d'A.

(1964), The Last Mycenaeans and their Successors, Oxford.

(1972), The Greek Dark Ages, London.

DEVOTO, G.

(1972), 'Non-classical languages of the Mediterranean region', in D. Daiches and A. Thorlby, eds, Literature and Western Civilization: the classical world, London.

DICKS, D.R.

(1954), 'Ancient astronomical instruments', JBAA, 64, 77-85.

(1960), The Geographical Fragments of Hipparchus, London.

(1970), Early Greek Astronomy to Aristotle, London.

DIETRICH, B.C.

(1970), 'Some evidence of religious continuity in the Greek Dark Age', BICS, 17, 16-31.

(1974), The Origins of Greek Religion, Berlin and New York.

(1975), 'The Dorian Hyacinthia: a survival from the Bronze Age', Kadmos, 14, 133-42.

DODDS, E.R.

(1951), The Greeks and the Irrational, Berkeley.

DOERMER, G.

(1883), De Graecorum sacrificulis qui 'hieropoioi' dicuntur, dissertation, Strassburg.

235 Bibliography

DOSSIN, G.
(1972), 'Membliaros - Anaphe', RBP, 50, 25-9.
DOUMAS, C.
(1974), 'The Minoan eruption of the Santorini volcano',
Antiquity, 48, 110-15.
(1976), 'Prehistoric Cycladic people in Crete', AAA, 9,
69-80.
See also excavation reports in AAA, AD, EAE, PAAH on Thera.
DOVER, K.J.
(1968), Lysias and the Corpus Lysiacum, Berkeley.
(1972), Aristophanic Comedy, London.
(1974), Greek Popular Morality, Oxford.
(1976), 'The freedom of the intellectual in Greek
society', Talanta, 7, 24-54.
(1978), Greek Homosexuality, London.
DOW, S.
(1960), 'The Greeks in the Bronze Age', article repr. in
G.S. Kirk, ed., The Language and Background of Homer,
Cambridge, 1964.
DUNBABIN, T.J.
(1948), The Western Greeks, Oxford.
(1957), The Greeks and their Eastern Neighbours, Society
for the Promotion of Hellenic Studies, suppl. 8.
EDELSTEIN, E.J. and EDELSTEIN, L.
(1945), Asclepius: a collection and interpretation of the
testimonies, Baltimore.
EDELSTEIN, L.
(1952), 'Recent trends in the interpretation of ancient
science', JHI, 13, 573-604.
(1967), 'Ancient medicine', in O. Temkin and C.L. Temkin,
eds, Selected Papers of Ludwig Edelstein, Baltimore.
EDELSTEIN, L. and KIDD, I.G.
(1972), Posidonius I. The fragments, Cambridge.
EDWARDS, G.P. and EDWARDS, R.B.
(1974), 'Red letters and Phoenician writing', Kadmos,
13, 48-57.
EHRENBERG, V.
(1969), The Greek State, 2nd edn, London.
EINARSON, B.
(1967), Notes on the development of the Greek alphabet',
CP, 62, 1-24.
ELSE, G.F.
(1957), Aristotle's 'Poetics': the argument, Harvard.
(1965), The Origin and Early Form of Greek Tragedy,
Harvard.
EVANS, A.J.
(1921-35), The Palace of Minos, London.
EVANS, J.D. and RENFREW, C.
(1968), 'Excavations at Saliagos near Antiparos', ABSA
suppl. 5.

FARNELL, L.R.
(1896; 1907; 1909), The Cults of the Greek States, I-II;
III-IV; V, Oxford.
(1921), Greek Hero Cults and Ideas of Immortality, Oxford.
FARRINGTON, B.
(1944; 1949), Greek Science, I; II, London; 2nd edn 1953.
FELLOWS, C.
(1852), Travels and Researches in Asia Minor, more
particularly in the Province of Lycia, London.
FESTUGIÈRE, A.-J.
(1954), Personal Religion among the Greeks, Berkeley.
FICK, A.
(1905), Vorgriechische Ortsnamen, Göttingen.
FINLEY, M.I.
(1970), Early Greece: the Bronze and Archaic Ages, London.
(1973), The Ancient Economy, Berkeley.
FORBES, R.J.
(1958-64 and 1964-6), Studies in Ancient Technology, VI-IX,
1st edn and I-V, 2nd edn, Leiden.
FORBES, W.T.M.
(1930), 'The silkworm of Aristotle', CP, 25, 22-6.
FORSDYKE, E.J.
(1957), Greece before Homer, London.
FOUCART, P.
(1873), Des Associations religieuses chez les Grecs, Paris.
FRAENKEL, H.
(1915), De Simia Rhodio, dissertation, Göttingen.
FRANCOTTE, H.
(1964), Mélanges de droit public grec, Rome.
FRASER, P.M.
(1953), 'An inscription from Cos', BSAA, 40, 35-62.
(1958), 'A Ptolemaic inscription from Thera', JEA, 44,
99-100.
(1972), 'Notes on two Rhodian institutions', ABSA, 67,
113-24.
FRASER, P.M. and BEAN, G.E.
(1954), The Rhodian Peraea and Islands, Oxford.
FRENCH, D.H.
(1973), 'Migrations and "Minyan" pottery in western
Anatolia and the Aegean', in BAMA 51-7.
FURNESS, A.
(1956), 'Some early pottery of Samos, Kalimnos and Chios',
PPS, 22, 173-212.
FURUMARK, A.
(1950), 'The settlement at Ialysos and Aegean history
c. 1550-1400 BC', OA, 6, 150-271.
GABRIEL, A.
(1932), 'La construction, l'attitude et l'emplacement du
colosse de Rhodes', BCH, 56, 331-59.

GALINSKY, G.K.
(1972), The Herakles Theme, Oxford.
GASK, G.
(1950), Essays in the History of Medicine, London.
GIFFLER, M.
(1939), 'The calendar of Cos', AJA, 43, 445-6.
GNAEDINGER, C.
(1892), De Graecorum magistratibus eponymis, dissertation, Strassburg.
GRAHAM, A.J.
(1964), Colony and Mother City in Ancient Greece, Manchester.
GRIFFITH, G.J.
(1935), The Mercenaries of the Hellenistic World, Cambridge.
GRUPPE, O.
(1887), Die griechische Kulte und Mythen in ihren Beziehungen zu den orientalischen Religionen, Leipzig.
GUARDUCCI, M.
(1939-40), 'Fu Prokles re di Thera?', ASSA, 1-2, 41-5.
GUTHRIE, W.K.C.
(1950), The Greeks and their Gods, London.
(1959), 'Early Greek religion in the light of the decipherment of Linear B', BICS, 6, 35-46.
(1962; 1965; 1969), A History of Greek Philosophy, I; II; III, Cambridge.
HALEY, J.B. and BLEGEN, C.W.
(1928), 'The coming of the Greeks', AJA, 32, 141-54.
HALLIDAY, W.R.
(1913), Greek Divination, London.
HARRIS, C.R.S.
(1973), The Heart and the Vascular System in Ancient Greek Medicine, Oxford.
HARRIS, H.A.
(1964), Greek Athletes and Athletics, London.
HASEBROEK, J.
(1933), Trade and Politics in Ancient Greece, London.
HEAD, B.V.
(1897), Catalogue of Greek Coins of Caria, Cos, Rhodes, etc. in the British Museum, London.
(1911), Historia Nummorum, 2nd edn, Oxford.
HEATH, T.L.
(1921), A History of Greek Mathematics, Oxford.
(1932), Greek Astronomy, London.
HÉDERVÁRI, P.
(1971), 'An attempt to correlate some archaeological and volcanological data regarding the Minoan eruption of Santorin', AD, 26, 1-15.

HERBRECHT, H.
(1886), De Sacerdotii apud Graecos Emptione Venditione,
disseration, Strassburg.
HERZOG, R.
(1898), 'Reisebericht aus Kos', AM (A), 23, 441-61.
(1901), 'Bericht über eine epigraphisch-archäologische
Expedition auf der Insel Kos im Sommer 1900', AA, 16, 130-40.
(1901), 'Das Heiligtum des Apollo in Halasarna', SBA, 470-94.
(1902), 'Kretikos Polemos', Klio, 2, 316-33.
(1903), 'Vorläufiger Bericht über die Archäologische
Expedition auf der Insel Kos im Jahre 1902; im Jahre 1903',
AA, 18, 1-13; 186-99.
(1904), 'Inscription grecque trouvée à Cos, CRAI, 164-73.
(1905), 'Vorläufiger Bericht über die Koische Expedition
im Jahre 1904', AA, 20, 1-15.
(1906), 'Dorier und Ionier', Philologus, 65, 630-6.
(1907), 'Aus dem Asklepieion von Kos', AR, 10, 201-28;
400-15.
(1922), 'Nikias und Xenophon von Kos', HZ, 125, 189-247.
(1931), Die Wunderheilungen von Epidauros, Leipzig.
(1932), Kos: Ergebnisse der Deutschen Ausgrabungen und
Forschungen, Berlin.
(1942), 'Symbolae Calymniae et Coae, RFIC, 20, 1-20.
HERZOG, R. and KLAFFENBACH, G.
(1952), 'Asylieurkunden aus Kos', ADAW, Klasse Sprache,
Lit., Kunst, 1.
HESTER, D.A.
(1957), 'Pre-Greek place-names in Greece and Asia Minor',
RHA, 61, 111-19.
(1968), 'Recent developments in Mediterranean "substrate"
studies', Minos, 9, 219-35.
HEWITT, J.W.
(1909), 'Major restrictions on access to Greek temples',
TAPA, 40, 83-91.
HILLER VON GAERTRINGEN, F.W.
(1893), 'Die samothrakischen Götter in Rhodos und
Karpathos', AM(A), 18, 385-94.
(1901), 'Eine Karneenfeier in Thera', Hermes, 36, 134-9.
(1902a), Thera, Untersuchungen, Vermessungen und
Ausgrabungen in den Jahren 1895-1902, Berlin.
(1902b), 'Die Götterkulte von Thera', Klio, 1, 212-27.
(1932), 'König Prokles von Thera', JDAI, 47, 127-34.
(1940), 'Alt-Thera vor der Grundung von Kyrene', Klio,
33, 57-72.
HOECKMANN, O.
(1975), Zu dem Kykladischen Gebäudemodell von Melos',
AM(A), 25, 269-99.
HOLLAND, L.B.
(1941), 'Axones', AJA, 45, 346-62.

HOLLEAUX, L.
(1917), 'Sur la guerre crétoise', REG, 30, 88-104.
HONEA, K.
(1975), 'Prehistoric remains on the island of Kythnos',
AJA, 79, 277-9.
HOOD, S.
(1970), 'The international scientific congress on the
volcano of Thera, 1969', Kadmos, 9, 98-106.
HOOKER, J.T.
(1977), Mycenaean Greece, London
HOPE SIMPSON, R.
(1965), A Gazeteer and Atlas of Mycenaean Sites, BICS
suppl. 16, London.
HOPE SIMPSON, R. and LAZENBY, J.F.
(1962; 1970a; 1973), 'Notes from the Dodecanese I; II;
III', ABSA, 57, 154-75; 65, 47-77; 68, 127-79.
(1970b), The Catalogue of Ships in Homer's Iliad, Oxford.
HOUWINK TEN CATE
(1973), 'Anatolian evidence for relations with the West
in the Late Bronze Age', in BAMA 141-61.
HUXLEY, G.L.
(1956), 'Mycenaean decline and the Homeric catalogue of
ships', BICS, 3, 19-30.
(1960), Achaeans and Hittites, Oxford.
(1969), Greek Epic Poetry, London.
ISLER, H.P.
(1973), 'An Early Bronze Age settlement on Samos',
Archaeology, 26, 170-5.
JACOBSEN, T.W.
(1973), 'Excavations in the Franchthi cave', Hesperia,
42, 45-88.
JACOBY, F.
(1959), 'Diagoras ho atheos', ADAW, 3, 3-8.
JACOPI, G.
(1928), 'Esplorazione del santuario di Zeus Atabyrios',
ClRh, 1, 88-91; see also 92-100.
(1929), 'Il tempio e il teatro di Apollo Eretimio', ClRh,
2, 77-116; see also 165-256.
(1932), 'Scavi e ricerche di Nisiro', ClRh 6-7, 475-552.
JAEGER, W.
(1945), Paideia: the ideals of Greek culture, Oxford.
(1963), Diokles von Karystos, Berlin.
JAMESON, M.H.
(1958), 'Inscriptions of Karpathos', Hesperia, 27, 122-4.
(1959), 'Inscriptions of Hermione, Hydra and Kasos',
Hesperia, 28, 109-20.
JEFFERY, L.H.
(1961), The Local Scripts of Archaic Greece, Oxford.
(1976), Archaic Greece, London.

JEFFERY, L.H. and MORPURGO-DAVIES, A.
(1970), 'Poinikastas and Poinikazein', Kadmos, 9, 118-54.
JENKINS, G.K.
(1972), Ancient Greek Coins, London.
JOHNSTON, A.
(1975), 'Rhodian readings', ABSA, 70, 145-67.
JOLY, R.
(1966), Le Niveau de la science hippocratique, Paris.
JONES, A.H.M.
(1937), The Cities of the Eastern Roman Provinces, London.
(1940), The Greek City from Alexander to Justinian,
Oxford.
JONES, W.H.S.
(1945), 'Hippocrates and the Corpus Hippocraticum', PBA,
31, 103-25.
(1947), The Medical Writings of Anonymus Londinensis,
Cambridge.
JOUANNA, J.
(1975), 'Approches actuelles de la collection hippocratique.
La méthode philologique', BAGB, 364-71.
KAMPS, W.
(1937), 'Les origines de la fondation cultuelle dans la
Grèce ancienne', AHDO, 1, 145-79.
KINKEL, G.
(1877), Epicorum Graecorum Fragmenta, Leipzig.
KIRCHHOFF, A.
(1877), Studien zur Geschichte des griechischen Alphabets,
3rd edn, Berlin.
KIRK, G.S.
(1970), Myth: its meaning and function in ancient and
other cultures, Berkeley.
(1972), 'Greek mythology. Some new perspectives', JHS,
92, 74-85.
(1974), The Nature of Greek Myths, Harmondsworth.
KIRKWOOD, G.M.
(1974), Early Greek Monody, CSCP, 37.
KLEINGÜNTHER, A.
(1933), 'Protos euretes', Philologus Supplbd.26.1.
KONSTANTINOPOULOS, G.
Excavation reports in AAA, AD, EAE, PAAH, on Rhodes and
the Dodekanese.
KONTORINI, V.
(1975a), 'Le roi Hiempsal II de Numidie et Rhodes', AC,
44, 89-99.
(1975b), 'Les concours des grands Éréthimia à Rhodes', BCH,
99, 96-117.
KRAAY, C.M.
(1976), Archaic and Classical Greek Coins, London.

KRETSCHMER, P.
(1896), Einleitung in die Geschichte der griechischen
Sprache, Göttingen.
(1925), 'Die protoindogermanische Schicht', Glotta, 14,
300-19.
KÜCHENMÜLLER, G.
(1928), Philetae Coi Reliquiae, Berlin.
LAFFRANQUE, M.
(1964), Poseidonios d'Apamée, Paris.
LANDELS, J.G.
(1978), Engineering in the Ancient World, London.
LAUMONIER, A.
(1958), Les Cultes indigènes en Carie, Paris.
LAURENZI, L.
(1941), Iscrizioni dell'Asclepieo di Coo', ClRh, 10,
25-40.
LAWALL, G.
(1967), Theocritus' Coan Pastorals, Cambridge, Mass.
LEAKE, W.M.
(1824), Journal of a Tour in Asia Minor, London.
LEVI DELLA VIDA, G.
(1938), 'Una bilingue Greco-Nabatea a Coo', ClRh, 9,
139-48.
(1939), 'Une bilingue gréco-palmyrienne à Cos', in Mélanges
Dussaud, 883-6.
LEVIN, S.
(1964), The Linear B Decipherment Controversy Re-examined,
New York.
(1972), 'Greek with substrate phenomena or "a jargon" -
what is the difference?', Kadmos, 11, 129-39.
LINDSELL,
(1936), 'Was Theocritus a botanist?', GR, 6, 78-93.
LLOYD, G.E.R.
(1963), 'Who is attacked in On Ancient Medicine?',
Phronesis, 8, 108-26.
(1964), 'Experiment in early Greek philosophy and
medicine', PCPS, 10, 50-72.
(1970), Early Greek Science, Thales to Aristotle, London.
(1973), Greek Science after Aristotle, London.
(1975a), 'Aspects of the interrelations of medicine, magic
and philosophy in ancient Greece', Apeiron, 9, 1-17.
(1975b), 'The Hippocratic question', CQ, 25, 171-92.
LONG, A.A.
(1974), Hellenistic Philosophy, London.
LONGRIGG, J.
(1963), 'Philosophy and medicine: some early interactions',
HSCP, 67, 147-75.
LONIE, I.M.
(1965), 'The Cnidian treatises in the Corpus Hippocraticum',
CQ, 15, 1-30.

LUCE, J.V.
(1969), The End of Atlantis, London.
(1972), 'More thoughts about Thera', GR, 19, 37-46.
(1976), 'Thera and the devastation of Minoan Crete: a new interpretation of the evidence', AJA, 80, 9-18.
MAHAFFY, J.P.
(1887), Greek Life and Thought, London.
MAIURI, A.
(1916), 'Nuove iscrizioni greche delle Sporadi meridionali, I: Iscrizioni del Museo Archeologico di Rodi', ASAA 2, 127-79.
Excavation reports in ASAA, ClRh on Rhodes and the Dodekanese; see especially: (1928) ClRh, 1, 99-117.
MARINATOS, S.
Excavation reports in AAA, PAAH (1968-74) on Thera.
(1933), 'La marine créto-mycénienne', BCH, 57, 170-235.
(1939), 'The volcanic destruction of Minoan Crete', Antiquity, 13, 425-39.
(1971), 'Life and art in prehistoric Thera', PBA, 57, 351-67.
(1973), 'Ethnic problems raised by recent discoveries in Thera', in BAMA, 199-201.
(1974), 'Late Minoan Thera', in Phylactopoulos, ed., 1974, 220-8 (survey).
MEIGGS, R.
(1972), The Athenian Empire, Oxford.
MEIGGS, R. and LEWIS, D.
(1969), A Selection of Greek Historical Inscriptions, Oxford.
MEILLET, A.
(1913), Apercu d'une histoire de la langue grecque, Paris.
MELLAART, J.
(1958), 'The end of the Early Bronze Age in Anatolia and the Aegean', AJA, 62, 9-33.
MENDOZA, J.
(1976), 'Cronologia de dos tratados del Corpus Hippocraticum', Emerita, 44, 171-88.
MERKELBACH, R. and WEST, M.L.
(1967), Fragmenta Hesiodea, Oxford.
MILLER, R.D.
(1939), The origin and original nature of Apollo, dissertation, Philadelphia.
MOGGI, M.
(1976), I sinecismi interstatali greci, Pisa.
MONACO, G.
(1941), 'Scavi nella zona micenea di Jaliso', ClRh, 10, 41-184.
MONEY, J.
(1973), 'The destruction of Acrotiri', Antiquity, 47, 50-3.

MOREAU, J.
(1962), Aristote et son école, Paris.
MORELLI, D.
(1959), 'I culti in Rodi', SCO, 8, 1-184.
MORRICONE, L.
(1950), 'Scavi e ricerche a Coo', BA, 35, 316-30.
(1952), 'I sacerdoti di Halios', ASAA, 11-13, 351-80.
(1965-6), 'Eleona e Langada: sepolcreti della tarda età
del Bronzo a Coo', ASAA, 27-8, 5-311.
(1972-3), 'Coo: scavi e scoperte nel "Serraglio" e in
località minori (1935-1943)', ASAA, 34-5, 139-396.
MUHLY, J.D.
(1974), 'Hittites and Achaeans: Ahhijawa redomitus',
Historia, 23, 129-45.
MÜLLER, K.O.
(1830, tr. H. Tufnell and G.C.Lewis), The History and
Antiquities of the Doric Race, Oxford.
MYLONAS, G.E.
(1966), Mycenae and the Mycenaean Age, Princeton.
MYRES, J.L.
(1930), Who were the Greeks?, Berkeley.
(1953), Geographical History in Greek Lands, Oxford.
NAVEH, J.
(1973), 'Some Semitic considerations on the antiquity of
the Greek alphabet', AJA, 77, 1-8.
NEUGEBAUER, O.
(1945), 'The history of ancient astronomy: problems and
methods', JNES, 4, 1-38.
(1950), 'The alleged Babylonian discovery of the
precession of the equinoxes', JAOS, 70, 1-8.
(1956), 'Notes on Hipparchos', in Studies presented to
Hetty Goldman, New York.
(1957), The Exact Sciences in Antiquity, 2nd edn,
Providence.
NEWTON, C.T.
(1862), A History of Discoveries at Halicarnassus, Cnidus
and Branchidae, London.
(1865), Travels and Discoveries in the Levant, London.
NILSSON, M.P.
(1906), Griechische Feste, Leipzig.
(1925, tr. F.J. Fielden), A History of Greek Religion,
Oxford.
(1932), The Mycenaean Origin of Greek Mythology,
Cambridge.
(1940), Greek Folk Religion, New York.
(1950), The Minoan-Mycenaean Religion and its Survival
in Greek Religion, 2nd edn, Lund.
(1951), Cults, Myths, Oracles and Politics in Ancient
Greece, Lund.

NINKOVICH, D. and HEEZEN, B.C.
(1965), 'Santorini tephra', CP, 17, 413-53.
O'CONNOR, J.B.
(1908), Chapters in the History of Actors and Acting in
Ancient Greece, Chicago.
OLIVER, J.R.
(1934), 'The sacrificing women in the temple of Asklepios',
BIHM, 2, 504-11.
OTTO, W.F.
(1933), Dionysos, Mythus and Kultus, Frankfurt.
PAGE, D.L.
(1959), History and the Homeric Iliad, Berkeley.
(1970), The Santorini Volcano and the Destruction of
Minoan Crete, London.
PALMER, L.R.
(1965), Mycenaeans and Minoans, 2nd edn, London.
PAPACHRISTODOULOU, C.I.
(1972), Istoria tes Rhodou, Athens.
PARKE, H.W.
(1977), Festivals of the Athenians, London.
PEEK, W.
(1969), 'Inschriften von der dorischen Inseln', ALA, 62, 34-51
PERSSON, A.W.
(1942), The Religion of Greece in Prehistoric Times, Berkeley.
PFEIFFER, R.
(1968), History of Classical Scholarship, Oxford.
PFISTER, F.
(1961), Greek Gods and Heroes, London.
PFLAUM, H.G.
(1971), 'Une inscription bilingue de Kos, et la perception
de la vicesima hereditatium', ZPE, 7, 61-8.
PHILLIPS, E.D.
(1973), Greek Medicine, London.
PHILLIPSON, C.
(1911), The International Law and Custom of Ancient
Greece and Rome, London.
PHYLACTOPOULOS, G.A., ed.
(1974; 1975, tr. P. Sherrard), History of the Hellenic
World: Prehistory and Protohistory; The Archaic Period,
London.
PICARD, C.
(1927), 'Sur la patrie et les pérégrinations de Demeter',
REG, 50, 320-69.
(1948), Les Religions préhelléniques, Paris.
PICKARD-CAMBRIDGE, A.
(1962), Dithyramb, Tragedy and Comedy, 2nd edn, rev.
T.B.L. Webster, Oxford.
(1968), The Dramatic Festivals of Athens, 2nd edn, rev.
J. Gould and D.M. Lewis, Oxford.

PITTINGER, J.
(1975), 'The mineral products of Melos in antiquity and their identification', ABSA, 70, 191-7.
POHL, R.
(1905), De Graecorum medicis publicis, inaugural dissertation, Berlin.
POHLENZ, M.
(1938), Hippokrates, Berlin.
POLAND
(1909), Geschichte des griechischen Vereinswesens, Leipzig.
POMERANCE, L.
(1975), 'Comments on the Vitaliano geological report', AJA, 79, 83-4.
POMEROY, S.B.
(1975), Goddesses, Whores, Wives, and Slaves: Women in classical Antiquity, London.
POULIANOS, A.N.
(1972), 'The discovery of the first known victim of Thera's Bronze Age eruption', Archaeology, 25, 229-30.
POWELL, J.U. and BARBER, E.A.
(1921; 1929; 1933), New Chapters in the History of Greek Literature, Oxford.
PRITCHETT, W.K.
(1946), 'Months in Dorian calendars', AJA, 50, 358-60.
PUGLIESE CARRATELLI, G.
(1939-40), 'Per la storia delle associazioni in Rodi antica', ASAA, 1-2, 147-200.
(1957a), 'Gli Asclepiadi e il sinecismo di Cos', PP, 12, 332-42.
(1957b), 'Epigrafi del demo coo di Isthmos', PP, 12, 442-4.
(1958a), 'Epigrafi del demo coo di Hippia', PP, 13, 418-19.
(1958b), 'Per la storia delle relazione micenee con l'Italia', PP, 13, 205-20.
(1963-4), 'Il Damos Coo di Isthmos', ASAA, 41-2, 147-202.
(1965), 'Ancora sul monarchos di Cos', PP, 20, 446-50.
(1969a), 'Epigrafi del demo coo di Isthmos', PP, 24, 128-33.
(1969b), 'Monarchos Coo e stephanephoros Calimnio', PP, 24, 372-4.
RADKE, G.
(1936), Die Bedeutung der weissen und schwarzen Farbe in Kult und Brauch der Griechen und Römer, dissertation, Berlin.
RAMSAY, W.M.
(1895-7), The Cities and Bishoprics of Phrygia, Oxford.

RAPP, G. and COOK, S.
(1973), 'Thera pumice recovered from LH II A stratum at Nichoria', AAA, 6, 136-7.
RAUBITSCHEK, A.E.
(1970), suppl. note to Jeffery and Morpurgo-Davies (1970).
RAVEN, J.E.
(1948), Pythagoreans and Eleatics, Cambridge.
RAWSON, E.
(1969), The Spartan Tradition in European Thought, Oxford.
REITZENSTEIN, R.
(1964), Geschichte der griechischen Etymologika, Amsterdam.
RENFREW, A.C.
(1972), The Emergence of Civilisation: the Cyclades and the Aegean in the Third Millennium BC, London.
(1973a), 'Linguistics and archaeology in Aegean prehistory', in BAMA, 5-15.
(1973b), 'Problems in the general correlation of archaeological and linguistic strata in prehistoric Greece: the model of autochthonous origin', in BAMA, 263-79.
(1977), 'A Linear A tablet fragment from Phylakopi in Melos', Kadmos, 16, 111-19.
RENFREW, C., CANN, J.R. and DIXON, J.E.
(1965), 'Obsidian in the Aegean', ABSA, 60, 225-47.
RICHTER, G.M.A.
(1929), 'Silk in Greece', AJA, 33, 27-33.
RIEMSCHNEIDER, M.
(1974), Rhodos. Kultur und Geschichte, Leipzig and Vienna.
ROBERT, L.
(1935), 'Notes d'épigraphie hellénistique', BCH, 59, 421-5.
(1936), 'Inscription trouvée à Kos', BCH, 60, 199-202.
(1940), Les Gladiateurs dans l'Orient grec, Paris.
(1963), Noms indigènes dans l'Asie Mineure gréco-romaine, Paris.
ROBERT, M.F.
(1939), 'Hippocrate et le clergé d'Asclépios à Cos', CRAI, 91-9.
ROSE, H.J.
(1930), Modern Methods in Classical Mythology, St Andrews.
ROSS, L.
(1840-5), Reisen auf den griechischen Inseln des ägäischen Meeres, Stuttgart.
(1852), Reisen nach Kos, Halikarnassos, Rhodos und der Insel Cypern, Halle.
ROSTOVTZEFF, M.
(1941), The Social and Economic History of the Hellenistic World, Oxford.

ROUSE, W.H.D.
(1902), Greek Votive Offerings, Cambridge.
SAKELLARIOU, M.B.
(1974), 'Linguistic and ethnic groups in Prehistoric
Greece, 364-89, in Phylactopoulos, ed., 1974.
SANDBACH, F.H.
(1975), The Stoics, London.
SCHLESINGER, A.C.
(1931), 'Associated divinities in Greek temples, AJA, 35,
161-9.
SCHWEGLER, K.
(1913), De Aischinis quae feruntur epistulis, dissertation,
Giessen.
SEGRE, M.
(1933a), 'Legge sacra di Stampalia', MC, 3, 136-40.
(1933b), 'Iscrizioni di Scarpanto', Historia, 7, 577-88.
(1933c), 'Kretikos polemos', RFIC, 11, 365-92.
(1934a), 'Iscrizioni del'Odeon di Coo', Historia, 8,
429-52.
(1934b), 'Grano di Tessaglia a Coo', RFIC, 12, 169-93.
(1935), 'Epigraphica. I Catalogo di libri da Rodi',
RFIC, 13, 214-22.
(1936a), 'Ancora sulla biblioteca del ginnasio di Rodi',
RFIC, 14, 40.
(1936b), 'Dedica votiva dell'equipaggio di una nave Rodia',
ClRh, 8, 227-44.
(1937a), 'Il culto di Arsinoe Filadelfo nelle città
greche', BSAA, 31, 286-98.
(1937b), 'La legge ateniese sull'unificazione della
moneta', ClRh, 9, 151-78.
(1937c), 'Osservazioni epigrafiche sulla vendita di
sacerdozio', RLo, 70, 1-42.
(1938a), 'Due lettere di Silla', RFIC, 16, 253-63.
(1938b), 'Due leggi sacre dell'Asclepieo di Coo', RIA, 6,
191-8.
(1940-1), 'Documenti di storia ellenistica, I Antigono
Dosone e Coo; III Le terre del re Perseo a Coo', RP, 17,
21-34; 37-8.
(1951), 'Rituali rodii di sacrifici', PP, 6, 153.
SEGRE, M. and HERZOG, R.
(1975), 'Una lettera di Corbulone ai Coi', PP, 30, 102-4.
SELTMAN, C.
(1955), Greek Coins, 2nd edn, London.
SEVERYNS, A.
(1960), Grèce et Proche-Orient avant Homère, Brussells.
SHERK, R.K.
(1966), 'Cos and the Dionysiac artists', Historia, 15,
211-16.

SHERWIN-WHITE, S.M.
(1975), 'A Coan domain in Cyprus', JHS, 95, 182-4.
SIDGWICK, H.
(1872; 1873), 'The Sophists', JP, 4, 288-307; 5, 66-80.
SIFAKIS, G.M.
(1967), Studies in the History of Hellenistic Drama,
London.
SIGERIST, H.E.
(1934), 'Notes and comments on Hippocrates', BIHM, 2,
190-214.
(1961), A History of Medicine, New York.
SMITH, D.R.
(1972), 'Hieropoioi and hierothytai on Rhodes', AC, 41,
532-9.
(1973a), 'The Coan festival of Zeus Polieus', CJ, 69,
21-5.
(1973b), 'The hieropoioi on Kos', Numen, 20, 38-47.
SMITH, W.D.
(1973), 'Galen on Coans versus Cnidians', BIHM, 41,
569-85.
SMYTH, H.W.
(1900), Greek Melic Poets, London.
SNODGRASS, A.M.
(1971), The Dark Age of Greece, Edinburgh.
SOKOLOWSKI, F.
(1954), 'Fees and taxes in the Greek cults', HTR, 47,
153-64.
(1955), Lois sacrées de l'Asie Mineure, Paris.
(1957), 'Partnership in the lease of cults in Greek
antiquity', HTR, 50, 133-43.
(1962), Lois sacrées des cités grecques, Paris.
SOLIN, H.
(1973), 'Zu den Namen der dorischen Inseln', ZPE, 10,
282-4.
SOLMSEN, F.
(1961), 'Greek philosophy and the discovery of the nerves',
MH, 18, 150-97.
STECKERL, F.
(1958), The Fragments of Praxagoras of Cos and his School,
Leiden.
STENGEL, P.
(1920), Die griechischen Kultusaltertümer, 3rd edn,
Munich.
STUBBINGS, F.H.
(1951), Mycenaean Pottery from the Levant, Cambridge.
SUSINI, G.
(1952-4), 'Tre iscrizioni inedite da Coo', ASAA, 30-3,
357-61.

(1963-4), 'Supplemento epigrafico di Caso, Scarpanto, Saro,
Calchi, Alinnia e Tilo', ASAA, 25-6, 203-92.
SWINDLER, M.H.
(1913), Cretan Elements in the Cults and Ritual of Apollo,
Pennsylvania.
SYME, R.
(1961), 'Who was Vedius Pollio?', JRS, 51, 23-30.
TATAKIS, B.N.
(1931), Panétius de Rhodes, Paris.
TEMKIN, O.
(1953), 'Greek medicine as science and craft', Isis, 44,
213-25.
THOMSON, G.
(1954), Studies in Ancient Greek Society. The Prehistoric
Aegean, 2nd edn, London.
THUMB, A.
(1909), Handbuch der griechischen Dialekte, Heidelberg.
TOMLINSON, R.A.
(1972), Argos and the Argolid, London.
TOZER, H.F.
(1890), The Islands of the Aegean, Oxford.
VAN GELDER, H.
(1900), Geschichte der alten Rhodier, Haag.
VAN STRAATEN, M.
(1962), Panaetii Rhodii Fragmenta, 3rd edn, Leiden.
VELIKOVSKY, I.
(1960), Oedipus and Akhnaton; myth and history, London.
VENTRIS, M. and CHADWICK, J.
(1953), 'Evidence for Greek dialect in the Mycenaean
archives', JHS, 73, 84-103.
VERMEULE, E.
(1964), Greece in the Bronze Age, Chicago.
VIAN, F.
(1963), Les origines de Thèbes: Cadmos et les Spartes,
Paris.
VITALIANO, C.J. and VITALIANO, D.B.
(1974), 'Volcanic tephra on Crete', AJA, 78, 19-24.
(1975), 'Reply to comments by Leon Pomerance', AJA, 79,
367-8.
VOLONAKIS, M.D.
(1922), The Island of Roses and her Eleven Sisters,
London.
VREEKEN, W.A.L.
(1953), De Lege quadam sacra Coorum, Groningen.
WAINWRIGHT, F.T.
(1962), Archaeology and Place-names and History, London.
WALBANK, F.W.
(1951), 'The problem of Greek nationality', Phoenix, 5,
41-60.
(1972), Polybius, Berkeley.

WARD-PERKINS, J.B.
(1974), Cities of Ancient Greece and Italy: Planning in
classical antiquity, London.
WARREN, P.
(1976), 'Did papyrus grow in the Aegean?', AAA, 9, 89-95.
WASSERSTEIN, A.
(1962), 'Greek scientific thought', PCPS, 8, 51-63.
WEBER, H.
(1969-70), 'Coae vestes', AM (I), 19-20, 249-53.
WEBSTER, T.B.L.
(1956), Greek Theatre Production, London.
(1964), Hellenistic Poetry and Art, London.
(1970), Studies in Later Greek Comedy, 2nd edn, Manchester.
(1974), An Introduction to Menander, Manchester.
WEHRLI, F.
(1969a; b; c), Die Schule des Aristoteles. Texte und
Kommentar, 2nd edn, Basle/Stuttgart: a, Eudemos von
Rhodos; b, Hieronymos von Rhodos; c, Phainias von Eresos,
Chamaileon, Praxiphanes.
WEST, M.L.
(1971), Early Greek Philosophy and the Orient, Oxford.
(1972), Iambi et elegi graeci ante Alexandrum cantati,
Oxford.
(1973), 'Greek poetry 2000-700 BC', CQ, 23, 179-92.
WIDE, S.
(1893), Lakonische Kulte, Leipzig.
WILAMOWITZ-MOELLENDORFF, U. VON
(1932-3), Der Glaube der Hellenen, Berlin.
(1894), 'Der Tragiker Melanthios von Rhodos', Hermes, 29,
150-4.
WILHELM, A.
(1926), 'Zu Inschriften aus Rhodos und Kos', AM (A), 51,
1-13.
(1941), 'Strabon über die Rhodier', RM, 161-7.
WILL, E.
(1956), Doriens et Ioniens, Paris.
WILLETTS, R.F.
(1955), Aristocratic Society in Ancient Crete, London.
(1962), Cretan Cults and Festivals, London.
(1974), Ancient Crete: A Social History, 2nd edn, London
and Toronto.
(1977), The Civilization of Ancient Crete, London.
WITHINGTON, E.T.
(1921), 'The Asclepiadae and the priests of Asclepius',
in C. Singer, ed., Studies in the History and Method of
Science, II, Oxford.
WOODBURY, L.
(1965), 'The date and atheism of Diagoras of Melos',
Phoenix, 19, 178-211.

WOODHEAD, A.G.
(1952), 'The state health service in Ancient Greece',
CHJ, 10, 235-53.
WOOTEN, C.
(1975), 'Le développement du style Asiatique pendant
l'époque hellénistique', REG, 88, 94-104.
WYCHERLEY, R.E.
(1962), How the Greeks Built Cities, London.
ZAPHEIROPOULOS, N. and ZAPHEIROPOULOS, P.
Excavation reports in AAA, AD, EAE, PAAH on Thera.

Names Index

Academy, 89-90, 93, 96, 103, 139; see also Plato
Ahhijawa, 25, 26
Aischines, 7, 52, 65, 92-3, 99-100, 129-30
Aischylos, 34, 66, 72, 133, 184
Alexander, 6, 8, 37-8, 81, 85, 126, 138, 172, 173-4, 198
Alexandria, 4, 15, 16, 17, 60, 64, 65, 81-9, 96, 98, 99, 101, 105, 113, 126, 131, 136, 138-40, 144
Alkmaion, 115, 117
Amorgos, 20, 205
Anaphe, 5, 6, 13, 15, 48, 54, 88, 160, 162, 164, 168-208
Anaxagoras, 113, 115, 181
Anaxandrides, 60-1, 75-8, 92
Andronikos, 104-5
Antagoras, 65, 66, 88, 89-90
Antheas, 79
Antigonos, Antigonids, 18, 38-9, 63, 89, 141
Antioch, 64, 126, 140
Antiphanes, 75
Antisthenes, 99
Aphrodite, 89, 153, 154, 156, 169, 174, 175, 176, 182, 184, 186, 187-8, 192, 197, 209-10; Basileia, 188; Eudie, 188; Hypakoos, 188;

Ourania, 188; Pandamos, 182, 186, 187-8; Paphia, 188
Apollo, 5, 18, 73, 83, 85, 108, 121, 157-9, 164, 169, 176, 177-9, 181, 187, 190, 191, 192, 194, 197, 202, 207, 210-12; Aigletes, 88, 164; Apotropaios, 177; Asgelatas, 164, 187; Dalios, 177, 178; Delphinios, 172, 178; Didymeus, 172, 177; Dromaios, 187; Epiknisios, 177; Epimelidios, 177; Erethimios, 158-9, 170, 177, 203, 204; Ixios, 158; Kalymnios, 177; of Kamyndos, 177; Karneios, 171, 177, 178, 188, 195, 198; Kyparissios, 170, 177; Lykeios, 157-8, 177; Maleatas, 177-8, 205; Megisteus, 177; Mylantios, 158, 177; Oulios, 177, 199; Pedageitnyos, 177; Petasitas, 178; Pharmakios, 177; Prostaterios, 177; Pythios, 171, 177, 178; Pyxios, 177; Sminthios, 172, Soter, 177; Stratagios, 177; Telchinios, 158

Apollodoros, 69, 159, 163,
   164, 167, 179
Apollonios Malakos, 105
Apollonios Molon, 102, 105
Apollonios of Perge, 140,
   142
Apollonios of Rhodes, 65,
   70, 86-9, 94, 164, 179
Appian, 38, 40, 41-4, 139,
   182
Aratos, 65, 89, 141, 143
Archimedes, 62, 140, 141,
   143
Argonauts, 28, 67, 88, 164,
   178
Argos, Argolid, 5, 22, 29,
   30, 39, 52, 55, 71, 153,
   159, 160, 163, 167, 171,
   178, 179, 182, 184, 187
Aristeides, 5, 44, 105, 124,
   208
Aristophanes, 19, 20, 21, 56,
   70, 73, 74, 75-7, 108,
   120, 121, 124, 182
Aristotle, 19, 20, 21, 32,
   59, 61, 67, 69, 71, 73-4,
   77-8, 79, 93-6, 104, 109,
   113, 116, 118, 120, 126,
   132, 136, 138, 140, 149,
   193-4, 195, 203-8
Arrian, 37, 126
Artemis, 160, 169, 177, 181,
   184, 212-13; Andromeda,
   160, 171; Aristoboule,
   166; Kekoia, 171; Orthia,
   166; Pergaia, 172, 197;
   Selasphoros, 176; Toxitis,
   172
Asklepiades of Bithynia, 127,
   129
Asklepiades of Samos, 81, 82,
   86
Asklepios, 18, 107-12, 121,
   124, 169, 170, 173, 177,
   178, 179-81, 186, 189,
   191, 192, 195, 197, 199,
   203, 204, 205, 206, 214;
   Asklepiadai, 108-12, 120,
   129, 175; Asklepieia, 79,

177; Asklepieion, 9, 12,
   18, 120-5
Astypalaia, 5, 6, 7, 11, 13,
   15, 34, 42, 79, 160, 167,
   168-208
Athena, 54, 59, 152, 159,
   166, 169, 176, 179, 181,
   183, 184-6, 192, 195,
   196, 215-16; Alseia, 170,
   185; Apotropaia, 185, 199;
   Areia, 185; Hyperdexia,
   185; Ktesia, 121; Lindia,
   12, 103, 171; Machanis,
   185; Nike, 173, 183, 204;
   Phratria, 185; Polias,
   185-6, 206; Soteira, 185;
   Telchinia, 158
Athenaios, 14, 15, 16, 18,
   21, 33, 58, 65, 70, 71,
   72, 75, 77, 79, 82, 83,
   87, 96, 105, 134, 152,
   161, 163, 166, 174, 205
Athens, 3, 4, 6, 7, 8, 10,
   15, 16-17, 18, 19, 21,
   32, 34, 35-7, 52, 55, 62,
   63-4, 66, 67, 68, 71-4,
   78, 80, 89-90, 90-3,
   99-100, 101, 103, 110,
   116, 135, 139, 144, 173,
   179, 181, 186, 187, 188,
   205
Attalids, 42, 64

Babylonians, 138, 142
Bakchylides, 63
Berossos, 141-2
Boiotia, 52, 59, 63, 67
Byzantium, 37, 39-40, 204

Cato, 16, 102, 126-7
Celsus, 105, 119, 145
Chalke, 5, 6, 13, 20, 34,
   168-208
Chios, 23, 37, 40, 66-7, 74,
   80, 116
Cicero, 8, 42, 43, 102-5
Corinth, 10, 42, 53, 66, 68,
   71, 74, 182

Crete, 5, 6, 7, 8, 19, 20,
  22-4, 28, 30, 31, 40, 43,
  50-1, 53-4, 65, 71, 83,
  85, 88, 90, 99, 153-5,
  160-1, 162-3, 168, 170,
  172, 182, 184, 191;
  Aptera, 128; Gortyn, 128;
  Knossos, 7, 12, 22, 23,
  66, 128, 162; Olous, 128
Cynics, 90, 103
Cyprus, 17-18, 21, 22, 31,
  38, 43, 51, 52, 53, 66,
  71, 153-4, 187, 207

Danaos, 153, 156, 159-60
Delos, 8, 18, 19, 34, 39,
  42, 43, 78, 95, 186, 205;
  Delian League, 7, 34-5,
  178
Delphi, 78, 111, 122, 128,
  164, 165, 176, 181, 191,
  205
Demeter, 15, 82, 107, 169,
  171, 184, 185, 188-9,
  192, 197, 205-6, 216-17;
  Karpophoros, 189;
  Olympia, 189; Soteira,
  189; Thesmophoros, 169,
  188-9
Demetrios Poliorketes, 38,
  42
Demokedes, 117, 126
Demokritos, 91, 99, 100,
  101, 110, 112, 116-17,
  120, 137, 139
Demosthenes, 7, 8, 16, 17,
  18, 37, 61, 110
Diagoras, 73-4, 91
Dieuchidas, 163
Dikaiarchos, 140
Dio Cassius, 11, 18, 40, 41,
  43
Dio Chrysostom, 10, 36, 43,
  44, 105
Diodoros, 9, 18, 27, 28,
  30, 36, 38, 41, 42, 98,
  153-63, 166-7, 179

Diogenes Laertius, 70, 89,
  95, 96, 169, 196
Diokles, 126
Diomedon, 176, 187, 190, 204
Dionysios Thrax, 95, 105
Dionysios, 10, 71-2, 81, 88,
  169, 172, 175, 176, 191-2,
  197, 217-18; Bakcheios,
  192; Epikarpios, 192;
  Kathegemon, 192; Pro
  Poleos, 192; Skyllitas,
  170, 192; Smintheus, 172;
  Theodaisios, 191;
  Thyllophorus, 170, 192,
  197-8, 203; Trieterikos,
  192; Dionysia, 78-9
Dosiadas, 65, 85
Dromeas, 83
Dromeas, 83

Egypt, 17-18, 31, 38, 39,
  66, 101, 156, 159-60,
  162, 174
Eleatics, 137
Empedokles, 61, 115, 117-19,
  143
Ephesos, 8, 81, 126, 177,
  189
Epicharmos, 60, 71, 77
Epicureans, 101, 103
Epidauros, 30, 52, 78, 121,
  124, 167, 171, 179, 189,
  205
Epimenides, 99
Epione, 180, 195, 203
Erasistratos, 126
Eratosthenes, 26, 109, 140,
  142-3
Ergias, 98, 161
Erinna, 86
Euboia, 52, 54, 63, 93
Euclid, 139
Eudemos, 81, 93-5, 96, 136,
  139
Eudoxox, 138, 140, 141
Eumelos, 66, 68
Euripides, 60, 64, 66, 74,

76, 95, 166, 181, 200
Eurypylos, 83, 164, 166,
   183

Galen, 91, 110, 121, 125,
   126, 127, 129, 133, 141,
   144, 145
Geminos, 104, 105, 131,
   144-5
Gorgias, 63, 91, 112
Gorgon, 98

Halikarnassos, 5, 33, 37,
   51-2, 54, 55, 57, 63,
   74, 117, 128, 176, 197,
   201
Hekataios, 61, 63, 69, 99,
   133, 149
Hekate, 171, 172, 176, 194;
   Enodia, 171; Phosphoros,
   171, 176; Soteira, 171;
   Stratia, 172
Hekaton, 103, 104
Heliadai, 153-63
Helios, 10, 43, 69, 99,
   155-6, 159, 169, 173,
   176, 179, 181-3, 192,
   197-8, 202, 218
Hera, 165, 184, 186, 187,
   192, 205; Ammonia, 174;
   Argeia, 187; Basileia,
   187; Dromaia, 187;
   Eleia, 187; Olympia, 187;
   Ourania, 187; Telchinia,
   158
Herakleides, 139-40
Herakleitos, 99, 115, 196
Herakles, 27-30, 68-9, 73,
   76, 83, 85, 88, 90, 152,
   164, 165, 169, 174, 176,
   189-90, 191, 192, 197,
   199, 207, 219; Diomedonteios, 176, 190
Hermes, 82, 121, 174, 190,
   192, 219-20; Hagemon,
   190; Kyllanios, 172, 190;
   Propylaios, 190

Hermesianax, 81, 83
Herodas, 17, 20, 60, 64,
   79-80, 82, 84, 94, 170,
   173, 204
Herodotos, 5, 26, 29-34, 51,
   57, 59, 61, 63, 66, 71,
   91, 107, 110, 117,
   159-60, 162
Herophilos, 126
Hesiod, 1, 66-7, 87, 134
Hestia, 184, 185, 186-7,
   192, 200, 203, 220;
   Boulaia, 186-7; Tamias,
   186
Hieronymos, 94-6, 99
Hipparchos, 101, 104, 123,
   131, 140-3, 144, 146
Hippias, 137
Hippodamos, 135
Hippokrates, 18, 91, 107-13,
   115
Hippokratic Corpus, 61-2,
   65, 90-1, 96, 113-25,
   133, 141, 170; Acut.,
   115; Aer., 114; Aff.,
   115; Aph., 114, 137;
   Art., 114; de Arte, 91,
   119; Carn., 117; Coac.,
   114; Cord., 125; Decent.,
   125; Ep., 34, 99-101,
   107, 116, 125; Epid., 8,
   91, 112, 116-7, 124, 129;
   Fract., 91, 114; Jusj.,
   117-8, 127; Lex, 119,
   130; Mochl., 114; Morb.
   Sacr., 114, 115, 117,
   130; Mul.114; Nat.Hom.,
   113, 118; Nat.Mul., 114;
   Off., 125; Praec., 125;
   Prog., 114; Prorrh., 114,
   117; Salubr., 17, 121,
   122-5; VC, 115; VM, 118,
   130
Hittites, 25-6, 48
Homer, 19, 25-30, 51, 59,
   66, 67, 69, 72, 82-3, 87,
   105, 134, 150, 162, 164,
   165, 166, 179
Hygieia, 108, 173, 180, 181,
   195, 197, 203

Iasos, 128
Ioklos, 167
Ion, 74, 116
Ionia, Ionians, 4, 6, 34,
    57, 63, 67, 132
Isokrates, 92, 95, 138
Italy, 60, 61, 66, 101, 115;
    Kroton, 117, 121, 126;
    Tarentum, 77; Thourioi,
    36, 63

Kadmos of Kos, 33
Kadmos of Phoenicia, 53, 54,
    133, 152, 153, 159-61,
    183, 191
Kallimachos, 61, 70, 82, 85,
    86, 88, 95
Kalymnos, 5, 6, 12, 13, 15,
    19, 23, 26-30, 34, 47,
    52, 55, 85, 121, 127,
    163, 166, 168-208
Karia, Karians, 29, 33, 37,
    41-2, 48, 49, 51-2, 105,
    111, 156-9, 162, 172,
    179, 182
Karpathos, 5, 6, 11, 13, 15,
    23, 26-30, 34, 39, 50-1,
    54, 128, 154, 168-208;
    Arkaseia, 185; Brykous,
    128-9; Eteokarpathioi,
    50-1; Potidaion, 185,
    186
Kasos, 5, 6, 13, 23, 26-30,
    34, 35, 39, 128, 160
Kastor, 31, 98
Kaunos, 30, 42-3
Keos, 8, 63, 91
Kimolos, 5, 13, 19, 134
Kinaithon, 68
Kleoboulos, 32, 70, 169
Knidos, 5, 36, 52, 61, 82,
    87, 111, 115, 126, 163
Kolophon, 31, 66, 81
Kos, passim; see esp.11-20,
    26-30, 34-8, 78-86, 120-3,
    168-77, 179-81; Aigele,
    127; Antimachia, 165;
    Astypalaia, 12;

Bourina, 9; Halasarna,
    47, 120, 177, 190, 197;
    Haleis, 9, 120, 127;
    Isthmos, 120, 127;
    Kyparissos, 18; Meropis,
    12, 48, 159; Pyxa, 9;
    Serraglio, 11, 30
Kronos, 153, 166
Kyrene, 31, 55, 121
Kythera, 5, 23, 74, 153
Kythnos, 22

Lade, 32, 98
Lapiths, 163; cf.153, 166
Leleges, 29
Lemnos, 50-1
Leros, 6, 26, 35
Lesbos, 23, 52, 59, 93, 94,
    156, 159, 189
Livy, 40, 41
Lucian, 10, 44, 102, 105,
    107, 205
Lucretius, 101, 143
Luwian, 48, 50
Lyceum, see Peripatetics
Lydia, 19, 32, 33, 51, 66,
    191
Lykia, 31, 41-2, 51, 157,
    158-9
Lykourgos, 29, 67
Lysias, 19, 63, 73, 92, 114

Macedon, Macedonia, 6,
    37-42, 58, 64-6, 72, 89,
    92-3, 101, 116, 126, 138,
    141
Machaon, 179, 180
Makareus, 98
Megara, 30, 52, 56, 71, 74
Melanippides, 66, 72-3
Melanthios, 74
Meleager, 90
Melissos, 35, 117-19, 137
Melos, 5, 6, 11, 13, 19,
    30-1, 35, 54, 56, 72-4,
    91, 157, 159, 162, 167,
    168-208; Phylakopi, 11,
    12, 23, 50, 162

Menander, 57, 62, 75-6, 80, 101
Menon, 109
Miletos, 6, 19, 25, 32, 52, 61, 63, 66, 85, 90, 99, 136, 198
Minos, Minoans, 7, 11, 23-5, 90, 152, 160-2, 170, 171, 184, 185, 188
Minyans, 30, 49
Mithridates, Mithridatic Wars, 21, 40, 42-3, 103, 139, 180
Mycenae, Mycenaeans, 4, 11, 12, 23-30, 31, 50, 52, 66, 68, 162, 170, 185

Naxos, 191
Nikias of Kos, 44, 176
Nikias of Miletos, 85, 125
Nisyros, 5, 6, 13, 16, 19, 26-30, 35, 36, 39, 154, 167, 168-208

Olympia, 36, 74
Ovid, 14, 15, 20, 82, 164

Panaitios, 101-4, 143
Panakeia, 108, 121, 180
Panyassis, 55, 69
Parmenides, 137
Paros, 189
Pausanias, 34, 36, 111, 152, 160, 166, 170, 179, 184, 187, 188
Peisandros, 55, 59, 66, 68-9
Peisinous, 68
Pelasgoi, Pelasgic, 49, 50, 51, 163
Peloponnese,   4, 5, 6, 11, 17, 29, 30, 31, 36, 39, 52, 55, 116, 166, 168, 171, 178, 182, see also Argos etc; Peloponnesian War, 34-6, 75

Pergamum, 41, 64, 90, 101, 121, 126, 130, 140, 205, 208
Peripatetics, 81, 90, 93-7, 99, 103-5, 138-9; see also Aristotle
Perseus, 160
Persia, Persians, 6, 32-4, 37, 51, 52, 100, 110, 117, 126, 172
Pherekydes, 90
Philinos, 126
Philip, 37, 40-1, 126
Philitas, 9, 18, 81-3, 95, 126, 139, 189
Philolaos, 62, 117
Philoxenos, 74
Phoenicians, 53-4, 90, 159-62
Pholegandros, 5, 13, 162, 177
Phrygia, Phrygians, 20, 31, 51, 191
Pindar, 5, 59, 63, 66, 83, 152, 155, 160, 161, 163, 167, 170, 179, 182
Plato, 51, 57, 61, 63, 64, 67, 70, 90, 93, 95, 96, 108-12, 113, 116, 119, 139, 137-8, 181, 182, 188, 205
Pliny, 4, 10, 11, 14, 16, 19, 20, 107, 142-3, 146
Plutarch, 33, 34, 35, 38, 64, 67, 70, 74, 102, 127, 156, 157, 164, 196
Podaleirios, 111, 121, 166, 179, 180
Pollux, 15, 20, 21
Polybios, 18, 38-42, 98, 99, 101, 143
Polybos, 112, 113
Polykrates, 32-3, 117, 126
Polyzelos, 98, 159, 163
Pompey, 43, 98, 102
Pontos, 16, 17, 39-40, 140
Poseidon, 54, 153-6, 159, 164, 166, 182, 183, 192, 195, 220-1; Asphaleios,

183; Gaiaochos, 183;
Gilaios, 154-5, 183;
Hippios, 103, 183;
Hippotas, 183; Kyreteios,
155, 183; Pelagios, 183;
Phytalmios, 183;
Porthmios, 183
Poseidonios, 92, 98, 101-4,
120, 131, 143-4, 145,
146
Praxagoras, 111, 126, 139
Praxiphanes, 94-6
Priene, 39
Prodikos, 91, 112
Protagoras, 63, 73, 115
Pserimos, 5, 6, 26
Ptolemies, 7, 18, 38, 42,
64, 68, 82, 85, 140,
174, 206
Ptolemy, 4, 28, 131-2, 141,
145
Pydna, 42, 101
Pylos, 50, 69
Pythagoras, Pythagoreans,
61-2, 107, 113, 117-18,
137
Pythokles, 176

Rhea, 15, 154-5, 170
Rhianos, 65, 88, 90
Rhinthon, 60, 77
Rhodes, passim; Achaia, 54,
161-2; Atabyros, 16, 140,
162-3; Brygindara, 147;
Ialysos, 5, 11, 25, 36,
54, 55, 57, 158, 159,
161-2, 163, 166, 168-208;
Kameiros, 5, 7, 11, 54,
55, 134, 155, 163,
168-208; Kamyndos, 47;
Kekoia, 171; Ladarma, 51;
Lartos, 19; Lindos, 5, 11,
31, 32, 35, 47, 52, 55,
71, 89, 103, 111, 152,
155, 159, 160, 168-208;
Lindian Chronicle, 12,
32, 94, 96, 98, 152-3;
Ophioussa, 48, 163;

Peraia, 5, 35, 39, 200,
206; Rhodos, 168-208;
Sminthe, Sminthia, 47;
Trianda, 23-4
Rome, Romans, 6, 7, 8, 16,
40-4, 58, 66, 101,
104-5, 126-7, 136, 144,
173, 176, 195, 202, 207;
Emperors, Augustus, 44,
78, 105, Tiberius, 44,
105, 180, Caligula, 186,
Claudius, 127, 180,
Trajan, 175, Hadrian, 8,
M.Aurelius, 127;
Emperor Worship, 173,
177, 189, 195, 202

Salamis, 33, 66
Samos, 4, 18, 23, 32-3, 35,
39, 41, 52, 61, 80, 81,
86, 117, 126, 128, 134,
201
Sappho, 59
Saros, 5, 13, 183
Seleukids, 18, 39, 40-1,
63, 101
Seriphos, 33, 64, 160
Seutloussa, 5, 13
Sicily, 5, 17, 20-1, 35-6,
56, 60, 62, 63, 64, 66,
75, 85, 115, 200; Akragas,
117; Gela, 31, 55, 171;
Syracuse, 72, 74, 84-5,
126, 140
Sikinos, 5, 54
Sikyon, 71, 74, 182, 187
Simias, 58, 81, 83-4, 85,
95
Simonides, 33, 59, 70, 72
Siphnos, 33, 135
Smyrna, 66, 140
Sokrates, 51, 63, 91, 92,
108, 111
Sokrates of Kos, 152
Sophokles, 35, 66, 72, 74,
92, 95, 107, 133, 135,
170, 181, 184
Sophron, 62, 79

Soranos, 107, 109-12
Sparta, 4, 5, 30, 32, 34, 36,
    52, 59, 61, 67, 68, 107,
    110, 166, 167, 168, 171,
    178, 195
Stoics, 95, 102-3, 143
Strabo, 4, 9-10, 14, 15-16,
    21, 28, 30-1, 36, 51, 65,
    67, 92, 94, 96, 103, 120,
    122, 133, 141, 143, 150,
    153, 155, 157-9, 167,
    177
Syme, 5, 6, 13, 19, 26-30,
    34, 39, 51, 157, 163,
    165, 178, 180, 200, 204,
    208
Syria, 90, 102, 104
Syros, 90

Tacitus, 43, 44, 127, 180
Telchines, 95, 152-6, 178
Telendos, 26
Telos, 5, 6, 13, 16, 39, 86,
    168-208
Tenos, 7, 86, 124
Teos, 31, 53
Thales, 32, 99, 107, 136-7
Thasos, 116
Thebes, Thebans, 50, 53, 57,
    159, 160
Themistokles, 33, 60, 64,
    72, 99
Theokritos, 5, 9, 14-15,
    60, 62, 66, 68, 82, 84-6,
    87, 88, 94, 125, 170,
    189
Theophrastos, 21, 93, 94, 96
Theopompos, 111, 121, 159
Thera, 5, 6, 7, 8, 11, 13,
    19, 21, 35, 39, 48, 53-5,
    58, 159-60, 164, 167,
    168-208; Akrotiri, 13,
    23-4, 30-1; Eleusis, 188
Therasia, 5, 6, 11, 15
Theseus, 68, 162, 187
Thessalos, 100, 112, 166
Thessaly, 6, 17, 22, 28-31,
    52, 66, 88, 110, 116,

    163-4, 166, 179-80, 183;
    Hypata, 180; Larissa,
    110, 116; Trikka, 121
Thrace, Thracians, 49, 51,
    63, 116, 191
Thucydides, 5, 29, 30, 31,
    32, 34, 35, 36, 51, 61,
    63, 91, 99, 110, 149,
    160, 162
Timachidas, 96, 98
Timocharis, 142
Timokreon, 33, 52, 59-60,
    70, 72
Tlepolemos, 153, 163, 165,
    166, 189
Troizen, 5
Troy, Trojan War, 6, 7, 12,
    26-30, 52, 66, 67, 111,
    164-6, 189

Vergil, 16, 141
Vitruvius, 142

Xenophon of Athens, 36, 51,
    72, 134
Xenophon of Ephesos, 10,
    44, 61
Xenophon of Kos, 127

Yiali, 7, 19

Zenodotos, 81, 82, 87
Zenon, 98, 99, 153, 161,
    163
Zeus, 14, 85, 88, 126, 153,
    159, 170-1, 176, 177,
    184, 186-7, 192, 195,
    196, 200, 221-3; Amalos,
    155, 184, 199;
    Apotropaios, 199;
    Astrapatas, 184;
    Astrapton, 184; Atabyrios,
    162, 184; Bronton, 184;
    Damatrios, 171; Drouthios,
    184; Eredimios, 170;

Hikesios, 184; Hyetios,
184; Hypsistos, 184;
Karpophoros, 170;
Kataibates, 184;
Keraunios, 184; Kronides
Anax, 171, 184; Ktesios,
121, Olympios, 184;
Ombrios, 184; Paian, 179;
Pasios, 176; Polieus, 111,
185-6, 201; Soter, 186;
Teleios, 186, 203

Subject Index

Aetiology, 88, 89, 97, 111,
150, 152, 165, 189
Alphabet, see Scripts
Anthology, Palatine, 70,
86, 89, 90
Arbitration, 21, 39
Architecture, 10, 23, 134-5
Associations, 158, 174-5,
191, 207
Astrology, 44, 131-2, 140-2
Astronomy, 94, 104, 105,
131-2, 136-46

Banks, 18
Biography, 91, 95, 99; Vitae,
86, 87, 92, 109-12, 135
Biology, 116, 120, 138, 146
Bronze Age, 4, 6, 7, 11,
23-30, 47-50, 53, 54, 59,
68, 151, 153-66, 170,
183; see also Minoans,
Mycenaeans

Calendars, 136, 145; local,
111, 169, 182, 185, 186,
201
Christianity, 173, 175, 181
Coinage, coins, 16, 32, 35,
36, 39, 57, 135, 152,
160, 162, 165, 169, 188,
190, 192

Colony, colonization, 3,
31, 34, 55, 166-7, 171,
200
Cult-titles, 3, 152, 172-3,
177-92, 194

Dark Age, 26-7, 30, 59, 67
Dedications, 56, 84, 156,
168-208
Demes, 6, 36, 39, 120,
128-9, 173, 207
Dialects, 4, 29, 52-3, 55,
56-62, 68, 83, 98, 114,
194; Aiolic, 52, 59, 61,
67; Arcado-Cyprian, 52,
59, 172; Attic, 52, 56-8,
61, 62, 135; Boiotian,
56, 57; Doric, 29, 52,
56-62, 63, 86, 122, 127;
Doric, of islands, 56-62;
of Crete, 58, 83; of
Lakonia, 56; of Megara,
56; of Sicily, 56, 58;
Ionic, 5, 52, 57, 59,
60, 61-2, 67, 91; Koine,
58, 60, 62, 114
Dithyramb, 71-4, 76, 79, 191
Doctors, see Medicine
Dorian Invasion, 27-30, 68
Drama, 66, 74, 88, 191-2;
actors, technitai, 7, 76,
78-9, 92, 129, 175, 191;

comic, 59, 60, 63, 73,
75-81, 101, 182, 191;
mime, 60, 62, 86; origins,
71-2; Roman, 77; satyric,
21, 71; tragic, 59, 63,
66, 74-5, 80-1, 107, 181,
191; in Greek West, 60,
71, 77
Dreams, 123-5, 133
Dye, 20, 134

Earthquakes, 18, 36, 39,
135, 154-5, 169, 183
Elegy, 82, 170, 189
Epic, 3, 59, 61, 63, 65,
66-9, 82, 85, 86, 88,
97, 152
Epigrams, 56, 83, 85-6, 87,
90, 179
Epistles, Aischines, 7, 52,
99-100; Hippokrates, 34,
100-1, 109-10, 116, 125,
130, 141
Epitaphs, 7, 52, 56, 70, 83,
90, 129
Eponyms, 178, 182, 186, 197,
204, 208
Experiment, scientific, 131-2

Festivals, 14, 68, 69, 79,
85, 129, 158, 168-208
Fish, 14, 15, 17, 39, 134
Folksong, 69, 70, 86
Frescoes, 19, 69, 160
Fruit, 9, 15, 17, 134
Fuller's Earth, 19, 134

Geography, 8, 88, 104,
137-46
Grain, 8, 16-18, 39
Gymnasia, 97, 112, 190

Herbs, 15-16
Heroization, 121, 174-6
Historians, local, 90, 98,
104

Homosexuality, 175
Honey, 8, 14, 15, 17

Indo-European, 48-9

Kolossos, 10, 38, 39, 135

Law, lawcourts, 7, 10, 17-18,
20, 21, 39, 80-1, 92, 99,
136
Libraries, librarians, 65,
81, 82, 86-7, 93, 96-7,
113
Linear A and B, see scripts
Lot, 196-8
Lyric, 59-61, 62, 63, 65,
69-71, 74, 83

Marble, 19, 134
Mathematics, 62, 93-4, 104,
107, 137-45
Medicine, 3, 82, 90, 96,
107-31, 132-3, 136, 139,
141, 145, 146, 170, 175;
anatomy, 108, 114;
cardiology, 117, 125;
embryology, 114, 117;
pathology, 108, 133;
physiology, 108, 112, 133,
137
Mercenaries, 38, 43, 51
Metallurgy, minerals, mining,
17, 19, 135, 146, 153-5
Music, 73, 74, 78, 81, 102,
135, 137
Myths, 3, 49, 51, 54, 67, 69,
74, 76-7, 83, 87, 97, 111,
115, 121, 133, 149-67,
168, 179, 181-2, 189, 191

Neolithic, 22-3, 28, 47

Observation, scientific,
131-2, 141, 144

Obsidian, 6–7, 19, 22–3
Officials, 6, 193–208
Olives, olive oil, 8, 14,
    15, 16, 17, 39, 134
Oratory, 21, 61, 63, 71,
    92, 113–14

Papyrus, 65
Parody, 56–7, 62, 77, 108
Patriotism, 60, 75, 81, 98,
    110, 152, 192
Patronage, 65–6, 78, 82,
    85, 136, 139, 140
Philology, 58, 83, 95, 98,
    105, 108, 137–8, 139
Philosophy: ethics, 94, 95,
    103, 137–8, 143; logic,
    104, 143; metaphysics,
    120, 137–8; natural
    (physics), 93–4, 107,
    136–7, 143; politics,
    94, 97, 137
Piracy, 7, 38, 39, 43, 51,
    164
Place-names, 47–50, 51
Pottery, 8, 12, 19, 22–5,
    30, 31, 135
Priests, 194–203
Publication, 65, 87, 113
Pumice, 19

Rhetoric, 73, 91–3, 96,
    99–101, 102–5, 108, 129,
    137, 138, 145, 146

Sacrifice, 14–15, 107, 159,
    168–208, esp. 200–1
Scripts: alphabetic, 3,
    53–6, 67; epichoric, 5,
    54–5; Linear A, 50;
    Linear B, 30, 48, 50, 52,
    170, 191

Sculpture, 43, 108, 135, 169
Seafaring, 6–8, 22–3, 36,
    69, 90, 135, 154
Silk, 20
Slaves, 35, 38, 80, 102,
    126, 129, 135–6, 165,
    199, 203
Sophists, 8, 63, 72, 73–4,
    91–2, 118, 137–8
Sponges, 19
Syncretism, 171, 174, 177,
    187, 195
Synoecism, 11, 12, 36, 135,
    168, 169, 173, 182, 185,
    188, 198

Taboos, 199
Technology, 3, 38, 133–6,
    139, 145
Temples, 10, 18, 97, 124–5,
    134, 158, 159, 158–208;
    temple archives, 120–2
Textiles, 19–21, 134
Theatres, 10, 78, 81, 92,
    158
Tourism, 10, 44
Trade, 3, 6, 7, 16–21, 25,
    31, 36, 39, 54, 174
Trees, 9, 18–19, 83, 134,
    170, 179, 186
Tribes, 29, 173, 207;
    Dymanes, 27, 177;
    Hylleis, 27, 190;
    Pamphyloi, 27; in Bronze
    Age, 27–9

Volcano, Thera, 11, 24, 48,
    154, 156

Water supply, 116, 134
Wine, 8, 16–17, 39, 134